The One Year Devotions for Moms

DEVOTIONS *for* MOMS

Ellen Banks Elwell

Tyndale House Publishers, Inc. Wheaton, Illinois

TYNDALE is a registered trademark of Tyndale House Publishers, Inc.

Tyndale's quill logo is a trademark of Tyndale House Publishers, Inc.

The One Year Devotions for Moms

Copyright © 2005 by Ellen Banks Elwell. All rights reserved.

Cover photograph © by Alexandra Grablewski/Getty Images. All rights reserved.

Interior photographs © by Stockbyte. All rights reserved.

Author photo © 2000 by Lewek Photography. All rights reserved.

One Year is a registered trademark of Tyndale House Publishers, Inc.

Some material previously published in *Quiet Moments of Hope for Moms, Quiet Moments of Encouragement for Moms, Quiet Moments of Wisdom for Moms,* and *Quiet Moments of Faith for Moms,* copyright © 1999 by Ellen Banks Elwell. All rights reserved.

Designed by Julie Chen

Library of Congress Cataloging-in-Publication Data

Elwell, Ellen Banks, date.
The one year devotions for moms / Ellen Banks Elwell.
p. cm.
Includes index.
ISBN 1-4143-0171-5 Softcover   ISBN 1-4143-0635-0 Hardcover
1. Mothers—Prayer-books and devotions—English. 2. Devotional calendars. I. Title.
BV4847.E557 2005
242′.6431—dc22   2004024025

Printed in the United States of America

10   09   08   07   06   05
7   6   5   4   3   2   1

To Joan Darnauer
and
Carol Pearce

ACKNOWLEDGMENTS

To my husband, Jim, and sons, Chad, Nate, and Jordan:

Thanks for helping in the kitchen, taking walks with me, praying for me, and humoring me. God was gracious to let me be in the same family with the four of you. I appreciate your permission to include some of our family's stories in this book. I love you all.

To my editor, Karin Buursma:

The first time I spoke with you on the phone, I knew I'd enjoy working with you. A few calls later, I discovered that your family lives in the red house just around the corner from my family! Thanks for being gracious, straightforward, encouraging, and insightful—all at the same time.

INTRODUCTION

When I was a young mom, I wanted to spend time with God each day—but I struggled to find a time that *worked*. Although I'm a morning person now, I wasn't then. Evenings weren't practical either, because after the children's bedtime ceremonies were completed, I was exhausted. There was one time of day, however, when the house was (usually) quiet, and that was right after lunch. For the sake of my sanity, I insisted that my boys either read or nap for one hour. On rare occasions when the hour stretched into two, I was blessed with a bonus.

Daily, I was faced with my need for encouragement, hope, wisdom, and faith. So I asked God for his help. I prayed, *God, if you'll allow my children to nap or read quietly for one hour, I will sit down and spend time with you each day.* God did help me—and I sat down most every day with a glass of iced tea or lemonade to read my Bible and pray. As a result of spending time with God, my soul grew rich and I was strengthened for the demands of being a mom.

Now I'm in my fifties and my youngest son is in high school. At this stage of my life, I enjoy rising early each morning to spend time with God. Instead of a glass of iced tea or lemonade, I drink hot coffee with vanilla creamer. And you know what? I still feel the need for encouragement, hope, wisdom, and faith. But years of spending time with God have convinced me that he is faithful to bless me with all of the above and more.

I'm glad you've picked up a copy of *The One Year Devotions for Moms*. I planned for this book to be simple and uncomplicated, so that you can begin reading it any day of the year. It doesn't matter when or where you choose to begin; all you need to do is locate today's date. Daily devotionals are planned around a weekly theme, so if you're interested in locating a particular subject, just refer to the topical index at the back.

Whatever time of day you choose, I hope that the devotional moments you spend pondering God's truth will enrich your life and strengthen you for your role as a mom. Blessings to you!

"May God bless you with his special favor and wonderful peace as you come to know Jesus, our God and Lord, better and better. As we know Jesus better, his divine power gives us everything we need for living a godly life. He has called us to receive his own glory and goodness!" 2 Peter 1:2-3

Ellen Banks Elwell
Wheaton, Illinois
2004

FAITH

FUTURE GENERATIONS WILL ALSO SERVE HIM. OUR CHILDREN
WILL HEAR ABOUT THE WONDERS OF THE LORD. HIS RIGHTEOUS
ACTS WILL BE TOLD TO THOSE YET UNBORN. THEY WILL HEAR ABOUT
EVERYTHING HE HAS DONE.

Psalm 22:30-31

When my children were in preschool and early elementary years, one of my favorite things to do was read to them. Whether we were sitting in a rocking chair or propped up in bed, it was fun to read and snuggle at the same time. Although we learned from many kinds of books, God's Word enriched us more than any other. Together, we witnessed God's wonders and provisions in other people's lives, and we were encouraged to believe he would provide for us, too.

I especially liked the story of baby Moses. The king of Egypt had instructed the Hebrew midwives to kill all of the Hebrew baby boys. Being a woman of faith, Moses' mother, Jochebed, put him in a basket and hid him among the reeds of a river. His older sister, Miriam, kept an eye on the basket until Pharaoh's daughter found Moses and adopted him. In God's plan, Miriam asked the princess if she should find a nurse for the child, and Moses' very own mother was able to raise him for some years before he was educated in Pharaoh's palace.

Imagine how often Jochebed must have retold that story to Moses and Miriam and their brother Aaron before Moses went to live in the palace. The siblings grew up hearing that God sees and God provides. Later in their lives God used them to lead his people out of Egypt. In the same way, we can encourage our children's faith by telling how God has provided for us. The time we spend encouraging them now will influence their leadership down the road.

God who sees and provides,
Thank you for blessing us with children to nurture and love. Thank you for
giving us your Word to be our guide. Please help us to notice your provisions
and then to rehearse them with our children, strengthening our faith and
encouraging theirs. Amen.

FAITH

> THEN HE SAID TO THOMAS, "PUT YOUR FINGER HERE
> AND SEE MY HANDS. PUT YOUR HAND INTO THE WOUND IN
> MY SIDE. DON'T BE FAITHLESS ANY LONGER. BELIEVE!" *John 20:27*

Although Thomas was one of Jesus' disciples, he had difficulty believing that Jesus had really risen from the dead. Hence the nickname "Doubting Thomas."

Thomas was not present when Jesus first appeared to his disciples after the Resurrection. When Thomas heard of Jesus' appearance, he said he wouldn't believe it unless he felt Jesus' hands and side. Seven days later they met, and Jesus invited Thomas to touch his wounds. Thomas's beautiful response—"My Lord and my God!"—prompted St. Augustine to say that Thomas doubted so that we might believe.

Thomas's struggle for faith offers us hope. If Jesus showed patience and willingness to help Thomas believe, he will do the same for us. If we or our children struggle with doubts that lead to questions, questions that lead to answers, and answers that lead to belief, then the doubts will have been productive. Doubts that stagnate rather than drive us to think more clearly about our faith tend to be nonproductive and may lead us to stubbornness. We're wise to beware of "camping out" in our doubts. It's interesting that in John 20:29, Jesus offered "extra credit" to the person who believes *without* seeing: "Then Jesus told him, 'You believe because you have seen me. Blessed are those who haven't seen me and believe anyway.'" Because we have God's Word and the witness of people like Thomas, we're inspired to believe.

Father,
We're grateful for your patience with Thomas and your patience with us when we doubt. Thank you that Thomas's experience helps us to believe in you. Amen.

FAITH

THEREFORE, SINCE WE HAVE BEEN MADE RIGHT IN GOD'S
SIGHT BY FAITH, WE HAVE PEACE WITH GOD BECAUSE OF WHAT
JESUS CHRIST OUR LORD HAS DONE FOR US. *Romans 5:1*

In a small farming town, a young family's two-story house caught fire in the middle of the night. Everyone in the family bolted out of the smoke-filled house into the front yard—except a five-year-old boy. The father stood in front of the house and looked up to see his crying son at a bedroom window, rubbing his eyes.

Knowing it would not be wise to go back into the burning house to rescue his son, the father yelled, "Jump, Son, and I'll catch you!" Sobbing, the boy replied to his father's voice, "I can't see you!" The father confidently yelled back, "But I can see *you*! Go ahead and jump." And the boy did. He jumped and was secure in his father's arms.

The choice this young boy made reminds me of the commitment we make when we decide to put our trust in Jesus. In the boy's helplessness, his father came to save him. In our helplessness, God came to save us. He didn't come to us because of our strength—he came to us because of our weakness.

As a result of Jesus' death and our faith, Romans 5:1-5 tells us we receive peace with God, access to God, hope, confidence amidst the daily trials of life, and a personal experience with God's love. If we realize that he died to save us from our sin, we see our helplessness and realize that jumping into his arms is a very wise choice. In fact, it's the only way we can live!

Father,
Thank you that you always see us, no matter where we are. Thank you that in our helplessness you sent Jesus to save us. Please help us to put our trust in you. Amen.

FAITH

THIS SAME GOD WHO TAKES CARE OF ME WILL SUPPLY ALL
YOUR NEEDS FROM HIS GLORIOUS RICHES, WHICH HAVE BEEN
GIVEN TO US IN CHRIST JESUS.

Philippians 4:19

While sorting through a pile of artwork from Chad's grade school years, I uncovered a meaningful treasure. On a piece of construction paper, Chad had drawn two ancient-looking oil jars, and next to them he had written the following poem:

> *The widow had no oil,*
> *For it had all been used.*
> *But then it flowed and flowed and flowed,*
> *For it had been renewed!*

Right around the time Chad wrote that poem, his friend Brad's father was tragically killed by a disgruntled employee, leaving Brad's mom to raise two young sons. Chad, along with the rest of our family, observed the many ways that God took care of Brad's family in the months and years after his dad's death.

I'll never forget the night that Brad's mom, Brenda, stopped by our home to deliver a gift. She had purchased small oil jars to give to each family who had been helpful to her and the boys after Dale's death. The oil jars hearkened back to the Old Testament story of Elisha and the widow (2 Kings 4:1-7). The widow in the Bible had also needed help to provide for her two sons, and God—through Elisha—used the empty oil jars of people around her to provide far more than she could have ever imagined. Brenda, Brad, and Andy had faith that God would take care of them, and—as is the case with God—his provisions proved to be even bigger than their faith.

Father,
Thank you that when we place our faith in you, you give us eyes to see beyond the visible. Thank you that you take care of us and supply our needs. In the name of Jesus, amen.

FAITH

AND NOW, JUST AS YOU ACCEPTED CHRIST JESUS AS YOUR
LORD, YOU MUST CONTINUE TO LIVE IN OBEDIENCE TO HIM.
LET YOUR ROOTS GROW DOWN INTO HIM AND DRAW UP NOURISHMENT
FROM HIM, SO YOU WILL GROW IN FAITH, STRONG AND VIGOROUS IN THE TRUTH
YOU WERE TAUGHT. LET YOUR LIVES OVERFLOW WITH THANKSGIVING FOR ALL HE
HAS DONE. DON'T LET ANYONE LEAD YOU ASTRAY WITH EMPTY PHILOSOPHY AND
HIGH-SOUNDING NONSENSE THAT COME FROM HUMAN THINKING AND FROM THE
EVIL POWERS OF THIS WORLD, AND NOT FROM CHRIST. *Colossians 2:6-8*

*P*astor Gary Dausey tells about a time his father asked him to cut sixty-four two-by-fours to a certain length. To get him started, Gary's dad cut one board as a pattern and asked Gary to cut all of them that size. So Gary used the pattern to cut the first board. Then he picked up the board he just had cut and marked the next board, used that board to mark the next, and continued in that manner until he was finished. It wasn't until he completed the project that he realized there was a problem: the last board was several inches longer than the pattern he had been given. Why? Because he hadn't used the pattern as his measuring stick. Gary was reminded that the pattern of faith we need for the foundation of our lives must be primary, not two or three generations away. We must go straight to the source.

As Christian moms, we desire to see our children develop in their faith. Just as our Christian life begins and grows through *our* faith in Christ, so theirs must begin and grow because of *their* faith in Christ. We can encourage this by nurturing our children's hearts through time in God's Word.

If our children are not rooted in Christ and grounded in God's Word, they can be drawn into beliefs that aren't true, resulting in unwholesome behavior and separation from God. We want our children to believe not only that Christ is important but that he is everything!

Father,
Thank you that the Bible provides nourishment for us. Please help us to point our children to personal faith in Christ through time spent in your Word.
Amen.

FAITH

AND WE KNOW THAT GOD CAUSES EVERYTHING TO WORK
TOGETHER FOR THE GOOD OF THOSE WHO LOVE GOD AND
ARE CALLED ACCORDING TO HIS PURPOSE FOR THEM.

Romans 8:28

*B*ob, would you please baste the turkey with the broth on the stove?" my mom called downstairs to my dad. "I'll be down in a few minutes." It was Thanksgiving morning, and my mom was preparing her scrumptious recipes for our family gathering.

When my mom came downstairs, ready to work on the lime-pear salad, she took the lid off the pan of pear juice. "Why is the pan empty?" she wondered. Quickly lifting the lid off the other pot on the stove, she discovered it was full of turkey broth. Uh-oh. Now my dad was in trouble. He had basted the turkey with pear juice.

"Did your mom ever ask your dad for help in the kitchen again?" you might ask. Yes, she did. The turkey our family ate that year was the tastiest and best-looking turkey we'd ever had. What began as a mistake and a disappoint-ment turned out to be a new family tradition. Now I baste my turkey with pear juice every year.

I'm reminded of other incidents in my life that included more serious disap-pointments, losses, or pain. At the time they made no sense to me, and my pre-dominant thoughts were, *How do I get out of this situation? How can I get this pain to stop?* or *Surely nothing good can ever come out of all this!* But I have seen God use those difficult circumstances to accomplish good things in my heart, and I have been encouraged to trust him more. As my friend Wanda says, "God does things in his time; and sometimes he even allows us to see the fruit of what he's doing in our time."

Faithful Father,
Thank you for the variety of ways that you work out your purposes in our
lives. It's encouraging to know that you work them together for good. Amen.

FAITH

FIGHT THE GOOD FIGHT OF THE FAITH. TAKE HOLD OF THE
ETERNAL LIFE TO WHICH YOU WERE CALLED WHEN YOU MADE
YOUR GOOD CONFESSION IN THE PRESENCE OF MANY WITNESSES.

1 Timothy 6:12, NIV

*D*uring times in our lives when we're struggling with doubts about God, it's good to remember that doubt is not the same as unbelief. Alister McGrath writes, "Unbelief is the decision to live your life as if there were no God. It is a deliberate decision to reject Jesus Christ and all that he stands for. But doubt is something quite different. Doubt arises within the context of faith. It is a wistful longing to be sure of the things in which we trust."[1]

It's comforting to learn that doubt is a natural part of growing in faith because faith is not easy. To fight for faith is not only to strive vigorously *for* it but also to struggle *against* our adversary, the devil. First Timothy 6:12 is set in a chapter that instructs us to do three things—flee, follow, and fight. We are to flee from pride, the love of money, and false teachings; follow after righteousness, godliness, faith, love, endurance, and gentleness; and fight *for* faith and *against* the world, the flesh, and the devil.

A mom who is depressed, whose husband is involved in addictive behavior, or whose child is hanging out with unwholesome friends has plenty of doubts and struggles—she's clearly in a fight. As we fight against the world, the flesh, and the devil through the power of God's Word and Spirit, we "take hold of . . . eternal life"—we grab it, setting our hope not on fleeting things but on God who gives eternal life and is himself hope.

Father,
Please give us strength as we fight the good fight of faith. Thank you that you have promised you will always be with us. Please help us to grab hold of your promises when doubts rise in our minds and hearts. Amen.

PRAYER

HANNAH WAS IN DEEP ANGUISH, CRYING BITTERLY AS
SHE PRAYED TO THE LORD.

1 Samuel 1:10

*H*ave you ever experienced times of grief, bitterness, or anguish, when you felt as though you were slipping? Hannah did. Back in the Old Testament book of 1 Samuel (1:1–2:21), we learn that Hannah was married to Elkanah, a Levite priest. He also had a second wife, named Peninnah. Each year the combined families made a trip to the Shiloh tabernacle, and each year the same thing happened: Elkanah celebrated his sacrifices by giving gifts to Peninnah and each of her children, but Hannah received only one for herself because she had no children. The Bible tells us that Peninnah laughed at Hannah's barrenness, making Hannah cry so much that she couldn't eat.

One evening in Shiloh, Hannah went over to the tabernacle. Out of her bitter grief and anguish, she cried out to the Lord. In the process of praying, she endured even *more* taunting because the priest mistook her sorrow for drunkenness! But something amazing happened after she poured out her heart to God. The priest gave her a blessing of peace, and after she left the tabernacle, she ate and her face was no longer downcast. After worshipping God together, the families went home, and Hannah became pregnant. We find Hannah's beautiful song of praise in 1 Samuel 2:1-10.

What's the lesson for us? In our heartache or anguish, we can cry out to the Lord, acknowledging that he is God and we are not. We can pour out our souls—grief, bitterness, and all. And after we bring him our requests, we can get on with our lives and worship God, thankful that he hears us.

Father,
Thank you for examples of women like Hannah, who experienced some of the same feelings of sorrow we have from time to time. Thank you that we can express our emotions to you and that you give us the grace and strength to stand up and move ahead. Thanks for your answers to our prayers. Amen.

PRAYER

AND SO WE KEEP ON PRAYING FOR YOU, THAT OUR GOD
WILL MAKE YOU WORTHY OF THE LIFE TO WHICH HE CALLED
YOU. AND WE PRAY THAT GOD, BY HIS POWER, WILL FULFILL ALL YOUR
GOOD INTENTIONS AND FAITHFUL DEEDS.   *2 Thessalonians 1:11*

I just sneaked into my son Nate's bedroom and straightened the blankets over his sleeping body—all six-feet-two of it. He returned home today from a mission trip to Bucharest, Romania. It is *so* good to have him home even if he is asleep. During the weeks he was gone, we were able to communicate through e-mail, and that was great. But I was thankful that I could pray for him all through the day and even sometimes when I woke up at night.

When I communicate with Nate through letters or e-mail, I catch up on the news. But when I pray for him, there's an added dimension to communication. I talk to Nate's Creator and my Creator, his Savior and my Savior, his sustainer and my sustainer. The God who is everywhere at once and who knows everything knows how much I care for Nate, and he hears my prayers on his behalf no matter what hour of the day or night it may be.

Whether our children are in our house, down the street, or across the world, we can communicate with God on their behalf, having confidence that God sees their bodies, minds, and hearts. Mark Twain once said, "I don't know of a single foreign product that enters this country untaxed except the answer to prayer." Prayer, unlike long-distance phone calls, does not cost money. We don't have to shop around for the best rates or the best times—we can talk to God anytime!

God who is everywhere and never sleeps,
Thank you that we can pray for our children anytime and anywhere.
Thank you that you are the God who sees and provides. Amen.

PRAYER

POUR OUT YOUR HEART LIKE WATER IN THE PRESENCE
OF THE LORD. LIFT UP YOUR HANDS TO HIM FOR THE LIVES
OF YOUR CHILDREN.   *Lamentations 2:19, NIV*

*P*astor Dennis Eenigenburg tells the childhood story of a time he returned home from school with a note from his elementary school teacher, who was concerned that Dennis perpetually talked back to her. His mother was becoming increasingly frustrated by his negative behavior at school, and she wasn't seeing much progress. This particular time, she stood looking at Dennis with tears in her eyes, and then she took his hand and led him to her bedroom. Although Dennis was expecting a well-deserved spanking, what he experienced was far more meaningful. His mother asked him to kneel down next to her as she prayed, and she asked God for wisdom to guide her son. As she prayed, she cried. Dennis was deeply moved. If his behavior was that important to his mom, he thought, he had to change. He reflects that no spanking he ever received had as much impact on him as kneeling next to his praying mother.

Haven't all of us moms, at some point, become frustrated by the behavior or attitudes of our children, our husbands, or ourselves? Perhaps we can relate to the verse above, which expresses the anguish of the Jewish people over the utter ruin of their city. Although most of us have not lived through the painful experience of having another nation conquer us, we sometimes experience anguish over a rebellious child, a husband we're concerned about, or an area in which we lack self-control in our own lives. Pouring our hearts out to God in these situations is the very best thing we can do.

Father,
Like the prophet Jeremiah, may we acknowledge our pain and call it to mind
with hope: "Because of the Lord's great love we are not consumed, for his
compassions never fail. They are new every morning; great is your faithful-
ness" (Lamentations 3:22-23, NIV). Amen.

PRAYER

THE LORD IS MY LIGHT AND MY SALVATION—SO WHY
SHOULD I BE AFRAID? THE LORD PROTECTS ME FROM DANGER—
SO WHY SHOULD I TREMBLE?

Psalm 27:1

One summer we took a family vacation to the Colorado Rocky Mountains. We spent an adventure-packed week surrounded by the spectacular Collegian Peaks, all of which were fourteen thousand or more feet. They towered above our A-frame cabin.

In the middle of the week, we decided to rent a four-wheel drive jeep to get into the back country. As we approached a rocky peak called "Tin Cup Pass" well above the timberline, we shut down the jeep to enjoy the quiet view. You can imagine our consternation when, after trying to restart the engine, we discovered that it not only wouldn't start, but the battery was quickly losing life. We were six miles from a ghost town, and we had a limited amount of food, water, and daylight. It was a frightening moment.

David, the writer of Psalm 27, faced many of his own harrowing "mountaintop experiences." Chased by jealous King Saul, David spent many of his early years as a leader running from one rocky mountain to the next, trying to stay one step ahead of his enemy.

Life feels like that sometimes. But David reminds us that the Lord is our light and salvation—so why should we fear? David found in the very rocks a picture of God. In Psalm 18:2 he says, "The Lord is my rock, my fortress, and my savior . . . in whom I find protection." We too can claim God's promise that he will provide for us whether it is light or dark. The Lord will supply all our needs, regardless of how high our feelings of anxiety or insecurity may rise.

There as a family on top of the mountain, we took one another's hands, reminded ourselves of God's faithfulness, and prayed for the Lord to protect us and help us get down the mountain. When we decided to try to start the jeep one last time, you can imagine our joy when the engine sprang back to life!

Sovereign Lord,
Thank you that no matter where we are, you are there with us, defending and
protecting us. In the name of Jesus, amen.

PRAYER

CONFESS YOUR SINS TO EACH OTHER AND PRAY
FOR EACH OTHER SO THAT YOU MAY BE HEALED. THE
EARNEST PRAYER OF A RIGHTEOUS PERSON HAS GREAT
POWER AND WONDERFUL RESULTS.

James 5:16

How many times each day do I encounter challenges that I could pray about? Often. How much time each day do I actually spend praying? Probably not enough. I'm presently aware of several crisis situations that family and friends are experiencing, and these concerns pop into my mind throughout each day. What do I learn from God's Word that can help me with these concerns?

It's interesting that the verse above begins with a call to confession. Sin brings great isolation to our lives. In the person perpetuating the sin, it produces selfishness; in others affected, it may produce unhealthy tendencies to hide the wrongdoing or protect the sinner. Confessing to each other removes these barriers and allows us to start afresh, focusing on God rather than ourselves.

Here are some practical ways of praying for specific needs:

- Pray using Scripture (see Psalm 25:8; 86:11; 119:37; 1 Thessalonians 5:23-24; Hebrews 13:20-21).
- Pray at specific times each day—perhaps during your children's naps or while you're fixing dinner.
- Leave Post-it notes on the mirror or above the kitchen sink to remind yourself of prayer requests.
- Use time alone in the car to pray.
- Remember that caring and doing are great, but the Bible promises that praying is powerful and effective!

Father,
Thanks for the reminder from your Word that our prayers can be powerful and effective. Thanks for those who pray for us. May we be faithful to do the same for our families and friends. Amen.

PRAYER

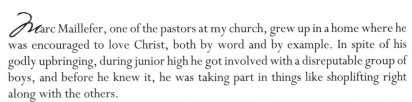

WHAT WE PRAY FOR IS YOUR RESTORATION TO MATURITY.

2 Corinthians 13:9

*M*arc Maillefer, one of the pastors at my church, grew up in a home where he was encouraged to love Christ, both by word and by example. In spite of his godly upbringing, during junior high he got involved with a disreputable group of boys, and before he knew it, he was taking part in things like shoplifting right along with the others.

Marc's mom mobilized many of the women of her church to pray for her son, and it was no secret to him. Some moms reading this devotional keenly understand the urgency of a parent's prayers for a struggling child. Nothing can bring us to our knees like feeling helpless in the face of challenges with our kids.

After eighth grade, Marc was invited to the Moody Church summer camp. Through the influence of God's Word and Spirit, Marc decided to aim his heart toward Christ and a wiser way of living.

One memory Marc says he will take with him to the grave is the image of his dad, sitting in his blue Volkswagen Bug, praying for Marc each morning before dropping him off for school. Marc is incredibly grateful to God for his faithfulness and for answering the prayers of his parents. He isn't the only one who's grateful—so is my family, because we have benefited from Marc's pastoral leadership.

When we pray for our children, we don't know how many people's lives they might touch in the future. Generations ago Abraham Lincoln said, "I remember my mother's prayers, and they have always followed me. They have clung to me all my life."

Father,
Thank you that you listen to the prayers of concerned parents. Where else would we turn? In Jesus' name, amen.

PRAYER

AND PRAY IN THE SPIRIT ON ALL OCCASIONS WITH ALL
KINDS OF PRAYERS AND REQUESTS. WITH THIS IN MIND, BE
ALERT AND ALWAYS KEEP ON PRAYING FOR ALL THE SAINTS.

Ephesians 6:18, NIV

This verse is so full of help for us on the habit of prayer that it's exciting to unpack all the instructions!

1. "Pray in the Spirit." At the outset of our prayers, we are wise to ask for the Spirit's help because, as Romans 8:26-27 explains, the Spirit helps us when we don't know how to pray and even when we think we do.
2. "Pray . . . on all occasions." When I was compiling *The Christian Mom's Idea Book,* one mom told me, "I pray at the sink, in the car, in the doctor's waiting room, with joy, with tears, through hardships, for the future, in all aspects and places of life."[2]
3. "Pray . . . with all kinds of prayers." One minute we might be thanking God, and five minutes later we may need to confess something to him. Sometimes we offer praise, and sometimes it's great to pray Scripture back to God.
4. "Keep on praying." Be persistent. My pastor, Kent Hughes, relates how he prayed for thirty years that his brother would come to Christ. One day when he was visiting, his brother said to Kent, "Let's talk about my soul." They ended up praying together, and his brother came to Christ!
5. "Praying for all the saints." Our prayers for fellow believers help them overcome the enemy and increase God's kingdom.

Prayer costs us no money, and the lines of communication are never overcrowded. What an incredible privilege it is to pray!

Father,
Thank you that when you teach us that we should pray, you also teach
us how to do it effectively. May we do it. Amen.

BIBLE

ALL SCRIPTURE IS INSPIRED BY GOD AND IS USEFUL TO
TEACH US WHAT IS TRUE AND TO MAKE US REALIZE WHAT IS
WRONG IN OUR LIVES. IT STRAIGHTENS US OUT AND TEACHES US TO DO
WHAT IS RIGHT. IT IS GOD'S WAY OF PREPARING US IN EVERY WAY, FULLY
EQUIPPED FOR EVERY GOOD THING GOD WANTS US TO DO. *2 Timothy 3:16-17*

I am grateful to have grown up in a home where the Word of God was honored and taught. My parents, Sunday school teachers, and youth leaders all treated the Bible with great respect; and as a result, my love for God's Word has grown through the years.

The New Testament character Timothy, a friend of the apostle Paul, was the son of a Gentile father and a Jewish-Christian mother. In spite of the fact that Timothy's father was probably not a believer, Timothy was taught the Scriptures from a very young age. His mother and grandmother gave him a great heritage. They not only taught him the truth, but they also guided him into spiritual understanding. The truth led him to a belief that ultimately brought him to salvation in Christ. Truth—faith—salvation. The pattern of Timothy's family is a pattern for us all.

God's Word brought Timothy to salvation, but it also provided everything he needed for effective Christian living.

F. B. Meyer writes, "In the stern experiences of life there is no stay that is comparable to the Holy Scriptures. . . . Whatever our need, we can find its solace and remedy here. Thus, we may live a complete life, finding in the Bible resources for all our emergencies."[3]

What experiences of life are you facing today? Spending time in God's Word will prepare you in every way so that you are equipped for every good thing God wants you to do. The Bible helps transform a new Christian into a mature person in Christ. The longer we live the Christian life, the more we realize our need for God's Word.

Father,
Thank you for the Bible. Thank you for the example of Timothy's mother and grandmother, who taught him to love and obey your Word. Please give us wisdom and grace with our children as we do the same. Amen.

BIBLE

YOUR WORD IS A LAMP FOR MY FEET AND A LIGHT
FOR MY PATH.
Psalm 119:105

*J*oanne Shetler, a missionary to the Balangao tribe in the northern part of the Philippines, was traveling by helicopter to deliver cement, glass, and nails for the tribe's new hospital clinic. As the helicopter descended, something went terribly wrong, and the helicopter crashed. At first Joanne feared she might burn to death, but after the Balangaos dug and yanked to get her out, she squirmed loose of the wreckage. Blood from gashes on her head mixed and hardened with the cement powder that covered her body, burning her eyes and filling her lungs.

While Joanne waited for help throughout the torturous night, some of the Balangao people worked their way through the throng, touched her hand, and prayed, "God, don't let her die—the Book's not done yet. Please let her live; the Book's not done yet." You see, Joanne was translating the Bible into the Balangaos' language so they could hear the words of the God who speaks. Because they were hungry to hear more of God's Word, they prayed for the life of the missionary who had been sent to them.

Joanne recovered from the accident and finished the translation of the Bible, and many lives were brought from darkness to light. When Joanne's work there was done and she was ready to board a plane home, Ama, a Balangao man, sent her home with this blessing: "Thank you. Thank you. Thank you for coming. I never would have known about God if you hadn't come."[4]

God who loves the whole world,
Thank you that your Word lights our path. May we read and study Scripture carefully, hiding it in our hearts so we can share it with others who also need to hear your words. Amen.

GOD'S LAWS ARE PERFECT. THEY PROTECT US, MAKE US
WISE, AND GIVE US JOY AND LIGHT. GOD'S LAWS ARE PURE,
ETERNAL, JUST. THEY ARE MORE DESIRABLE THAN GOLD. THEY ARE
SWEETER THAN HONEY DRIPPING FROM A HONEYCOMB. FOR THEY WARN US AWAY
FROM HARM AND GIVE SUCCESS TO THOSE WHO OBEY THEM.   *Psalm 19:7-11, TLB*

*W*arning our children away from harm and pointing them toward success is what we want to do for them, right? We teach them not to touch the stove because we don't want them to be burned. We instruct them not to play in the street because we don't want them to get hit by a car. We teach them to do their homework and study for tests so they can enjoy the rewards of learning. We give them tangible laws to follow because we want the best for them.

Most parents set these guidelines because they care deeply about their children. But I'm amazed at how many parents present their kids with "ideas" as opposed to laws.

I was disheartened by a recent newspaper article written by a parent who said that abstinence before marriage is a fine idea, but that it is only an opinion—not a hard-and-fast rule. What's the natural result of that approach? In a recent survey of three thousand couples conducted by *Bride's* magazine, only 4 percent of the women and one percent of the men reported that they were virgins when they married.

What would happen if I taught my child that not exceeding the speed limit is only an opinion? He could cause an accident. God didn't give ten opinions on Mt. Sinai—he gave the Ten Commandments, all of which point to Christ, who is the ultimate fulfillment of all God's requirements.

It shouldn't surprise us that God gave us laws for our spiritual well-being. Just as we physically protect our children, God has graciously established laws for our *spiritual* protection. His laws are based on truth and goodness—a sign of his great love and care.

Father,
Thank you that as we obey your Word, we experience protection, wisdom, joy,
and light. Help us not to chafe at the boundaries you have set but to embrace
them. Amen.

BIBLE

> YOU ARE MY REFUGE AND MY SHIELD; YOUR WORD IS MY
> ONLY SOURCE OF HOPE. *Psalm 119:114*

*O*ver the years I've prayed that my sons would grow in their love for God and his Word, but sometimes I forget that it's often the challenges of life that send us running there.

I'll never forget the afternoon I picked up one of my sons from high school and could tell by the way he walked to the car that he'd had a dismal day. After he told me about a big disappointment (his girlfriend had informed friends at school that she was breaking up with him before she told him), I redirected our van to Taco Bell. As the mother of boys, I've discovered that a favorite snack often helps promote good conversation. When we returned home and sat at the kitchen table, I listened to his feelings and tried to encourage him the best I could.

Later that afternoon, I walked upstairs to check on my son in his bedroom, and I noticed that his eyes were red. As I sat down next to him, I noticed something else. On his desk was his open Bible. When I asked him what he was reading, he said, "Hebrews 13:5, where God promises that he will never leave us or forsake us." Then it was my turn to get misty eyes.

That experience reminded me why it's important to saturate a child's life with reverent knowledge of God's Word. Then, when they need hope, they know exactly where to turn. Ruth Graham wisely wrote: "If our children have the background of . . . unshakable faith that the Bible is indeed the Word of God, they will have a foundation that the forces of hell cannot shake."

Father,
Help us to cherish the Bible so that our children will cherish it, too.
Thanks for the encouragement your Word brings to people of all ages.
In Jesus' name, amen.

BIBLE

THE RAIN AND SNOW COME DOWN FROM THE HEAVENS AND
STAY ON THE GROUND TO WATER THE EARTH. THEY CAUSE THE
GRAIN TO GROW, PRODUCING SEED FOR THE FARMER AND BREAD FOR
THE HUNGRY. IT IS THE SAME WITH MY WORD. I SEND IT OUT, AND IT ALWAYS
PRODUCES FRUIT. IT WILL ACCOMPLISH ALL I WANT IT TO, AND IT WILL PROSPER
EVERYWHERE I SEND IT.   *Isaiah 55:10-11*

*R*ainfall makes a difference. In the central areas of South America, which receive over sixty inches of rainfall a year, life-forms flourish. But in places like
northern Africa, which receives less than ten inches of rainfall a year, the land is
dry and treeless.

I love the verses from Isaiah that liken rain and snow to God's Word. I especially appreciate the progression of the action: the precipitation comes down,
stays, waters, causes grain to grow, produces seed, and makes bread. That's what
rain and snow do for people, and that's what God's Word does for us.

It *comes down*. It may come during a church service, or while a mother reads a
Bible story at bedtime, or through a neighborhood Bible study.

It *stays*. Just as moisture is absorbed into the ground, God's Word is absorbed
into our hearts.

It *waters*. Revelation 22:17 (NIV) says, "Whoever is thirsty, let him come; and
whoever wishes, let him take the free gift of the water of life." God's Word refreshes us and gives us life.

It *causes grain to grow*. When God's Word sprouts in our hearts, it's like the
grain—first the stalk appears, then the head, and then the full kernel, producing
more seed. Growth takes time.

It *produces seed*. The new seed dies, takes root, sprouts, and grows as it is nurtured. As we share God's good news with others, the seeds of his truth are multiplied in their hearts. God's Word is necessary for all these stages of growth.

It *produces bread*; it *gives life*. The Word of God leads us to an eternal relationship with Jesus, who is the Bread of Life (John 6:35).

Father,
Thank you for the rain and snow you provide to water the earth. Thank you for
your Word, which points us to a growing relationship with Jesus, the Bread of
Life. May we be faithful in guiding our children to your Word. Amen.

BIBLE

I REJOICE IN YOUR WORD LIKE ONE WHO FINDS
A GREAT TREASURE.

Psalm 119:162

*O*f all the birthday parties our sons were invited to, I think the most creative one involved a treasure hunt. After the boys arrived at the Howards' home and got settled, Mr. Howard read them their first clue in the form of a riddle. The first riddle helped the kids figure out where to look for the second clue (in a copy of *Treasure Island* at the public library), and so on. Some of the subsequent locations were the Popcorn Shop, Dairy Queen, the baseball card shop, and one or two others. Each destination seemed more exciting than the last. The very last riddle led the boys back to the Howards' house, where they spied a huge treasure chest, overflowing with candy and prizes for everyone!

The image of a treasure hunt is a good way to describe my love for the Bible, which has grown over the years. It began with Bible stories I heard from my parents and Sunday school teachers as a child. My youth leaders and pastors continued opening up God's Word to me, and then three of my college years were spent studying at Moody Bible Institute. But my most meaningful times in the Bible have been and continue to be the quiet moments I spend each day "panning for gold"—and I always find some. "Truly, I love your commands more than gold, even the finest gold" (Psalm 119:127).

As good as the stops are along the way, the final destination of the "hunt" in the Bible—the treasure—is Christ. "In [Christ] lie hidden all the treasures of wisdom and knowledge" (Colossians 2:3).

Father,
Thank you for the treasure of your Word. Thank you that you sent
Jesus—your treasure—to die for us. In Christ's name, amen.

BIBLE

ALL MEN ARE LIKE GRASS, AND ALL THEIR GLORY IS LIKE
THE FLOWERS OF THE FIELD. THE GRASS WITHERS AND THE
FLOWERS FALL, BECAUSE THE BREATH OF THE LORD BLOWS ON THEM.
SURELY THE PEOPLE ARE GRASS. THE GRASS WITHERS AND THE FLOWERS FALL, BUT
THE WORD OF OUR GOD STANDS FOREVER.

Isaiah 40:6-8, NIV

I have always loved reading these verses from Isaiah because of the last phrase: "but the word of our God stands forever." Those few words remind me that God's Word has an *eternal* shelf life. Unlike grass or flowers, it never dies. Throughout the Bible we are likened to grass as a reminder of our human frailty. Lest we get to thinking we are invincible and will live here forever, God's Word points out that our earthly lives are temporary.

In Palestine, grass is green from April through October, when there's plenty of rain. But when the dry season comes, the grass dries up and withers. Flowers provide us with another example of the transience of our lives. Flowers are beautiful and wonderful. They bud, sprout, and burst forth with color and aroma. When flowers from our gardens hit that bursting point, we sometimes cut them, bringing them into our houses to enjoy in a vase or an arrangement. But whether we leave them growing outside or bring them inside, individual flowers and blooms very quickly begin to droop. Their color and fragrance fade.

When we contrast the length of bloom our lives have with the length of bloom the Scriptures have, we realize that we can never put too much emphasis on God's Word. In all the demands of motherhood, it's so easy for us to let other seemingly urgent things crowd out our reading, meditating upon, and praying over God's Word. But in the context of eternity, what is most lasting and important?

God of the Bible,
Thank you for the incredible value and life of your Word. May we make time
each day to read it, and then may we choose to obey it. Amen.

FRIENDSHIP

> A FEW DAYS LATER MARY HURRIED TO THE HILL COUNTRY
> OF JUDEA, TO THE TOWN WHERE ZECHARIAH LIVED. SHE
> ENTERED THE HOUSE AND GREETED ELIZABETH.   *Luke 1:39-40*

Think about your close friendships. What are some of the ingredients that make them special? My list includes common values, enjoyable companionship, mutual respect, shared circumstances, and exchanged confidences.

In Luke 1 we read that during the months before and after the births of John the Baptist and Jesus, Elizabeth and Mary formed a special friendship based first on their common values. The Bible explains that Elizabeth was obedient to God's Word. And in Mary's reaction to the angel's announcement, we see evidence of her humility, belief in God, and willingness to be his servant.

The circumstances these women shared were remarkably similar. Both women's pregnancies were announced by angels, and both were unusual—Elizabeth's because she was old, and Mary's because she was a virgin. Both women were obedient to God and were willing to be his servants.

I like how Luke described the way Mary "hurried" to the town where Elizabeth lived. That's how it is when we enjoy the companionship of another woman—we can't *wait* to share our news!

Mary and Elizabeth must have had many cups of tea and hours of deep conversation as they shared the secrets of their own experiences—the angels, the announcements, the wonder, and the pregnancies. The mutual respect between these two women was fascinating. If they had been petty or selfish women, there might have been some jealousy. But instead we find Elizabeth, who was full of God's Spirit, blessing Mary, and Mary, who was full of belief, praising God. They were truly soul mates whose souls were aligned first with God and then with each other. These two women of faith left an exquisite example of Christian friendship for us today.

Father,
Thank you for the companionship, respect, shared circumstances, and
confidences modeled in the friendship of Mary and Elizabeth. Please provide
us with the blessing of Christian friends and give us grace to be the best friend
we can be. Amen.

FRIENDSHIP

YOUR OWN SOUL IS NOURISHED WHEN YOU ARE KIND,
BUT YOU DESTROY YOURSELF WHEN YOU ARE CRUEL.

Proverbs 11:17

I've heard a story of a young soldier in World War I who asked his officer to allow him to go out into the no-man's-land between the trenches. He wanted to bring back one of his comrades who lay grievously wounded. "You can go," said the officer, "but it's not worth it. Your friend is probably dead, and you will throw your own life away." But the man went. Somehow he managed to get to his friend, hoist him onto his shoulder, and bring him back to the trenches. The two of them tumbled in together and lay at the bottom.

The officer looked very tenderly at the would-be rescuer, and then he said, "I told you it wouldn't be worth it. Your friend is dead, and you are mortally wounded."

"It was worth it, though, sir," the soldier said.

"How do you mean, 'worth it'? I tell you, your friend is dead."

"Yes, sir," the boy answered, "but it was worth it because when I got to him he was still alive, and he said to me, 'Jim, I knew you'd come.'"

Isn't that the kind of friend each of us desires? That kind of friend sees a need, is willing to get involved, and acts unselfishly. All of us have opportunities to be that kind of friend.

In God's gracious plan, we are sometimes the givers and sometimes the receivers. Healthy friendships involve a certain degree of both and are worth more than their weight in gold.

Father,
Thank you for the wonderful gift of friendship. Please prompt us to be aware
of those who might be lonely or new to our communities and be willing to
bring grace into their lives. And may we be sensitive to the hurts and needs of
our friends around us. Amen.

FRIENDSHIP

THE GREATEST LOVE IS SHOWN WHEN PEOPLE LAY DOWN
THEIR LIVES FOR THEIR FRIENDS.   *John 15:13*

What kind of a friend was Jesus? Several years ago I worked my way through the Gospels to find an answer to that question. Here are some of my discoveries:

1. Jesus took initiative—he called out to Peter and Andrew.
2. He spent time (lots of it) with those he taught. And he talked about the really important things in life.
3. He reached out and touched the man with leprosy, showing his compassion.
4. Jesus associated with sinners. When the Pharisees asked him about this, he explained that it's not the healthy who need a doctor—it's the sick people.
5. He was honest with his friends and separated himself from false flattery.
6. He was protective of people's souls, not of things.
7. He served his friends, leaving them an example by washing their feet.
8. He prayed for his friends, that they would be united as he and the Father are, that they would be kept from Satan's power, and that they would be made pure and holy through the Word. This is a great model of how to pray for our children and their friends.
9. He was selfless; he ultimately sacrificed his lifeblood for sinners— for us.
10. Jesus selected friends carefully. He did not choose people who pretended to be good when they weren't, or people who were so obsessed with detailed regulations that they lost sight of justice and the love of God. While he still loved these people, he didn't turn to them for companionship.

What a great example of friendship Jesus left for all of us!

Father,
Thank you that you are the best friend we could ever have. Thanks that you call us your friends if we obey you. Please help us to be a good friend. Amen.

FRIENDSHIP

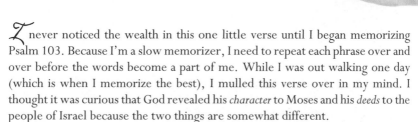

He revealed his character to Moses and his deeds to
the people of Israel.   *Psalm 103:7*

I never noticed the wealth in this one little verse until I began memorizing Psalm 103. Because I'm a slow memorizer, I need to repeat each phrase over and over before the words become a part of me. While I was out walking one day (which is when I memorize the best), I mulled this verse over in my mind. I thought it was curious that God revealed his *character* to Moses and his *deeds* to the people of Israel because the two things are somewhat different.

Although character and deeds are related, it's more intimate to know something about a person's character than his actions. If I explained my son Jordan's *deeds* to you, I might say, "He golfs, he goes to high school, he goes to youth group at church, and he plays the trumpet, guitar, and accordion." That would tell you what he does. But what if I described Jordan's *character*? What if I told you that he is kind, patient, polite, entertaining, and innovative? Wouldn't you know more about him?

When we describe someone's deeds, we convey their achievements, their acts, and their accomplishments. But when we describe that person's character, we convey their individuality, their disposition, and their personality. Pondering the contrast between deeds and character has prompted me to ask questions about my own relationship with God. Do I, like the people of Israel, concern myself mainly with his deeds? Or do I, like Moses, concern myself also with God's character?

> *Father,*
> *Thank you that our relationship with you can go beyond knowing what*
> *you've done. We're thankful that we can get to know who you are. In Jesus'*
> *name, amen.*

FRIENDSHIP

A FRIEND IS ALWAYS LOYAL, AND A BROTHER IS BORN
TO HELP IN TIME OF NEED.   *Proverbs 17:17*

*G*od's Word reminds me that knowledge alone is not enough for spiritual growth. I also need the grace of friendships.

When I consider my close friendships, three things come to mind. First, mutual love. None of us is perfect, so we're not looking for perfection, but it's important to respect some of our friend's qualities. Second, mutual trust. Friends can rely on each other to keep confidences, help out when needed, and do what they say they're going to do. Because friendships are built on mutual respect and trust, God warns us in Proverbs 22:24-25, "Keep away from angry, short-tempered people, or you will learn to be like them and endanger your soul." Third, shared conversations and experiences. Whether funny and lighthearted or deep and serious, we accumulate memories of sharing and caring. Of course, having each experienced the common denominator of God's love and grace adds an eternal element to our friendships.

The book *A Confident Woman* defines a friend like this: "A friend is someone to whom I do not have to explain myself. Such a friendship offers unspeakable comfort. Friendship can also be redemptive, for friends can act as mediators of God's presence and invite us into the embrace of God's grace."[5]

Over the seasons of our life, it's good to look for a balance in friendships. Are we frequently on the giving end? Are we frequently on the receiving end? It's healthy for us to experience some of both.

One of our roles as moms is helping our children learn to develop healthy friendships. We can do this by modeling strong relationships, by praying for their friendships, and by guiding and encouraging them to make healthy choices for themselves—one choice at a time.

Father,
Thank you for blessing us with redemptive friendships. Help us trust you
to bring these relationships into our lives in your time. Amen.

FRIENDSHIP

THEN DAVID BOWED TO JONATHAN WITH HIS FACE TO THE GROUND. BOTH OF THEM WERE IN TEARS AS THEY EMBRACED EACH OTHER AND SAID GOOD-BYE, ESPECIALLY DAVID. AT LAST JONATHAN SAID TO DAVID, "GO IN PEACE, FOR WE HAVE MADE A PACT IN THE LORD'S NAME. WE HAVE ENTRUSTED EACH OTHER AND EACH OTHER'S CHILDREN INTO THE LORD'S HANDS FOREVER."

1 Samuel 20:41-42

During the 2004 Summer Olympics held in Athens, we saw a striking gesture of friendship. Two fiercely competitive Americans were swimming in the same event. At the end of the race Michael Phelps, a swimmer who had already won four gold medals, triumphed over Ian Crocker, who had yet to win his own gold medal. Along with the victory, Phelps had earned a position in the men's four-hundred-meter medley relay final, and would almost assuredly win yet another medal. To the world's great astonishment, Phelps volunteered to give up his place to Crocker so that his teammate would have a chance to win at least one gold medal for himself. What an act of kindness and friendship!

Phelps's unselfish gesture reminds us of a similar friendship in the Old Testament—that of David and Jonathan. Jonathan, the son of King Saul, was next in line for the throne by virtue of his family. Yet, having been given God's word that David would be the next king, he did not rebel against God's plan but rather embraced David as his dearest friend.

Jesus said, "The greatest love is shown when people lay down their lives for their friends. You are my friends if you obey me" (John 15:13-14). He spoke these words the night before his death, an event that supremely demonstrates true friendship and opens the door to a relationship with God himself through our obedience of faith. Jesus commends such active love to us. He challenges us to give away our lives to others, just as Jonathan was willing to give up the kingdom to David, the man God chose.

Lord,
Help me today to be a true friend to those around me, willing to give of
myself for the benefit of others. In the name of Jesus, my true friend, amen.

FRIENDSHIP

AND ELISHA SAID, "BORROW AS MANY EMPTY JARS AS YOU
CAN FROM YOUR FRIENDS AND NEIGHBORS."   *2 Kings 4:3*

*H*ave you ever gone through a time in your life when you felt lonely but found it difficult to reach out for companionship? I have. At a period in my life when I felt depressed and discouraged, reaching out felt risky. I feared what might happen if I didn't sense acceptance from the other person.

Philip Yancey and Tim Stafford see some good in this condition. They write, "I believe God created us incomplete, not as a cruel trick to edge us toward self-pity, but as an opportunity to edge us toward others with similar needs. His whole plan for us involves relationships with others: reach out to the world around us in love. Loneliness, that painful twinge inside, makes us reach out."[6]

With all the hustle and bustle of our schedules as moms, we have a fair amount of physical companionship—especially when the children are young. But it's easy to feel lonely, even when there are lots of bodies in the room, if our soul hasn't had enough opportunity to knit with a friend or companion. God built this need into us.

Think of the woman Jesus described who lost a silver coin and upon finding it rejoiced with friends. Or remember the widow ministered to by Elisha who was instructed to ask all her friends and neighbors for jars to hold the oil that was about to be miraculously multiplied. Asking her friends for their help may have felt risky and humbling, but I like to imagine the joy and excitement they all shared in the experience.

When we get to feeling lonely, we can present our need to God because he cares, sees, and provides. But we can also then call a friend or someone we'd like to get to know and put something on the calendar!

Father,
Thank you that you intend for us to need other people. Thank you that you
understand our loneliness because you experienced it yourself when you lived
on earth. May we do our part in connecting with others around us. Amen.

HOPE

We wait in hope for the Lord; he is our help and our shield. In him our hearts rejoice, for we trust in his holy name. May your unfailing love rest upon us, O Lord, even as we put our hope in you.

Psalm 33:20-22, NIV

Have you ever waited for something very important? For a parent to know Christ? For a child to complete cancer treatments? For a husband who has strayed from God's truth to return? Waiting is difficult. The Old Testament character Joseph spent a fair amount of his life waiting. I've often wondered what his life was like—first in the dry well where his brothers dumped him before they sold him to Ishmaelite traders, and then as he waited again before he arrived in Egypt and was sold to Potiphar, one of Pharaoh's officials. But the Bible tells us that God was with Joseph and that Joseph experienced success in all that he did.

Even when he was falsely accused and sent to prison, Joseph knew God showed him extra kindness through the prison warden. After two more years of waiting, Joseph was not only called out of prison to interpret Pharaoh's dream, but he was put in charge of Pharaoh's palace and ultimately the whole land of Egypt. Joseph was eventually reunited with his family in a miraculous way that only God could have arranged! (Read more of Joseph's story in Genesis 37, 39–45.)

Was Joseph waiting on his brothers? The Ishmaelites? Potiphar? Yes, but he was also waiting on God. The influence and even forgetfulness of some of those individuals was all part of God's larger plan for the world. Are you experiencing a time of waiting in your life? Remember, we're not only waiting on people or a process—we're waiting on God.

God who sees and provides,
Waiting sometimes feels hopeless and pointless. But we find encouragement
in seeing your faithfulness to other people who waited on you. May we
experience your unfailing love as we put our hope in you. Amen.

HOPE

FOR EVERYTHING THAT WAS WRITTEN IN THE PAST
WAS WRITTEN TO TEACH US, SO THAT THROUGH ENDURANCE
AND THE ENCOURAGEMENT OF THE SCRIPTURES WE MIGHT
HAVE HOPE.   *Romans 15:4, NIV*

I once had a part-time job playing violin for services at a funeral home. I sat through many sermons from a variety of religious perspectives. Some messages were downright depressing, but the ones I appreciated contained words of hope. Not hollow, fluffy words, but words that came from God's Word. The Bible consistently gives us encouragement that lasts.

Based on Romans 15:4, I believe that a large part of our hope comes from the *encouragement* of God's Word. Sometimes we read it ourselves, other times we hear God's Word taught at church or a Bible study, and hopefully our friends encourage us with it from time to time. Not long ago I was feeling in a panic after receiving some bad news, but when I opened my Bible to Psalm 94:19 and read, "When doubts filled my mind, your comfort gave me renewed hope and cheer," I was encouraged.

Endurance is the other aspect of hope mentioned in Romans 15:4. God graciously gives us choices, and one of our choices is to endure instead of giving up. Endurance is the act, power, or quality of carrying on despite hardships or difficulties. We can give our children lots of encouragement on their homework, but unless they choose to *do* it—to endure—they have no hope of doing well. Hope is like that for us too. We receive encouragement from God's Word, but we must also choose to carry on!

> *Father,*
> *Thank you for the encouragement we receive from your Word. May we choose to endure with your help and strength. Amen.*

HOPE

FROM THE DEPTHS OF DESPAIR, O LORD, I CALL FOR YOUR
HELP. HEAR MY CRY, O LORD. PAY ATTENTION TO MY PRAYER. . . .
O ISRAEL, HOPE IN THE LORD; FOR WITH THE LORD THERE IS UNFAILING
LOVE AND AN OVERFLOWING SUPPLY OF SALVATION.
Psalm 130:1-2, 7

I admire the psalmist for writing with such refreshing honesty: "From the depths of despair, O Lord, I call for your help." Admitting my pain to God, to myself, and to others is not a sign of weakness, although it might feel that way at times. Rather, it's a sign of honesty and integrity.

The "depths of despair" describes a low point. However we arrive there, it feels like a place of weakness. Sometimes we despair because of circumstances, sometimes we despair because of choices—ours or our children's—and sometimes we don't understand why we feel such despair. Whether our discouragement involves sadness, anger, or numbness about health, money, or relationships, being in the depths leaves us feeling isolated and—at times—even distant from God. This is precisely when we need him the most! G. K. Chesterton said, "When belief in God becomes difficult, the tendency is to turn away from him, but—in heaven's name—to WHAT?"

The psalmist acknowledged both his fear *and* his trust in God. It's reassuring that he struggled toward a proper perspective in the middle of his conflicting feelings. I do too. He dealt with his despair in a healthy way by calling out to God, counting on God for help, and hoping in God's Word. His pattern has guided me at points of despair in my own life. God did not disappoint the psalmist, and he hasn't disappointed me either.

Father,
Thank you that it's safe to bring our fears to you. Thank you for your promise to watch over those who hope in your unfailing love. Amen.

HOPE

WHEN EVERYTHING IS READY, I WILL COME AND GET
YOU, SO THAT YOU WILL ALWAYS BE WITH ME WHERE I AM.

John 14:3

*P*eter Marshall knew a mom whose young son was critically ill and facing death. The mother had spent hours nursing him and playing with him, knowing that the boy's days on earth were short. One day the boy asked his mother what it would be like to die. After the mother prayed for wisdom and composure, she said, "Kenneth, do you remember when you were a tiny boy how you used to play so hard all day that when night came you were too tired even to undress? You would tumble into your mother's bed and fall asleep. That was not your bed; it was not where you belonged. You would only stay there a little while. Much to your surprise, you would wake up and find yourself in your own bed in your own room. You were there because someone had loved you and taken care of you. Your father had come with big strong arms and carried you away. Kenneth, darling, death is just like that. We wake up some morning to find ourselves in the other room—the room where we belong—because the Lord Jesus loved us and died for us."

With a peaceful face, the lad looked up at his mother. She knew that he understood and that there would be love and trust in his little heart as he went to meet the Father in heaven. He never asked any more questions, and he died peacefully several weeks later. His strong heavenly Father had taken the boy to be with him.

Father,
Thank you that your hope and peace come to the hearts of believers
of all ages as we trust in your death and resurrection on our behalf. Amen.

"For I know the plans I have for you," says the Lord.
"They are plans for good and not for disaster, to give
you a future and a hope."

Jeremiah 29:11

I just received a royalty check from Hope Publishing Company yesterday. The name of the company holds extra meaning to me because of the hope God brought to me during an especially trying time of my life.

My early thirties included some cloudy times of sadness and depression. Without recounting the surrounding events, it's enough to say that my life seemed to have lost its joy. One day my friend Shirley sent me an encouraging note in the mail, ending with the verse written above.

Several months later I received a phone call from the senior editor of Hope Publishing, saying their company wanted to publish a new series of praise books for student pianists. He asked if I'd be interested in compiling and arranging one book. I was flattered, but my response was, "I've never done that before." The editor replied, "Why don't you send us two arrangements and let us decide."

I did my best, sent in the arrangements, and waited. About a month later an envelope came from Hope Publishing. I thought, *Here's my "Thanks but no thanks" letter.* I was shocked when I read the letter, which said, "Here's the contract. Would you please do a whole book?" I still remember sitting down on the couch, having a good cry, and thanking God for blessing me with a huge affirmation of hope. The experience was one of many that reminded me that God really cares about me.

Father,
Thanks for providing bright rays of hope at times when our lives seem overcast with dark clouds. Thank you that you are the God of hope. Amen.

HOPE

NOTHING IS IMPOSSIBLE WITH GOD. *Luke 1:37*

*T*he angel's announcement of the virgin birth had the word *impossible* written all over it. Mary wasn't married, she hadn't experienced sexual relations, and she was probably no older than fourteen. Furthermore, Nazareth, Mary's hometown, was an unlikely location for an important proclamation such as this. Not even mentioned in the Old Testament, Nazareth was despised by the people in Judah.

When the angel Gabriel visited Mary, he gave her a lot of information in a short amount of time. He told her that she was favored by God, that God was with her, that she would give birth to a son, and that she should name him Jesus. This would not be just any son—he would be the Son of God, and his kingdom would never end!

Mary's response provides a pattern for us to follow. She didn't say, "This is impossible!" She said, "How will this be?" In other words, how will this be possible? She understood what would happen, but she didn't understand *how* it would happen.

Are you facing an impossible situation? Do circumstances seem hopeless or insurmountable? Examine the angel's answer to Mary. The angel announced that the Holy Spirit would overshadow her, and she would experience the transforming power of God's presence. He encouraged her with news that Elizabeth, her very old cousin, was also pregnant—another seeming impossibility. With God, nothing is impossible.

As believers, we have the presence of God's Spirit, who specializes in transforming and encouraging our hearts. May we, like Mary, ask "How?" and submit to God's transforming power in our lives.

Father,
Forgive us for too often responding to difficulties with "This is impossible!"
instead of looking to you and asking, "How, God?" Thanks for your Spirit
who teaches and encourages us. Amen.

HOPE

THIS IS WHAT THE LORD SAYS: "CURSED ARE THOSE WHO
PUT THEIR TRUST IN MERE HUMANS AND TURN THEIR HEARTS
AWAY FROM THE LORD. THEY ARE LIKE STUNTED SHRUBS IN THE
DESERT, WITH NO HOPE FOR THE FUTURE. THEY WILL LIVE IN THE BARREN
WILDERNESS, ON THE SALTY FLATS WHERE NO ONE LIVES. BUT BLESSED ARE THOSE
WHO TRUST IN THE LORD AND HAVE MADE THE LORD THEIR HOPE AND
CONFIDENCE. THEY ARE LIKE TREES PLANTED ALONG A RIVERBANK, WITH ROOTS
THAT REACH DEEP INTO THE WATER. SUCH TREES ARE NOT BOTHERED BY THE HEAT
OR WORRIED BY LONG MONTHS OF DROUGHT. THEIR LEAVES STAY GREEN, AND
THEY GO RIGHT ON PRODUCING DELICIOUS FRUIT."

Jeremiah 17:5-8

If I was thinking of launching a landscaping company and I asked my children whether I should locate it in the desert or next to a riverbank, they would say, "Well, that's a no-brainer!" The first location would spell doom; the second would predict success. Each of us has a similar choice about where we will locate the landscape of our life. Will we place our hope in mere humans, or will we place it in the Lord? The way we live out the answer to that question concludes whether our hearts will be empty or full.

"Where do you want to place your hope?" Jeremiah asks us. "In a fallible person who might live for about eighty years, or in the all-powerful Creator who lives forever?" How we answer his question determines whether we will look like a measly, undersized bush or a flourishing plant. It determines whether we will live a life that's unproductive or a life that's abundant. Do we want to be depleted and empty, or do we want to be full? I vote for full.

Father,
Thanks for vivid descriptions of things like shrubs, trees, deserts, and river-
banks that remind us to put our trust in you. Amen.

LISTENING

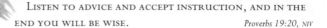

LISTEN TO ADVICE AND ACCEPT INSTRUCTION, AND IN THE
END YOU WILL BE WISE. *Proverbs 19:20, NIV*

Naaman, a commander of the Syrian army, was cured of leprosy through the prophet Elisha. In spite of the fact that Naaman was a prominent man, he came down with leprosy, a despised disease. A young Israelite slave girl in his household, who had been captured on a raid, had apparently done a lot of listening in her home and "church" while growing up. She suggested to Naaman's wife that the prophet Elisha might be able to heal Naaman's leprosy. Naaman's wife listened and mentioned the idea to her husband. Naaman listened and spoke to his superior, the king of Aram. The king listened and sent a letter with Naaman to the king of Israel. The king of Israel, however, didn't do such a hot job of listening. He tore his robes and suggested that the whole thing was a silly trick.

But Elisha listened. When he heard about the king's reaction, Elisha sent him a message suggesting that Naaman come to see him. Then the king listened, and Naaman came to Elisha's house with horses and chariots. When Elisha sent a messenger to Naaman saying, "Wash yourself seven times in the Jordan River," Naaman didn't listen. He went away in an angry rage because he thought the cure was beneath his dignity. But when Naaman's servants reasoned with him and asked him to reconsider, he listened—and was healed.

All of this listening began with a girl who obviously grew up in a family and community of faith, where she was taught to listen to God. How amazing that it all started with the faith of a child who listened!

Father,
May we be listening always to you and your Word, ready to heed the good
advice of godly people around us. Amen.

LISTENING

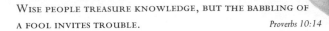

WISE PEOPLE TREASURE KNOWLEDGE, BUT THE BABBLING OF
A FOOL INVITES TROUBLE. *Proverbs 10:14*

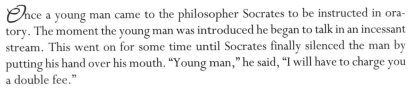

*O*nce a young man came to the philosopher Socrates to be instructed in oratory. The moment the young man was introduced he began to talk in an incessant stream. This went on for some time until Socrates finally silenced the man by putting his hand over his mouth. "Young man," he said, "I will have to charge you a double fee."

"A double fee? Why is that?"

Socrates replied, "Because I will have to teach you two sciences. First, the science of holding your tongue; and then the science of using it correctly."[1]

I used to think that if I wasn't talking, I was listening. But I'm learning that listening is making an *effort* to hear something, and paying close attention in the process. When I dropped off my sixth-grade son for his first day of classes in middle school, I said, "Have a great day! I'll pray, and you listen." Listening is an underrated art. It's not something we do with our ears only; if we're really listening, our minds and hearts are involved as well.

Listening is an essential gift for every mom to give her child. It doesn't cost money, but it does cost time! Ross Campbell, in his book *How to Really Love Your Child*, says that if a child doesn't receive focused attention from his parents, he experiences increased anxiety. The message the child receives is that everything and everyone else is more important than he is.

When we listen to our children, they feel a sense of value and importance. That's a good skill for moms to practice.

Father,
Help us to be quiet long enough for us to empathetically listen to our
children. Amen.

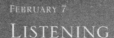

LISTENING

> BUT GOD DID LISTEN! HE PAID ATTENTION TO MY
> PRAYER.
>
> *Psalm 66:19*

I'll never forget God's answer to a prayer I prayed in my freshman year of college. I wanted to attend an Urbana missions conference over winter break, but I didn't want to burden my parents for the money since they were already paying my college bills. So I decided to ask God to provide the money if he wanted me to attend.

Several weeks later my mom called from home. She said that I must have forgotten to cash one of my summer paychecks because the company I worked for had inquired about the outstanding check. I explained to my mom where I kept my pay stubs, and when she looked in the shoebox in my closet, sure enough, there was the uncashed check sitting on top of all the pay stubs. Not only did the check pay for the missions conference, but it also covered my transportation there and back!

Knowing that God heard my prayer and cared enough to provide was a huge encouragement that built up my faith and prompted me to keep praying.

"Prayer is an exchange of confidence: we assume the stance of a trusting child and pray with faith that is matched by obedience. God remembers our frailty, loves us as his children, hears and answers our prayers."[2]

God wants our thanks and praise when we experience his listening and his provision. In Psalm 50:14-15, we're taught, "What I want . . . is your true thanks to God; I want you to fulfill your vows to the Most High. Trust me in your times of trouble, and I will rescue you, and you will give me glory."

Father,
Thank you that you, an infinite and holy God, listen to us in spite of the fact that we are deeply flawed and many times ungrateful. May we run to you first in our moments of need, and may we encourage our children to do the same. Amen.

LISTENING

As you enter the house of God, keep your ears open and your mouth shut! Don't be a fool who doesn't realize that mindless offerings to God are evil. And don't make rash promises to God, for he is in heaven, and you are only here on earth. So let your words be few.

Ecclesiastes 5:1-2

Have you ever spent time with a person who talked incessantly and rarely came up for air? Who bounced from one thought to the next to the next to the next? Whose endless flow of words left you wishing that there was a STOP button you could push? (I realize that many three-year-olds fit into this category, but even three-year-olds can be taught to be quiet for short periods of time.)

We tend to feel anxious and agitated around such people because we feel trapped, used, or controlled. We sense that the person we're listening to is hardly aware of us.

I wonder how God feels when I rush into his presence and rattle off my words, feelings, and requests. I wonder how he feels when I forget who he is and fail to show him appropriate reverence and respect. Oh, I know there are times when I'm overwhelmed and I want to pour out my heart to God. My earthly friends offer me patience and understanding at times like that, and I have no doubt that God's ears are open to my cries too. But am I? Am I mostly talking and rarely listening? That kind of pattern doesn't bode well with friends and family, and in these verses from Ecclesiastes, Solomon explains it doesn't bode well with God, either.

It's obvious that the psalmists felt comfortable expressing their thoughts and feelings to God. But they were also in the habit of stopping, looking, and listening. We're wise to follow their lead—to "Be silent, and know that I am God!" (Psalm 46:10).

Father,
May we never get so busy that we don't take time to listen to you. Amen.

LISTENING

> GOD DOESN'T LISTEN TO SINNERS, BUT HE IS READY TO
> HEAR THOSE WHO WORSHIP HIM AND DO HIS WILL.   *John 9:31*

> LISTEN! THE LORD IS NOT TOO WEAK TO SAVE YOU, AND HE IS
> NOT BECOMING DEAF. HE CAN HEAR YOU WHEN YOU CALL. BUT THERE IS A
> PROBLEM—YOUR SINS HAVE CUT YOU OFF FROM GOD. BECAUSE OF YOUR SIN, HE
> HAS TURNED AWAY AND WILL NOT LISTEN ANYMORE.   *Isaiah 59:1-2*

*G*od listens to us. He heard the Israelites groaning in bondage, he heard Hannah crying out in barrenness, and he heard David facing Goliath in battle.

But there are times when God does not listen, and we are wise to be aware of the conditions involved. Amazingly, John 9:31 (quoted above) was not spoken by a religious leader, but by a blind man who received sight when Jesus healed him. The blind man had apparently grown up hearing the Scriptures and knew some of the verses from Job, Proverbs, and Isaiah that teach this awesome truth.

Jesus healed the blind man on the Sabbath, and instead of the "religious" Pharisees being pleased for the blind man, they grilled him and his parents, trying to get them to say something that would either get them excommunicated or discredit Jesus. There was a serious attitude problem here. Look at the contrast between the heart of the Pharisees and the heart of the blind man:

Pharisees (Spiritual Blindness)	**Blind Man** (Spiritual Insight)
Pride	Humility
No concern for others	Compassion for others
Condemnation	Forgiveness
Hopelessness	Hope
Insensitivity to sin	Desire to repent and change
Anger	Love [3]

The Pharisees thought they were spiritually wise, yet they failed to realize that God would not listen to them because they were not devoted to him. From the blind man, we learn that the person God listens to is the person who does his will.

Father,
Please forgive us for the times we've been more concerned with outward show than inward devotion to you. May we come to you with humility, being assured that you will hear us. Amen.

LISTENING

MY CHILD, HOW I WILL REJOICE IF YOU BECOME WISE. YES,
MY HEART WILL THRILL WHEN YOU SPEAK WHAT IT RIGHT
AND JUST.

Proverbs 23:15-16

My oldest son, Chad, owns a twelve-year-old white Pontiac Bonneville. It's served him well during his post-college years, carrying him to camping trips on the West Coast, friends' weddings on the East Coast, and back and forth to the high school where he teaches every day. But with over 160,000 miles on his car, he suspected that it might be approaching its demise. Recently, after his car failed an emissions test, Chad concluded that the car had indeed reached the end of the line.

When Chad showed me the charts and graphs he received from the Illinois Vehicle Inspection Station, I better understood the reason for emissions testing. The inspection station tests cars for carbon monoxide (a toxic gas) and hydrocarbons (unburned fuel that causes smog and contributes to eye and throat discomfort). A dictionary definition of the word *emit* is "to utter or exhale." After I read that, I got to wondering, *What would happen if we moms were required to have periodic emissions testing on our speech? What if someone listened to us and tested the words that we utter throughout the day?*

Would our words be full of kindness, truth, wisdom, and blessing? Or would they be found to be full of criticism, rumors, flattery, and anger? Although we probably all have days that we would fail the test, here's the good news: our problem with words is one of the reasons Jesus died for us. As we confess our sin and look to him for wisdom with our words, he will help us. A failed "emissions" test doesn't mean the end of the line for us! If we turn to Jesus, he will help us with necessary repairs.

> Father,
> Please forgive us for times when our speech might have failed an emissions test. We want the words we utter each day to be words of truth, wisdom, blessing, and kindness. Thank you for the help that your Spirit gives us. In Jesus' strong name, amen.

LISTENING

THE EYES OF THE LORD WATCH OVER THOSE WHO DO RIGHT, AND HIS EARS ARE OPEN TO THEIR PRAYERS. BUT THE LORD TURNS HIS FACE AGAINST THOSE WHO DO EVIL.

1 Peter 3:12

When I meet famous people, I'm not so amazed that they would say something to me, but I am amazed when they *listen* to me. How much more comforting to know that the God who created the world and died for me also listens to me! God is not like a corporate executive who cloisters himself in a faraway office, not wishing to be involved in his employees' lives. The Bible teaches that he hears and listens to us. Astounding! If you are presently wondering if God is listening, be encouraged by these verses:

> *I am praying to you because I know you will answer, O God. Bend down and listen as I pray. Show me your unfailing love in wonderful ways. You save with your strength those who seek refuge from their enemies. Guard me as the apple of your eye. Hide me in the shadow of your wings. (Psalm 17:6-8)*

> *I cried out to the Lord in my suffering, and he heard me. He set me free from all my fears. (Psalm 34:6)*

> *Come and listen, all you who fear God, and I will tell you what he did for me. For I cried out to him for help, praising him as I spoke. If I had not confessed the sin in my heart, my Lord would not have listened. But God did listen! He paid attention to my prayer. (Psalm 66:16-19)*

> *Father,*
> *Thank you so much that you listen and that you never sleep. May we assure our children that you listen to them. Amen.*

LOVE

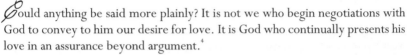

BUT GOD SHOWED HIS GREAT LOVE FOR US BY SENDING
CHRIST TO DIE FOR US WHILE WE WERE STILL SINNERS.

Romans 5:8

Could anything be said more plainly? It is not we who begin negotiations with God to convey to him our desire for love. It is God who continually presents his love in an assurance beyond argument.[4]

If we ever feel doubtful of God's love and care, it's good to remember that he loved us even when our hearts were cold toward him.

Sometimes, for an hour or two or for a day, I am prompted to look for all the ways God seeks to show his love to me. We talk about seeking God, but we sometimes forget how much he seeks us—constantly. We see his love in the air we breathe, the day and the night, the beauty of the seasons, the magnificent way he created our bodies to function, the plants and animals he created for our food and enjoyment—and the list goes on.

But most of all, his love was revealed when Jesus died for us "while we were still sinners." It's the redemptive aspect of his love that ministers health to my soul. He didn't wait until I was "good enough." His loving plan for all of us is to *redeem* us—to save us from a state of sinfulness and restore us with honor, worth, and reputation that are all based on *him*!

And redemptive love doesn't stop with us. God's plan is for the world, and when we accept his redemption for our souls, we desire to teach our children about God's love.

> *Father,*
> *Thank you that you loved us before we even thought about you! May our*
> *gratefulness prompt us to service that begins with our family. Amen.*

LOVE

MY COMMAND IS THIS: LOVE EACH OTHER AS I HAVE
LOVED YOU. GREATER LOVE HAS NO ONE THAN THIS, THAT
HE LAY DOWN HIS LIFE FOR HIS FRIENDS. YOU ARE MY FRIENDS
IF YOU DO WHAT I COMMAND. I NO LONGER CALL YOU SERVANTS, BECAUSE A
SERVANT DOES NOT KNOW HIS MASTER'S BUSINESS. INSTEAD, I HAVE CALLED YOU
FRIENDS, FOR EVERYTHING THAT I LEARNED FROM MY FATHER I HAVE MADE
KNOWN TO YOU. YOU DID NOT CHOOSE ME, BUT I CHOSE YOU AND APPOINTED
YOU TO GO AND BEAR FRUIT—FRUIT THAT WILL LAST. THEN THE FATHER
WILL GIVE YOU WHATEVER YOU ASK IN MY NAME. THIS IS MY COMMAND:
LOVE EACH OTHER.   *John 15:12-17, NIV*

How do we understand love, and how do we measure it? With five words: "as I have loved you." Jesus left both a standard and a personal example for us to follow. He doesn't ask us to do anything he hasn't already done.

First, he laid down his life for us (15:13). In order for me to love, I may need to forfeit something valuable to me for the sake of another person. This may involve giving up some of my desires or expectations, or experiencing a greater or lesser degree of inconvenience.

Second, Jesus contrasted servants and friends to teach us that he not only treats us kindly, but he also shares his very thoughts with us (15:15). He has chosen to commune with us and be close to us. This must have been very difficult for him to do with his disciples when he knew that some would doubt him, betray him, deny him, or run away from him. His example inspires us to continue to commune with a husband who disappointed us or a child who disobeyed us.

Third, Jesus took initiative and action with his disciples. He did not sit back and wait for them to come to him, but he reached out to them (15:16). Our families will remember us most for how we cared and reached out to them.

How we follow Christ's example needs to be thought through with integrity and honesty, asking God for his wisdom, strength, and grace. Because when we choose to love, the world sees that we are God's disciples.

Father,
Thank you that you love us perfectly. Please forgive us for the lack of love we sometimes have for others. We need the warmth of your love in hearts that would be cold without you. Amen.

LOVE

FOLLOW GOD'S EXAMPLE IN EVERYTHING YOU DO,
BECAUSE YOU ARE HIS DEAR CHILDREN. LIVE A LIFE FILLED
WITH LOVE FOR OTHERS, FOLLOWING THE EXAMPLE OF CHRIST, WHO
LOVED YOU AND GAVE HIMSELF AS A SACRIFICE TO TAKE AWAY YOUR SINS. AND
GOD WAS PLEASED, BECAUSE THAT SACRIFICE WAS LIKE SWEET PERFUME TO HIM.

Ephesians 5:1-2

Two of my former piano students, Corrie and Sydney, are sisters. They look alike, and they talk alike. They are darling and polite; they both have gentle southern accents and sweet dispositions. Why? They are imitators of their parents, both in the way they dress and the way they act.

The way we learn to love is by imitating Christ. How does he love? When Jesus gave himself as a sacrifice for sinners—for us—he brought great joy to the heart of God. That's who we should imitate, and that's how we should love—sacrificially. It's not hard to love a person who treats us well or a person we respect. But what about the opposite? Jesus wasn't treated well by mankind—we crucified him. And how much respect could he have felt toward people who denied him and abandoned him? But he still loved mankind so much that he *died* for us!

So what does sacrificial love look like? It involves forfeiting something we value highly for the sake of someone we believe to have a greater value or claim—God and his kingdom. We may choose to forfeit a dream, a comfort, a convenience, or some of our time and money because we want to show God's love to another, bringing great joy to the heart of God. We imitate God through a life of giving and serving. As moms, our giving and serving begins in our home.

Father,
Your example would be impossible for us to follow if you hadn't also promised us your presence and your strength in our lives. May we look to you daily, so our children will see your love in us. Amen.

LOVE

FOR SINCE WE WERE RESTORED TO FRIENDSHIP WITH GOD
BY THE DEATH OF HIS SON WHILE WE WERE STILL HIS ENEMIES,
WE WILL CERTAINLY BE DELIVERED FROM ETERNAL PUNISHMENT
BY HIS LIFE. SO NOW WE CAN REJOICE IN OUR WONDERFUL NEW RELATIONSHIP
WITH GOD—ALL BECAUSE OF WHAT OUR LORD JESUS CHRIST HAS DONE FOR US IN
MAKING US FRIENDS OF GOD.   *Romans 5:10-11*

My five-year-old son, Jordan, and I were walking home from the park hand in hand. He must have been enjoying our time together because he looked up at me and said, "Mommy, you're loveful and beautiful and heartful." "Jordan, would you say that again?" I asked as my heart did a little flip. "You're loveful and beautiful and heartful," he repeated. "Would you tell me that every day for the rest of my life?" I asked, laughing. Although I had never heard of *loveful* or *heartful*, I now think they are some of the most wonderful words in the language—Jordan's five-year-old language. I am still warmed by the memory of his words.

As wonderful as Jordan's words were, I realize that they were spoken on a day when he was five, life was wonderful, and Mom seemed perfect. On rare occasions when he repeats those words today (he's now a young man who knows that life can be difficult and that Mom is not perfect), the words mean even more.

On days when I don't feel particularly loved, secure, or confident, I remember God's *objective* words. According to Romans 5:10-11, the love that prompted Christ to die for me while I was still his enemy is the same love that is available to me today through the presence of God's Spirit in my heart. Those have to be the most loving words I've ever heard.

Father,
Thank you for sending your son to die for us. The only way we'll ever begin
to love others like you have loved us is by staying close to you. In the name
of Jesus, amen.

LOVE

**MOST IMPORTANT OF ALL, CONTINUE TO SHOW DEEP LOVE
FOR EACH OTHER, FOR LOVE COVERS A MULTITUDE OF SINS.**

1 Peter 4:8

> *Ah, the beauty of being at peace with another, neither having to weigh thoughts
> or measure words, but spilling them out just as they are; chaff and grain together,
> certain that a faithful hand will keep what is worth keeping, and with a breath of
> kindness blow the rest away.* Arab proverb

The Christian's "love muscle" is called on to have amazing elasticity and flexibility. The wife of a company president sits and applauds her husband at a banquet where he is honored for his accomplishments, and yet she has also known him to lose his temper and act selfishly. We cheer on our child who is given a great honor at her school, fully aware of that child's foibles and inconsistencies (as she is of ours). I'm thankful for friends and family who have seen me at both my better and worse moments but love me just the same.

Love covers. So where do we draw the line between showing a healthy amount of love that covers sins and ignoring sins to the point of enabling a person to continue in destructive behaviors or addictions?

Because of our sinful nature, we all have shortcomings and inconsistencies. As they surface from time to time, we stretch and forgive others as we hope they will do for us. However, if repetitive behaviors become destructive or addictive, God has given us healthy ways of dealing with bigger issues. In these cases, we are not wise to roll over and ignore the problems. (See Matthew 18:15-17; Luke 17:3; or Ephesians 5:3-11.)

Father,
*Please give us grace to have flexible love muscles for daily family life and
courage to deal with larger problems that demand special attention. Amen.*

LOVE

IF ANOTHER BELIEVER SINS AGAINST YOU, GO PRIVATELY
AND POINT OUT THE FAULT. IF THE OTHER PERSON LISTENS
AND CONFESSES IT, YOU HAVE WON THAT PERSON BACK. BUT IF
YOU ARE UNSUCCESSFUL, TAKE ONE OR TWO OTHERS WITH YOU AND GO BACK
AGAIN, SO THAT EVERYTHING YOU SAY MAY BE CONFIRMED BY TWO OR THREE
WITNESSES. IF THAT PERSON STILL REFUSES TO LISTEN, TAKE YOUR CASE TO THE
CHURCH. IF THE CHURCH DECIDES YOU ARE RIGHT, BUT THE OTHER PERSON
WON'T ACCEPT IT, TREAT THAT PERSON AS A PAGAN OR A CORRUPT TAX
COLLECTOR.

Matthew 18:15-17

It's not difficult to love someone when things in the relationship are going well. But what happens when it feels like that person is our enemy? Sadly, we sometimes experience circumstances that are very unjust. Someone may have stolen from us, or our husband or friend might be involved in immoral behavior. Does God really expect us to love *them*?

God has not left us without provision for these situations. His Word instructs us what to do when another believer has blatantly sinned against us.

First, we go to the person one-on-one. We don't go with the goal of winning an argument; we go with the goal of speaking the truth in love (Galatians 6:1; Ephesians 4:15). This means telling the person how she has sinned against us and what effect her behavior has had. This meeting may be enough to get things moving on the right track. If so, the relationship is on its way to restoration. If not, there's another step.

Second, we ask for help and counsel from one or two other mature believers, going to the offender together. When sin isn't dealt with, it spreads, and so does the circle of people that it influences.

If steps one and two don't prompt confession and repentance, the third step is to take the matter to the church. By this time, if the offender has not repented, she forfeits her position of spiritual sister and is not held in close fellowship.

The goal of these loving but tough steps is restoration of the person and the relationship, and for this we hope and pray.

Father,
Life's situations are sometimes extremely challenging, and we're thankful that
you have not left us without help from your Word. Please give us extra
strength and wisdom to meet the challenges that come our way. Amen.

LOVE

May your roots go down deep into the soil of God's marvelous love. And may you have the power to understand, as all God's people should, how wide, how long, how high, and how deep his love really is. May you experience the love of Christ, though it is so great you will never fully understand it. Then you will be filled with the fullness of life and power that comes from God.

Ephesians 3:17-19

Some time ago my husband and a friend had breakfast together. His friend posed the question, "When we get to heaven, what do you think is going to be the biggest surprise of all?" After thinking it over, my husband replied, "I think we'll be surprised by the overwhelming depth of God's love for us."

In today's passage, Paul's prayer for the Ephesians explores the scope of God's love—how wide, how long, how high, and how deep it is. Paul wants us not only to have an intellectual understanding of the love of Christ but also to experience that love. He tells us that Christ's love is so great that we will never fully understand it! Thankfully, we can experience it even without understanding it.

The shore of a great ocean is one of the best places to think about the extremes of God's love. As far as our eyes can see to the left, to the right, and straight across, there is no end in sight. What a wonderful picture of the extent of God's love.

A songwriter puts it this way:

> Could we with ink the ocean fill
> And were the skies of parchment made,
> Were every stalk on earth a quill
> And every man a scribe by trade,
> To write the love of God above
> Would drain the ocean dry,
> Nor could the scroll contain the whole
> Tho' stretched from sky to sky.[5]

Father,
Please fill us with your love that is deep and wide so that we will live a full life for you. In Jesus' name, amen.

LIGHT

FOR THOUGH YOUR HEARTS WERE ONCE FULL OF DARKNESS, NOW YOU ARE FULL OF LIGHT FROM THE LORD, AND YOUR BEHAVIOR SHOULD SHOW IT! FOR THIS LIGHT WITHIN YOU PRODUCES ONLY WHAT IS GOOD AND RIGHT AND TRUE. TRY TO FIND OUT WHAT IS PLEASING TO THE LORD. TAKE NO PART IN THE WORTHLESS DEEDS OF EVIL AND DARKNESS; INSTEAD, REBUKE AND EXPOSE THEM. IT IS SHAMEFUL EVEN TO TALK ABOUT THE THINGS THAT UNGODLY PEOPLE DO IN SECRET. BUT WHEN THE LIGHT SHINES ON THEM, IT BECOMES CLEAR HOW EVIL THESE THINGS ARE. AND WHERE YOUR LIGHT SHINES, IT WILL EXPOSE THEIR EVIL DEEDS. THIS IS WHY IT IS SAID, "AWAKE, O SLEEPER, RISE UP FROM THE DEAD, AND CHRIST WILL GIVE YOU LIGHT."

Ephesians 5:8-14

Imagine for a moment the contrast between a sunny day at the beach and a day spent crawling around in dark underground caverns. God's Word teaches us that a Christian's life ought to be as different from the world as light is from darkness.

Jesus is the source of our light. As he said in John 8:12, "I am the light of the world." Light imagery is used throughout the New Testament, and in Ephesians 5:8 (NIV), faithful followers of Christ are called "children of light." God always deals with us in terms of our position. He knows that once we walked in darkness, but now, through our faith in Christ, we have become children of light. Our position in Christ is the basis for our behavior. Whereas darkness produces sin, the light of Christ produces "goodness, righteousness and truth." Our children know we are not perfect, but when we moms are children of the light, *our* children will see evidence of goodness, righteousness, and truth in us.

I love the words of a contemporary song included in some of our hymnals:

I want to walk as a child of the light;
I want to follow Jesus.
God set the stars to give light to the world;
The star of my life is Jesus.
In him there is no darkness at all;
The night and the day are both alike.
The Lamb is the light of the city of God:
Shine in my heart, Lord Jesus.[6]

God of light,
Please shine in our hearts as we follow you. Amen.

LIGHT

JESUS SAID TO THE PEOPLE, "I AM THE LIGHT OF THE WORLD.
IF YOU FOLLOW ME, YOU WON'T BE STUMBLING THROUGH THE
DARKNESS, BECAUSE YOU WILL HAVE THE LIGHT THAT LEADS TO LIFE."

John 8:12

While watching some recent TV coverage of downhill skiing, I enjoyed seeing the colorful outfits of the skiers racing down the white hills. During one run the TV screen went gray, and I could see nothing. Then gradually I could make out *some* activity, although not very clearly. Ten or fifteen seconds later, everything was clear and bright again. The announcer explained what had happened: The skier began his run in the sun, went through a patch of dense fog, and then skied into another area of hazy mist before coming back out into the sun. As you can imagine, I enjoyed the event best when I could see it clearly.

Our lives are like that. Sin has a way of making things hazy, cloudy, or dark. We need the light of Jesus to lift the fog and darkness and help us see our way clearly. We don't find a clearly lit path by following rules—we find it by following *him*. The more time we spend getting to know God through reading his Word, the more his light will shine in our hearts.

When light can easily pass through a material—a piece of glass, for example—we describe it as *transparent*. Materials such as waxed paper that let only some light through are *translucent*. Other materials, such as bricks, do not let any light pass through. These are *opaque*. As Christian moms, we can be transparent if we follow Jesus closely. When we follow his light, it shines through with brightness and color to those around us.

Father,
May we follow you closely so that your light will fill us and we will reflect you to our children. Amen.

LIGHT

> YOUR EYE IS A LAMP FOR YOUR BODY. A PURE EYE LETS
> SUNSHINE INTO YOUR SOUL. BUT AN EVIL EYE SHUTS OUT THE
> LIGHT AND PLUNGES YOU INTO DARKNESS.   *Luke 11:34*

*H*uman eyes are the most sophisticated cameras in the whole world. They were graciously given to us by our Creator; we did not have to pay for them. Light is traveling all around us, but we wouldn't be able to see it if our eyes couldn't bend the light and form images.

When a ray of light first meets the eye, it falls on the cornea, which bends the light so it will go through the pupil and iris to the flexible lens. The lens adjusts so that light patterns focus correctly on the retina. From there the image is carried to the brain by the optic nerves. The brain decodes all these messages and tells us what we are seeing. God has made us amazingly complex!

In the same way that light surrounds our physical bodies, God's light shines all around our souls. But before it can change us, it must enter our lives. In Psalm 119:130 we read, "As your words are taught, they give light; even the simple can understand them."

Since our eyes are organs of vision, we must be careful about what we observe, and as moms we also need to protect the eyes of our children. It's our responsibility to seek out the wholesome and to run from the destructive. Of course, our eyes should daily be in God's Word, because only the Word of God, used by the Spirit of God, has the power to bend the light of Jesus into our souls.

Light of the World,
Thank you that your light is always available and that it gives us understanding. May our eyes turn away from the unwholesome things of this world but spend time reading your Word, which changes us when it enters our lives. Amen.

LIGHT

I COULD ASK THE DARKNESS TO HIDE ME AND THE LIGHT
AROUND ME TO BECOME NIGHT—BUT EVEN IN DARKNESS I
CANNOT HIDE FROM YOU. TO YOU THE NIGHT SHINES AS BRIGHT
AS DAY. DARKNESS AND LIGHT ARE BOTH ALIKE TO YOU.   *Psalm 139:11-12*

One of my favorite childhood memories was taking a summer trip to the Shaffers' cottage in Lake Nebagamon, Wisconsin. The two highlights of the week were going to Bridgeman's for ice cream and visiting the town dump. "The dump?" you might ask. "What's so great about visiting the town dump?"

The town dump was a good place to see bears. After dark, we parked our car a short distance from the dump, turned off the headlights, and listened for sounds of animal life. When we heard rustling or banging, the driver of the car would turn on the lights so we could see what was going on. Most of the time all we saw was raccoons, but sometimes the car beams exposed bears. Great excitement! In the darkness, we had no idea what we were hearing, but when the lights of the car shone in front of us, we were able to spot the animals. It was the light that made things clear.

On this earth, we experience both light and darkness—depending on the time of day and season of the year. But God is not limited by darkness. He dwells in light and he sees us all the time, no matter where we are. He not only sees us but he knows everything about us. His light is always on, because he *is* light. How comforting—especially for a child—to know that we can never be lost to God.

Father,
Thank you for the security that your light brings to our lives. Amen.

LIGHT

DON'T HIDE YOUR LIGHT UNDER A BASKET! INSTEAD, PUT IT ON A STAND AND LET IT SHINE FOR ALL. IN THE SAME WAY, LET YOUR GOOD DEEDS SHINE OUT FOR ALL TO SEE, SO THAT EVERYONE WILL PRAISE YOUR HEAVENLY FATHER. *Matthew 5:15-16*

My pastor, Kent Hughes, had an interesting experience when flying back to Chicago from a missions conference in California. He had been busy the whole week and was looking forward to reading C. S. Lewis's *Letters to Malcolm*, but as he got on the plane he prayed, "Lord, if you want me to share Christ with someone, I'm willing." The seat next to him was already occupied by a young man who was reading an Isaac Asimov novel. Pastor Hughes took out his book and said, "Are you enjoying your book?" The result? He didn't even notice the jet taking off or the in-flight meal as he shared Christ with this young man. It was the shortest trip to Chicago he had ever taken. He was so caught up in a divine appointment that he left his copy of *Letters to Malcolm* on the plane!

Being a light for Christ is often not convenient or easy. John the Baptist was certainly an example of that. John was sent out to be a witness to Jesus Christ, telling people that the Light had come into the world. There were three important things that John the Baptist taught (as quoted or implied in John's Gospel), and they are important for us to understand if we want to be witnesses for Jesus:

1. Jesus is eternal (John 1:15).
2. Jesus is full of grace and truth (John 1:16-17).
3. Jesus is the way to God (John 1:18).

Our focus must always be on *Jesus*.

Father,
May we be good students of your Word so that we will be ready to share your light and truth with others who do not know you. Amen.

LIGHT

BUT THIS PRECIOUS TREASURE—THIS LIGHT AND POWER THAT
NOW SHINE WITHIN US—IS HELD IN PERISHABLE CONTAINERS,
THAT IS, IN OUR WEAK BODIES. SO EVERYONE CAN SEE THAT OUR
GLORIOUS POWER IS FROM GOD AND IS NOT OUR OWN. *2 Corinthians 4:7*

*I*t's easy to fall into a false belief that in order for us to reflect the light of Jesus, we need to be in a position of strength. But God says that his strength is made perfect in our weakness (2 Corinthians 12:9). It's probably much more obvious that way. A story from Susan Hunt's book *A True Woman* illustrates this principle.

Susan recounts that when her friend Sharon was diagnosed with cancer, Sharon's response was, "I am confident that God will use this to take me deeper into his love for me." Susan didn't see Sharon again until after she'd had surgery and several rounds of chemotherapy. She was surprised at what she saw. Yes, Sharon's body and hair were thinner, but she was amazed at how Sharon glowed with peace and love. She looked absolutely radiant. Susan said, "Sharon, you must have been spending some incredible time with God." In the midst of Sharon's weakness, God's glory was reflected.

If our weak bodies are God's temple and he dwells in us, then his strength will be reflected in our circumstances and our relationships. As we spend time with God, his presence will radiate to those around us.

> God of light and power,
> Thank you that we don't need to feel embarrassed about our lack of strength,
> health, wealth, or intelligence. Thank you that your light can shine forth
> from our weak, perishable bodies. Amen.

LIGHT

LORD, YOU HAVE BROUGHT LIGHT TO MY LIFE; MY
GOD, YOU LIGHT UP MY DARKNESS.   *Psalm 18:28*

Taking a tour in a big dark cave would be great fun for three young boys, right? That's what my friend Cindy Cochrum and her husband thought. On their way back from Florida, they saw road signs advertising various caves in Kentucky, so they decided to stop and take a tour.

After waiting in line for a while, their family joined a bigger tour group. They all followed a guide as they began their descent into the cave. The guide was the only person with a lantern, and as he explained how easy it was to become lost or disoriented in a cave, one of Cindy's sons became increasingly frightened. When the guide announced that he was going to turn off his lantern so they could see how dark it really was, Cindy's son panicked. The light went out, and her young son cried for his dad and reached out in the darkness, hoping to latch on to one of his dad's arms or legs.

Thankfully, the light of the lantern soon reappeared, and the boy was relieved. Their guide led them out of the cave, and the sunlight seemed more brilliant to Cindy's son than anything he'd ever seen.

Sometimes we feel frightened by the darkness of depression, a marital challenge, or an impending move to another part of the country. Calling out and reaching out for our heavenly Father is the best thing we can do. Even when we can't feel him, he is there. And he promises us that someday the darkness will be gone and we will live with him in brilliant light forever, because he is light.

Father,
Sometimes our lives feel as dark as though we were trapped in a cave. But we thank you for the promise of your presence and your light. Please help us to reach out to you. In the name of Jesus, who is the Light of the World, amen.

PERSEVERANCE

ONE DAY JESUS TOLD HIS DISCIPLES A STORY TO ILLUSTRATE
THEIR NEED FOR CONSTANT PRAYER AND TO SHOW THEM THAT
THEY MUST NEVER GIVE UP. "THERE WAS A JUDGE IN A CERTAIN CITY,"
HE SAID, "WHO WAS A GODLESS MAN WITH GREAT CONTEMPT FOR EVERYONE.
A WIDOW OF THAT CITY CAME TO HIM REPEATEDLY, APPEALING FOR JUSTICE
AGAINST SOMEONE WHO HAD HARMED HER. THE JUDGE IGNORED HER FOR A
WHILE, BUT EVENTUALLY SHE WORE HIM OUT. 'I FEAR NEITHER GOD NOR MAN,'
HE SAID TO HIMSELF, 'BUT THIS WOMAN IS DRIVING ME CRAZY. I'M GOING TO
SEE THAT SHE GETS JUSTICE, BECAUSE SHE IS WEARING ME OUT WITH HER
CONSTANT REQUESTS!'"

Luke 18:1-5

Although the judge in this parable had no interest in the widow's situation, the widow kept coming to the courtroom of the judge. She was not asking for punishment or revenge on her adversary—she was looking for justice. If it hadn't been for the woman's persistence, the judge might not have been persuaded to do anything. But because her visits were tiresome and annoying, the judge decided to deal with the matter. Moms understand these kinds of requests.

We are meant to see a huge contrast between the unjust judge in this parable and our just and merciful God. If out of the purely selfish motive of being rid of an annoying woman an ungodly judge would grant a defenseless woman her request, how much more will a God who is full of truth and grace hear and answer the prayers of his children, whom he loves?

The emphasis in this parable is not intended to encourage us to weary God with our requests (we can't), but rather to assure us that he is very willing to take care of his children. Someone has said, "The purpose of prayer is not to get man's will done in heaven, but to get God's will done on earth." It is good for us to be persistent, as long as we want God's will and aren't selfishly demanding our own agenda.

God,
Thank you for parables in the New Testament that help us to understand how
much you love us. Because we know you do, may we come to you often with
our needs and requests, persevering in faith and prayer. Amen.

PERSEVERANCE

BY FAITH HE [MOSES] LEFT EGYPT, NOT FEARING THE
KING'S ANGER; HE PERSEVERED BECAUSE HE SAW HIM WHO
IS INVISIBLE.

Hebrews 11:27, NIV

We often think of perseverance as straining and gritting our teeth to get a job done. We're correct in realizing that a person who perseveres is not a person who quits and that diligence and persistence are necessary for achieving our goals and living out our beliefs. But too often we act as though all the strength to persevere must come from *us*. Remembering that *we* are not our only resource for perseverance is wonderfully encouraging.

One day a little boy was trying to take the lid off of a peanut-butter jar. The little guy was wincing and straining, but he couldn't make the lid budge. His mom smiled and said, "Are you using all of your strength?"

"Yes, Mommy, I'm using all of my strength!"

"I don't think you are," his mom replied, "because you haven't asked me to help you! I'm your mom, and I'm happy to share my strength with you."

Sometimes we're like that little boy. But when we see how small we are and how big God is, we're prompted to run to him. When we do, we experience his great power to help us. Moses remembered the God who spoke to him in the burning bush. He remembered the God who changed a rod into a serpent. And when the time came for Moses to do the very hard task of leaving Egypt and leading his people, "he persevered because he saw him who is invisible."

Father,
Thank you for your great strength. May we continue to persevere because we are looking to you. May we encourage our children to look to you for strength as well. Amen.

PERSEVERANCE

DON'T GET TIRED OF DOING WHAT IS GOOD. DON'T GET
DISCOURAGED AND GIVE UP, FOR WE WILL REAP A HARVEST
OF BLESSING AT THE APPROPRIATE TIME.   *Galatians 6:9*

*A*s a young mom, I remember coming to the end of some days feeling extremely inadequate for the job. Reflecting back on the day, I'd think of the times I'd been impatient. I'd think of times I wished I'd dropped whatever I was doing to play with the kids. Some nights, I felt so weary of waking up with a fussy baby that I wasn't sure how I would find the strength to keep going.

Perseverance keeps us going when we feel like quitting. It prompts us to stick with the task even when we'd rather run the other direction. Sheer grit and will-power are helpful in the short run, but we need something more significant to keep us going in the long run. The Bible promises a prize—or, as Galatians 6:9 expresses it, a "harvest of blessing." A harvest is a crop, a consequence, or a return on our investment.

One of my short-term prizes has been to see my sons grow in Christian character. But the long-term blessing will come someday when I—and my children—realize the prize of eternal life with Christ. Someday we will live and reign with him, and like a good farmer, I want us to enjoy the fruit of our labors!

Corrie ten Boom, a humble Dutch woman who along with her family hid Jews in her home during the Nazi invasion of Holland, had lots of opportunities to work on perseverance. Landing in a concentration camp, there were times that she felt like giving up hope. But she didn't. Corrie wrote, "When a train goes through a tunnel and it gets dark, you don't throw away your ticket and jump off. You sit still and trust the engineer."

I'm sure glad now that I didn't "jump off the train" during the toddler years. They were certainly trying (for me they were the most difficult years of child raising), but now I'm reaping some of the harvest.

> *Father of the harvest,*
> *Please help us to plant well and persevere so that we will reap a harvest*
> *of blessing. Amen.*

PERSEVERANCE

WE GIVE GREAT HONOR TO THOSE WHO ENDURE UNDER
SUFFERING.

James 5:11

*D*o you have a child who is going through great emotional or physical turmoil? Are you experiencing financial difficulties? Do you ever have days when you feel like throwing in the towel? Sufferings—especially those that are ongoing—wear us down and challenge our perspective.

Pastor and author Kent Hughes suggests that our character and moral development are largely dependent on the experience of suffering: "We children of God seldom trust God as we do when we are in big trouble. Troubles knock secondary things away. They sharpen our focus and increase our grip on God."[1]

Some of the sufferings I've experienced have produced unique opportunities for service to Christ that never would have been possible if I hadn't suffered and persevered—imperfect as my perseverance was. When I look at those opportunities in retrospect, I'm grateful for glimpses of God's good plan. Other sufferings I've undergone haven't made sense to me even in hindsight. For those unanswered questions, I draw great comfort from Bible characters like Job, Joseph, Hannah, and Daniel. All of them waited and persevered, and God blessed them for it. We honor them now when we recount their stories, realizing that many of them experienced little or no honor during their trials.

When sufferings come, we won't always know the answer to the question "Why?" but we do know whom to run to for strength to persevere.

God,
Where can we run when there seems to be trouble all around us? To you!
Please help us to trust you more, draw near to you, and commune with you, so
that we can keep going and not throw in the towel. Amen.

PERSEVERANCE

JOB IS AN EXAMPLE OF A MAN WHO ENDURED PATIENTLY.
FROM HIS EXPERIENCE WE SEE HOW THE LORD'S PLAN FINALLY
ENDED IN GOOD, FOR HE IS FULL OF TENDERNESS AND MERCY.

James 5:11

*C*an you imagine having ten children, and then losing *all* of them the same day? Job did.

Job was a prosperous man in every way. He was healthy and wealthy, and he feared God. Satan thought that Job would remain faithful to God only if he prospered financially, and God permitted Job to be tested. Hardship after hardship came to him; he lost his children, his cattle, his servants, and he was left penniless. Yet "in all of this, Job did not sin by blaming God" (Job 1:22).

Although it's hard to imagine things getting any worse, they did. God allowed Job to be afflicted with painful sores from head to toe, but even when Job's wife suggested that he give up his faith, Job said, "Should we accept only good things from the hand of God and never anything bad?" (Job 2:10).

Satan's argument about Job's life (and about all our lives) was that "no one serves God for who he is, but for what he or she can get."[2] But when everything was taken away from Job, he said, "I came naked from my mother's womb, and I will be stripped of everything when I die. The Lord gave me everything I had, and the Lord has taken it away. Praise the name of the Lord!" (Job 1:21).

In the end, God blessed Job with spiritual humility and abundant physical blessings. But in the middle of a terrible situation, Job persevered with faith even when he didn't understand the reasoning behind his suffering.

Father,
You know how weak we are. Even when we persevere, we have our moments of tears and questions, just like Job. Please help us to remember that the trials and hardships we experience now are part of a much bigger plan that we don't always understand. May we see your grace and compassion even in the midst of hard times. Amen.

PERSEVERANCE

FOR IF WE ARE FAITHFUL TO THE END, TRUSTING GOD
JUST AS FIRMLY AS WHEN WE FIRST BELIEVED, WE WILL
SHARE IN ALL THAT BELONGS TO CHRIST. BUT NEVER FORGET THE
WARNING: "TODAY YOU MUST LISTEN TO HIS VOICE. DON'T HARDEN YOUR HEARTS
AGAINST HIM AS ISRAEL DID WHEN THEY REBELLED."

Hebrews 3:14-15

*E*ven though I'm not a sports fan, I found it exciting to watch the Chicago Bulls when they won multiple championships several years ago. Who could fail to appreciate the energy and drive the team had, led by the greatest basketball player ever, Michael Jordan? In one particularly memorable game, Jordan was ill. What was amazing was that after dragging himself onto the court, he somehow had the perseverance to continue to make the shots!

The children of Israel lacked perseverance many times. After God delivered them from Egypt and miraculously provided for them on their way to the Promised Land, the people faltered when they learned of "giants in the land" that they would need to defeat. They quickly forgot God's presence. Time after time God had overwhelmed their enemies and surely would do so again, but they failed to persevere in their faith that God cared for them and had good plans for them.

Sometimes we and our children find it easier to persevere in the lesser things of life, like a game of basketball, a hobby, or exercise. We overlook the most important perseverance of all—our perseverance of faith. But the prize for choosing to be strong in faith will be much greater than a gold championship ring. The prize will be sharing "in all that belongs to Christ."

Lord,
Give us the grace today to stay strong in our faith. Help us to know how much
you value us. May we remember all the good you want for our lives, if we will
only trust in you. In the faithful name of Jesus, amen.

PERSEVERANCE

IF YOU THINK YOU ARE STANDING STRONG, BE CAREFUL,
FOR YOU, TOO, MAY FALL INTO THE SAME SIN. BUT REMEMBER
THAT THE TEMPTATIONS THAT COME INTO YOUR LIFE ARE NO DIFFERENT
FROM WHAT OTHERS EXPERIENCE. AND GOD IS FAITHFUL. HE WILL KEEP THE
TEMPTATION FROM BECOMING SO STRONG THAT YOU CAN'T STAND UP AGAINST IT.
WHEN YOU ARE TEMPTED, HE WILL SHOW YOU A WAY OUT SO THAT YOU WILL
NOT GIVE IN TO IT.   *1 Corinthians 10:12-13*

*I*t's reassuring for us to realize that encountering temptation is not a sin, because even Jesus was tempted (Hebrews 4:15). But the way we respond to temptation indicates our spiritual state.

When we experience temptations of the body, God has already provided us with a way of escape. Adrian Rogers calls it "the King's highway—two legs and a hard run." When Joseph realized that Potiphar's wife was trying to seduce him, he fled. First Corinthians 6:18 tells us, "Run away from sexual sin!" We're not told to fight—we're told to flee!

We are taught to deal with temptations of the soul by reflecting on God:

> Turn your eyes upon Jesus,
> Look full in his wonderful face,
> And the things of earth will grow strangely dim,
> In the light of his glory and grace.[3]

If we're experiencing God in our lives, we won't quickly run to substitutes.

When Peter questioned Jesus' mission and said he shouldn't have to die, Jesus told him, "Get away from me, Satan! You are a dangerous trap to me. You are seeing things merely from a human point of view, and not from God's" (Matthew 16:23). We can say the same in the name of Jesus Christ.

When we encounter temptation we do not want to be "like an ox going to the slaughter or like a trapped stag . . . a bird flying into a snare" (Proverbs 7:22-23). Instead, we can flee, focus on God, and pray.

> God our Savior,
> Thank you that because you lived on this earth as a man, we know that you
> understand temptation. Thank you that you left us a pattern and that we
> have the presence of your Spirit. May we walk closely with you so that we will
> find strength to make good choices. Amen.

FEAR

CAST ALL YOUR ANXIETY ON HIM BECAUSE HE CARES
FOR YOU.   *1 Peter 5:7, NIV*

First Peter 5:7 was one of the earliest Bible verses I memorized as a child, and it is a verse I have taught to my children. But even when we have *memorized* a verse from the Bible, it doesn't mean we have yet learned the lesson and seen it worked out in our lives. God wants us to cast all our anxiety on him. Other words for anxiety are fear, apprehension, doubt, fretfulness, panic, nervousness, or uncertainty. We've all been there, haven't we? Perhaps you're there now because your husband lost his job, you are caring for an ailing parent, or you're worried that your child might get into an accident.

One of the reasons God permits difficulties in our lives is to present us with opportunities to learn and exercise lessons of faith. We read in Mark 4 that Jesus had been teaching his disciples when they got into a boat together on the Sea of Galilee and promptly encountered a violent storm. Even though (1) Jesus had told the disciples they were going to the other side of the lake, (2) he was with them, and (3) he was calm, they still cried out to him, "Teacher, don't you even care?" (v. 38). We sometimes do the same thing!

After Jesus calmed the storm, he spoke to his disciples about the unbelief in their hearts. He was more concerned about the problem *within* them than the problems *around* them. This God who is in control wants us to cast (throw, fling, heave, or thrust) our anxieties and fears on him because he cares for us.

God who is in control of everything,
Thank you that you welcome our worries and fears. Thank you that you are
not indifferent to our cries, but that you care for us. Amen.

FEAR

I AM LEAVING YOU WITH A GIFT—PEACE OF MIND AND
HEART. AND THE PEACE I GIVE ISN'T LIKE THE PEACE THE
WORLD GIVES. SO DON'T BE TROUBLED OR AFRAID.

John 14:27

*J*esus' instructions not to be fearful, anxious, or in a panic are often a challenge for me. When difficulties happen in my life or the lives of my family, I sometimes react fearfully, losing perspective about my resources in Christ.

The Bible teaches us that there's a big difference between the peace the world gives and the peace Christ gives. The world bases its peace on its resources, while God's peace depends on relationships. The world depends on personal ability, but the Christian depends on spiritual adequacy in Christ. In the world, peace is something a person hopes for or works for; but to the Christian, peace is God's wonderful gift, received by faith. Unsaved people enjoy peace when there is an absence of trouble, but Christians can enjoy peace *in spite of trials* because of the presence of the Holy Spirit.

Warren Wiersbe writes, "People in the world walk by sight and depend on the externals, but Christians walk by faith and depend on the eternals. The Spirit of God teaches us the Word and guides us (not drags us!) into the truth."[4] In the midst of fearful times, I need to return to that truth to give me proper perspective and to calm my heart. Through the Bible, God's Spirit shares his peace, love, and joy, and that is what calms my fearful heart.

God's Spirit and God's Word offer great help and hope to any Christian mom dealing with fear!

> *Father,*
> *Please forgive us for acting fearfully. May we be thankful for your Spirit, who is our Counselor, and your Word, which is our guide. And may we look to you instead of focusing on obstacles or difficulties. Amen.*

FEAR

> WHO ARE THOSE WHO FEAR THE LORD? HE WILL SHOW
> THEM THE PATH THEY SHOULD CHOOSE. *Psalm 25:12*

What are some of your fears as a mom? Through twenty years of motherhood, I've experienced plenty of my own. The first one I remember was, "How will I know what to *do* with this little person when I bring him home from the hospital?" Apparently, God helped me figure it out, because Chad grew up safely and presently teaches high school physics. Now it's *his* turn to figure out what to do with a whole classroom.

While I was pregnant with my second child, I feared that I wouldn't be able to love that child as much as I loved my firstborn. I smile now because as soon as I started taking care of Nate, my fear dissolved in the middle of my busyness. The third time around, I feared that I wouldn't be able to squeeze in much one-on-one time with our youngest child. Now that the first two have graduated from college, my husband and I spend all kinds of one-on-one time with Jordan. He gets more time with us than the other two ever did.

Although my fears were probably common, they weren't particularly helpful. But one fear is—the fear of the Lord. The Bible teaches that fearing the Lord doesn't mean being scared of him or avoiding him. Instead, it's seeing God for who he is and responding to him with reverent and affectionate obedience. Part of fearing him is presenting our fears to him—fears about our kids, schedules, husbands, health, jobs, and relationships. When we trust him with our fears, we discover that he is faithful to help us choose good paths. Fearing God helps us to put our other fears in proper perspective.

Father,
Thank you that we can trust you with our fears. Help us always to respond to you with the reverence and obedience you deserve—and may that give us the right view of our lives. Amen.

FEAR

ELIJAH WAS AFRAID AND FLED FOR HIS LIFE. HE WENT TO
BEERSHEBA, A TOWN IN JUDAH, AND HE LEFT HIS SERVANT THERE.
THEN HE WENT ON ALONE INTO THE DESERT, TRAVELING ALL DAY.
HE SAT DOWN UNDER A SOLITARY BROOM TREE AND PRAYED THAT HE MIGHT DIE.
"I HAVE HAD ENOUGH, LORD," HE SAID. "TAKE MY LIFE, FOR I AM NO BETTER THAN
MY ANCESTORS."

1 Kings 19:3-4

Do you know how much fear a man can feel when he's threatened by a woman? A lot. Elijah, an Old Testament prophet, was a man of great faith. In 1 Kings 18 we read that he stood up to wicked King Ahab, asked God to send down fire, and struck down 850 false prophets. A man of faith, Elijah experienced some incredible victories.

But in the very next chapter we see Elijah as a man of *fear*. Queen Jezebel was not happy when she heard that 850 of her prophets had been killed, and she promised to take revenge on Elijah. In spite of the great victory he had just experienced, the prophet fled eighty miles to the town of Beersheba. Elijah left his servant there and traveled alone into the wastelands—one lonely and despondent man. He was so exhausted physically and emotionally that when he lay down to sleep, he prayed that God would take away his life. Elijah was in trouble here. He had taken his eyes off God and had fixed them on himself.

As God so often does, he graciously protected and ministered to Elijah. The Lord sent an angel to give him food to strengthen him for his journey to Mt. Horeb, where God spoke to Elijah and reminded him of his great power, using wind, an earthquake, and finally a quiet voice. Elijah learned that God can be trusted always—when there are great displays of power and when things are quiet.

What are you afraid of? What is overwhelming in your life? God can be trusted *always*. Our job is to keep our eyes on him.

God of the fire and the still, small voice,
It's reassuring to know that even great prophets of the Bible struggled with
fear and disillusionment. Whether our fears relate to our children, husbands,
finances, or anything else, may we turn to you in our times of fear so you can
strengthen and encourage us. Amen.

FEAR

SINCE THE CHILDREN HAVE FLESH AND BLOOD, HE TOO
SHARED IN THEIR HUMANITY SO THAT BY HIS DEATH HE
MIGHT DESTROY HIM WHO HOLDS THE POWER OF DEATH——THAT
IS, THE DEVIL——AND FREE THOSE WHO ALL THEIR LIVES WERE HELD IN SLAVERY BY
THEIR FEAR OF DEATH.   *Hebrews 2:14-15, NIV*

Sometimes we joke that we'd rather die than have a root canal. But the fear of death is a real fear that must be faced, sooner or later, by every human being. A mom reading this might have received news that one of her family members has only a few months to live. Another mom might have a child asking questions about death or may have just buried her own mother.

The author of the book of Hebrews wrote to people who were immobilized by their fear of death, and he encouraged them with some truths that encourage our hearts today. First of all, Jesus shared our humanity. We all connect back to Adam. But just as sin was brought into the world by Adam, righteousness came through Jesus Christ, who was born into our world as God's Son. He experienced death and suffering too. And when we believe in Christ, he calls us his brothers and sisters!

Second, when Jesus died (with human flesh just like ours, nailed and bleeding on a cross), he called out to God, in faith, "Father, into your hands I commit my spirit" (Luke 23:46, NIV). The last words he spoke on earth were words of dependence, and those must be our thoughts and words also. Jesus needed to exercise faith in suffering too.

Finally, Jesus' death on the cross destroyed the power of death, and his resurrection promised our union with him in eternal life! If we ponder the reality of these truths, our hearts will be encouraged.

Lord Jesus,
Thank you that you didn't leave us on earth as orphans, but you died so we could have life. Even though our physical bodies will someday die, may we be encouraged that you shared our humanity and trusted God, and because of your resurrection, we will share in your eternal life! Amen.

FEAR

HE SAID, "LISTEN, KING JEHOSHAPHAT! LISTEN, ALL YOU
PEOPLE OF JUDAH AND JERUSALEM! THIS IS WHAT THE LORD
SAYS: DO NOT BE AFRAID. DON'T BE DISCOURAGED BY THIS MIGHTY ARMY,
FOR THE BATTLE IS NOT YOURS, BUT GOD'S."

2 Chronicles 20:15

Jehoshaphat, king of Judah, was about to face a combined army of the Moabites and the Ammonites, two ancient enemies of Israel. When Jehoshaphat received news from some of his men that enemy troops were advancing, he was alarmed.

When we sense an army of trouble coming upon us—whether it's financial difficulties, health problems, or a crisis in our family—what is our reaction? Panic, fear, anger? These are normal human reactions, but we run into trouble if we get stuck there. Any of those reactions, left unchecked, will only add to the confusion and intensity of the problems confronting us.

Notice some excellent choices Jehoshaphat made in this situation (see 2 Chronicles 20:1-30):

- He resolved to ask the Lord for guidance.
- He encouraged the people to fast and pray.
- In front of the people, he rehearsed who God is and what he had done in the past. Then he asked for God's help, admitting that the people did not know what to do, but that their eyes were upon God.

Through a prophet, God told the people not to be discouraged or afraid, pointing out that the battle was not theirs—it was his. They then gave thanks and praise to God even before they saw who was going to win the battle.

The amazing conclusion is that the enemies were thrown into confusion, killing each other, and Jehoshaphat and his people were saved! When faced with trouble or crisis, may we, like Jehoshaphat, remember to pray and praise, waiting to see what God will do.

Father,
Thank you for examples of people who, though fearful and imperfect like we are, made some wise decisions to trust you. Thanks for lessons from the past that remind us that you are faithful. Amen.

FEAR

"I AM GOD," THE VOICE SAID [TO JACOB], "THE GOD
OF YOUR FATHER. DO NOT BE AFRAID TO GO DOWN TO
EGYPT, FOR I WILL SEE TO IT THAT YOU BECOME A GREAT NATION
THERE. I WILL GO WITH YOU DOWN TO EGYPT, AND I WILL BRING YOUR
DESCENDANTS BACK AGAIN."

Genesis 46:3-4

I've heard the story of a man who attempted to cross the frozen St. Lawrence River in Canada. Unsure whether the ice would hold him, the man first tested it by laying one hand on it. Then he got down on his knees and gingerly began making his way across the ice. When he got to the middle of the frozen river, trembling with fear, he heard a noise behind him. Looking back, he saw a team of horses pulling a carriage down the road toward the river. Upon reaching the bank, the horses didn't stop but bolted right onto the ice and drove past him—while he cowered on all fours.

Sometimes we feel the same fear this man did. We come up against an obstacle or a frightening experience, and we are uncertain about how to proceed or where to place our confidence. At times like these, it's good for us to be reminded of the faith journeys of other people who trusted God.

Jacob, an Old Testament patriarch, thought his son Joseph was dead. When he found out that Joseph was still alive in Egypt, his mind and heart must have been doing somersaults. Since Jacob was such an old man, the thought of moving to Egypt was likely a fearful one. But notice how God graciously anticipated Jacob's fears. "I am God," he reminded Jacob. And then he told Jacob not to be afraid and assured him of his presence. What a great reminder for any of us who feel frightened or even paralyzed by fear today: he is God. We need not be afraid, for he is with us!

God who keeps promises,
Thank you that you kept your promises to people like Jacob. May we be
encouraged not to be afraid but to trust you in all the events of our lives too.
Amen.

CHRIST'S PASSION

CHRIST ALSO SUFFERED WHEN HE DIED FOR OUR SINS ONCE
FOR ALL TIME. HE NEVER SINNED, BUT HE DIED FOR SINNERS
THAT HE MIGHT BRING US SAFELY HOME TO GOD.

1 Peter 3:18

*E*ver since Adam and Eve chose to sin back in the Garden of Eden (see Genesis 3), suffering has been part of human existence. To suffer is to experience agony, distress, intense pain, or great sorrow. Some people suffer from illness, others lose a child in an accident, some are betrayed, and others lose everything they own in a flood or a war. But Jesus experienced unparalleled suffering.

As we learn in Isaiah 53, Jesus was despised and rejected, he carried all our sorrows, he was pierced for our transgressions, he was led like a lamb to the slaughter, and he bore the sins of the whole world.

Look through the eyes of a mother to get a glimpse of Jesus' suffering: "What mother's sufferings were ever equal to Mary's? Jesus was only thirty-three, her firstborn, the son of her strength. There he hung before her eyes, but she was helpless."[5] Mary stood at the foot of the cross and watched Jesus bleeding, but she couldn't tend to his wounds. Jesus was thirsty, and Mary couldn't give him a drink. The arms that were stretched out on a cross were arms that had frequently given Mary a hug. What agony for Mary that day; nails pierced Jesus' hands and a sword pierced her soul.

I hope I never forget that although Pilate issued the official order sentencing Jesus to death by crucifixion, Jesus bore the weight of all my sin as well. I deserved the wages and penalties for my sin, and yet Jesus suffered them for me. What a wonderful Savior!

Jesus,
Thank you for paying the penalty for our sin and suffering for our sin. May
we offer you our devotion in return. Amen.

CHRIST'S PASSION

THEN THEY NAILED HIM TO THE CROSS. THEY GAMBLED
FOR HIS CLOTHES, THROWING DICE TO DECIDE WHO WOULD
GET THEM.

Mark 15:24

Many people today hang attractive crosses on the walls of their homes or on a chain around their neck. But the cross on which Jesus died was anything but attractive. During the period of history when Jesus lived on earth, people sentenced to death by crucifixion were first beaten with leather lashes, often losing a great deal of blood before they were forced to carry the upper beam of their cross to the execution site. This was the case with Jesus. When the crossbeam was laid on the ground, Jesus' hands were nailed to the beam with spikes, and then his body, probably unclothed, was hoisted up. When the crossbeam was attached to a vertical stake, his feet were nailed into place.

Many Jews of Jesus' time didn't believe that the world could be saved through such a seemingly bizarre plan, and many people alive today feel the same way. But God's Word teaches us that the best news the world has ever heard came from a graveyard. Jesus Christ, the sinless Son of God, died on the cross in the place of you and me. Before rising from the dead with eternal life, he experienced the separation from God that we deserved because of our sin.

It is in the death of Jesus that we see how much God loves us. As a result of this great love, we can be reconciled both to God and to each other.

Because of his death, we have life and hope.

Father,
Thank you that because of Jesus' death on the cross, I can have a relationship
with you. Thank you that I can be reconciled to others around me too because
of the example and power Jesus provides for us. Amen.

CHRIST'S PASSION

AT NOON, DARKNESS FELL ACROSS THE WHOLE LAND UNTIL
THREE O'CLOCK. AT ABOUT THREE O'CLOCK, JESUS CALLED OUT
WITH A LOUD VOICE, *"Eli, Eli, lema sabachthani?"* WHICH MEANS, "MY
GOD, MY GOD, WHY HAVE YOU FORSAKEN ME?"

Matthew 27:45-46

It wasn't until I began attending a church that affirms the Apostles Creed each Sunday morning that I ever gave much thought to the fact that Jesus actually experienced hell. Together with our human father, Adam, we should be the ones going to hell for our sins. But Jesus suffered in our place. He experienced hell so we could experience heaven. The physical torture that Jesus experienced was awful enough, but far worse for him was becoming in his soul the sin that he hated. Second Corinthians 5:21 says, "God made him who had no sin to be sin for us, so that in him we might become the righteousness of God" (NIV).

Michael Horton writes, "He who was the truth would become the world's most inveterate liar. He who was too pure to look upon a woman to lust would become history's most promiscuous adulterer."[6] It is no wonder that Jesus, as he prayed in the Garden of Gethsemane with such agony of spirit that sweat drops of his blood fell to the ground, told his disciples that his soul was crushed with grief to the point of death.

Later on the cross, Jesus spoke the words, "My God, my God, why have you forsaken me?" If we choose to believe in his provision for us, we will never have to speak those words ourselves. Jesus became God's enemy in hell so we could become God's friends, singing "Hallelujah, what a Savior!"

Father,
We can never thank you enough for sending Jesus to be our Savior. Amen.

CHRIST'S PASSION

THEN THE ANGEL SPOKE TO THE WOMEN. "DON'T
BE AFRAID!" HE SAID. "I KNOW YOU ARE LOOKING FOR
JESUS, WHO WAS CRUCIFIED. HE ISN'T HERE! HE HAS BEEN
RAISED FROM THE DEAD, JUST AS HE SAID WOULD HAPPEN. COME, SEE WHERE
HIS BODY WAS LYING."

Matthew 28:5-6

*T*he resurrection of Jesus is the capstone of all his teaching and ministry, proving to the disciples and to us that he really is the Son of God. The classic images of the Resurrection are a stone rolled away from the entrance to Jesus' tomb, grave-clothes left behind, an earthquake, and an angel speaking to the women at the tomb. In contrast to the Crucifixion, where everything appeared to be coming to a grinding halt with Jesus' death, his resurrection was surrounded by a frenzy of activity that included Jesus' friends running back and forth in breathless excitement.

Without the Resurrection, our Christian beliefs and hopes would be meaningless. Our lives can be transformed only by the same power that overcame evil and death and raised Christ from the dead! Because Jesus was raised from the dead, just as he and the Scriptures both promised, we can believe that he will accomplish everything else he has promised us in his Word.

Even Jesus' disciples struggled at first with understanding his resurrection, and we today are no different. Some think the Resurrection is a fairy tale but are willing to examine it further. If we are serious about wanting to know the truth, we will eventually encounter Jesus personally; and as we enter into a personal relationship with him, we begin to experience his power to change our lives.

Father,
Thank you that because of Jesus' resurrection we have hope both for this life
and for eternity. Please help us to communicate this hope to our children in
gracious actions and words. We are grateful that the power that raised Jesus
from the grave is the same power that changes us and helps us as we trust in
you. Amen.

CHRIST'S PASSION

THEN JESUS LED THEM TO BETHANY, AND LIFTING HIS
HANDS TO HEAVEN, HE BLESSED THEM. WHILE HE WAS BLESSING
THEM, HE LEFT THEM AND WAS TAKEN UP TO HEAVEN. THEY WORSHIPED
HIM AND THEN RETURNED TO JERUSALEM FILLED WITH GREAT JOY. AND THEY
SPENT ALL OF THEIR TIME IN THE TEMPLE, PRAISING GOD.   *Luke 24:50-53*

I find it reassuring that Jesus remained on earth for forty days after his resurrection to minister to his disciples. The Jewish leaders' official position on the Resurrection was that Jesus wasn't alive—they said his disciples had just stolen Jesus' dead body. It was very important that the disciples be able to refute that lie. The disciples' spiritual power was dependent on Jesus' resurrection, because if Jesus had remained dead, they would have had no message of hope to share.

Some people may wonder why Jesus went back to heaven. Wouldn't it have been better for him to stay on earth and preach his message? But if he hadn't left, the Holy Spirit—God himself—would not have come to dwell in the believers' hearts. Jesus assured his disciples that the Holy Spirit would give ordinary believers extraordinary power through his work in their lives.

Before Jesus' death and resurrection, the disciples had worried too much about the positions, privileges, and politics of God's kingdom. After the Resurrection, Jesus spoke to them about what was most important—the coming of God's kingdom to people's *hearts*.

The ascended Jesus still plays a huge role in the lives of believers. He intercedes for us, petitioning God on our behalf and bringing us into relationship with God as a result of our faith in him. He's also our advocate before the Father, offering forgiveness when we confess our sins (Hebrews 7:25).

The Savior who was spat on, humiliated, and crucified on the cross was lifted up to the heavens and now prays for us and offers us forgiveness!

> *Father,*
> *Thank you for the reassurance you gave to the disciples after Jesus' resurrection, and thanks for the reassurance we have today of the presence of your Spirit in our lives. May we talk to our children about what is most important in life—the coming of God's Kingdom to our hearts. Thank you that Jesus intercedes on our behalf. Amen.*

CHRIST'S PASSION

HE PERSONALLY CARRIED AWAY OUR SINS IN HIS OWN
BODY ON THE CROSS SO WE CAN BE DEAD TO SIN AND LIVE FOR
WHAT IS RIGHT. YOU HAVE BEEN HEALED BY HIS WOUNDS!

1 Peter 2:24

About six months before *The Passion of the Christ* was released, my husband and I were invited to preview the movie in London, where we visited a British distributor. I enjoyed going out to lunch with my husband's colleagues before the viewing, but I wasn't particularly looking forward to seeing the movie. I was skeptical of what Hollywood would do with the Bible, and I was also pretty sure that the movie was going to show more gore than I had ever seen. It did, and there were times when I looked down or closed my eyes. But I was relieved that for the most part the movie seemed true to Scripture. Because it contained so much truth and because the gospel is important to me, I entered into the experience.

As I watched the movie, I contemplated Jesus' agony in the garden. I wept over his humiliation. I was warmed by the flashbacks, which pictured the incredible love Jesus showed to sinners in general, and his disciples in particular. As sad as Peter's betrayal was, I sat there thinking, *I'm a sinner too.* And when the movie showed Jesus being beaten, forced to carry his cross, and then crucified, I was so overcome with emotion that I wanted to stand up and yell, "STOP!" But then I remembered why he did it—why he went through such passion and suffering. He did it because he loves us so much. He did it because he wanted us to be able to die to sin and live for what is right. I felt overwhelmed by his love.

After the movie, as I walked out onto the busy streets of London, I thought, All of eternity will not be long enough to praise Christ for what he did for me!

Father,
I am grateful for your wonderful plan to bring us life through Christ's death.
I don't ever want a day to go by where I don't thank you for Christ's death
and resurrection, which made it possible for me to be healed. In Jesus' precious
name, amen.

CHRIST'S PASSION

AND SO, DEAR BROTHERS AND SISTERS, WE CAN BOLDLY
ENTER HEAVEN'S MOST HOLY PLACE BECAUSE OF THE BLOOD
OF JESUS. THIS IS THE NEW, LIFE-GIVING WAY THAT CHRIST HAS
OPENED UP FOR US THROUGH THE SACRED CURTAIN, BY MEANS OF HIS DEATH
FOR US. AND SINCE WE HAVE A GREAT HIGH PRIEST WHO RULES OVER GOD'S
PEOPLE, LET US GO RIGHT INTO THE PRESENCE OF GOD, WITH TRUE HEARTS
FULLY TRUSTING HIM. FOR OUR EVIL CONSCIENCES HAVE BEEN SPRINKLED
WITH CHRIST'S BLOOD TO MAKE US CLEAN, AND OUR BODIES HAVE BEEN WASHED
WITH PURE WATER. *Hebrews 10:19-22*

What kind of window coverings do you use in your home? My favorites are the floral valances hanging in my living room. When my family first moved into our home, the valances helped pull all of our colors together. And when we re-painted our walls taupe, my neighbor suggested tea-staining the valances to get a new effect. It worked nicely, so the valances are still hanging.

During the time that Jesus was on earth, a heavy curtain hung in the Temple and separated the Holy Place (which only priests could enter) from the Most Holy Place (which only the high priest could enter, and then only once a year to make amends for the sins of the people). This curtain holds a significant place in the story of Jesus' crucifixion.

Matthew 27:50-53 explains that at the very moment Jesus died, while an earthquake opened some graves and saints rose from the dead, the curtain in the temple was torn from top to bottom! Only God could have done that. This Passion event holds great symbolism for us: Since that moment when the curtain was torn, the way to God has been opened. All of us may come to him.

The curtain is no longer necessary. There is no more need for temples, altars, or animal sacrifices, because Jesus—through his death for our sins—provided the way to God. This is huge! Any person who has trusted in Christ's death and resurrection can communicate directly with God—anytime and anywhere. Have you placed your faith in Christ's death for your sin on the cross? Are you enjoying the access Christ offers you to the presence of God?

Father,
Thank you for the image of a torn curtain, reminding us that if we place our
faith in Jesus' death and resurrection, nothing holds us back from communi-
cating directly with you. In Jesus' name, amen.

CHRIST'S GIFTS

I PRAY THAT YOU WILL BEGIN TO UNDERSTAND THE
INCREDIBLE GREATNESS OF HIS POWER FOR US WHO BELIEVE
HIM. THIS IS THE SAME MIGHTY POWER THAT RAISED CHRIST
FROM THE DEAD AND SEATED HIM IN THE PLACE OF HONOR AT GOD'S RIGHT HAND
IN THE HEAVENLY REALMS. NOW HE IS FAR ABOVE ANY RULER OR AUTHORITY
OR POWER OR LEADER OR ANYTHING ELSE IN THIS WORLD OR IN THE WORLD
TO COME.

Ephesians 1:19-21

Although Jesus had remained silent throughout his trial before the Crucifixion, he did answer one of the high priest's questions: " 'Tell us if you are the Christ, the Son of God.' 'Yes, it is as you say,' Jesus replied. 'But I say to all of you: In the future you will see the Son of Man sitting at the right hand of the Mighty One and coming on the clouds of heaven' " (Matthew 26:63-64, NIV).

This declaration of Jesus is a gift to us, holding great meaning for our personal faith. Why? First, there is immense significance in the fact that Jesus is now sitting at the right hand of God the Father. Michael Horton writes, "In the ancient world, the emperor would sometimes seal the treaty between his empire and a lesser kingdom by a regal ceremony in which the local king would take his place at the right hand of the emperor, the place of power and authority. Thus, he would be adopted in a sense by the great king as a son."[7]

Second, we know that Jesus has ascended to sit at the right hand of God, but in the same breath he said he would come "on the clouds of heaven"—a great promise to us that he is coming back!

Finally, God's Word also assures us that we will reign with him if we have put our faith in him. "For if, by the trespass of the one man, death reigned through that one man, how much more will those who receive God's abundant provision of grace and of the gift of righteousness reign in life through the one man, Jesus Christ" (Romans 5:17, NIV).

Father,
Thank you that your mighty strength that raised Jesus from the dead and seated him at your right hand is the same power you share with us to deal with all the challenges of family life. Amen.

CHRIST'S GIFTS

AND GOD HAS PUT ALL THINGS UNDER THE AUTHORITY OF
CHRIST, AND HE GAVE HIM THIS AUTHORITY FOR THE BENEFIT
OF THE CHURCH. AND THE CHURCH IS HIS BODY; IT IS FILLED BY CHRIST,
WHO FILLS EVERYTHING EVERYWHERE WITH HIS PRESENCE.   *Ephesians 1:22-23*

*O*ne Sunday when a young friend was worshipping with our family, she leaned over and asked, "Since this isn't a Catholic church, why does the Apostles' Creed say, 'I believe in one holy catholic Church'?" I briefly explained that the word *catholic* means general or worldwide, as opposed to specific.

The Bible teaches that Jesus calls the church his bride and that the universal church includes all believers, gathered under the head of Christ. Being united with other believers is not something *we* do—Christ has already accomplished it. It is another one of his gracious gifts. We are miraculously united to other Christians because God has united us to his Son. The church is not our idea but God's.

It's comforting to read in John 17 that the night Christ was betrayed, his prayer to God the Father was for the salvation and protection of his church. What amazing love! If he could be so concerned about his church immediately before his incomprehensible suffering, imagine his concern now as he sits in heaven at God's right hand.

God's church is both visible and invisible. The visible is what humans can see—people worshipping God in church buildings and homes all around the world. But we do not know who in their innermost being worships him and who does not. God alone knows our hearts, and he sees the invisible church—those who love him and obey him. He uses these people to spread his Good News and build up the faith of his children.

Father,
Thank you that even in heaven Jesus prays for your church here on earth—for our joy, protection, purity, and unity. May we be faithful members of your invisible church, no matter where we worship and serve you visibly. Amen.

CHRIST'S GIFTS

BUT WHEN THE FATHER SENDS THE COUNSELOR AS MY
REPRESENTATIVE—AND BY THE COUNSELOR I MEAN THE
HOLY SPIRIT—HE WILL TEACH YOU EVERYTHING AND WILL
REMIND YOU OF EVERYTHING I MYSELF HAVE TOLD YOU.   *John 14:26*

The Holy Spirit, one of the three members of the Godhead, has the role of connecting people and God. As we spend time in God's Word, the Holy Spirit comes alongside us to plant truth in our minds, convince us of God's will, and point out where we are straying from it. What an awesome gift! When I think of how much money my husband and I have spent putting our sons through college, I'm amazed that there is no cost for the divine instruction of the Holy Spirit.

When we come to Christ and experience a spiritual birth, the Holy Spirit helps us to see God's Word with new eyes. It's as though the words of Scripture jump straight from the page into our hearts, and we begin to understand God's purposes in ways we never did before.

A Bible commentary explains it this way: "Theologians use the term illumination to describe the Holy Spirit's process of helping believers understand Scripture. Without God, sinful people are unable to recognize and obey divine truths."[8]

Counselor is one of many titles given to Christ throughout the Bible. After we come to faith in Christ, God's Holy Spirit becomes our Counselor. A counselor, according to the dictionary, is a person who gives advice and guidance. Because there is nothing the Holy Spirit does not know, he is the supreme Counselor. He will give us the best advice and guidance available because he understands us much better than we could ever understand ourselves. The Holy Spirit is the most qualified Counselor in the universe because he knows us, loves us, encourages us, is patient with us, and prays for us. How thankful we are for his presence in our lives!

Father,
We need divine guidance every day to meet the challenges of motherhood in particular and life in general. Thank you that the Holy Spirit knows us completely. Please counsel us in your ways and give us your guidance and help. Amen.

CHRIST'S GIFTS

BUT LET ME TELL YOU A WONDERFUL SECRET GOD HAS
REVEALED TO US. NOT ALL OF US WILL DIE, BUT WE WILL ALL
BE TRANSFORMED. IT WILL HAPPEN IN A MOMENT, IN THE BLINKING OF
AN EYE, WHEN THE LAST TRUMPET IS BLOWN. FOR WHEN THE TRUMPET
SOUNDS, THE CHRISTIANS WHO HAVE DIED WILL BE RAISED WITH TRANSFORMED
BODIES. AND THEN WE WHO ARE LIVING WILL BE TRANSFORMED SO THAT WE WILL
NEVER DIE. *1 Corinthians 15:51-52*

I wish that as part of today's reading I could enclose a CD of Handel's *Messiah*—specifically, the bass recitative and solo of "The Trumpet Shall Sound." Being a musician, I get goose bumps when I hear that piece; the marriage of the biblical text to the music creates strong feelings of anticipation. (If you have a recording at home, listen to it with your Bible open to 1 Corinthians 15 and get ready for a meaningful worship experience!)

In order to explain the resurrection of the dead, Paul used the picture of a seed (vv. 35-38). When a seed of any kind is sown in the ground, it first dies and then rises as something much more beautiful. The same is true of the caterpillar, which becomes a butterfly—helpful in explaining the Resurrection to a child. So it is with our bodies too. They are sown weak, but they are raised strong. They are sown as natural bodies, but they are raised as spiritual bodies.

What does all that mean to us *today*? It's sobering to realize that *every* human being who ever lived in a human body will have an eternal spiritual body. But the question is, what kind? Those who have trusted and obeyed Christ will receive the gift of heavenly bodies, and those who have turned their backs on Christ will have bodies suited to their environment in hell.

If we believe what the Bible teaches us about the Resurrection, we will want to trust Christ now and use our bodies to the glory of God.

Gracious Father,
Thank you that someday you will transform our frail bodies. We want to use them for your glory while we're here on earth. Amen.

CHRIST'S GIFTS

SINCE YOU HAVE BEEN RAISED TO NEW LIFE WITH CHRIST,
SET YOUR SIGHTS ON THE REALITIES OF HEAVEN, WHERE
CHRIST SITS AT GOD'S RIGHT HAND IN THE PLACE OF HONOR
AND POWER. LET HEAVEN FILL YOUR THOUGHTS. DO NOT THINK ONLY ABOUT
THINGS DOWN HERE ON EARTH. FOR YOU DIED WHEN CHRIST DIED, AND YOUR
REAL LIFE IS HIDDEN WITH CHRIST IN GOD.

Colossians 3:1-3

*I*t is incorrect to think that the gift of everlasting life begins only when our body dies. For the person who trusts Christ as their Savior, everlasting life begins *immediately*, giving us a portfolio of riches that we sometimes don't realize are available.

Michael Horton, in his book *We Believe*, suggests that the Christian life involves a cycle. Because the law leads us to despair, we run to Christ. As we abide in Christ, we bear fruit because we share in his Resurrection power. Then we are lifted out of despair and into joy because the realities of Christ give us confidence for this life on earth. Lest we get too comfortable, we need to hear the law again, reminding us that even our best work is no match for Christ's righteousness. Then we run to him again. Gradually, we realize that "it is the intrusion of the coming age into the present, not the gradual improvement of the sinful nature, that is responsible for our new life and growth in Christ."[9]

When we first put our faith in Christ, we become a new creation. God tells us that the old passes away and the new arrives. God's Word guides us into truth, and the presence of his Spirit is our "down payment" on the life to come. So we don't have to wait for physical death or the Rapture before we experience everlasting life. Our faith in Christ makes it a present reality!

Father,
Thanks that the gift of everlasting life is something we begin to experience as soon as we trust Christ. Thanks that we receive your Spirit as a hint of the riches to come. Amen.

CHRIST'S GIFTS

YOU FATHERS—IF YOUR CHILDREN ASK FOR A FISH, DO
YOU GIVE THEM A SNAKE INSTEAD? OR IF THEY ASK FOR AN EGG,
DO YOU GIVE THEM A SCORPION? OF COURSE NOT! IF YOU SINFUL
PEOPLE KNOW HOW TO GIVE GOOD GIFTS TO YOUR CHILDREN, HOW MUCH
MORE WILL YOUR HEAVENLY FATHER GIVE THE HOLY SPIRIT TO THOSE WHO
ASK HIM.

Luke 11:11-13

*O*ur ten-year-old son, Jordan, was about to have surgery to repair a broken femur sustained in a skateboarding accident. My husband, Jim, and I were standing next to our son's bed in a holding area of the hospital, waiting for him to be wheeled into the operating room. One of our pastors and a church elder had just left after praying with Jordan.

While we were waiting, Jordan looked up at Jim and me and said, "You know that electric guitar I've been wanting?" My husband and I nodded, knowing exactly where this was headed. "Well . . . do you think you could buy it for me now?" You know the old saying "Timing is everything"? Jim was out buying the electric guitar before Jordan even came home from the hospital. When we told sixteen-year-old Nate what Jordan had requested, Nate said, "I would have asked for a car!"

As parents, we want to please our children and give them good gifts. How much more must God want to bless his children? The gift Jim and I gave to Jordan sits up in his bedroom closet, and he still plays it every now and then. But the gift that God most wants to give to his children—the Holy Spirit—is the gift that keeps on giving.

Jordan had it right—he looked to his parents in dependence for the gift he wanted. How much more will God give his Spirit to those of us who ask!

Father of all gifts,
Thank you for the joy that giving gifts to our children brings. May we be quick to depend on you and be thankful each day for the gift of your Spirit's power and presence in our lives. Amen.

CHRIST'S GIFTS

BUT WHEN THE HOLY SPIRIT CONTROLS OUR LIVES, HE
WILL PRODUCE THIS KIND OF FRUIT IN US: LOVE, JOY, PEACE,
PATIENCE, KINDNESS, GOODNESS, FAITHFULNESS, GENTLENESS,
AND SELF-CONTROL.

Galatians 5:22-23

When my family vacationed on the island of St. Thomas one summer, all three of our sons decided to take up windsurfing for the week. "Let's give it a try," they said after sitting on the beach watching experienced windsurfers bounce and glide over the waves. The guys quickly learned that windsurfing is much more difficult than it looks. Anyone who steps onto a surfboard with a sail discovers that previous experience with aerodynamics and hydrodynamics is desirable.

My husband and I spent many hours that week watching our three sons get on and fall off the boards. By the end of the week, they were actually able to get the boards moving, with the help of the wind. When the wind got going, the boys said that the experience was exhilarating. If there had been no wind, though, there could have been no movement.

Jesus described God's Spirit as the wind that brings us new life (John 3:8). Just as we cannot predict or control the wind, neither can we predict or control God's Spirit. We don't actually see the wind when it moves, but we see its effects. We see a flag flapping, trees swaying, or a beach chair tumbling over the sand. In a similar way, when the Holy Spirit moves, we don't actually see him. But when he controls our lives, we see love, joy, peace, patience, kindness, goodness, faithfulness, gentleness, and self-control.

I'm thankful that these life-changing effects—the fruit of God's Spirit—do not require previous experience in aerodynamics or hydrodynamics. They result from faith in Christ.

Father,
Thank you that the presence of your Spirit in our hearts produces evidence
that we know you. In Jesus' name, amen.

SALVATION

FOR THE GRACE OF GOD HAS BEEN REVEALED, BRINGING
SALVATION TO ALL PEOPLE.   *Titus 2:11*

During the summer, my sons and I used to spend time at our community's swimming pool whenever the weather allowed. I was impressed with the many lifeguards stationed every few feet around the pool. Usually they were a quiet presence, but one day my youngest son and I saw a lifeguard perform the service she was trained to do—deliver a swimmer from difficulty and drowning.

A little girl around the age of five had jumped off the highest diving board. After entering the water, she surfaced but was thrashing and gasping for air, unable to swim from the middle of the pool over to the edge. The lifeguard blew her whistle, promptly jumped in, rescued the little girl, and delivered her to the edge of the pool. Once the child was out of the water, she was visibly upset but all right. Everyone nearby heaved a sigh of relief!

My son had heard the word *salvation* many times, but that day he had a mental picture of it—deliverance from difficulty or death. Just as every swimmer in the pool was within sight of a lifeguard, so every person in the world is within sight of God. Salvation through Jesus has appeared to *all*, and all of us need to realize that we cannot make it through life on our own. The Bible teaches that for us to experience salvation, we need to believe that Jesus is God and turn to him in saving faith.

Through a common experience of going to the pool, we witnessed a not-so-common rescue. It was a reminder to me and to my son that God's plan for the whole world is salvation.

> *God,*
> *We're thankful whenever a person is rescued from difficulty or distress. Thank you that because of your death on the cross, you have offered us salvation. Amen.*

SALVATION

YET THEY CANNOT REDEEM THEMSELVES FROM DEATH
BY PAYING A RANSOM TO GOD. REDEMPTION DOES NOT
COME SO EASILY, FOR NO ONE CAN EVER PAY ENOUGH TO LIVE
FOREVER AND NEVER SEE THE GRAVE. THOSE WHO ARE WISE MUST FINALLY DIE,
JUST LIKE THE FOOLISH AND SENSELESS, LEAVING ALL THEIR WEALTH BEHIND.

Psalm 49:7-10

When I drove several hours to my son's state band competition today, I was thankful for expressways that have divided traffic going opposite directions. Many accidents have been avoided because of separation from oncoming cars. I realize that we spend our lives trying to avoid many things; we design airbags to help prevent serious injuries in car crashes, and we invent anesthesia to avoid pain. But none of our efforts can ever help us avoid eventual death. We can postpone it perhaps, but never avoid it.

We can't purchase an escape from death with either time or money, and we can't purchase eternal life either. Each person who lives on this earth has a penalty to pay for sin, but it can't be worked off with good deeds or paid off with money. God's Word tells us that human souls are far too precious to be ransomed by earthly wealth.

So if time or money can't rescue us, what can? *Christ's blood through faith!* Romans 3:25 (TLB) teaches, "For God sent Christ Jesus to take the punishment for our sins and to end all God's anger against us. He used Christ's blood and our faith as the means of saving us from his wrath." It's great to design airbags and invent painkillers, which improve the quality of our short years on earth. But we would do well to spend more time thinking about ways to improve the quality of people's *forever* lives—time spent with Jesus that doesn't end.

Father,
Thank you that you place such great value on our souls. And thank you for offering salvation through faith in Christ's blood. Amen.

SALVATION

HERE IS A SAMPLE OF JOHN'S PREACHING TO THE CROWDS
THAT CAME FOR BAPTISM: "YOU BROOD OF SNAKES! WHO
WARNED YOU TO FLEE GOD'S COMING JUDGMENT? PROVE BY THE WAY
YOU LIVE THAT YOU HAVE REALLY TURNED FROM YOUR SINS AND TURNED TO
GOD. DON'T JUST SAY, 'WE'RE SAFE—WE'RE THE DESCENDANTS OF ABRAHAM.'
THAT PROVES NOTHING. GOD CAN CHANGE THESE STONES HERE INTO CHILDREN
OF ABRAHAM."

Luke 3:7-8

In John the Baptist's task of preparing the way for Jesus, he went straight to the root issue—he called people to repentance. He taught that there will be a future judgment and warned that the only way to avoid God's wrath is to turn from sin and trust God. To repent is to have a change of mind or attitude that includes a reversal of previous thinking or conduct. John told the people that God wasn't impressed with their religious profession if their lives didn't produce fruit. They needed to know there would be a judgment before they could receive God's grace.

John's job was to "make straight in the wilderness a highway for our God" (Isaiah 40:3, NIV). In ancient times, roads were built whenever a king traveled. His subjects built highways so his chariot would not get stuck in the mud or sand. Just as those subjects prepared roads for their king, John was preparing the way for Jesus by preaching that all people needed salvation.

John reminded the people of his day that salvation wasn't inherited as a result of being descendants of Abraham. Likewise, it's important for us to teach our children that their salvation is not inherited from us. Rather, it is a result of *their* repentance—a change in mind or attitude going the opposite direction from sin and destruction. And when the posture of our children's hearts leans toward repentance, their lives will show evidence of changed minds and attitudes.

Father,
Thank you that repentance produces fruit in our lives. May we point our children toward you so they will experience personal repentance and salvation through a relationship with you and will produce fruit for your kingdom. Amen.

SALVATION

"COME NOW, LET US REASON TOGETHER," SAYS THE LORD.
"THOUGH YOUR SINS ARE LIKE SCARLET, THEY SHALL BE
AS WHITE AS SNOW; THOUGH THEY ARE RED AS CRIMSON,
THEY SHALL BE LIKE WOOL."

Isaiah 1:18, NIV

I'm grateful that God has presented us with images in the Bible that we can easily understand—images like darkness, light, fire, and water. Think, for example, about color. If I were to say, "Black . . . red . . . white . . . green . . . gold" slowly enough, you would be able to visualize each of those colors in your head.

God's use of color in the Bible was one of the seeds that brought me to Christ as a young child. Most people who decide to follow Christ make that decision over a period of time, after a series of seeds are planted in their heart. That's the way it was for me. My parents talked about my need for Christ, and I read about Christ's death and resurrection in the Bible. The seed involving color was planted when one of my Sunday school teachers demonstrated my need for Christ with a simple song and a wordless book:

> *My heart was black with sin until the Savior came in [black for sin].*
> *His precious blood, I know [red for blood] has washed it white as snow*
> *[white for cleansing].*
> *And in his Word I'm told [green for growth] I'll walk the streets of gold*
> *[gold for heaven],*
> *What a wonderful, wonderful day—He washed my sins away.*

As mothers, we plant seeds of God's truth in our children's minds while we pray for their hearts. One of my pastors, Chris Castaldo, says, "We prayerfully and intentionally cooperate with God and others in sharing redemptive truth, with a view to leading unbelievers one step closer to Jesus Christ." I'm thankful for simple images like color that God uses to help us see our need for salvation.

> *Father,*
> *Thank you that in your good plan, Jesus gave his life to free us from sin. Help us to make the most of the opportunities you give us to plant seeds of faith in others' lives. Amen.*

SALVATION

> LORD, IF YOU KEPT A RECORD OF OUR SINS, WHO, O LORD, COULD EVER SURVIVE? BUT YOU OFFER FORGIVENESS, THAT WE MIGHT LEARN TO FEAR YOU.
>
> *Psalm 130:3-4*

The story is told in Spain of a father whose relationship with his teenage son had become strained. The son ran away from home. His father, however, began a journey in search of his rebellious child. Finally, in Madrid, in a last desperate effort to find him, the father put an ad in the newspaper. It read: "Dear Paco, meet me in front of the newspaper office at noon. All is forgiven. I love you. Your father." The next day at noon in front of the newspaper office eight hundred Pacos showed up, all seeking forgiveness and love from their fathers.

The Bible teaches that God forgives sins completely. Although sin deserves punishment because it violates God's holy character, he is also a God of grace and pardon who *initiates* forgiveness and salvation.

Before God can forgive sin, two conditions must be met. A blood sacrifice must be made, and a person must have a repentant heart. In Old Testament times, animal sacrifices were made over and over to cover sin, pointing ahead to Christ. And when Jesus came, he became a once-for-all sacrifice—the just for the unjust.

Before we meet Christ, we are all Pacos needing to meet our fathers in front of the newspaper office. But the beauty of Christ's forgiveness is that we can receive it anytime and anywhere, as long as we have admitted our sin and trust in his blood.

Father,
Thank you so much for your complete forgiveness. May our lives show how much we appreciate your amazing gift of salvation. Amen.

SALVATION

THE SPIRIT OF THE LORD IS UPON ME, FOR HE HAS
APPOINTED ME TO PREACH GOOD NEWS TO THE POOR. HE
HAS SENT ME TO PROCLAIM THAT CAPTIVES WILL BE RELEASED,
THAT THE BLIND WILL SEE, THAT THE DOWNTRODDEN WILL BE FREED FROM THEIR
OPPRESSORS, AND THAT THE TIME OF THE LORD'S FAVOR HAS COME. *Luke 4:18-19*

When Jesus taught in his hometown, he chose to read a passage from Isaiah's prophecy (see Isaiah 61), demonstrating salvation's balance between grace and truth. Since we moms desire to point our children to Christ, it's good for us to think about the balance ourselves:

1. The truth is that we're all poor, but the grace is that God has given us his riches.
2. The truth is that on our own we're all prisoners to sin, but the grace is that there is freedom in Christ.
3. The truth is that left to ourselves we are spiritually blind, but the grace is that God can give us sight.
4. The truth is that we are oppressed, but the grace is that by faith in Jesus' death for us, we can be released from oppression.

Imagine a poor orphan child discovering that his parents had left a special bank account for all his needs. Imagine a child locked up in a room but then being freed by the one person who had the key. Imagine a child being chased by a bully until the police officer arrested the bully. We are all that child!

The truth is that we're very needy, but the grace is that Jesus loved us so much that he provided for our needs when he died on the cross. God's salvation makes us very rich.

Father,
Thank you for the best gift in the world—the gift of salvation through Jesus' blood. Thank you that when we place our faith in you, you bless us with spiritual riches, freedom, sight, and release from oppression. Amen.

SALVATION

FOR GOD IN ALL HIS FULLNESS WAS PLEASED TO LIVE IN
CHRIST, AND BY HIM GOD RECONCILED EVERYTHING TO HIMSELF.
HE MADE PEACE WITH EVERYTHING IN HEAVEN AND ON EARTH BY MEANS
OF HIS BLOOD ON THE CROSS.

Colossians 1:19-20

I reserve one small drawer in my dresser for papers and notes that hold special meaning to me. Recently I noticed that the drawer was getting a little messy, so I decided to sort through the contents, getting rid of whatever I could and tidying the rest.

As you might imagine, I got caught up in reading the notes and appreciating the memories. One item that I'll never part with was given to me by my oldest son, Chad, when he was six. It consists of several small pieces of notebook paper that Chad cut, fashioned, and taped into the shape of a cross. On the cross, Chad drew a stick figure picture of Jesus, with nails through his hands and feet—and a smile on his face.

"The cross," says Dietrich Bonhoeffer, "is God's truth about us, and therefore it is the only power which can make us truthful. When we know the cross, we are no longer afraid of the truth." Embracing the truth of the cross has made a difference in Chad's priorities. Because of the cross, Chad finds service to Christ more important than money, power, or pleasure. Because of the cross, Chad cares about other people's hearts. I'm grateful the cross of Christ had an impact on Chad's young heart at the age of six and that it continues to have an impact on him today at twenty-six.

Father,
Thank you that we can have peace with you because of Jesus' death on the
cross. Thank you that the truth of the cross is life changing. In the precious
name of Jesus, amen.

PEACE

> I WILL LIE DOWN IN PEACE AND SLEEP, FOR YOU ALONE,
> O LORD, WILL KEEP ME SAFE.
>
> *Psalm 4:8*

When I was in my early thirties, my husband traveled a fair amount for his job. I was not accustomed to being alone at night and found that I wasn't sleeping very well. When I mentioned my situation to a friend, she related an experience I'll never forget.

Theo and her husband were missionaries to West Africa—Americans living in a foreign culture. Security was an issue even when her husband was around, but when he traveled on occasion, she felt apprehensive at night. One morning while her husband was away on a trip, she awoke to discover that she had left a door to the courtyard not only unlocked but *open* the night before. After checking through the house and realizing that everything was all right, she reasoned that if God could take care of her and keep her safe when the door was open overnight, then she need not worry about being home alone. From then on when her husband was gone at night, she remembered Psalm 4:8.

We read in Mark 4 that Jesus and his disciples were in a boat on the Sea of Galilee when a fierce storm suddenly came up. In the middle of the storm, Jesus was able to continue napping. Why? Because he knew that God would care for him.

Are you experiencing storms in your life? Are any of your children struggling at school or with friends? Remember that God wants us to come to him for refuge. He is our peace. He is our security.

Father,
Instead of worrying and being fearful, may we run to you when we feel insecure, realizing that you want to give us your peace. Amen.

PEACE

I AM LEAVING YOU WITH A GIFT—PEACE OF MIND AND
HEART. AND THE PEACE I GIVE ISN'T LIKE THE PEACE THE
WORLD GIVES. SO DON'T BE TROUBLED OR AFRAID.

John 14:27

H. G. Spafford was a dedicated Christian who lived during the 1800s. Although he was a businessman, today he is remembered for words he penned during an excruciatingly painful time in his life. He had just suffered a financial reversal and was leaving for England with his family. He sent his wife and four daughters ahead on the SS *Ville du Havre.* In the middle of the ocean, the ship carrying his family collided with another ship and sank quickly, with 230 people losing their lives. Spafford's four daughters were drowned, but his wife was rescued. The message she wired to her husband read, "Saved alone." Spafford felt incredible grief; he had lost all four of his daughters to the sea, and his wife was on the other side of the world, alone. But out of his grief he penned some amazing words that still encourage us today:

> *When peace like a river attendeth my way,*
> *When sorrows like sea-billows roll;*
> *Whatever my lot, Thou hast taught me to say,*
> *"It is well, it is well with my soul."*[1]

Father,
Thank you that you share your peace with us in a much different way than we expect. It's always available—even in the worst of times. May we be devoted to you consistently so that we will experience your peace consistently. Amen.

PEACE

> TURN AWAY FROM EVIL AND DO GOOD. WORK HARD AT
> LIVING IN PEACE WITH OTHERS.
>
> *1 Peter 3:11*

*B*ecause baseball was always a love of our son Nate's life (and still is), Jim and I anticipated that he would play all the way through twelfth grade. Somewhere in the middle of high school, though, he lost his zest to play. His coach used foul language and yelled a lot, and Nate felt demoralized by that behavior. While watching Nate's spirits slump lower and lower, Jim and I listened to him and prayed for him. We also encouraged him to speak with his coach one-on-one. That wasn't easy to do, but he did it. He used the *AAA* approach that our family has adopted for such times: affirmation, assertion, action.

Nate affirmed his coach for his good qualities, spoke assertively of how discouraged he felt by the foul language and yelling, and asked his coach to please cut out the offensive behavior. Although the coach thanked him for coming to talk and apologized for his behavior, there was no significant change. Nate finished that season well but decided not to play high school baseball after that.

Nate's decision was a difficult one. He loved baseball, and he didn't want to be a quitter. But sometimes making a decision to get out of something demoralizing is a strong and peace-loving thing to do. God's help and wisdom shows us the right path to take. "Seek his will in all you do, and he will direct your paths" (Proverbs 3:6).

Father,
Sometimes our life situations are confusing and full of unrest. Please give us
wisdom on how to turn away from evil and how to live in peace. In Jesus'
name, amen.

PEACE

A HEART AT PEACE GIVES LIFE TO THE BODY, BUT ENVY
ROTS THE BONES.

Proverbs 14:30, NIV

*T*his verse displays a contrast that gets our attention—the difference between life and decay, stemming from peace or envy. Throughout the Bible, peace is described as hope, trust, and quiet in the soul that is brought about by reconciliation with God through faith in Christ. Quite the opposite, however, is the picture of envy. To be an envious person is to be discontented, dealing with resentment and unfulfilled yearning.

I recently came across a newspaper article detailing some of the recent scientific studies suggesting that religious faith benefits health. These studies don't go to God's Word as their authority, but they rely on data that is demonstrating to the world the truth of what the believer already knows: our personal faith in God through Christ helps us grow in peace. The further we progress in our faith, the more settled we become. This isn't to say that we don't ever become sick, encounter serious problems in our families, or have anxious thoughts, but we have an anchor for our souls. When the ship of our life feels as though it's being tossed about and we're not sure where we are, it's comforting to know that whatever happens to us here, we'll someday be safe in heaven's harbor with God forever. *That's* peace.

Do things in your life feel out of control? Do you lack a compass amidst storms in your life? Jesus came to seek and save people who were lost. Run to him. Run to his Word. To be in relationship with him is to experience peace.

Father,
Thank you that we can experience peace through a relationship with you.
Please help us to model your peace in our homes. Amen.

PEACE

I HAVE TOLD YOU ALL THIS SO THAT YOU MAY HAVE PEACE
IN ME. HERE ON EARTH YOU WILL HAVE MANY TRIALS
AND SORROWS. BUT TAKE HEART, BECAUSE I HAVE OVERCOME
THE WORLD. *John 16:33*

*M*any people think of peace as being the absence of conflict, but Jesus taught a different kind of peace. He never claimed that we would experience peace only in times of quiet because as Christians, we live in a constant war zone. Our enemy, the devil, seeks to destroy us and undermine our faith, and as long as we are alive, we are not in a parade—we are in a battle.

The peace that Jesus offers us is found *in him*, as opposed to the tribulation that is found *in the world*. Romans 5:1 tells us, "Therefore, since we have been justified through faith, we have *peace* with God through our Lord Jesus Christ" (NIV, italics mine). The peace that Jesus brings is a combination of hope, trust, and quiet in our minds and souls, which can be realized even when life experiences are *not* peaceful.

Peace, perfect peace, in this dark world of sin?
The blood of Jesus whispers peace within.
Peace, perfect peace, by thronging duties pressed?
To do the will of Jesus, this is rest.
Peace, perfect peace, with sorrows surging round?
On Jesus' bosom naught but calm is found.
Peace, perfect peace, our future all unknown?
Jesus we know, and He is on the throne.
Peace, perfect peace, death shadowing us and ours?
Jesus has vanquished death and all its powers.
It is enough: earth's struggles soon shall cease,
And Jesus, call us to heav'n's perfect peace.[2]

Father,
Thank you for the hope, trust, and peace that only you can bring to our hearts and minds as we depend on you. Amen.

PEACE

DON'T WORRY ABOUT ANYTHING; INSTEAD, PRAY ABOUT
EVERYTHING. TELL GOD WHAT YOU NEED, AND THANK HIM
FOR ALL HE HAS DONE. IF YOU DO THIS, YOU WILL EXPERIENCE GOD'S
PEACE, WHICH IS FAR MORE WONDERFUL THAN THE HUMAN MIND CAN
UNDERSTAND. HIS PEACE WILL GUARD YOUR HEARTS AND MINDS AS YOU LIVE
IN CHRIST JESUS.

Philippians 4:6-7

> *Worry is a thin stream of fear trickling through the mind. If encouraged, it cuts a
> channel into which all other thoughts are drained.*   Arthur Somers Rocke

The stream of worry is built one drop or one thought at a time. Worry is made
up of many, many anxious thoughts. It's not enough to say to ourselves, *Stop worrying!* Left on our own, we'll come back to our fears. However, God gives us
something specific to do when we feel anxious or worried. He tells us to present
our requests to him about *everything*, and we are to give them over to him in three
ways:

1. Prayer—talking to God about the situation
2. Petition—making a request to an authority
3. Thanksgiving—expressing our gratitude

When we present something—like an award or a gift—to someone, there's
often some ceremony involved. In the same way, we literally need to hand over
our worries and get rid of them. We do this by coming to God, calling on his authority as God, thanking him for the things he's already done, and expressing our
confidence in him for the future. As we make that presentation, an exchange
takes place. We hand over our worry, and God's peace comes to guard our
hearts. The word *guard* is used here as a military term, so we might picture a sentinel watching over our hearts and minds.

As always with God, he gives us the better end of the deal. We give him our
worries, our requests, and our thanks, and he gives us his peace.

> *God, my authority,*
> *I confess my worry, and I hand it over to you. Thank you that you are in
> control and that you hear me. Please give me your peace to stand guard over
> my heart and mind. Thanks for all you've done for me in the past and all
> that you will do in the future. Amen.*

PEACE

YOU WILL KEEP IN PERFECT PEACE ALL WHO TRUST
IN YOU, WHOSE THOUGHTS ARE FIXED ON YOU! TRUST IN
THE LORD ALWAYS, FOR THE LORD GOD IS THE ETERNAL ROCK.

Isaiah 26:3-4

Some years ago our family rented a cottage at Honey Rock Camp in northern Wisconsin. The cottage was far off the beaten path—down a gravel road, off a smaller dirt lane, and nestled amidst some fragrant pine trees. Set on a little rise, the cottage overlooked a small river and came complete with a rope tied to a tree limb above—perfect for swinging and plunging into the river. What an ideal place to take three young boys!

In the early morning and at dusk the river was especially still. At times it became a mirror, reflecting the trees, sky, and everything else above it. The river was the perfect picture of peace.

Many times in life, things aren't as serene as the river outside our cottage. The storms of life churn up the water, we begin to feel overwhelmed, and it may seem as though we'll be carried away by strong currents.

But Jesus said, "I am leaving you with a gift—peace of mind and heart. And the peace I give isn't like the peace the world gives. So don't be troubled or afraid" (John 14:27). He said this shortly after he reminded Philip that those who had seen him had really seen the Father. Jesus was identifying himself with the Great Jehovah, God the Father.

When the rivers of our lives are churning, Jesus reminds us that we must fix our thoughts on him—on his strength, love, and faithfulness. We must choose to rest in his care and good plans for our lives.

The hymn writer Frances Havergal put it this way:

> *Like a river glorious is God's perfect peace,*
> *Perfect, yet it floweth fuller ev'ry day,*
> *Perfect, yet it groweth deeper all the way.*
> *Stayed upon Jehovah, hearts are fully blest—*
> *Finding as He promised perfect peace and rest.* [3]

Lord God,
Thank you for the peace you offer us as we trust in you. Help us to keep our thoughts fixed on you. In Jesus' name, amen.

He who fears the Lord has a secure fortress, and
for his children it will be a refuge. *Proverbs 14:26, NIV*

*H*ave your children ever made "forts" inside or outside your home? My kids have had forts at sleepovers made out of blankets duct-taped to tables and chairs. They have also built snow forts. Their largest project was a three-level tree fort in the backyard that took three summers to build.

A fort for our kids is a cozy place where they can play, but a fort or fortress in the military sense is much more substantial—it's a place of strength and security. God tells us that when we respect and acknowledge him, *he* is our fortress. Because of God's presence in our lives, the strength and security he provides can be experienced in any location.

Corrie ten Boom was a Dutch woman whose parents feared the Lord. During the Nazi invasion of Holland during World War II, Corrie's family hid Jewish people in their home so those people wouldn't be sent to the Nazi concentration camps. Sadly, Corrie and her family ended up in those very camps because of their help to the Jews. Corrie's fortress—her refuge in God—was sometimes experienced in her father's watch shop, sometimes on a cramped train ride, sometimes in the secret room of their home, and sometimes in the bunks of a concentration camp. Her fortress wasn't a physical dwelling. Rather, it was the security of her relationship with God.

We often spend time and money on our actual dwelling places, which has some value. But how much more important it is that we teach our children to be in awe of God, who is our ultimate security and fortress in all of life—our refuge wherever we may be.

Father,
Thank you that the security we have in you doesn't depend on where we are or where we live. Thank you that we carry it in our souls. Amen.

SECURITY

I HAVE SET THE LORD ALWAYS BEFORE ME. BECAUSE HE
IS AT MY RIGHT HAND, I WILL NOT BE SHAKEN. THEREFORE
MY HEART IS GLAD AND MY TONGUE REJOICES; MY BODY ALSO
WILL REST SECURE.

Psalm 16:8-9, NIV

What mom *doesn't* experience times of insecurity or uncertainty? Now in my fifties, I still have occasional days when I feel insecure. But in my early adult years, I had more of those days, and I sometimes thought I was one of very few moms who questioned her worth. Now that I'm older, I know differently. Every mom who is honest with herself admits that she has some of those days. In order to be truly secure, we're wise to keep these two truths from God's Word in balance constantly:

1. It was the awfulness of our personal sin that made the death of Christ necessary.
2. God loved us so much that he sent his Son to *die* for us.

When we concentrate on one and not the other, we get out of balance—we either get too proud or too insecure.

Security begins when we say, like the psalmist in the verses above, "I keep the Lord (not self) always before me." Thinking too much about ourselves can get us into trouble. If we think too highly of ourselves, we begin feeling smug and proud; if we belittle ourselves, we begin feeling discouraged. Thoughts of what God has done for us, however, give us a healthy perspective. Gladys Hunt writes, "God has redeemed us; we can lift up our heads and shout praises. God's love is an in-spite-of kind of love—the kind of love that is safe, that lets us dump our load honestly before him, assured of his constancy."[*]

Now that's a great start toward security!

God,
Thank you that we don't find our sense of security by looking inward at ourselves, but that we start by looking up to you. Thanks that you cared for us so much that you died for us and wanted us to be your friends forever. You are "God with us." Amen.

SECURITY

CAN A MOTHER FORGET HER NURSING CHILD? CAN SHE
FEEL NO LOVE FOR A CHILD SHE HAS BORNE? BUT EVEN IF THAT
WERE POSSIBLE, I WOULD NOT FORGET YOU! SEE, I HAVE WRITTEN
YOUR NAME ON MY HAND.

Isaiah 49:15-16

Those of you moms who have nursed children from your breasts probably have a picture of security in your mind. I remember times that my babies were oh-so-fussy—either tired, hungry, or just plain-old cranky—and the only thing that seemed to satisfy them was putting them to my breast. They often fell asleep there. Even if the room had been full of mothers, *I* was the one who had what the baby needed.

This mental picture of a mother who has power to feed and settle a baby gives us a glimpse into the meaning of El Shaddai, one of the names of God used in the Old Testament. *El* stands for might or power, and *Shaddai* describes the power of all-bountifulness. *Shaddai* came from the Hebrew word *Shad*, meaning "breasted."

If anyone can understand how the title "Breasted" came to mean "Almighty," it's a mother. Kay Arthur writes, "A babe is crying—restless. Nothing can quiet it. Yes! The breast can. . . . The breast can give it fresh life, nourishment. By her breast the mother has almost infinite power over the child."[5]

In an even more secure and everlasting way, God is our El Shaddai, the one who pours himself out for us when we run or cry out to him.

El Shaddai,
Milk from mothers' breasts eventually dries up, but your supply of nourish-
ment is everlasting. Thank you that there is always plenty for us all. Amen.

SECURITY

I KNOW THE LORD IS ALWAYS WITH ME. I WILL NOT BE
SHAKEN, FOR HE IS RIGHT BESIDE ME.   *Psalm 16:8*

Someone listed in *Who's Who* has no guarantee against feelings of insecurity. Although it sounds like an oxymoron, just because a person is well-known doesn't mean he or she necessarily feels secure.

A famous person in the Bible had a huge problem with insecurity. Saul came from a rich and influential family, and the Bible describes him as the most handsome man in Israel (1 Samuel 9:1-2). Notice, though, what Saul says to Samuel when they first meet: "I'm only from Benjamin, the smallest tribe in Israel, and my family is the least important of all the families of that tribe!" (1 Samuel 9:21).

The first king of Israel, Saul was often tossed back and forth between his feelings and his convictions, and he frequently gave in to an inferiority complex. I wonder if instead of *suffering* from an inferiority complex, he wasn't really *choosing* an inferiority complex. It's easy to do that. Like Saul, we can slide into the choice of being more us-focused than God-focused. When that happens with some frequency, we tend to plan and interpret most of life in terms of ourselves, forgetting that the purpose of our life on earth is to serve God and bring glory to him.

The more Saul was consumed with himself, the more arrogant, jealous, and insecure he became. Imagine how different life would have been for Saul if he, like David, had focused on God. We will never find the cure for our insecurity by looking within ourselves. "The cure of our insecurity," wrote Betsy Childs, "is not to become more secure in ourselves, but more confident in God."

Lord,
Thank you for your strong presence that brings us security as we trust in you.
In Jesus' name, amen.

SECURITY

FOR EVERY TIME YOU EAT THIS BREAD AND DRINK THIS CUP,
YOU ARE ANNOUNCING THE LORD'S DEATH UNTIL HE COMES
AGAIN.   *1 Corinthians 11:26*

Just about every year my parents invite all four of their children and each of our families to spend a few days together at a local hotel right after Christmas. Each family unit stays in their own suite, and my parents stay in a conference room suite, which ends up being like Grand Central Station with lots of food and games. The adults have time to sit around and talk while the kids play games, explore the hotel, and swim in the pool. What a feeling of security and warmth for all of us! The older I get, the more I appreciate my parents' generosity in providing the time for us all to be together as a family.

At church this morning, I also experienced great security and warmth as I shared in the Lord's Supper. Along with the rest of the believers in my church family—one little part of the body of Christ—I partook of the bread and wine (grape juice) with the purpose of remembering Christ, receiving strength from him, and rededicating myself to his purposes.

The Greek word for Communion means *fellowship*, *participating*, and *sharing*. What security there is in remembering together that we have been delivered from sin because of Christ's death and in being reminded again of his presence and power to help us. What anticipation we feel for a day yet to come when we will experience the *ultimate* in security—sharing Communion together with Christ in heaven!

Father,
Thank you for the security of being a part of your family and sharing
Communion with other believers, our brothers and sisters in Christ. May we
never take it lightly but always be reminded of your great love for us and your
great power to help us. Amen.

SECURITY

THE CHILDREN OF YOUR PEOPLE WILL LIVE IN
SECURITY. THEIR CHILDREN'S CHILDREN WILL THRIVE IN
YOUR PRESENCE.
Psalm 102:28

Security [n]: Protection, care, refuge

One of our church's pastors, Todd Augustine, recently returned from a short missions trip to Japan. During the two weeks that Todd was away, his wife, Cindy, and their two young daughters went to visit Cindy's mom in Georgia.

Driving down a rural Georgia road, Cindy, her mom, Eleah (six), and Katie (four) heard a huge crash on the top of their van. They were passing through a wooded, mountainous area, and apparently a tree up on the hillside had rotted and fallen—on them. A split second earlier and the large trunk would likely have gone through their windshield. *God protects.*

After Cindy brought the van to a stop and checked on her mom and daughters, she was thankful that there had been no serious injuries—only minor scrapes and cuts from broken glass. It could have been so much worse.

The first woman to stop and help them was especially warm and friendly, and Eleah looked up at the woman and said, "Do you know Jesus?" "I sure do, honey," the woman replied, "and I'm praying for you right now!" *God cares.*

Seven thousand miles away, Todd woke up at 4 a.m. with the strong sense that he should call home. When he called, Eleah answered and relayed the whole story. Todd said, "In my utter helplessness over not being there to comfort my wife and daughters, I felt totally dependent on God's care for the lives of those dearest to me." *God is our refuge.*

How comforting to know that whether we are in the same room with our family or seven thousand miles away, we can always find our security in God.

> Father,
> Thank you that there is great security in being your child. Thanks for the protection, care, and refuge you bring to our lives—especially the many times when we're not even aware of it. In the name of Jesus, amen.

Security

Even if my father and mother abandon me, the Lord will hold me close.   *Psalm 27:10*

If you were asked to illustrate the word *security* as it relates to a child, what would you describe? I might describe a little boy jumping into his father's arms, knowing that his dad would catch him. Or I might envision a mother holding her sleeping baby snugly against her chest. Security is freedom from risk, danger, anxiety, or fear, and we mothers work at providing it for our children.

Sadly, we sometimes hear of parents who do the opposite. I recently heard a news report of a young couple who, after a dispute in their car, left their ten-month-old baby alongside a busy Chicago expressway. Thankfully, a doctor on his way to work saw the baby and took her to the hospital, where she was found to be in good physical condition. At the time of the news report, the state was seeking foster parents for the child.

What's your mental picture of security? I've lived long enough to know that my picture isn't money, a house, a job, a spouse, or health. My picture has me running into God's arms, knowing that he cares for me even though he also is available for everyone else in the world who wants to spend time with him. No matter what kind of disappointment or rejection any of us has experienced, we know that if we come to God, he will *never* forsake us. That's the ultimate in security.

Lord,
Thank you for always being ready to receive us. Thank you that we can run to you at any time about anything, because you are our Creator, and you know us inside out. Thank you that you never forsake us. Amen.

ANIMALS

THE LORD IS MY SHEPHERD; I SHALL NOT WANT. HE MAKES ME TO LIE DOWN IN GREEN PASTURES; HE LEADS ME BESIDE THE STILL WATERS. HE RESTORES MY SOUL; HE LEADS ME IN THE PATHS OF RIGHTEOUSNESS FOR HIS NAME'S SAKE. YEA, THOUGH I WALK THROUGH THE VALLEY OF THE SHADOW OF DEATH, I WILL FEAR NO EVIL; FOR YOU ARE WITH ME; YOUR ROD AND YOUR STAFF, THEY COMFORT ME. YOU PREPARE A TABLE BEFORE ME IN THE PRESENCE OF MY ENEMIES; YOU ANOINT MY HEAD WITH OIL; MY CUP RUNS OVER. SURELY GOODNESS AND MERCY SHALL FOLLOW ME ALL THE DAYS OF MY LIFE; AND I WILL DWELL IN THE HOUSE OF THE LORD FOREVER.

Psalm 23, NKJV

One time a little boy was heard misquoting this verse. He said, "The Lord is my shepherd—what more shall I want?" He had the right idea.

The animal most frequently mentioned in the Bible is a sheep. Sheep are basically helpless creatures that depend on their shepherds for food, rest, and protection. Although they are kept in flocks, some sheep have a tendency to wander off and get into trouble. As much as we do not like to admit it, human beings are a lot like sheep. We are stubborn, we tend to follow the crowd, we are fearful, and we sometimes get into things that we shouldn't. Like sheep, we need someone to follow—someone who cares for us and wants to protect us.

It is interesting that the meaning or significance of all seven of the Old Testament names for God is seen in Psalm 23: The Lord will provide. The Lord will heal or restore. The Lord our peace. The Lord our righteousness. The Lord is there. The Lord our banner. The Lord my shepherd.

On days when we feel the strain of our family's financial pressures, we can thank God that he is the Lord who provides. When we feel tension or conflict in a family relationship, we can thank him that he is the Lord our peace. At times when we feel confused and uncertain, we can thank God that he is our shepherd. Not only is he the God who knows me, but he is the God who provides everything I need.

Great Shepherd,
Thank you that you see all our needs and that you provide for us. May we run to you first whenever we feel needy. Amen.

ANIMALS

SO [THE SPIES] SPREAD DISCOURAGING REPORTS ABOUT THE
LAND AMONG THE ISRAELITES: "THE LAND WE EXPLORED WILL
SWALLOW UP ANY WHO GO TO LIVE THERE. ALL THE PEOPLE WE
SAW WERE HUGE. WE EVEN SAW GIANTS THERE, THE DESCENDANTS OF ANAK.
WE FELT LIKE GRASSHOPPERS NEXT TO THEM, AND THAT'S WHAT WE LOOKED
LIKE TO THEM!"

Numbers 13:32-33

In response to God's instructions, Moses sent twelve spies into Canaan, a land that God had promised to give to the Israelites. The spies were asked to scout things out and bring back a report, as well as samples of some of the crops. Upon returning, they described the land as *magnificent*. One single cluster of grapes was so big that it took two of the spies to carry it back on a pole between them. But they also observed walled cities and giants. Two of the spies, Caleb and Joshua, said, "Let's go!" The other ten said, "No, not against people their size—we felt like *grasshoppers* in comparison to them!"

What a contrast! The two spies who believed God's promise responded with courage, saying that the Israelites could certainly conquer the land. The ten who didn't believe responded with fear. God vowed that of those twelve spies, only Caleb and Joshua would live to enter the Promised Land.

I wonder what my perspective would have been if I had been one of the twelve spies. Would I have seen myself as a grasshopper? It's tempting to rehearse my fears instead of looking to God.

Sometimes we see ourselves as grasshoppers in comparison to the problems we face. Rehearsing the promises of God like Caleb and Joshua did would be a good choice: "The Lord loves us, he keeps his promises, he is with us. Don't be afraid!"

Father,
On days when our problems seem to tower over us, may we choose to reflect on
your promises instead of our fear. Amen.

ANIMALS

WHAT IS THE PRICE OF FIVE SPARROWS? A COUPLE
OF PENNIES? YET GOD DOES NOT FORGET A SINGLE ONE
OF THEM. AND THE VERY HAIRS ON YOUR HEAD ARE ALL
NUMBERED. SO DON'T BE AFRAID; YOU ARE MORE VALUABLE TO HIM THAN A
WHOLE FLOCK OF SPARROWS.

Luke 12:6-7

Sparrows are common birds. To the casual observer, it may seem that a sparrow is a sparrow is a sparrow. But when I looked up *sparrow* in *North American Wildlife*, I discovered seventeen different varieties, and there are probably more. Because I am a musician, I was particularly interested in the song sparrow, which has more than thirty subspecies. Their songs often begin with a few regularly spaced notes, followed by a trill, and end with a jumble of notes. Amazingly, no two song sparrows sing exactly the same tune!

Jesus taught that God cares about each sparrow. He also taught that each of us is worth much more than a sparrow to him. Too many times we judge our worth by what we believe others think of us. That kind of thinking gets us into trouble because our value then depends on how we look, what we achieve, or how well we perform. When we look to God for our worth, we receive from him a deep sense of belonging. It gives me great comfort to know that if God cares for even the most common of birds, just think how much he cares for me!

God,
Thank you that you have given worth to everything you created. Please help us never to forget how valuable we are to you, and also how valuable our children are to you. Amen.

ANIMALS

**THE GODLY ARE CONCERNED FOR THE WELFARE OF THEIR
ANIMALS.** *Proverbs 12:10*

My youngest son, Jordan, came home from grade school one afternoon to discover that his favorite hamster, Ethel, had delivered fourteen babies. There was great excitement in the Elwell house that day and for some days to follow. Whether we're talking humans or hamsters, *all* of God's new creations are a marvel.

After a few weeks, the hamsters began venturing out of their nest, and we were able to see what they looked like. "Mom!" Jordan yelled from the basement one day, "Come quick! Something's wrong with one of Ethel's babies." I ran downstairs. Looking into the cage, I realized that one of the threads from the nest had wrapped around the baby's tiny toe, cutting off circulation and causing that little toe to balloon to the size of the hamster's head. "Let's call the vet," I said. Medical meltdowns are not my specialty, whether they involve kids or animals.

There's nothing like an emergency to help us appreciate another person's professional skills. The vet snipped the thread with microscopic scissors, applied antibiotic ointment to the affected area, and—surprisingly—wrote NO CHARGE on the statement. "I didn't have the heart to charge you anything," she said. "Those little babies are so cute!"

I find it interesting that the God who rescued his children from drowning in the Red Sea and cared for his children like a compassionate mother tells us that we are like him when we are concerned about the welfare of our animals. What a kind God we have!

> *Father,*
> *Thank you for the tender and compassionate love you show to us. Please help us to imitate you in the way we treat people and animals alike. Amen.*

ANIMALS

TAKE A LESSON FROM THE ANTS, YOU LAZYBONES.
LEARN FROM THEIR WAYS AND BE WISE! EVEN THOUGH
THEY HAVE NO PRINCE, GOVERNOR, OR RULER TO MAKE THEM
WORK, THEY LABOR HARD ALL SUMMER, GATHERING FOOD FOR THE WINTER.

Proverbs 6:6-8

Although ants are small, they are very wise. They almost make us look lazy. They work day and night, they store up food, and they build their mounds three or four times higher (comparatively speaking) than the Egyptian pyramids are to us. When ants are sick, they care for each other, and in the winter they eat what they saved in the summer.

Ants have one of the most elaborate social organizations in the animal world. Thousands of ants live in a communal nest, each one having its own task to perform. These workers gather, make, and store food for both the adults and the larvae.

Living near fields of grain and carrying seed into their private storehouses, the ants described in Proverbs 6 are harvester ants. When cold weather comes, these ants swarm together and hibernate. They have enough food stored up during the winter to last until the next harvest. God gave ants an amazing ability to solve problems and plan ahead. For example, if the grain they stored gets wet, they haul it out to dry in the sun.

These tiny creatures are included in the Bible as examples for us. They are busy, they plan ahead, and they work together. The next time you're out on a walk with your child and you see an ant, take the opportunity to discuss some of the lessons we can learn from these tiny creatures.

God,
Thank you that we learn important lessons about life from some of your tiniest creatures. Like the ants, help us to be diligent in the work you've given us to do. Amen.

ANIMALS

HE GIVES POWER TO THOSE WHO ARE TIRED AND WORN
OUT; HE OFFERS STRENGTH TO THE WEAK. EVEN YOUTHS WILL
BECOME EXHAUSTED, AND YOUNG MEN WILL GIVE UP. BUT THOSE WHO
WAIT ON THE LORD WILL FIND NEW STRENGTH. THEY WILL FLY HIGH ON
WINGS LIKE EAGLES. THEY WILL RUN AND NOT GROW WEARY. THEY WILL
WALK AND NOT FAINT.

Isaiah 40:29-31

Eagles are majestic birds, and even though certain types are considered endangered species, the God who created them and gives life to them knows the address of every eagle alive. Eagles build their nests in trees or cliffs—high places that are inaccessible—and they add to their nests each year, using sticks, weeds, and dirt. Sometimes a nest ends up weighing over a thousand pounds, and some nests have been reported to measure up to fifteen feet deep! In these deep nests, a female eagle hatches two eggs, only one of which usually survives to be an adult.

A mother eagle carries her eaglet on her back until it masters the art of flying. Moses spoke of this picture from nature to remind us how God cares for his people: "Like an eagle that rouses her chicks and hovers over her young, so he spread his wings to take them in and carried them aloft on his pinions" (Deuteronomy 32:11). God has probably delivered us from more than we could ever imagine.

An eagle can soar for hours at a time while searching for prey. It rides wind currents, rarely moving its wings. God promises us that if we hope in him, he will provide some of that soaring time as well. It would be great if we could soar all the time, but that's not how life works. Sometimes we soar, sometimes we run, sometimes we walk, and sometimes we stumble and fall. But the Lord promises to replenish our strength as we hope in him.

> *God who knows every eagle's address,*
> *Thank you for the beauty of an eagle's flight. As we hope in you, please help*
> *us to soar; but help us to look to your strength during times of weariness as*
> *well. Amen.*

ANIMALS

THEN THE LORD SAID TO MOSES, "GO TO PHARAOH ONCE AGAIN AND TELL HIM, 'THIS IS WHAT THE LORD SAYS: LET MY PEOPLE GO, SO THEY CAN WORSHIP ME. IF YOU REFUSE, THEN LISTEN CAREFULLY TO THIS: I WILL SEND VAST HORDES OF FROGS ACROSS YOUR ENTIRE LAND FROM ONE BORDER TO THE OTHER. THE NILE RIVER WILL SWARM WITH THEM. THEY WILL COME UP OUT OF THE RIVER AND INTO YOUR HOUSES, EVEN INTO YOUR BEDROOMS AND ONTO YOUR BEDS! EVERY HOME IN EGYPT WILL BE FILLED WITH THEM. THEY WILL FILL EVEN YOUR OVENS AND YOUR KNEADING BOWLS. YOU AND YOUR PEOPLE WILL BE OVERWHELMED BY FROGS!'"   *Exodus 8:1-4*

When I was in fifth grade, I was required to write a report on an animal of my choice. I settled on the frog. That report sparked such an interest in frogs that I began a collection. By the time I went off to college, I had more than seventy-five frogs in the form of stuffed animals, salt shakers, glass figurines, and so on.

In the Bible, God sometimes used animals to carry out his missions—frogs included. Because Pharaoh wouldn't listen to God's instructions to let his people go, God sent ten plagues on the Egyptians—the second of which was frogs. Although more than twenty-five hundred species of frogs and toads exist, Bible scholars presume that the frogs described in Exodus 8 were probably marsh frogs of the *Rana ridibunda* species. These particular frogs are described as noisy and gregarious, growing about six inches long. They prey on small birds and mammals, and they breed (rapidly) in the spring, which is about the time of year that the plagues began.

To ancient Egyptians, frogs were symbols of the goddess of life and birth. God, however, used the plague of frogs—and the eventual stinking heaps of *dead* frogs—to demonstrate *his* power. "When I show the Egyptians my power and force them to let the Israelites go, they will realize that I am the Lord" (Exodus 7:5).

My frog collection of years ago is long gone, but I'm still fascinated that God chose frogs to accomplish his purposes.

Father,
Thank you for your awesome power that is evident in the way you use animals for your purposes. Thank you that we can share that awe with our children.
Amen.

ATTITUDE

MAY THE LORD BLESS YOU AND PROTECT YOU. MAY THE
LORD SMILE ON YOU AND BE GRACIOUS TO YOU. MAY THE
LORD SHOW YOU HIS FAVOR AND GIVE YOU HIS PEACE.

Numbers 6:24-26

The words we choose and the attitudes we use in speaking to our children about their future hold tremendous influence on how they will think and act as adolescents and adults.

If a child grows up hearing positive words of confidence, encouragement, and blessing from a parent, those words will stick when the child begins to have those inevitable questions about his or her worth during adolescence.

The opposite is also true. If children grow up hearing negative words of criticism, nagging, and sarcasm from a parent, those words will also stick—sometimes for the rest of their lives. The way we reflect on who our children are now and who we think they will become has more impact on them than we probably realize.

Gary Smalley and John Trent write, "When it comes to predictions about their future, children are literalists—particularly when they hear predictions from their parents, the most important people from an earthly perspective in their lives."[6]

Here are a few ways to encourage our children and help them see God's blessing for their lives:

When a child has had a bad day at school, decide together to pray daily that God will bring some special blessing or encouragement to that child's life, thanking him together when he does.

As a son or daughter displays characteristics that will be admirable in marriage or fatherhood or motherhood someday, point them out, and then remind him or her that you pray regularly for his or her future spouse, wherever that person may be.

Pray the verses above for your child at bedtime or when he or she is leaving on a trip.

> *Father,*
> *In the same way that we leave a church service encouraged by a hopeful benediction, please help us to encourage our children to see your blessing and hope in their lives. Amen.*

ATTITUDE

HOW DO YOU KNOW WHAT WILL HAPPEN TOMORROW?
FOR YOUR LIFE IS LIKE THE MORNING FOG—IT'S HERE A
LITTLE WHILE, THEN IT'S GONE. WHAT YOU OUGHT TO SAY IS,
"IF THE LORD WANTS US TO, WE WILL LIVE AND DO THIS OR THAT."

James 4:14-15

In James 4:13-17 James warned believers that boasting and self-confidence are dangerous. A group of believers were bragging about their plans and the success they were expecting, announcing they were planning to go into the city, set up a business, and return as very wealthy people. Their attitude was anything but humble; rather, it was downright proud, and God hates pride.

James warned this proud group of people that their arrogance was foolish for two reasons. First, how did they know what would happen tomorrow? Only God knows what will happen in the future, and any person who thinks he or she also knows is basically claiming to be God. Second, James reminded believers that our lives here on earth are likened to a mist or a vapor, neither of which gives the impression of permanence. As quickly as a mist comes into view, it disappears or evaporates.

Our lives are so brief that we cannot afford to live carelessly or aimlessly. The proper attitude for a mom who follows Christ to have is: "If it is the Lord's will, we will live and do this or that." Those may also be words that we speak to our children, but most important, they need to be lived out in a life that trusts God. We cultivate this kind of life by spending time daily, praying and asking God that *his* will be done in our lives, just like the pattern he left for us in the Lord's Prayer.

Father,
Sometimes we rush ahead and make plans without asking you for wisdom and direction. We know that you are in control and we are not. May we look to you regularly so that the things that are important to you become important to us. Amen.

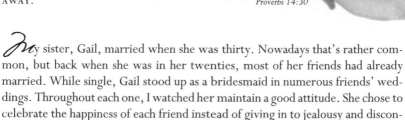

ATTITUDE

A RELAXED ATTITUDE LENGTHENS LIFE; JEALOUSY ROTS IT
AWAY.
Proverbs 14:30

My sister, Gail, married when she was thirty. Nowadays that's rather common, but back when she was in her twenties, most of her friends had already married. While single, Gail stood up as a bridesmaid in numerous friends' weddings. Throughout each one, I watched her maintain a good attitude. She chose to celebrate the happiness of each friend instead of giving in to jealousy and discontent. She chose to have a relaxed attitude.

Gail also displayed a relaxed attitude when she and Rick married. As they planned their wedding, they hired a company to videotape both the wedding and reception. The videographer showed up early on their wedding day and taped a lot of the preparations. Throughout the day, she captured special moments of the wedding and reception with people as young as the flower girl and as old as Great-Grandma.

When Gail and Rick returned from their honeymoon, the video company called them with some bad news. By mistake, the videographer had left the videotape in her camera for her next customer's wedding, taping over all of Gail and Rick's festivities. When my sister and her husband heard what had happened, they were terribly disappointed. But they also acknowledged that it was an unintentional mistake and that they were thankful for all the happy memories they did have—both in their minds and in other photos. They chose not to be resentful, and their mature attitude was a good example to our whole family.

The book of Proverbs teaches that if we have a relaxed perspective, our lives may be lengthened. That's not a literal promise, of course, but it's a general principle of existence here on earth—a principle that certainly improves our lives. A side benefit to cultivating this attitude is that we become more pleasant to be around!

> *Father,*
> *It's easy to complain and have a sour attitude when things don't go the way we hope. Please help us to shun discontentment and embrace a relaxed outlook. Amen.*

ATTITUDE

I WILL BLESS THOSE WHO HAVE HUMBLE AND CONTRITE
HEARTS, WHO TREMBLE AT MY WORD.   *Isaiah 66:2*

In the opening verses of Isaiah 66, God condemned outward show in worship. He said that he needed no temples built by human hands or sacrificial animals for food; rather, he desired repentant and believing hearts. God said that if a person brought an animal sacrifice without the proper attitude of repentance and faith, the sacrifice to him was an abomination that was as serious as murder!

The *Life Application Bible* contrasts two distinct groups of people: ". . . humble persons, who have a profound reverence for God's messages and their application to life, with those who choose their own ways. God shows mercy to the humble, but he curses the proud and self-sufficient."[7]

God said that the person he blesses is the one who is "humble," has a "contrite heart," and "trembles" at his Word. In this day when our society encourages us to be assertive and look out for ourselves, we need God's wisdom and help in balancing personal responsibility with dependence on God.

Humility is honored throughout the Bible. In Mary's *Magnificat*, the same truth emerged: God scatters the proud but lifts up the humble. *Contrite* is a word we don't often hear. A person who is contrite is sorrowful or remorseful over sin in his or her heart. As for *trembling*—does the truth of God's Word ever bring tears to our eyes or cut our hearts to the quick? What a reminder for us—God blesses the humble!

Father,
Forgive us for our pride. Sometimes we make choices that take us in the oppo-
site direction of humility and contrition. May we ask your forgiveness and
turn to your Word so that we will value the attitudes that you value. Amen.

ATTITUDE

IN EVERYTHING YOU DO, STAY AWAY FROM COMPLAINING
AND ARGUING, SO THAT NO ONE CAN SPEAK A WORD OF BLAME
AGAINST YOU. YOU ARE TO LIVE CLEAN, INNOCENT LIVES AS CHILDREN
OF GOD IN A DARK WORLD FULL OF CROOKED AND PERVERSE PEOPLE. LET
YOUR LIVES SHINE BRIGHTLY BEFORE THEM.

Philippians 2:14-15

These verses about complaining and arguing seem to refer back to the Old Testament book of Deuteronomy, specifically to a prayer of Moses. In Deuteronomy 32 Moses began his prayer by recounting the greatness of God—God is the Rock, his ways are perfect, all his ways are just, and he is a faithful God who does no wrong.

But sadly, Moses went on to lament that the people had acted corruptly toward God. No longer were they acting like God's children, but as a result of their complaining, they had become a warped and crooked generation. Moses asked, "Is this the way you repay the Lord, O foolish and unwise people? Is he not your Father, your Creator, who made you and formed you?" (v. 6, NIV).

Have you ever had a talk like that with one of your children? Something like, "All the time and love I spend in taking care of you, providing for you, feeding you, doing your laundry, driving you around—and you think you can treat me like *that*? No way!" God had a much bigger stake in the lives of the children of Israel. He was not just their parent—he was their Creator, and he was God!

Although we don't like to hear our children complain and argue, we sometimes complain and argue ourselves. When we do, we lose some of our luster before a watching family and a watching world. May God help us stay away from complaining and arguing so that we will reflect Christ more effectively.

Father,
Please forgive us for complaining and arguing. Help us to remember that by doing this we are choosing to walk down a crooked path. Instead, may we be grateful and praise you, so that we will more effectively reflect Christ to our children! Amen.

ATTITUDE

You have heard that the law of Moses says, "Do not murder. If you commit murder, you are subject to judgment." But I say, if you are angry with someone, you are subject to judgment! If you call someone an idiot, you are in danger of being brought before the high council. And if you curse someone, you are in danger of the fires of hell.

Matthew 5:21-22

For years I found it easy to zip right through this passage, thinking, *I don't need to concern myself with that. After all, I've never murdered anyone.* That was when murder was something I had only read about in the newspaper.

A few years ago, a young man whom my family is acquainted with murdered his sister-in-law. When my husband and I received the shocking, tragic news, I remember thinking, *I don't have a place in my brain to understand and process the news I've just heard.* Sometimes our shock at news like this settles into a sense of superiority—until we read Bible verses like those above. Jesus explained that a person who commits murder is subject to judgment. All of us know that. But Jesus went on to explain that if I'm angry enough with a person that I curse him or even call him an idiot or a moron, I'm in danger of the fires of hell. Whoa! That makes me squirm. I'm not in the habit of calling others idiots or morons, but I've felt and thought that way about people before.

There is a time and a place for righteous anger. Jesus demonstrated that in John 2 when he cleared the Temple. But the danger Jesus addressed here is unrighteous anger that is more like malignant contempt for another human being. These verses encourage me to confess my attitudes of spiritual superiority and run to Jesus, who is my only hope of salvation, righteousness, and grace.

Father,
Your Word cuts right through our pride and speaks to attitudes of our hearts.
Please forgive us and help us to love others the way you love. Amen.

ATTITUDE

Now your attitudes and thoughts must all be constantly changing for the better. Yes, you must be a new and different person, holy and good. Clothe yourself with this new nature.

Ephesians 4:23-24, TLB

*T*hroughout the Bible are references to taking off one garment and putting on another. It's possible for a believer to be a new person in Christ who sometimes reverts to wearing the dirty clothing of the old person. God has given us a new wardrobe, but we have to make the choice to put on the new garments.

When we first trust Christ, we embark on a lifelong adventure of change. Transformation in our attitudes and thoughts doesn't happen immediately. As we follow God, we will change constantly. The same is true for our children, and when we see them demonstrating growth in attitudes through good choices and actions, it's wise for us to affirm them.

Just recently I sent notes to all three of my sons (even the two living at home), calling attention to areas of growth that I appreciated. One had begun tithing—a generous attitude. One had taken his younger brother out for lunch—a kind attitude. One had been faithfully praying for a person with deep needs—a compassionate attitude.

Our attitudes will change in healthy ways as we saturate our minds with the truth of God's Word and pray for that truth to be worked out in our lives. This will no doubt result in confession of sin as dark corners of our hearts are exposed to the light of Christ. If we are serious about growing, improved attitudes and thoughts will be noticeable in our lives.

Father,
Thank you for the hope of change! Thank you that as we spend time in your Word and ask for your help, we will see a difference in our attitudes and thoughts. Amen.

WORDS

HE WHO GUARDS HIS MOUTH AND HIS TONGUE KEEPS
HIMSELF FROM CALAMITY.   *Proverbs 21:23, NIV*

*D*uring the Middle Ages, a young man approached a monk and confessed, "I've sinned by making slanderous statements about another person. What should I do?" The monk replied, "Put a feather on every doorstep in town." That's exactly what the young man did. Then he came back to the monk and asked, "Is there anything else I should do?" The monk said, "Yes. Go back and retrieve all those feathers." The young man was upset and cried, "But that's not possible! The wind has probably blown the feathers all over town!" The wise monk responded, "In the same way, your slanderous words are impossible to retrieve."

To slander is to speak falsely of someone and hurt his or her reputation. This can happen in many different ways, possibly most often when we jump to conclusions (or join our children in jumping to conclusions) about another person. If the conclusion we come to regarding someone else is false, we have been guilty of slander.

Sometimes we forget that slander is prohibited in the ninth commandment: "You shall not give false testimony against your neighbor" (Exodus 20:16, NIV). The commandments about murder, stealing, or adultery seem to stand out more, but God hates slander because the devil does it too—about us! Satan is called the great accuser because he opposes Christians and accuses us before God.

Since we don't like the idea of being falsely accused, we're wise to be careful about protecting the reputations of others. Once the feathers are distributed, they can't be easily retrieved.

Father,
Please help us to guard our mouths from slandering others. Amen.

WORDS

WITH THE TONGUE WE PRAISE OUR LORD AND FATHER, AND
WITH IT WE CURSE MEN, WHO HAVE BEEN MADE IN GOD'S
LIKENESS. OUT OF THE SAME MOUTH COME PRAISE AND CURSING. MY
BROTHERS, THIS SHOULD NOT BE. CAN BOTH FRESH WATER AND SALT WATER
FLOW FROM THE SAME SPRING? MY BROTHERS, CAN A FIG TREE BEAR OLIVES, OR A
GRAPEVINE BEAR FIGS? NEITHER CAN A SALT SPRING PRODUCE FRESH WATER.

James 3:9-12, NIV

If you have a telephone in your home, you probably have many telemarketers
bombarding you each week. Sometimes I receive as many as four or five sales
calls in one day! Some of the callers can be quite persistent, so my response requires determination mixed with graciousness.

I have noticed that the callers are frequently caught by surprise if I answer on
the first ring. This past week I picked up one call after the first ring and answered,
"Hello!" I heard silence, and then a man used the name of God in a disgusted way.
I repeated, "Hello?" a second time. Then, a bit startled, the man turned on his
professional phone voice, said, "Well, hello, Mrs. Elwell," and launched into his
pitch.

No matter how fine a salesman he was, he lost me back at the beginning of the
call because of the way he spoke God's name. At a point when he stopped to take
a breath, I kindly explained that I had no need for his product, and in addition I
had been offended by the way he had spoken God's name into the telephone at
the outset of the call. In a sugary voice he said, "God *bless* you, ma'am!" and hung
up. The tone at the end of the call sure didn't match the words at the beginning.

Our children are listening to us each day to see how consistent *we* are. Since
the words that come out of our mouths reveal what's in our hearts, what are our
words saying about our hearts?

Father,
"Set a guard over my mouth, O Lord; keep watch over the door of my lips"
(Psalm 141:3, NIV). Amen.

WORDS

GUIDE MY STEPS BY YOUR WORD, SO I WILL NOT BE
OVERCOME BY ANY EVIL.   *Psalm 119:133*

A young man who hoped to be chosen as a steamboat pilot on the Mississippi River was nearing the end of his job interview. The interviewer, curious to discover if the young man was aware of the dangers of the river, asked if he knew where all the rocks were. The young man wisely responded, "No, sir, I do not know where all the rocks are, but I know where they *aren't*." He got the job.

As moms, we need help navigating the river of motherhood. Although each of our routes is slightly different, wisdom to know where the rocks *aren't* is available to us all. It's available in the form of words—God's words. "For the Lord grants wisdom! His every word is a treasure of knowledge and understanding" (Proverbs 2:6, TLB). God's words give us discernment for what it true, right, and lasting. His words are more valuable than gold or silver. His words are something we need to hear every day of motherhood—even after our kids have left home!

Just as we need a recipe to bake a cake or instructions to locate the correct soccer field for a child's game, we need the words of the Bible for all the situations that motherhood brings our way. We need them to help us avoid rocks like jealousy, selfish ambition, and angry outbursts. And most of all, we need them to point us to Christ, who is the source of all wisdom.

Faithful Guide,
Thanks for the gift of your Word. We would be lost without it. Amen.

WORDS

THE TALK OF FOOLS IS A ROD FOR THEIR BACKS, BUT THE
WORDS OF THE WISE KEEP THEM OUT OF TROUBLE.   *Proverbs 14:3*

I remember one exciting Christmas as a child when one of my younger sisters received a Chatty Cathy doll. If we pulled the cord on the doll's back, she spoke preset sentences. What fun we had! In real life, though, God has not programmed us with only a few phrases that we must repeat throughout our lives (although our kids might accuse us of repetition sometimes). He gave us the words of the language we have learned. How precious to choose words for their creativity, not for protection or harm. To inspire us in our choices, let's look at what God's Word has to say about our words:

> *Evil words destroy one's friends; wise discernment rescues the godly.*
> *(Proverbs 11:9)*

> *The godly speak words that are helpful, but the wicked speak only what is*
> *corrupt. (Proverbs 10:32)*

> *Kind words are like honey—sweet to the soul and healthy for the body.*
> *(Proverbs 16:24)*

> *Fire goes out for lack of fuel, and quarrels disappear when gossip stops.*
> *(Proverbs 26:20)*

> *In the end, people appreciate frankness more than flattery. (Proverbs 28:23)*

> *Wise people treasure knowledge, but the babbling of a fool invites trouble.*
> *(Proverbs 10:14)*

> *A gossip goes around revealing secrets, but those who are trustworthy can keep a*
> *confidence. (Proverbs 11:13)*

> *Your own soul is nourished when you are kind, but you destroy yourself when you*
> *are cruel. (Proverbs 11:17)*

> *Father,*
> *With the inspiration of your Word and the strength of your help, may we*
> *choose words today that protect our children, not harm them. Amen.*

WORDS

A GENTLE ANSWER TURNS AWAY WRATH, BUT HARSH
WORDS STIR UP ANGER.   *Proverbs 15:1*

*B*efore our third son was born, my husband and I and our two sons took a week's vacation to Petoskey, Michigan. The second day of our vacation, I had a severe allergic reaction and ended up in the local hospital for three days while my husband tried to occupy Chad and Nate, then seven and five. Let's say it was not one of our more enjoyable vacations! I felt alone, scared, and disappointed that our plans were ruined, and Jim had to play "Mr. Mom" for those days. But any troublesome experience also has lessons for good that we can take away with us, and this event was no exception.

I shared my hospital room with an elderly woman who was confused, to put it mildly. Although the curtain between our beds was drawn shut, for three days I heard a variety of nurses and doctors coming and going throughout the day and night. One thing I'll never forget was the effect that the medical professionals' words had on the elderly woman, confused though she was. Gentle and soft words, even when spoken firmly and directly, were able to get a whole lot more cooperation from the woman than harsh, unpleasant ones.

That principle also holds true for us as moms. In dealing with our children, choosing words and tones that are considerate and compassionate will reap better results than words that are rough and strident.

Father,
May our words be gentle and not harsh. Amen.

WORDS

GIVE THANKS TO THE LORD, FOR HE IS GOOD! HIS FAITHFUL
LOVE ENDURES FOREVER. HAS THE LORD REDEEMED YOU? THEN
SPEAK OUT! TELL OTHERS HE HAS SAVED YOU FROM YOUR ENEMIES.

Psalm 107:1-2

*Y*oung children often get their words mixed up. My kids used to say *hangaburger* instead of hamburger and *skabetti* instead of spaghetti. Perhaps one of the more memorable word slips for our two-year-old son, Chad, was his version of a children's praise song. Instead of "Praise him, Praise him, all ye little children," he sang "Praise him, Praise him, *naughty* little children." When one of our friends from church heard Chad singing the incorrect—albeit cute—version of the song, he remarked, "Well, he does have his theology straight."

Only in heaven does God hear perfect praise. This side of heaven, there's just no such thing. If we waited until we were "good enough," praise would never happen. But isn't that the point? Isn't that exactly why we praise him? None of us *are* good enough! We praise God because of what he has done in sending Jesus to die on the cross for our sins and provide forgiveness, healing, and hope for us all.

Seeing God take care of me and provide for me in the middle of my neediness is one thing that prompts me to praise him. In fact, I've noticed that great trials often prompt great praise. When I see how strong and righteous God is compared to how weak and needy I am, it's hard to keep that kind of good news to myself.

Father,
Thank you that you love us so much that you want to hear our imperfect
praises. May we be willing to speak out and tell others what you have done for
us. In Jesus' name, amen.

WORDS

SOME PEOPLE MAKE CUTTING REMARKS, BUT THE WORDS
OF THE WISE BRING HEALING. *Proverbs 12:18*

*I*n his collection of short stories *Ragman and Other Cries of Faith*, Walter Wangerin provides us with a wonderful lesson about spiders that illustrates an amazing spiritual truth to us and to our children. He explains that sometimes a female spider becomes a widow for a surprising reason: she eats other spiders who come her way! When a would-be husband shows up in her house, her visitor becomes a corpse and her dining room becomes a morgue. This picture of a spider that eats other spiders becomes a sobering image of how destructive evil words can be. Wangerin says, "This world is populated by walking caskets because countless lives have been dissolved and sucked empty by another's words."[1]

We know that words can kill because most of us have been on both the giving and the receiving end. As a mom I want to be careful how I speak to my own children and what I say about them to others, because words can build my children up or tear them down. In our families it's one thing to hear a life situation discussed with discernment, but it's another thing to hear it recounted with criticism. When we judge another, God tells us we're setting ourselves above him—an arrogant, scary place to be. We want our words to encourage people's souls, not dissolve them.

Father,
Please forgive us for the times our words have hurt other people. May we not set ourselves above your law by criticizing and judging others. Amen.

MOTHERS AND WIVES

LOOK! THE VIRGIN WILL CONCEIVE A CHILD! SHE WILL GIVE
BIRTH TO A SON, AND HE WILL BE CALLED IMMANUEL
(MEANING, GOD IS WITH US).   *Matthew 1:23*

*W*hether it's Mother's Day or Christmas, I enjoy pondering the fact that Jesus had a mother. When we look at the New Testament accounts of the life of Christ, we don't have to search far to see the important role his mother had in his life. Over time though, her role changed. The way she handled that shifting role leaves a great example for us.

Mary's love for Jesus was obvious. She wrapped him in swaddling clothes in Bethlehem. She and Joseph fled with him to Egypt. They watched his wisdom and independence blossom. In Jesus' adult years—when Mary witnessed him turn the water into wine at a wedding—her role as a mom seemed to change. She stepped back and acknowledged his authority. She continued to follow him on his trips as he ministered to people around him. On one of those trips, when he announced that his mother and brothers were not those connected to him by flesh and blood but those who were part of the family of faith (Luke 8:21), she was presented with another aspect of her role change: in addition to being Jesus' mother, she was his disciple as well. It's obvious that she accepted that position, because she followed Jesus to his death and stood at the foot of his cross. After the Resurrection, Mary was also present in the upper room, where she waited for the Holy Spirit along with the other disciples.

When we struggle as moms, when we're unsure of our roles, when we need wisdom and help for a particular stage, it is so comforting to remember that the one to whom we pray is also one who had a mother!

Jesus,
Thank you that you understand our challenges from both a human and a divine perspective. May we look to you for help and wisdom when we deal with things that you observed and experienced yourself. Thank you that you are "God with us." Amen.

MOTHERS AND WIVES

[A VIRTUOUS WIFE] CAREFULLY WATCHES ALL THAT
GOES ON IN HER HOUSEHOLD AND DOES NOT HAVE TO BEAR
THE CONSEQUENCES OF LAZINESS.   *Proverbs 31:27*

Whenever I speak to groups of young moms, I reassure them that I found the early years of motherhood to be the most challenging. I think I felt that way for a couple of reasons. One was that during the years my children were young, I experienced many, many interruptions. Another reason was that when they were little, I didn't seem to have a lot to show for all my efforts at the end of any given day. If you can identify with any of these feelings, you'll enjoy the following story:

> *Too many times women are made to feel that they should apologize for being mothers and housewives. In reality, such roles can be noble callings. When I was on the faculty of the University of Pennsylvania, there were gatherings from time to time to which faculty members brought their spouses. Inevitably, some woman lawyer or sociologist would confront my wife with the question, "And what is it that you do, my dear?" My wife, who is one of the most brilliantly articulate individuals I know, had a great response: "I am socializing two homo-sapiens in the dominant values of the Judeo-Christian tradition in order that they might be instruments for the transformation of the social order into the teleologically prescribed utopia inherent in the eschaton." When she followed that with, "And what is it that you do?" the other person's "a lawyer" just wasn't that overpowering.*[2]

I love that story! We can become so weary of doing the menial tasks that it's easy to lose sight of the great privilege God has given us—to influence and mold young lives for his Kingdom.

> *Lord of life,*
> *Thank you for the gift of children. We are so rich. Please empower us with your love, strength, and wisdom so we will raise children who will help to further your Kingdom. Amen.*

MOTHERS AND WIVES

NOW GLORY BE TO GOD! BY HIS MIGHTY POWER AT WORK
WITHIN US, HE IS ABLE TO ACCOMPLISH INFINITELY MORE THAN
WE WOULD EVER DARE TO ASK OR HOPE. *Ephesians 3:20*

*P*erhaps some of you are reading today's devotional while you're nursing an infant. As you hold that small gift from God in your arms, it's hard to imagine that he or she might begin walking in about a year. And it's almost impossible to imagine that your child—in twenty-some years—might graduate from college and begin a career. But they often do, and it's never too early for a mom to begin praying about her children's future plans.

When our oldest son, Chad, was a senior in college, my husband and I were excited to see how God would provide a job for him. One of his college classmates, Rachel, went to church with a partner in an engineering firm who asked, "Do you know any responsible engineering majors who are graduating from your college?" Several weeks and an interview later, Chad had his first job with Sargent and Lundy.

During Nate's senior year of college, he was invited to go home to Atlanta, Georgia, with his friend Nate Zacharias. Nate's dad, Ravi, is a Christian apologist and speaker. At the time our Nate visited, Ravi was looking for an assistant to travel with him as he spoke around the world. Toward the end of the weekend, Ravi offered Nate the job, and he accepted. Nate has since shared in some amazing ministries in many different countries around the globe.

As we look back at God's provisions for Chad and Nate, we are no less grateful today than we were at the time God provided. We praise him for the way his mighty power accomplishes his purposes in our children's lives—and we continue praying.

Father,
Thank you for specific glimpses of your mighty power. We pray that you will
continue to work out your plans in our lives and in our children's lives. In the
powerful name of Jesus, amen.

MOTHERS AND WIVES

A NAGGING WIFE IS AS ANNOYING AS THE CONSTANT
DRIPPING ON A RAINY DAY. TRYING TO STOP HER COMPLAINTS
IS LIKE TRYING TO STOP THE WIND OR HOLD SOMETHING WITH
GREASED HANDS.

Proverbs 27:15-16

We've all seen sitcoms or comic strips about dominating mothers or wives, and we've probably known a few in real life. Not surprisingly, the Bible includes some accounts of dominating and difficult-to-live-with women that we can learn from.

We read in Genesis 27 that Rebekah played manipulative games with her husband, Isaac, and encouraged her son Jacob to deceive his father into giving him a blessing that was intended for Jacob's brother. Later on in the book of Genesis, when Potiphar's wife unsuccessfully tried to seduce Joseph and Joseph fled, Mrs. Potiphar screamed and made up a story that blamed the "Hebrew slave" for attempting to harm *her*.

Another woman of evil influence was Delilah, who connived to deceive Sampson so that he could be robbed of his strength and delivered over to her partners in crime (Judges 16). And then there's Jezebel, who pushed her husband towards pagan religious practices (1 Kings 16).

In terms of numbers, Solomon's wives stand out to us as obvious examples of women who brought harm—not help—to their husbands; 1 Kings 11:4 records that Solomon's one thousand wives and concubines "turned his heart to worship their gods."

A woman who has used her influence over men for deception, evil, or destruction is not a pretty picture, and yet it is not difficult for us to repeat those behaviors in our own families. Only the wisdom and strength of God will help us avoid falling into these negative patterns ourselves. May we humbly ask for his help each day!

Father,
"May the words of my mouth and the thoughts of my heart be pleasing to you, O Lord, my rock and my redeemer" (Psalm 19:14). Amen.

MOTHERS AND WIVES

WIVES, IN THE SAME WAY BE SUBMISSIVE TO YOUR
HUSBANDS SO THAT, IF ANY OF THEM DO NOT BELIEVE THE
WORD, THEY MAY BE WON OVER WITHOUT WORDS BY THE BEHAVIOR
OF THEIR WIVES, WHEN THEY SEE THE PURITY AND REVERENCE OF YOUR LIVES.

1 Peter 3:1-2, NIV

Some would interpret these verses as handing a wife the role of a doormat, but as we take a closer look, that's not what we find. A wife is not a powerless woman; rather, she is much more powerful than she sometimes realizes. In these verses Peter was speaking to the woman in the Roman world.

A note in the *Life Application Bible* reads, "Under Roman law, the husband and father had absolute authority over all members of his household, including his wife. If he disapproved of her new beliefs, she could endanger her marriage by demanding her rights as a free woman in Christ."[3] Peter's encouraging words were intended for Christian women. He reassured them that their responsibility was not to preach to their husbands, but to show them loving service—the kind of love and service that Christ showed the church.

The woman who thinks she can persuade her husband with *words* is mistaken. Rather, he is influenced by the way she conducts herself—her ethics, her habits, her morals, and her interactions with others. Peter refers to both purity and reverence. *Purity* means being free from pollution, abuse, or contamination. *Reverence* includes awe for God, respect for others, and the realization that God created us with great value.

Wives are instructed to support their husbands but not to allow abuse. Allowing mistreatment of any kind to go on contradicts God's instruction to be pure, meaning "free of abuse or pollution." Whether a husband is an unbeliever or a believer who is acting like an unbeliever, actions speak louder than words.

Father,
May we never forget the tremendous influence and persuasion that we have as wives. Please help us to grow in purity and reverence, remembering that our behavior can be winsome. Amen.

MOTHERS AND WIVES

WE DON'T GO AROUND PREACHING ABOUT OURSELVES; WE PREACH CHRIST JESUS, THE LORD. ALL WE SAY ABOUT OURSELVES IS THAT WE ARE YOUR SERVANTS BECAUSE OF WHAT JESUS HAS DONE FOR US. FOR GOD, WHO SAID, "LET THERE BE LIGHT IN THE DARKNESS," HAS MADE US UNDERSTAND THAT THIS LIGHT IS THE BRIGHTNESS OF THE GLORY OF GOD THAT IS SEEN IN THE FACE OF JESUS CHRIST.   *2 Corinthians 4:5-6*

After World War II, German students volunteered to help rebuild a cathedral in England, one of many casualties of the Luftwaffe bombings. As the work progressed, debate broke out on how to best restore a large statue of Jesus with His arms outstretched and bearing the familiar inscription, "Come unto Me." Careful patching could repair all damage to the statue except for Christ's hands, which had been destroyed by bomb fragments. Should they attempt the delicate task of reshaping those hands?

Finally the workers reached a decision that still stands today. The statue of Jesus had no hands, and the inscription now reads, "Christ has no hands but ours."[4]

Over the years, we use our hands to point out many things to our children. While reading a book to a toddler, we point to a cow, asking, "What's that?" While baking chocolate chip cookies with a daughter, we point to the recipe to determine how much sugar we need. While riding in the car with our student driver, we point to the upcoming exit ramp and suggest moving into the right lane.

Of all the things moms point their children to, nothing is as important to their well-being as pointing them to Christ. We point them to the Light of the World because we don't want them to stumble in the darkness. We point them to the Bread of Life because we don't want them to be spiritually hungry. We point them to the Savior because we don't want them to live as slaves to sin. Nothing compares with the privilege of pointing our children to Christ.

God,
Thank you that you sent us light when you sent Christ—and thank you that you allow us to be your hands in this world. Please equip us for the privilege we've been given of pointing our children to Christ. In Christ's name, amen.

MOTHERS AND WIVES

WE WILL NOT HIDE THESE TRUTHS FROM OUR CHILDREN
BUT WILL TELL THE NEXT GENERATION ABOUT THE GLORIOUS
DEEDS OF THE LORD. WE WILL TELL OF HIS POWER AND THE
MIGHTY MIRACLES HE DID.
Psalm 78:4

*M*ax Jukes lived in New York. He did not believe in Christ or in Christian training. He refused to take his children to church, even when they asked to go. He has had 1,026 descendants; of those, 300 were sent to prison for an average term of thirteen years, 190 were public prostitutes, and 680 were admitted alcoholics. His family, thus far, has cost the state in excess of $420,000. They made no measurable contributions to society.

Jonathan Edwards lived in the same state at the same time as Jukes. He loved the Lord and saw that his children were in church every Sunday as he served the Lord to the best of his ability. He has had 929 descendants, and of these 430 were ministers, 86 became university professors, 13 became university presidents, 75 authored good books, and 7 were elected to the United States Congress. One was vice president of his nation. His family never cost the state one cent but has contributed immeasurably to the life of plenty in this land today.[5]

What kind of heritage are we leaving for *our* children? Down the road, we'd all like to pass on some kind of monetary inheritance or a few pieces of furniture that will hold sentimental value. But we'd be wise to focus more on the inheritance with a value that cannot be measured.

Will we pass down a love for God and his Word; an example of truth, love, and mercy; and a grateful heart? These are the most valuable gifts we can give.

Father,
In our busy days as moms, please help us to think ahead to the kind of inheritance we wish to leave for our children. Help our words and actions to match.
Amen.

GOD

FATHER TO THE FATHERLESS, DEFENDER OF
WIDOWS—THIS IS GOD, WHOSE DWELLING IS HOLY.

Psalm 68:5

The Bible teaches us that when we put our faith in God, we become children of God, and God is our Father. The dictionary defines a father as a man who begets, raises, or nurtures a child, and God is faithful to do all of that for us. He created us, gives us his nature, provides for us, and loves us deeply. Some women, myself included, have gratefully experienced those things from their earthly father; but sadly, not every woman's father has lovingly raised or nurtured her. Some women have experienced their father's death, abandonment, or abuse.

It is challenging for these women to understand the God of the Bible. But since injustices, large or small, cross all our paths from time to time, we are wise to realize that God's Word, not our own package of life experiences, must frame our faith.

Michael Horton writes, "While in practice we cannot help but be influenced in our views of God's fatherhood by our earthly experiences, the Good Father can heal our broken images."[6]

Reading God's Word helps us see that we can run to God confidently because he is our faithful Father. (If you struggle with understanding God's father-love for you, reading John 10:1-30 may give you hope and encouragement.)

Father,
Thank you that as we read your Word, it frames our faith and helps us to
understand what a wonderful Father you are to us. Amen.

GOD

JOSEPH IS A FRUITFUL TREE, A FRUITFUL TREE BESIDE A
FOUNTAIN. HIS BRANCHES REACH OVER THE WALL. HE HAS
BEEN ATTACKED BY ARCHERS, WHO SHOT AT HIM AND HARASSED HIM.
BUT HIS BOW REMAINED STRONG, AND HIS ARMS WERE STRENGTHENED BY THE
MIGHTY ONE OF JACOB, THE SHEPHERD, THE ROCK OF ISRAEL. MAY THE GOD
OF YOUR ANCESTORS HELP YOU; MAY THE ALMIGHTY BLESS YOU WITH THE
BLESSINGS OF THE HEAVENS ABOVE, BLESSINGS OF THE EARTH BENEATH, AND
BLESSINGS OF THE BREAST AND WOMB.   *Genesis 49:22-25*

Almighty (*El Shaddai*) is one of the names given to God in the Old Testament. It
means "sufficient and mighty," acknowledging God as a source of blessing. This
name for God appears in the accounts of two particular Old Testament characters, Joseph and Ruth, who led very difficult lives.

I suppose it's not too hard to think of God as sufficient, all-powerful, and a
source of blessing on sunny days when we're healthy, there's money in the
checking account, and our kids are doing well. But what about the gloomy days
when it feels like the rug has been pulled out from underneath us?

Joseph was left in a pit and traded for money by his brothers, taken to a foreign country, falsely accused, and sent to jail. And yet he acknowledged God's
power and later experienced his blessings—wisdom, a high position of influence, responsibility, the ability to interpret dreams, a wife and children, relief
from famine, and a miraculous reunion with his brothers and father that only God
could have orchestrated.

Ruth didn't have it easy either. Her husband and father-in-law died, leaving
her and her mother-in-law as widows who struggled for existence. But after
Ruth chose to stay with her mother-in-law, God blessed Ruth with a husband and
eventually gave them a son who became the grandfather of King David!

The next time we face a difficult day and struggle with seeing God as sufficient, all-powerful, and full of blessing, perhaps we would be wise to read the
stories of Joseph and Ruth and be encouraged anew by God's almighty power.

Father,
Thank you that you left us with accounts of people who dealt with difficult
circumstances and found your mighty power to be more than just enough.
They were blessed abundantly, and we are too. Amen.

GOD

> I LOOK UP TO THE MOUNTAINS—DOES MY HELP COME
> FROM THERE? MY HELP COMES FROM THE LORD, WHO MADE
> THE HEAVENS AND THE EARTH!
>
> *Psalm 121:1-2*

*W*hat do we do when we make something? If we make a cake with our children, we cause it to exist by combining all the ingredients, mixing them, and then baking. If we make a piece of pottery, we shape some clay with our hands or a machine. If we make laws, we institute or establish them.

When God made heaven and earth, he introduced the wonderful process of creativity. He caused things to happen. He shaped. He established. He brought life into existence. He caused matter to assume specific functions and act in specific ways.

But there's a huge difference between what we make and what God made. When we make a cake or a piece of pottery, we start with ingredients, but God made something out of nothing. I love the questions God asked Job in Job 38:4-7 (TLB): "Where were you when I laid the foundations of the earth? Tell me, if you know so much. Do you know how its dimensions were determined, and who did the surveying? What supports its foundations, and who laid its cornerstone, as the morning stars sang together and all the angels shouted for joy?" It's quite clear that God is God, and we are not!

When we encounter challenges and difficulties in our lives, how comforting and encouraging to realize that we can run to our Creator—the one who can make something out of nothing—asking him to bring order to our sometimes chaotic existence here on earth.

Father,
Thank you that heaven and earth are full of your glory! Thank you for giving
us abilities to be creative with things that you brought into being. We know
that you alone can bring order to our existence here on earth. Amen.

GOD

ON THE LAST DAY, THE CLIMAX OF THE FESTIVAL, JESUS
STOOD AND SHOUTED TO THE CROWDS, "IF YOU ARE THIRSTY,
COME TO ME! IF YOU BELIEVE IN ME, COME AND DRINK! FOR THE
SCRIPTURES DECLARE THAT RIVERS OF LIVING WATER WILL FLOW OUT
FROM WITHIN."

John 7:37-38

When you hear the word *thirsty,* what thoughts come to your mind? I think of
the New Guinea impatiens plant that's hanging and flourishing outside the front
door of my home. It must be hearty, because I'm not the world's greatest gardener.

As long as I give my New Guinea impatiens plant about one-half gallon of
water a day, it's happy and vibrant. If I miss a day or two of watering, the leaves
begin to sag. If I miss more than a couple of days, especially in hot weather, the
plant droops into an all-out wilt and looks as though it's about to die. That happened once this summer when my family and I went away for a weekend. When
we returned home, I could just about hear my plant crying for water. I promptly
gave it a good, long drink, and within several hours its droopy leaves perked up.

What a graphic picture that thirsty plant was to me! I have a desperately needy
heart that is also thirsty for God. Over the years, I've settled into the refreshing
habit of satisfying my spiritual thirst through time with God each morning. If I
miss out on that time for whatever reason, my soul begins to wilt and droop.
Spending time with God—through reading his Word and talking to him—renews my heart without fail.

Father,
Thank you that your living water quenches our thirsty souls. In Jesus' name,
amen.

GOD

THE SAVIOR—YES, THE MESSIAH, THE LORD—HAS BEEN
BORN TONIGHT IN BETHLEHEM, THE CITY OF DAVID!

Luke 2:11

When we watch movies that are set in past centuries of English history, it's not unusual to hear a subject addressing a king as "My Lord," acknowledging a man of renowned power or authority. Although the word *Lord* is short, it is packed with tremendous meaning throughout the Bible. The Old Testament word for God is translated "Lord" in our English versions of the Bible because in late Old Testament times Jews chose not to pronounce the sacred name of God but to say instead "my Lord." Because Jesus taught believers to speak in a familiar way to God, we now address God by many names when we pray—Lord, Shepherd, Redeemer, Provider, Father, and more, stemming from the original names of God included in Old Testament accounts.

Probably the most important name for God in the Old Testament was Jehovah, meaning "I am who I am."

One of my reference books reads, "His 'I am' expresses the fact that he is the infinite and original personal God who is behind everything and to whom everything must finally be traced."[7]

Other names in honor of the Lord that are included in the Old Testament are: *Jehovah-Jireh* ("The Lord will provide"), *Jehovah-Nissi* ("The Lord is my banner"), *Jehovah-Shalom* ("The Lord is peace"), *Jehovah-Shammah* ("The Lord is there"), *Jehovah-Tsebaoth* ("The Lord of hosts"), and *Jehovah Elohe Yisrael* ("The Lord God of Israel").

When we address God as Lord and teach our children to address him as Lord, we recognize him as the only one who has infinite power to provide strength, peace, and security in our lives just as he has for others in the past.

Father,
Thank you for the honor of your name. May we teach our children always to have great respect for you as our Lord, Shepherd, Provider, and Redeemer.
Amen.

GOD

THEREFORE, SINCE WE HAVE BEEN MADE RIGHT IN GOD'S
SIGHT BY FAITH, WE HAVE PEACE WITH GOD BECAUSE OF WHAT
JESUS CHRIST OUR LORD HAS DONE FOR US. BECAUSE OF OUR FAITH,
CHRIST HAS BROUGHT US INTO THIS PLACE OF HIGHEST PRIVILEGE WHERE WE
NOW STAND, AND WE CONFIDENTLY AND JOYFULLY LOOK FORWARD TO SHARING
GOD'S GLORY.   *Romans 5:1-2*

The only way to know or worship God is through belief in his Son, Jesus Christ. We might be tempted to think that a lot of people in the world know God—if the determining factor were how much they mention his name. How often we hear people exclaiming, "Thank God it's Friday!" or "For God's sake." I often wonder if people who speak God's name that way have any idea that we can actually know him through Jesus Christ.

Christ has paved the way for us to know God. The whole story of the Bible shows how God took initiative to bring us to himself through Christ. The plan was promised in the Old Testament and fulfilled in the New Testament. As we study the life, teaching, person, and work of Jesus, we learn that he has many titles—including Wonderful Counselor, the Mighty God, the Everlasting Father, and the Prince of Peace (Isaiah 9:6). But the three main ministries he carries out are those of prophet, priest, and king.

As prophet, he reveals God's character and will to the world. As priest, instead of offering continual animal sacrifices, he offered himself once for all for the sins of the world. And as king, he will someday return to earth in triumph to set up his kingdom. God becomes known to us not because of our efforts, but as a result of how he revealed himself in Jesus Christ.

Father,
Thank you that when we believe in Jesus, we are reconciled to you. We're grateful that Jesus came to earth and showed us the path to you. May we encourage our children—both by our lives and our words—to be reconciled to you. Amen.

GOD

YOU FORMED THE MOUNTAINS BY YOUR POWER AND
ARMED YOURSELF WITH MIGHTY STRENGTH. YOU QUIETED
THE RAGING OCEANS WITH THEIR POUNDING WAVES AND SILENCED
THE SHOUTING OF THE NATIONS. THOSE WHO LIVE AT THE ENDS OF THE EARTH
STAND IN AWE OF YOUR WONDERS.

Psalm 65:6-8

My friend Ruthie just returned home from a vacation to the Canadian Rocky Mountains. When she showed me her pictures of the snowcapped mountains, colorful wildflowers, and clear-as-glass lakes, the words that came to mind were *majestic* and *glorious*.

When Jim and I and our sons take vacations to the ocean—whether it's the emerald waters of Gulf Shores, Alabama, or the aqua waves of Hallandale, Florida—our pictures prompt descriptive words like *mighty* or *awesome*.

We humans have a penchant for wonder. We are captivated by spectacular sights like a peacock spreading its wings or a porpoise leaping in the ocean. But we finite humans also need glimpses of how wonderful God is—and that's what nature gives us. I think that's why many of the words we use to describe mountains or oceans are words that the Bible uses to describe God. If the mountains and the oceans are *this* glorious, and the Bible tells us that God formed the mountains and quieted the raging oceans, God must be much more awesome than anything we could ever imagine!

Visiting the mountains or the ocean with our children gives us incredible opportunities to witness the power and majesty of God. As J. I. Packer phrased it, "The world dwarfs us all, but God dwarfs the world."

God of the mountains and the oceans,
Thanks for the beauty you created in the world, all of which points back to
you. Amen.

GRACE

What do you think the Scriptures mean when they say that the Holy Spirit, whom God has placed within us, jealously longs for us to be faithful? He gives us more and more strength to stand against such evil desires. As the Scriptures say, "God sets himself against the proud, but he shows favor to the humble." So humble yourselves before God. Resist the Devil, and he will flee from you.

James 4:5-7

Someone has said, "Man is born broken. He lives by mending. The grace of God is glue." Grace is what we all long for, isn't it? We all long to be shown mercy, love, compassion, and patience. The healthiest people in the world are those who are experiencing the grace of God and are learning to pass it on to others. I guess that also means that the healthiest people in the world are not proud but humble, because proud people don't think they need grace, and they certainly can't pass on to others what they haven't experienced themselves.

The devil, however, doesn't like grace. He prefers for us to be proud. His questions for the believer are, "Why keep so closely to the narrow way and the humble path? Why not be more self-assertive? Why not express yourself as fully as you can, and find power and enjoyment in that self-expression?"[8] He knows that if we don't take God seriously and submit to him in humility, we'll remain broken people.

And so we see that the path to grace is through faith that resists the devil. When we put our faith in Christ, we humble ourselves, and grace can come only to the humble.

Father,
We ask forgiveness for our pride. May we daily submit ourselves to you and resist the devil. Thank you for your grace. Amen.

GRACE

> FOR IT IS BY GRACE YOU HAVE BEEN SAVED, THROUGH
> FAITH—AND THIS NOT FROM YOURSELVES, IT IS THE GIFT
> OF GOD.
>
> *Ephesians 2:8, NIV*

Grace is the favor and kindness of God shown to us in spite of the fact that we don't deserve it. Grace cannot be purchased or earned because it is a *gift*. But like any gift, it can't be appreciated or experienced unless it is accepted. When we accept God's grace by faith, we become victorious, generous, courteous, and strong.

We are *victorious* because we have already been raised from the grave of sin and seated with the risen Lord. Sadly, we often forget that we have received this gift of victory over our sinful nature.

We are *generous* because we have received God's gift of grace, and we want to follow his example. I remember one year when my dad shared one of his bonuses from work with all four of us children. He didn't have to, but in his gratitude he wanted to. When we receive God's grace, we feel the same way—we want to share it with others.

God's grace makes us *courteous*. Because God has not been critical and angry with us, we avoid being that way with others.

Finally, God's grace makes us *strong*. The beauty of God's strength is that it is made perfect in our weakness. God's strength was shown through giving sight to a blind man and through David's small sling, and it can be exhibited in our weakness when we present ourselves as vessels of his grace.

Because of God's gracious gift to us—his Son—we can share the blessings of victory, generosity, courtesy, and strength in our interactions with our children, our husbands, and our friends. God's grace makes us *rich!*

Father,
The more we get to know you, the more we appreciate your grace. Thank you for your indescribable gift! Amen.

GRACE

Do not be carried away by all kinds of strange teachings. It is good for our hearts to be strengthened by grace, not by ceremonial foods, which are of no value to those who eat them.

Hebrews 13:9, NIV

I have read this verse many times before, but when I read it in my morning devotional time recently, three words jumped out at me—"strengthened by grace." More often I see the words *amazing, abounding,* or *healing* tied together with *grace,* but *strengthened* was a new thought. To strengthen something is to encourage or enlarge it.

Our hearts need to be encouraged, enlarged, and strengthened because they are so often discouraged, small in faith, and weak. All the way through the Bible, we are taught to look to God for his help and strength, and nothing prompts us to do that more than our neediness. God doesn't want us to approach him with pride—his grace goes to the humble.

My pastor, Kent Hughes, explains that in the same way the earth's water system operates on gravity, so does grace. He calls it the spiritual "gravity of grace." Try to picture the waters of the Niagra rolling over the falls and dropping into the river below. Then the river continues to flow down even lower to its tributaries, and lower yet to land that needs water for crops. God's grace does the same thing. It rolls off the proud in heart but is appreciated most keenly by people who are lowly in heart. There, it brings growth and blessing. James 4:6 (NIV) reads, "God opposes the proud but gives grace to the humble."

Kent Hughes writes, "The unbowed soul standing proudly before God receives no benefit from God's falling grace. It may descend upon him, but it does not penetrate, and drips away like rain from a statue. But the soul lying before God is immersed—and even swims—in a sea of grace."[9]

Strengthening grace comes to the humble—to those who admit their need.

Father,
Thanks that when we admit our neediness to you, you strengthen and enlarge our hearts with your unending grace. Amen.

GRACE

For the grace of God has been revealed, bringing salvation to all people. And we are instructed to turn from godless living and sinful pleasures. We should live in this evil world with self-control, right conduct, and devotion to God, while we look forward to that wonderful event when the glory of our great God and Savior, Jesus Christ, will be revealed. He gave his life to free us from every kind of sin, to cleanse us, and to make us his very own people, totally committed to doing what is right.

Titus 2:11-14

*G*race brings salvation.

All of God's promises and saving work that he has shown since the beginning of the human race have revealed his grace. All of his blessings and all of his gifts have been planned to bring men and women to repentance. One of the purposes of Jesus' death on the cross was to redeem us from iniquity, but according to Titus that wasn't the only reason. He also wanted to purify us and encourage us toward good works.

Grace teaches us to say no to ungodliness.

To be inwardly godly is to be self-controlled. We can only control our actions and emotions with our will as we depend on God's Spirit to govern our lives (Galatians 5:22-23). As we experience God's grace, we will live honest, faithful, straightforward, and trustworthy lives outwardly among those around us. Godly living displays itself with much more than words—it demonstrates the reality and power of a vital union with God.

Grace causes us to look for the blessed hope.

Knowing that Jesus will return for us is a big incentive to live holy lives. We can draw on his riches now, but we know that when he comes again, we'll share his wealth and his kingdom forever.

What a privilege we experience through God's grace—that of being changed in so many ways!

Father,
Thank you that your grace brings us salvation, godliness, and hope. May we never forget how much all of that cost you. Amen.

GRACE

BE CAREFUL! WATCH OUT FOR ATTACKS FROM THE DEVIL,
YOUR GREAT ENEMY. HE PROWLS AROUND LIKE A ROARING LION,
LOOKING FOR SOME VICTIM TO DEVOUR. TAKE A FIRM STAND AGAINST
HIM, AND BE STRONG IN YOUR FAITH. REMEMBER THAT YOUR CHRISTIAN
BROTHERS AND SISTERS ALL OVER THE WORLD ARE GOING THROUGH THE SAME
KIND OF SUFFERING YOU ARE. IN HIS KINDNESS GOD CALLED YOU TO HIS ETERNAL
GLORY BY MEANS OF JESUS CHRIST. AFTER YOU HAVE SUFFERED A LITTLE WHILE,
HE WILL RESTORE, SUPPORT, AND STRENGTHEN YOU, AND HE WILL PLACE YOU
ON A FIRM FOUNDATION.

1 Peter 5:8-10

*A*ny mom who has ever felt despair will appreciate the following words from
Lewis B. Smedes' book *How Can It Be All Right When Everything Is Wrong?*

> *Grace does not make everything right. Grace's trick is to show us that it is right
> for us to live; that it is truly good, wonderful even, for us to be breathing
> and feeling at the same time that everything clustering around us is wholly
> wretched. . . . Grace is not a potion to charm life to our liking; charms are
> magic. Grace does not cure all our cancers, transform all our kids into winners,
> or send us all soaring into the high skies of sex and success. Grace is rather an
> amazing power to look earthy reality full in the face, see its sad and tragic edges,
> feel its cruel cuts, join in the primeval chorus against its outrageous unfairness,
> and yet feel in your deepest being that it is good and right for you to be alive on
> God's good earth. Grace is power, I say, to see life very clearly, admit it is some-
> times all wrong, and still know that somehow, in the center of your life, "It's all
> right." This is one reason we call it amazing grace. . . . Grace is the one word for
> all that God is for us in the form of Jesus Christ.*[10]

Grace doesn't take away our problem, but it allows us to experience God
alongside us while we are in the midst of it. And he promises to "restore, support, and strengthen" us.

> *Father,*
> *Sometimes it does feel like life is all wrong. Thank you that you understand
> every circumstance of each mom reading this, and that you will come to us
> and meet us with your grace in our moment of need, if we will just ask. Amen.*

GRACE

AFTER BREAKFAST JESUS SAID TO SIMON PETER, "SIMON
SON OF JOHN, DO YOU LOVE ME MORE THAN THESE?" "YES,
LORD," PETER REPLIED, "YOU KNOW I LOVE YOU." "THEN FEED MY
LAMBS," JESUS TOLD HIM. JESUS REPEATED THE QUESTION: "SIMON SON OF JOHN,
DO YOU LOVE ME?" "YES, LORD," PETER SAID, "YOU KNOW I LOVE YOU." THEN
TAKE CARE OF MY SHEEP," JESUS SAID. ONCE MORE HE ASKED HIM, "SIMON SON OF
JOHN, DO YOU LOVE ME?" PETER WAS GRIEVED THAT JESUS ASKED THE QUESTION A
THIRD TIME. HE SAID, "LORD, YOU KNOW EVERYTHING. YOU KNOW I LOVE YOU."
JESUS SAID, "THEN FEED MY SHEEP."   *John 21:15-17*

These verses are encouraging for any Christian mom who's wondered, *How can I
nurture my children spiritually when I've struggled spiritually myself?* The scene in
which John 21:15-17 took place was pregnant with grace for Jesus' disciples—and it is for us, too.

Some days before the breakfast on the shore, Peter had denied Christ three
times and wept bitterly afterward. He knew he had failed, and so did Jesus. Now
Jesus appeared to his disciples for the third time after his death and resurrection.
It was gracious of Jesus to approach Peter with the goal of restoration, though his
straightforward questions probably left Peter feeling very uncomfortable. True
friends speak the truth in love, and that is a grace of sorts.

Just as Peter denied Jesus three times, Jesus asked Peter three times, "Do you
love me?" Bottom line: Jesus wanted to know if Peter was serious about his love
for Christ. Jesus graciously offered Peter a chance to demonstrate his love
through service.

Like Peter, we moms have sometimes failed Christ. We too need to grieve
over our sin, repent (turn around and go the other direction with no intention to
return), and concentrate on the most important thing—loving Christ. As we
love him, our joyful service will be the natural result of our love. Our service to
Christ is an outgrowth of his grace to us.

*Gracious Savior,
Like Peter, all of us fail you at various times. Thank you for your loving grace
that seeks us out, confronts us with truth, and offers us restoration. In Jesus'
name, amen.*

GRACE

THE LORD IS MERCIFUL AND GRACIOUS; HE IS SLOW TO
GET ANGRY AND FULL OF UNFAILING LOVE.   *Psalm 103:8*

It was a busy Saturday morning at the Elwell house when twelve-year-old Jordan asked if he could invite a couple friends over to "jam" on their musical instruments. "We're going to practice up in the attic," Jordan announced. I didn't like the idea and suggested they practice in the basement, but my husband said, "Oh, let's let them do it—there's nothing they can hurt up there."

While the boys were upstairs "jamming," I left the house for a short while to run an errand. When I returned, my husband met me at the door. "We had a little problem while you were gone," he said. "What happened?" I asked. "Well, the good news is that no one is hurt." He continued, "The bad news is that one of the boys slipped in the attic, crashed halfway through the rafters, and left a big hole in our bedroom ceiling."

I was mad. I wanted to lash out with, "I told you it wasn't a good idea!" I didn't say the words, but I'm sure that my attitude conveyed them nonetheless. For the next hour, I quietly went about my work in the kitchen while Jim went about his—preparing the ceiling for a repair. After an hour or so, I had calmed down enough to sit and talk about it. I even managed to catch glimpses of humor in the situation. And of course we laugh about it now, but it took me awhile.

For all the stubbornness and rebellion we humans have shown to God, the Bible consistently describes him as gracious, slow to get angry, and abounding in steadfast love and mercy. My reactions are so different from his! I'm learning that I can't summon those character traits on my own. Only as I trust Christ for help am I able to grow more like him in the area of grace.

Gracious Father,
Please forgive me for times I haven't been gracious and slow to anger. Thank you that you share your grace with me. Amen.

PURITY

DON'T LET ANYONE THINK LESS OF YOU BECAUSE YOU ARE
YOUNG. BE AN EXAMPLE TO ALL BELIEVERS IN WHAT YOU
TEACH, IN THE WAY YOU LIVE, IN YOUR LOVE, YOUR FAITH,
AND YOUR PURITY.

1 Timothy 4:12

To be pure is to be free from mixture or pollution, having a uniform composition. How do we encourage this kind of purity in our children so they will be an example to others? Psalm 119:9 asks and answers that question: "How can a young person stay pure? By obeying your word and following its rules."

To be pure, we also need to be cleansed. We ask God to do part of the cleansing process, and we take personal responsibility for another part.

We come to God asking him to create in us a new and clean heart. His promise in 1 John 1:9 assures us that he will: "But if we confess our sins to him, he is faithful and just to forgive us and to cleanse us from every wrong."

But the other part of cleansing is our responsibility. We must put out of our lives those things that cause us to sin. There are thoughts, places, movies, and reading material that would be destructive to our purity and our children's purity; so we must take responsibility to stay away from them or get rid of them. It's not right to sit back and wait for God to get rid of these when we can do so ourselves.

When we choose purity by spending time in God's Word and experiencing cleansing, we reap the beautiful result of being able to love others and influence them for God's kingdom.

Father,
Thank you for the promise of 1 Timothy 1:5 that when we have "a pure
heart, . . . a good conscience, and a sincere faith" (NIV), we can love others.
Please strengthen us as we encourage our children to spend time in your Word
and to be cleansed of impurities so they can be a positive influence for your
Kingdom. Amen.

PURITY

MAY GOD HIMSELF, THE GOD OF PEACE, SANCTIFY YOU
THROUGH AND THROUGH. MAY YOUR WHOLE SPIRIT, SOUL
AND BODY BE KEPT BLAMELESS AT THE COMING OF OUR LORD JESUS
CHRIST. THE ONE WHO CALLS YOU IS FAITHFUL AND HE WILL DO IT.

1 Thessalonians 5:23-24, NIV

What is sanctification?

"Sanctification is the process of God's grace by which the believer is separated from sin and becomes dedicated to God's righteousness. Accomplished by the Word of God and the Holy Spirit, sanctification results in holiness, or purification from the guilt and power of sin."[11]

How does sanctification take place?

It is God who sanctifies us, and the tools he uses are his Word and his Spirit. We cannot do it ourselves, but we do have a responsibility. Our part is to decide—wholeheartedly—that we want to be separated from sin, and then present ourselves to God. If I want my son's dress pants cleaned, I take them to the dry cleaner; likewise, if I want to be sanctified, I need to present myself to God and be prepared for change. I would never hand the pants to the dry cleaner and ask for only one leg of the garment to be cleaned. In order for my life to be sanctified, God needs all of me too.

This process isn't fast—it begins when we present ourselves to God and ends only when we get to heaven. But God promises that if we make ourselves available to him, he will be faithful to sanctify us.

Father,
I give all of myself to you—my body, my mind, and my soul. Amen.

PURITY

PUT ME ON TRIAL, LORD, AND CROSS-EXAMINE ME.
TEST MY MOTIVES AND AFFECTIONS. FOR I AM CONSTANTLY
AWARE OF YOUR UNFAILING LOVE, AND I HAVE LIVED
ACCORDING TO YOUR TRUTH.
Psalm 26:2-3

We would have no need of an examination if we were sinless. The psalmist David's very request that God examine him was an admission that he already knew he was a sinner. If David hadn't valued God's truth and if he hadn't desired fellowship with his Creator and sustainer, he wouldn't have asked for examination; he would have avoided it and run the other direction. Asking God to examine us, observe us, analyze us, and check our health is a hard thing to do, but a very good thing nevertheless. It shows that we desire a close and loving relationship with the Father. After David asked God to examine him, he asked God to purify his mind and heart. Our thoughts and affections begin in the mind, and they travel to our hearts. To be purified is to be cleansed from impurities and objectionable elements.

David's desire for close fellowship with God is a wonderful pattern for us—a request to be examined, tried, and purified. It's good for our children to hear us asking God to purify *our* minds and hearts.

Father,
Thank you that you are a God who is slow to anger and abounding in mercy.
Because we have experienced your mercy, may we regularly come to you with
open hearts. We want to be moms with pure hearts and minds. Amen.

PURITY

AND NOW, DEAR BROTHERS AND SISTERS, LET ME SAY ONE
MORE THING AS I CLOSE THIS LETTER. FIX YOUR THOUGHTS ON
WHAT IS TRUE AND HONORABLE AND RIGHT. THINK ABOUT THINGS THAT
ARE PURE AND LOVELY AND ADMIRABLE. THINK ABOUT THINGS THAT ARE
EXCELLENT AND WORTHY OF PRAISE.

Philippians 4:8

One day when I was a child, my family was getting ready for a day trip with some church friends to the sand dunes. Mom had cooked a fancy lunch of chicken breasts and potato salad. She had even baked a pie for dessert. As we were walking out the door, my mom said, "Bob, would you please take the trash out to the garage before we leave?" My dad dutifully picked up the bag that he *thought* was the garbage and placed it inside a trash can in our garage.

When my family arrived at the dunes a couple of hours later, we quickly discovered that the bag in our trunk was not the bag of food we thought it was. It was just a bag full of garbage. My mom felt heartsick when she and my dad discovered the mix-up, though she has fun telling the story now.

I can't imagine any of us sitting down to a meal of garbage and actually ingesting it into our bodies. We're much more sanitation-conscious than that. But do we take the same precautions with our—and our children's—eyes, ears, and minds? Are we careful to filter out the things we see, hear, and think about, so that we keep garbage out of our hearts? "No one would allow garbage at his table," said Fulton John Sheen, "but many allow it served into their minds." Let's not mix up the food with the garbage.

Father,
We want to pursue purity in our lives, not garbage. Thank you that as we trust you, you share your righteousness with us. In Jesus' name, amen.

PURITY

COME NEAR TO GOD AND HE WILL COME NEAR TO YOU.
WASH YOUR HANDS, YOU SINNERS, AND PURIFY YOUR
HEARTS, YOU DOUBLE-MINDED.   *James 4:8, NIV*

There are some things in the Christian life that only God can do. But there are also things in the Christian life that God asks *us* to do. James 4:8 urges us to come near to God with the promise that he will also come near to us. How do we come near to him? We speak to him, listen to him, and receive his love and power. My pastor, Kent Hughes, says, "Inch toward God, and he will step toward you. Step toward God, and he will sprint toward you. Sprint toward God, and he will fly to you!"[1]

James also urges us to look into our hearts. Whether we've read something we had no business reading, spoken impatiently to a child, or gossiped about a friend, our hearts need cleansing each day.

As our souls encounter sin throughout the day, we are wise to purify them by exposing our hearts to Christ's cleansing.

How many times do you think you wash your hands each day? eight? ten? twelve? Washing our hands is a process of cleansing that we repeat throughout the day, ridding them of the germs and dirt we come into contact with. Whether we've been feeding oatmeal to a baby, making cookie dough with our toddler, or planting tulip bulbs with an older child, our hands come into contact with food and dirt that we want to get rid of. Keeping our souls clean requires frequent washing too. For cleansing of our hands, we go to the sink; for cleansing of our hearts, we go to Christ.

As we move toward Christ, he moves toward us. He helps us see things in our lives that shouldn't be there, and his power provides the strength to get rid of them.

Father,
We wash our hands many times each day, and we remind our children to do the same. May we also come to you each day for cleansing of our hearts as it is necessary, so that our hearts will be pure. Amen.

PURITY

How can a young person stay pure? By obeying your word and following its rules.   *Psalm 119:9*

*D*o we sometimes concern ourselves more with the purity of the water we drink than with the purity of our hearts? We make sure that our drinking water is clean, filtered, and sanitized. When we travel to foreign countries, we drink bottled water; we wouldn't think of drinking water from the tap. But over the course of our lives, how protective are we about the purity of our hearts—and our children's hearts?

Proverbs 4:23 cautions us to guard our hearts above everything else. How do we do that? God's Word points out a safe PASS to take:

P—Pray
A—Ask for help
S—Stay away from trouble
S—Scripture

Pray—Hebrews 4:14-16 reminds us that Jesus understands our temptations because he was tempted just like we are. But he died for us, conquered sin and death, and now prays for us before God. We can boldly ask him to deliver us from temptation.

Ask for help—We should ask a female Christian friend to hold us accountable and to pray with and for us, especially when we're struggling (Galatians 6:2).

Stay away from trouble—Stay away from situations (reading material, people, activities, immodest clothes, etc.) that might tempt us to sin (1 Timothy 6:11).

Scripture—Face temptation with Scripture, just like Jesus did when he was tempted by Satan. For example, if complaining is a temptation for us, we can memorize Philippians 2:14.

Pure drinking water is good, but pure hearts are more important. "Put everything into the care of your heart," wrote Dallas Willard, "for it determines what your life amounts to."

Father,
Please help us to care for our—and our children's—hearts. Amen.

PURITY

JESUS REPLIED, "YOU HYPOCRITES! ISAIAH WAS
PROPHESYING ABOUT YOU WHEN HE SAID, 'THESE PEOPLE
HONOR ME WITH THEIR LIPS, BUT THEIR HEARTS ARE FAR AWAY.
THEIR WORSHIP IS A FARCE, FOR THEY REPLACE GOD'S COMMANDS WITH THEIR
OWN MAN-MADE TEACHINGS.'"

Mark 7:6-7

At the point in Jesus' ministry when he spoke these words to the Jewish religious leaders, they were openly hostile to him. They were in the habit of looking for something to criticize. The verses above were Jesus' response to the Pharisees when they asked why his disciples didn't participate in ceremonial hand-washing, which had been a tradition of the Jewish elders. These ceremonial hand-washings were not commanded in the Mosaic law, nor were they done for personal cleanliness. Instead, the Pharisees used them as a way to separate themselves from the "unclean" common people and make themselves look especially religious. The tradition probably had a good beginning—reminding the Jewish people that they were set apart for God's purposes—but as the years went on, it became a statement of pride and contempt.

Jesus addressed two issues, and they are important for us to look at closely, both in our lives and the lives of our children.

1. Man-made traditions are not more important than God's truth. Sadly, human nature sometimes holds on to human ideas and ignores God's wisdom.
2. The true source of purity is what is in a person's heart, not outward obedience to certain rules. No matter how many times we wash the outside of our body, only the blood of Jesus can make our hearts clean on the inside. *That* is the reason Jesus died for us.

God,
You look at our hearts, and you know what is there. Thank you that your Son's blood can cleanse our hearts and make us spotless from the inside out. Please help us to teach our children that purity of heart is more important than following man-made traditions. Amen.

EXAMPLE

THOSE WHO CONTROL THEIR ANGER HAVE GREAT UNDER-
STANDING; THOSE WITH A HASTY TEMPER WILL MAKE MISTAKES.

Proverbs 14:29

As Christian moms, we want to be good examples to our children in the area of patience. Having said that, many of us feel that impatience is a daily struggle.

I heard a story once about a man whose car stalled in heavy traffic as the light turned green. All his efforts to start the engine failed, and a chorus of honking behind him made matters worse. He finally got out of his car, walked back to the first driver, and said, "I'm sorry, but I can't seem to get my car started. If you'll go up there and give it a try, I'll stay here and blow your horn for you!"

The honking drivers displayed quick tempers and folly. Patient people are usually people of understanding. Because they are not looking out only for themselves, they are generally not hasty or impulsive. When pain, difficulty, or annoyance come into their lives, they are willing to stand back and attempt to evaluate a situation with some degree of calm.

Quick-tempered people, on the other hand, become angry or irritable very easily. They don't have a good perspective on any given situation, which stems from their lack of thought about other people's needs.

The more we grow in Christ, the more patient we become, because patience is one of the evidences that God's Spirit is present and working in our lives.

Father,
Please help us learn what it means to be patient. We want to be good
examples to our children. Amen.

EXAMPLE

WHEN JESUS SAW HIS MOTHER STANDING THERE BESIDE
THE DISCIPLE HE LOVED, HE SAID TO HER, "WOMAN, HE IS
YOUR SON." AND HE SAID TO THIS DISCIPLE, "SHE IS YOUR
MOTHER." AND FROM THEN ON THIS DISCIPLE TOOK HER INTO HIS HOME.

John 19:26-27

In contrast to the Roman soldiers whose job required them to be present at Jesus' crucifixion, John and Jesus' mother, Mary, were there because of love. Jesus and John had been close friends, and Mary and Jesus shared a love that few others understood. In addition to the typical memories that mothers and sons share, Mary and Jesus both knew they were part of God's plan for the world—his plan to establish relationship between God and humans.

Even as he was dying, Jesus left us an example for our own relationships: He *noticed*, *spoke*, and *provided*. Jesus *noticed* his mother and his friend. In spite of the fact that he was very near death and had been hanging on the cross for hours, he noticed. What amazing, selfless love! I sometimes fail to notice others' needs just because I am tired.

Even though it took great physical effort, Jesus *spoke*. He said to Mary, "Woman, he is your son," and to the disciple, "She is your mother." How touched Mary must have felt that Jesus was using some of his last words to remind her of how much he cared for her.

Jesus *provided* for Mary by asking John to take her home with him. Mary was a widow at that time, and Jesus exercised love and responsibility in wanting to make sure his mother had food and shelter.

Jesus' example of noticing, speaking, and providing is one we can follow in all of our friendships and family relationships.

Lord Jesus,
Thank you that even when you were close to death, you noticed, you spoke,
and you provided. May we follow your example. Amen.

EXAMPLE

AND YOU YOURSELF MUST BE AN EXAMPLE TO THEM BY
DOING GOOD DEEDS OF EVERY KIND. LET EVERYTHING YOU DO
REFLECT THE INTEGRITY AND SERIOUSNESS OF YOUR TEACHING.

Titus 2:7

After urging (nagging?) my sons for many years to do things like brush their teeth, say please and thank you, and use their napkins at the dinner table, I'm pleased to report that I have no reason to remind them anymore—at twenty-six, twenty-four, and eighteen they do these things automatically.

There's something very rewarding about seeing young children remind someone else to follow the behavior we've urged them to practice. I remember seeing this happen one spring day when Chad was three or four. We had just returned home from the grocery store, and Chad had a leftover piece of bread in his hand. While I was in the kitchen putting away groceries, I heard Chad start to cry outside. I ran to the back door and saw that the piece of bread he had set down in his wagon was now being carried off in the beak of a big, black crow! As I walked over to console Chad, he put his hands on his little hips and yelled up to the crow, "Birdie, what do you say?" I'm not sure whether Chad wanted to hear a "thank-you" or an "I'm sorry," but clearly this crow needed to say something!

As moms, we are models, patterns, and illustrations to our children. The habits we display to them, for better or for worse, are the habits they will most likely adopt in their own lives. And then—sometimes in surprising ways—they will model those habits for others. "The first gift we can bestow on others," wrote Thomas Morell, "is a good example."

> *Father God,*
> *Thank you for the Bible, which teaches us how to live with integrity. May we imitate you, so that our children will have good examples to follow. In the name of Jesus, amen.*

EXAMPLE

REMEMBER YOUR LEADERS WHO FIRST TAUGHT YOU THE
WORD OF GOD. THINK OF ALL THE GOOD THAT HAS COME
FROM THEIR LIVES, AND TRUST THE LORD AS THEY DO.

Hebrews 13:7

*T*his short verse is packed with three instructions involving the past, the present, and the future. First, "Remember your leaders"—the ones who spoke God's Word to you. I am thankful for childhood memories of Pastor and Mrs. Rushing, the Browns, the Heggelands, my parents, Mary Waldo, Jacky Riley, the Bevers, Roger and Jan Creamer, the Thompsons, the Anchas, and more. From my adult years I think of Beth Raney, Jack and Theo Robinson, Kent and Barbara Hughes, and others from whom I have heard God's Word. None of these people are perfect, but I am grateful they have been faithful in their lives and in their commitment to teach God's Word, whether it was in a children's Sunday school class, a youth group, a Bible study, or a Sunday morning worship service. Who has had a significant spiritual influence in your life?

"Think of all the good that has come from their lives." To the best of my knowledge, the leaders I mentioned above have continued to walk with God. Unfortunately, this is not the case with all leaders who call themselves Christians, and such a change can be devastating to people who have sat under their teaching. If the outcome of a leader's life is spiritually ugly, disobedient, or rebellious, it's difficult to follow the third instruction.

"Trust the Lord as they do" or, as the NIV says, "Imitate their faith." Imitating involves copying, duplicating, or mirroring. This verse is sobering for those of us who are in positions of leadership—whether we're moms, youth leaders, teachers, or Bible study leaders. Is our faith worth imitating? If they're not old enough already, our children will someday be remembering, considering, and imitating our faith.

> *Father,*
> *May we be good examples to our children, their friends, and all those over whom we're in leadership. May we remember that they will be remembering us, considering us, and imitating us. Amen.*

EXAMPLE

ALL PRAISE TO THE GOD AND FATHER OF OUR LORD JESUS
CHRIST. HE IS THE SOURCE OF EVERY MERCY AND THE GOD
WHO COMFORTS US. HE COMFORTS US IN ALL OUR TROUBLES SO THAT
WE CAN COMFORT OTHERS. WHEN OTHERS ARE TROUBLED, WE WILL BE ABLE TO
GIVE THEM THE SAME COMFORT GOD HAS GIVEN US. YOU CAN BE SURE THAT THE
MORE WE SUFFER FOR CHRIST, THE MORE GOD WILL SHOWER US WITH HIS
COMFORT THROUGH CHRIST.

2 Corinthians 1:3-5

When my friend Marty was dying of cancer and had only a month to live, she gave me a copy of the book *A Shepherd Looks at Psalm 23* by Phillip Keller. When I read the book, I realized why Marty had been so encouraged by the author. His wife had been sick with cancer for two years before she died, and he wrote not as an example of a life untouched by difficulty, but rather as an example of one who had walked through pain and loss himself.

He wrote that during his wife's illness and even after her death, he was amazed at the strength and solace that God's Spirit graciously brought to his life. In the process of going through his own dark valley with God's help, he was being prepared to minister to others.

If you've gone through a valley in the past and have experienced God's comfort, you will readily identify with the author. If you're presently going through a valley, pray and ask God to send you comfort in ways that only he can orchestrate. And then don't be surprised if—at some point down the road—he uses you to bring comfort to someone else in the valley.

Keller writes, "Only those who have been through such dark valleys can console, comfort or encourage others in similar situations."[2]

Do we want the valleys? No! But when we experience God's faithfulness and comfort even in the valleys, we can be living examples of that to others.

God even in the valleys,
Thank you that as we experience troubles, you are faithful to give us your comfort and compassion. Thank you that when we have received it and experienced it ourselves, we can comfort others with the comfort we received from you. Amen.

EXAMPLE

So take a new grip with your tired hands and stand firm on your shaky legs. Mark out a straight path for your feet. Then those who follow you, though they are weak and lame, will not stumble and fall but will become strong.

Hebrews 12:12-13

In May 2003 I attended the memorial service of Dr. Andrew Chong. As I listened to four of Andrew's children speak of the godly example their father left for them, I wished that the whole world could have been there to hear them. With his wife Catherine's permission, I am sharing some of her children's comments here.

Karen: "My dad delighted in me, and because of the way he loved me, I can better understand the way God loves me. My dad told me, 'Think of God as your Daddy, except know that he loves you infinitely more.'"

David: "I remember one night when my dad prayed, 'Thank you, Jesus, for saving me, thank you for living in me, thank you for my family, thank you for the cross, thank you for sending your Son to die for me. Thank you for a new life.'"

Sarah: "Dad, we'll always remember you for your humble heart and your wise words . . . for settling our hearts when we were so unsure, and teaching us that we need God's wisdom more than anything."

Paul: "Multiple social workers had recommended to my mom and dad that they put Cindy, our disabled sister, into an institution. Instead, my dad wrote in his journal, 'I know I can't do that. I can't put away my own kid, the one God gave me to minister to and nurture and love. . . . Cindy, YOU are our ministry. May God give us grace to serve you as we serve the Lord Jesus.'"

And serve Christ he did, by his example to his children.

Father,
Thank you for the example of parents like Andrew. Please give us your help to walk a straight path in front of our children. In the strong name of Jesus, amen.

EXAMPLE

A WOMAN WHO IS BEAUTIFUL BUT LACKS DISCRETION IS
LIKE A GOLD RING IN A PIG'S SNOUT.

Proverbs 11:22

*W*hether you prefer pants to skirts and whether you're in your twenties or your forties, you'll probably agree that advertising for women's clothing sometimes exceeds appropriate limits. "How much power does advertising wield with respect to shaping the culture? Jan Kurtz, Curator of American Advertising Museum in Portland, Oregon reports, 'Advertising is a very conscious attempt to depict a fantasy lifestyle, so it exacerbates the cultural trends.'"[3]

How much power does advertising wield? A lot. How much power does God's Word wield? A lot more. Advertising aims to change the outside of us (buying, eating, dressing, exercising), while the Word of God aims to change the inside of us (thinking—attitudes that produce behavior). God's Word teaches discretion and modesty, in contrast to much of the advertising we see today.

Discretion and *modesty* are big words that set big examples. Discretion includes being able to make responsible decisions, including practicing self-restraint in speech and behavior. A woman who exercises discretion looks honestly at the circumstances and sees the potential consequences of her words and actions. And modesty? Although advertisers may not always choose modesty, Christian women must (see 1 Timothy 2:9). Modesty includes not attempting to call attention to ourselves and exercising caution in speech, dress, and behavior.

Where will we get our example of a proper feminine life—from advertising or from God's Word? Our choice determines the kind of example we will be to our children.

Father,
Thank you for instructive words in the Bible about discretion and modesty.
May we choose to exercise them in our lives so we will be good examples to our
daughters and sons. Amen.

RIGHTEOUSNESS

WHEN CALAMITY COMES, THE WICKED ARE BROUGHT
DOWN, BUT EVEN IN DEATH THE RIGHTEOUS HAVE A
REFUGE. . . . RIGHTEOUSNESS EXALTS A NATION, BUT SIN IS A
DISGRACE TO ANY PEOPLE.   *Proverbs 14:32, 34, NIV*

The word *righteousness* comes from a root word that means "straightness." Righteousness is upright and holy living that follows God's standards. God is perfectly righteous, and so all righteousness comes from him. That's why Proverbs 3:5-6 instructs us, "Trust in the Lord with all your heart and lean not on your own understanding; in all your ways acknowledge him, and *he will make your paths straight*" (NIV, emphasis added).

As we trust in Christ, he shares his righteousness with us. Our character becomes more like his, and our status is elevated—we become children of God. That's how righteousness *exalts* people. Isn't that what we want for ourselves and our children? We can't buy this with money, but rather we choose to trust Christ, and he imparts his righteousness to us.

Righteousness not only *exalts* us, but it *protects* us. Parents and children who choose to share the righteousness of Christ find refuge in him. He is a source of protection, shelter, help, relief, and comfort in times of trouble or hardship.

> *O my people, trust in him at all times. Pour out your heart to him, for God is our refuge. (Psalm 62:8)*

> *Those who live in the shelter of the Most High will find rest in the shadow of the Almighty. This I declare of the Lord: He alone is my refuge, my place of safety; he is my God, and I am trusting him. (Psalm 91:1-2)*

Righteousness elevates us and protects us, but not because of our own merit. As we trust in Christ, he shares *his* righteousness with us; then we are exalted and protected.

Righteous God,
Thank you that because of our relationship with you, we can experience your righteousness. May we continually trust you so that we will be gracious examples of your righteousness to our families. Amen.

RIGHTEOUSNESS

OH, THE JOYS OF THOSE WHO DO NOT FOLLOW THE ADVICE
OF THE WICKED, OR STAND AROUND WITH SINNERS, OR JOIN IN
WITH SCOFFERS. BUT THEY DELIGHT IN DOING EVERYTHING THE LORD
WANTS; DAY AND NIGHT THEY THINK ABOUT HIS LAW. THEY ARE LIKE TREES
PLANTED ALONG THE RIVERBANK, BEARING FRUIT EACH SEASON WITHOUT FAIL.
THEIR LEAVES NEVER WITHER, AND IN ALL THEY DO, THEY PROSPER. BUT THIS IS
NOT TRUE OF THE WICKED. THEY ARE LIKE WORTHLESS CHAFF, SCATTERED BY THE
WIND. THEY WILL BE CONDEMNED AT THE TIME OF JUDGMENT. SINNERS WILL
HAVE NO PLACE AMONG THE GODLY. FOR THE LORD WATCHES OVER THE PATH OF
THE GODLY, BUT THE PATH OF THE WICKED LEADS TO DESTRUCTION.   *Psalm 1*

Psalm 1 is rich in word pictures. It invites us to envision a crossroads, two
paths, a Bible, a tree, a stream, fruit, green leaves, and garbage blowing in the
wind.

The crossroads reminds us that we have a choice to make. There are only two
paths in life—God's way of righteousness or the way of rebellion and destruction. Which are we on?

The images of the person who chooses God's way are rich indeed. Someone
who spends time in God's Word is likened to a tree, planted by a river, that bears
fruit and prospers. In other words, he is growing, lasting, and bringing life to
others. This person develops love for the Bible because spending time in God's
Word is the way she figures out how to follow God. Meditating means reading
and thinking about what we've read, looking to apply it to our lives. The Bible
brings us great hope, and the more we know of God's Word, the more wisdom
we'll have to handle the daily decisions of motherhood in particular and life in
general.

The path of the wicked is not pretty—it is a picture of garbage. Chaff is an
outer shell that has to be removed to expose the valuable grain inside. In Bible
times, after stalks of grain were cut and crushed, they were thrown into the air.
The chaff blew off as garbage, while the good grain fell to the earth.

We all have a choice to make. Will we choose godliness or garbage?

Father,
Thank you that you promise to bless the person who chooses your way. May
we choose the way of righteousness, not the way of garbage. Amen.

RIGHTEOUSNESS

WE SHOULD BE DECENT AND TRUE IN EVERYTHING WE
DO, SO THAT EVERYONE CAN APPROVE OF OUR BEHAVIOR.
DON'T PARTICIPATE IN WILD PARTIES AND GETTING DRUNK, OR IN
ADULTERY AND IMMORAL LIVING, OR IN FIGHTING AND JEALOUSY. BUT LET THE
LORD JESUS CHRIST TAKE CONTROL OF YOU, AND DON'T THINK OF WAYS TO
INDULGE YOUR EVIL DESIRES.

Romans 13:13-14

As Christians, we know we should stay away from the behaviors listed in this verse. But when people are alienated from God, these behaviors are inevitable.

What is the antidote to these sinful behaviors? It's the righteousness of Christ. His righteousness is not something we work hard to attain by doing good things or attempting to get rid of the bad. Rather, we exchange our filthy garments for a robe of righteousness.

If one of our children came in from playing outside—covered from head to toe with mud—would we hand him a scrub brush and say, "Go to work on your clothes and clean off every last spot"? Of course not. We'd help clean him up and provide a fresh change of clothes. That's essentially what Jesus did for us by living a sinless life, dying on the cross to pay the price for our sin, and being raised by God from the dead. Isaiah 61:10 says, "I am overwhelmed with joy in the Lord my God! For he has dressed me with the clothing of salvation and draped me in a robe of righteousness."

Every woman or child who trusts in Christ exchanges her rags for Christ's righteousness!

Righteous Father,
Thank you that we can be robed with your righteousness as we trust in you.
May we never forget that you paid for our new garment with your lifeblood.
Amen.

RIGHTEOUSNESS

"TWO MEN WENT TO THE TEMPLE TO PRAY. ONE WAS A
PHARISEE, AND THE OTHER WAS A DISHONEST TAX COLLECTOR.
THE PROUD PHARISEE STOOD BY HIMSELF AND PRAYED THIS PRAYER: 'I THANK
YOU, GOD, THAT I AM NOT A SINNER LIKE EVERYONE ELSE, ESPECIALLY LIKE THAT
TAX COLLECTOR OVER THERE! FOR I NEVER CHEAT, I DON'T SIN, I DON'T COMMIT
ADULTERY, I FAST TWICE A WEEK, AND I GIVE YOU A TENTH OF MY INCOME.' BUT
THE TAX COLLECTOR STOOD AT A DISTANCE AND DARED NOT EVEN LIFT HIS EYES
TO HEAVEN AS HE PRAYED. INSTEAD, HE BEAT HIS CHEST IN SORROW, SAYING,
'O GOD, BE MERCIFUL TO ME, FOR I AM A SINNER.' I TELL YOU, THIS SINNER, NOT
THE PHARISEE, RETURNED HOME JUSTIFIED BEFORE GOD. FOR THE PROUD WILL BE
HUMBLED, BUT THE HUMBLED WILL BE HONORED."   *Luke 18:9-14*

Whenever we feel confident of our own righteousness and look down on other
people, we are in a most dangerous place. Jesus addressed this parable to a
self-righteous audience, teaching that pride disqualifies us from experiencing the
righteousness of God. Only God is the standard for righteousness.

> He is the Rock; his work is perfect. Everything he does is just and fair. He
> is a faithful God who does no wrong; how just and upright he is!
> (Deuteronomy 32:4)

The contrast between the Pharisee and the publican was huge. The Pharisee
stood up in the middle of the Temple, wanting to be noticed, while the tax collector stood at a distance, wishing to be out of the way. The Pharisee bragged
about himself and noted the sins of others, while the tax collector beat on his
breast and confessed his own sin. The Pharisee went home condemned by his
pride, while the publican went home justified and saved by his faith.

Jesus did not take issue with the behavior of the Pharisee; he took issue with
the self-righteous attitude of his heart. The lesson here for us is that God desires
simplicity, humility, and faith—not fanfare, bragging, and confidence in our
self-righteousness. If we exalt ourselves, we will eventually be humbled; but if
we humble ourselves before God, we will eventually be exalted.

> Father,
> Forgive us for taking note of the sins of others instead of confessing our own
> sins to you. May we daily choose a heart posture of humility. Amen.

RIGHTEOUSNESS

THE WAY OF THE RIGHTEOUS IS LIKE THE FIRST GLEAM OF
DAWN, WHICH SHINES EVER BRIGHTER UNTIL THE FULL LIGHT
OF DAY. BUT THE WAY OF THE WICKED IS LIKE COMPLETE
DARKNESS. THOSE WHO FOLLOW IT HAVE NO IDEA WHAT THEY ARE STUMBLING
OVER.

Proverbs 4:18-19

In the verses above, we see quite a contrast between the way of the righteous and the way of the wicked. The word *way* clearly indicates a method of moving from one place to another. If I go to Florida, I don't just happen to wake up there one morning. I arrive there because I made a choice either to fly or to drive. The same principle holds true for righteous or wicked living—we make choices that determine which direction we will go.

Righteousness means holy living that conforms to God's standards, and it's impossible for us to attain on our own. Because God is the source of all righteousness, he *is* the standard. The path of righteousness is not hidden. It is well-defined because Christ has already blazed the trail for us. Whenever we spend time with him through his Word or prayer, if we choose to obey, we experience the gleam of dawn—an indication that there is more light to come. The more time a mom spends with Christ, the more she shines, reflecting the light of Christ to her family.

Wicked is a word we tend to relegate to fictional characters, like the Wicked Witch of the West in *The Wizard of Oz*. But the word is found throughout the Bible, and it describes a person who habitually practices sin. "The way of the wicked" is absent of light or clarity, and the people on that path commit sin with regularity. But there is hope. The presence of Jesus can bring righteousness and light to a dark heart that is stumbling for lack of a straight path, because Jesus *is* our righteousness.

Father,
Thank you that the path to righteousness is not a secret, but that your
righteousness is equally available to all who want you. Amen.

RIGHTEOUSNESS

For God made Christ, who never sinned, to be the offering for our sin, so that we could be made right with God through Christ.

2 Corinthians 5:21

One Saturday my son Jordan stopped at a garage sale, where he spotted a distortion pedal for an electric guitar. Because he'd been looking around on eBay long enough to know that distortion pedals are worth a fair amount, he purchased it for four dollars. After returning home and checking it out on eBay, he discovered that the particular model he had purchased was one of the oldest and best ever made. It was worth much more than he'd thought. He put it up for sale on eBay, and the next day (I'm not making this up) he sold it for 350 dollars!

eBay is built on the principle of exchange. You put an item up for sale and wait to see what another person is willing to pay for it. All of us make exchanges every day—one dollar for a bagel and a cup of coffee, several dollars for a gallon of milk, and so on. Most things in our world can be exchanged or traded for a price.

Not righteousness. We can never earn enough money to buy righteousness, nor can we ever do enough good deeds to earn it. But gaining righteousness *does* involve a trade of sorts. What's the trade? Our sin. The *Life Application Study Bible* explains it this way: "In the world, bartering works only when two people exchange goods of relatively equal value. But God offers to trade his righteousness for our sin—something of immeasurable worth for something completely worthless."⁴

The righteousness of Christ, God's priceless gift to us, comes only through faith in Christ's death and resurrection.

Father,
Thank you for sending your Son to die for us so that we could be made
righteous. We praise you for giving us such an incredible gift when we have
done nothing to deserve such kindness. In your Son Jesus' name, amen.

RIGHTEOUSNESS

WE ARE ALL INFECTED AND IMPURE WITH SIN. WHEN WE
PROUDLY DISPLAY OUR RIGHTEOUS DEEDS, WE FIND THEY
ARE BUT FILTHY RAGS.   *Isaiah 64:6*

How do you use rags in your house? I keep a few small rags underneath my kitchen sink for polishing silver pieces. I store others in the bathroom closet and use them for cleaning floors.

If I was trying to come up with an image for righteous deeds, I might have said, "Righteous deeds look like a pure white linen tablecloth," or "Righteous deeds look like crystal clear water flowing from a stream." But when God, through Isaiah, described our "righteous deeds," he said that they look like filthy rags. Yuck!

Isaiah's ugly picture of rags is not intended to make us despair. The name *Isaiah* means "the salvation of Jehovah." The prophet Isaiah was sent to the nation of Judah to expose the people's sin and explain that God's salvation would come through the Messiah. He wanted them to see that no amount of clean living or good deeds was enough to save them from God's wrath over sin, but that God's righteousness comes to our hearts when we humbly repent of our sin and trust in him for salvation.

The fairy-tale character Cinderella wouldn't have had a lovely gown to wear to the ball if her fairy godmother hadn't stepped in to help. Up until that point, all Cinderella owned were raggedy clothes. We're a bit like Cinderella in that sense. Whether we're kids or adults, God tells us that our best efforts are like rags. But Christ has provided us with snow-white garments of *his* righteousness. It's totally a gift of his grace.

Righteous Father,
We have no clue how far short of your righteousness we come. Thank you that having a relationship with you depends on our faith in Jesus' death and not on our good works. In Jesus' name, amen.

HUMILITY

MARY RESPONDED [TO ELIZABETH], "OH, HOW I PRAISE THE
LORD. HOW I REJOICE IN GOD MY SAVIOR! FOR HE TOOK NOTICE
OF HIS LOWLY SERVANT GIRL, AND NOW GENERATION AFTER GENERATION
WILL CALL ME BLESSED. FOR HE, THE MIGHTY ONE, IS HOLY, AND HE HAS DONE
GREAT THINGS FOR ME. HIS MERCY GOES ON FROM GENERATION TO GENERATION,
TO ALL WHO FEAR HIM. HIS MIGHTY ARM DOES TREMENDOUS THINGS! HOW HE
SCATTERS THE PROUD AND HAUGHTY ONES! HE HAS TAKEN PRINCES FROM THEIR
THRONES AND EXALTED THE LOWLY. HE HAS SATISFIED THE HUNGRY WITH GOOD
THINGS AND SENT THE RICH AWAY WITH EMPTY HANDS. AND HOW HE HAS HELPED
HIS SERVANT ISRAEL! HE HAS NOT FORGOTTEN HIS PROMISE TO BE MERCIFUL. FOR
HE PROMISED OUR ANCESTORS—ABRAHAM AND HIS CHILDREN—TO BE MERCIFUL
TO THEM FOREVER."
                                                                    Luke 1:46-55

Humility jumps from the page as we read what Mary said (or sang) to her cousin
Elizabeth, reflecting on God's promise to make her the mother of the Messiah.
What a beautiful snapshot of a humble heart. Notice some of the ingredients of
humility included in her song:

1. Humility involves moving the focus off ourselves. Mary didn't praise
   herself—she praised God. She spoke of him as her Savior and Lord and
   acknowledged that he was mighty, holy, and merciful.
2. Humility doesn't mean insecurity. Mary acknowledged God's power and
   love, which she had felt in her own life.
3. Humility shows us where we fit in the big picture. Mary understood that
   she was part of a much bigger plan than just her days on earth. She knew
   she was involved in a design that God had for the world. It's easy for us
   to get caught up in our own agenda and forget that we are here to serve.
4. Humility springs from our innermost being. Mary saw that things are not
   always as they appear. What's important to God is not the position we
   hold before our peers, but rather the state of our inmost thoughts about
   God. That's where humility begins.

Father,
*Thank you for the beautiful song that Mary sang in praise to you. May we
learn from her example of humility and be an example to our children of a
mom who praises you out of an overflowing heart. Amen.*

HUMILITY

BUT WHEN [NEBUCHADNEZZAR'S] HEART AND MIND
WERE HARDENED WITH PRIDE, HE WAS BROUGHT DOWN
FROM HIS ROYAL THRONE AND STRIPPED OF HIS GLORY.

Daniel 5:20

To be a person of humility is to exhibit modesty in behavior, attitude, and spirit, not demonstrating arrogance or pride. An Old Testament king who was anything but humble, Nebuchadnezzar had captured Jerusalem, destroyed the Temple, and carried the people of Judah into captivity. He had also set up a golden statue of himself and required all his subjects to worship it! Although the prophet Daniel warned King Nebuchadnezzar to repent and change his ways, the king refused to heed his advice.

We read in Daniel 4:30 that Nebuchadnezzar made an arrogant declaration about himself: "Is not this the great Babylon I have built as the royal residence, by my mighty power and for the glory of my majesty?" (NIV). While he was finishing his pompous statement, a voice from heaven told him that his authority would be taken away, and he would live with the wild animals and eat grass like cattle. Tell this story to your children the next time you're driving down a country road and see some cattle. Old Nebuchadnezzar experienced a bit of a lifestyle change! Because the king did not humble himself before God, God brought the path of humiliation to him, giving him yet another opportunity to change.

The good news is that he did have a change of heart. The king learned that he was nothing and God was everything. When we have that kind of perspective, pride and arrogance dissolve. Nebuchadnezzar looked up to heaven, saying, "Now I, Nebuchadnezzar, praise and exalt and glorify the King of heaven, because everything he does is right and all his ways are just. And those who walk in pride he is able to humble" (Daniel 4:37, NIV). Humility before God restores our dignity and sanity, resulting in a changed life that praises God.

Father,
What a merciful God you are! Even when Nebuchadnezzar overdosed on his own pride, you graciously restored him once he took his eyes off himself and looked to you. May we do the same. Amen.

HUMILITY

I TELL YOU, THIS SINNER, NOT THE PHARISEE, RETURNED
HOME JUSTIFIED BEFORE GOD. FOR THE PROUD WILL BE
HUMBLED, BUT THE HUMBLE WILL BE HONORED.

Luke 18:14

*O*ne of the few times my family watches TV is during the Olympics. We are drawn to various aspects of the Games, but we especially enjoy learning about the athletes who are competing. Some seem personable and humble; others appear proud and even arrogant. One such athlete was recently quoted in the newspaper as saying, "Defiance is fun!" Hmmm. There was nothing endearing to us about that.

In Luke 18:9-14, Jesus told the story of two men who went to the temple to pray. One went to brag about how good he was, and the other went to admit his sin and beg for mercy. Curiously, the one who bragged left with more distance between himself and God than when he walked in. But the man who came recognizing his sin and begging for mercy was pronounced justified by God. He was brought into a *closer* relationship with God.

In the Olympics, I'd rather watch the interview of a humble person than a proud person. In my home, I'd rather have my child approach me with a humble attitude than an attitude of pride. Apparently God feels the same way about us. When he observes our thoughts, our words, and our deeds, does he see humility or pride? Humility is endearing to God.

> *Father,*
> *Hardly a day goes by that we don't struggle with pride of some sort. We*
> *confess it to you. Thank you for pictures in the Bible that help us to see how*
> *much you value humility. In Jesus' name, amen.*

HUMILITY

YES, I AM THE VINE; YOU ARE THE BRANCHES. THOSE WHO
REMAIN IN ME, AND I IN THEM, WILL PRODUCE MUCH FRUIT.
FOR APART FROM ME YOU CAN DO NOTHING.   *John 15:5*

In an essay on humility, Søren Kierkegaard suggests that we imagine an arrow racing on its course. Suddenly it halts in its flight, perhaps to see how far it has come, how high it has soared above the earth, or how its speed compares to that of another arrow (or to admire the gracefulness with which it flies). At that very moment it falls to the ground. Even so, the philosopher insists, self-preoccupation is dangerous and self-destructive.

Self-preoccupation is as different from abiding in Christ as darkness is from light. To be preoccupied with myself is to become self-focused, diminished, and weak, because on my own I have no source of strength. But to be preoccupied with Christ—to abide in him—means that my life is others-focused, enlarged, and strong through God's limitless store of power. Abiding in Christ is what I want to do, but without the daily commitment of spending time with him, I drift back into self-preoccupation.

God asks us to be occupied with him and his kingdom. When we focus on *him* and forget ourselves, we find that he has already secured our significance for us. "This significance is not based on performance, power, prosperity, or position, but in the person of the living God releasing Christ within us."[5]

Father,
Forgive us for being so preoccupied with ourselves. May our children see us
focusing on you and your Kingdom and growing in humility. Amen.

HUMILITY

FOR THE PROUD WILL BE HUMBLED, BUT THE HUMBLE
WILL BE HONORED. *Luke 14:11*

Children love the Old Testament story of David and Goliath. I used to sing the song "Only a Boy Named David" to my boys most nights at bedtime when they were little guys. Goliath, a Philistine giant and the epitome of pride, had been out strutting, stepping out of the battle lines, and shouting defiantly at the Israelites. The Philistines occupied one hill, and the Israelites occupied another, with a valley in between them. Goliath wanted the Israelites to send out one man to fight him, but the whole Israelite army was terrified of the giant!

Enter David—the picture of humility. David was a simple shepherd who had faithfully performed his tasks as a "nobody." In fact, not long before this account, God had sent the prophet Samuel to the house of David's father, Jesse, saying that one of Jesse's sons would someday be the king of Israel. As the prophet was presented the "most likely" candidates from oldest to youngest, Samuel said no to seven sons and then asked, "Are these *all* of your sons?" Jesse answered, "No, the youngest is out tending the sheep." And—you know the story—the young shepherd David was the one Samuel was looking for!

Humanly speaking, the battle plan didn't make sense. Goliath should have won the fight easily, but in God's plan David felled the giant with a stone from his slingshot. As we live in a highly competitive society that rewards the biggest and best, may we not be tricked into thinking that strong and proud is good, and weak and humble is bad. May God's Word remind us that a posture of humility and service is the right posture for us.

God of surprises,
Thank you that through your Word we are reminded that you honor faithful
service—not proud strutting. May we be faithful today in many small ways.
Amen.

HUMILITY

> BUT HE SAID TO ME, "MY GRACE IS SUFFICIENT FOR YOU,
> FOR MY POWER IS MADE PERFECT IN WEAKNESS."
>
> *2 Corinthians 12:9, NIV*

When I encounter problems and difficulties in my life, too often my initial approach is to work hard at being strong. I like to see myself as a person who is resilient physically, mentally, emotionally, and spiritually. But I have discovered that even the best of my strength is no match for many of the challenges of my life here on earth.

I'm also tempted to focus on myself when I'm in a crisis. I feel sorry for myself, spend time thinking about myself, and try to protect myself. But when I spend great amounts of time thinking about myself and not a lot of time thinking about God, I'm in trouble.

The apostle Paul is a great example to me of a humble person. God was able to use Paul tremendously to further his kingdom, and he didn't do it because Paul was strong. God told Paul in the verse above, "My grace is sufficient for you, for my power is made perfect in weakness."

Hebrews 11 reminds us of Gideon, Barak, Samson, Jephthah, David, and the prophets, who because of their faith saw their weakness turned into strength (see verse 32). God can use us when we realize we're *not* strong on our own and admit our weakness before him. We ask him to take our frail offerings and use them to increase *his* kingdom, not ours.

Father,
The message we get in our culture today is, "Be strong!" But you tell us that we're wise to admit our weakness, run to you, and wait to see your power and strength worked out in our frail beings. May our children see your strength because they see us turning to you in times of need. Amen.

HUMILITY

DON'T BE SELFISH; DON'T LIVE TO MAKE A GOOD IMPRESSION
ON OTHERS. BE HUMBLE, THINKING OF OTHERS AS BETTER THAN
YOURSELF. . . . YOUR ATTITUDE SHOULD BE THE SAME THAT CHRIST
JESUS HAD. THOUGH HE WAS GOD, HE DID NOT DEMAND AND CLING TO HIS
RIGHTS AS GOD. HE MADE HIMSELF NOTHING; HE TOOK THE HUMBLE POSITION OF
A SLAVE AND APPEARED IN HUMAN FORM. AND IN HUMAN FORM HE OBEDIENTLY
HUMBLED HIMSELF EVEN FURTHER BY DYING A CRIMINAL'S DEATH ON A CROSS.

Philippians 2:3, 5-8

Throughout the Bible, we're reminded that "the Lord supports the humble, but he brings the wicked down into the dust" (Psalm 147:6). That same thought appears in Psalm 18:27—"You rescue those who are humble, but you humiliate the proud." Clearly, God hates pride and values humility.

If we want to improve our sewing, cooking, decorating, or parenting skills, thousands of books are available to help us. But if we want to learn how to be humble, where do we go? I've never run across a book titled *Humility 101* in my local bookstore.

The Bible tells us that the place to go—the person to look at—is Jesus. There's no better role model for any of us. In Philippians 2, we discover that humility begins with an attitude—one that looks up at God and up at other people. When we look at our holy, powerful God, there's only one direction to look, and that's up! Our biggest problem is that we don't spend enough time looking at him. And when we look at other people, we sometimes look down, but that's not the right direction.

When the attitude of humility is present in our hearts, the actions of humility seem to follow. Instead of demanding, we begin serving. Instead of clinging to our rights, we begin thinking about others. Even though Jesus was God, he didn't demand and cling to his rights. Instead, he took the humble position of a slave, to the point of death on a cross—for us. By looking at Jesus' attitude and actions, we find the only perfect example of humility.

Father,
Each day we face many opportunities to practice humility, but it doesn't come naturally to us. Please help us look to your example and your strength and make the choice to serve others. In Christ's name, amen.

WORK

FOR WE ARE GOD'S MASTERPIECE. HE HAS CREATED US
ANEW IN CHRIST JESUS, SO THAT WE CAN DO THE GOOD
THINGS HE PLANNED FOR US LONG AGO.   *Ephesians 2:10*

Work. To some the word sounds depressing. To others it sounds energizing. I believe that our perspective on life and eternity helps determine our attitude toward work.

While on an airplane flight, I picked up the March 1998 copy of *Hemisphere* magazine and read an article about Millard Fuller, the founder of Habitat for Humanity. At age twenty-nine, Fuller became a millionaire while working as a lawyer and was living with a pretty fancy roof over his head. But after a marital crisis, he and his wife decided to downscale and seek a path of service. They searched for a way to make their lives count for God's work in the world.

Discovering that one great need in our nation was housing for low-income families, they began a program of building houses for the poor. Fuller stated that the majority of volunteers who work with Habitat do so because of religious motivation. He calls it the "theology of the hammer." Putting their faith into action, people use hammers as tools that demonstrate love.

As a mother, I don't have to search very far before I find ways that my life can count for God's work in the world. I prepare meals and pray that God's Word will nourish my children's souls. I do laundry and pray for the purity of my children. I encourage Christian character in them, praying that God will use them to build Christian families. The important thing is that all our work is done with a goal of furthering God's Kingdom.

God,
Thank you for examples of people who want their lives to count for you. May our lives count for you as we serve you inside and outside our homes. Amen.

WORK

MAY THE FAVOR OF THE LORD OUR GOD REST UPON US;
ESTABLISH THE WORK OF OUR HANDS FOR US—YES, ESTABLISH
THE WORK OF OUR HANDS.   *Psalm 90:17, NIV*

I was amazed at the amount of space the word *work* is given in the dictionary—one and a half columns! But then I got to thinking that a whole lot of my life is spent working—giving physical or mental effort toward the production or accomplishment of some task or goal. I have invested hours of work in my children's lives—nursing, feeding, holding, singing, dressing, reading, putting together puzzles, going to church, driving, hosting friends, cooking, praying, listening, talking, doing laundry, and providing music lessons. Those are all part of a mother's work. Is it producing or accomplishing something? You bet! What a joy for a mom to see her children growing, maturing, and accomplishing things on their own.

It's especially meaningful to think that my work has not only been aimed at the years of my children's life spans. Because I am in relationship with the eternal God, my work has been aimed toward eternity. When I look, with gratitude, at the choices my sons are making in their late teens and early twenties, I understand a little bit of what it means to see my work *established*, as mentioned in the above verse. To establish something is to make it firm and secure, to place or settle it in a secure position or condition. As moms, that is the goal of our work.

No matter what stage of motherhood we're at or how many mistakes we've made, we can pray that God will help us focus our work of motherhood on eternity.

Father,
May we realize that the work we do today has an impact on eternity. Amen.

WORK

THE CROWD WAS LISTENING TO EVERYTHING JESUS SAID.
AND BECAUSE HE WAS NEARING JERUSALEM, HE TOLD A STORY
TO CORRECT THE IMPRESSION THAT THE KINGDOM OF GOD
WOULD BEGIN RIGHT AWAY. HE SAID, "A NOBLEMAN WAS CALLED AWAY TO A
DISTANT EMPIRE TO BE CROWNED KING AND THEN RETURN. BEFORE HE LEFT, HE
CALLED TOGETHER TEN SERVANTS AND GAVE THEM TEN POUNDS OF SILVER TO
INVEST FOR HIM WHILE HE WAS GONE."   *Luke 19:11-13*

*S*omething new jumped out at me when I read Jesus' parable of the king's servants today. I knew that the parable focused on three servants who had been
given money to invest. What I forgot was that money had been given to *ten* servants—not just three. Surprisingly, we never find out what happened to the
other seven.

In the parable, a nobleman informed ten servants that he was going away to be
crowned king, but that he would return. Before he left, he gave each of the servants some money to invest while he was gone. When the king returned, he summoned the servants and asked what they had done with his money. The parable
recounts that the first two who reported to him had invested the money and
gained a profit, but the third had kept it in secret because of his fear.

The whole point of investing is that we contribute money to make more
money. The *Dean Witter Guide to Personal Investing* reports that if a thirty-year-old
begins investing $150 a month at 10 percent interest, by the time he or she is
sixty-five, the investment will have grown to about $574,000. Sounds good!

As a follower of Christ, I too have been given resources to help build and ex-
pand God's Kingdom. God has blessed me with life, breath, energy, time, children, his Word, his church, his Spirit, gifts, meaningful work, and an income.
How am I managing those gifts? How am I contributing to those gifts? What kind
of return is God getting on his investment in me?

Father,
*We want to be faithful servants. Please help us to manage your resources well.
In Jesus' name, amen.*

WORK

GIVE HER THE REWARD SHE HAS EARNED, AND LET HER
WORKS BRING HER PRAISE AT THE CITY GATE.

Proverbs 31:31, NIV

*W*hat might a description for a mom look like if it appeared in a local newspaper?

> *Wanted: A creative and patient woman to be a cook, chaplain, good listener, fashion consultant, decorator, recreation expert, teacher, chauffeur, psychologist, nurse, artist, gardener, economist, communication advisor, entertainer, purchasing agent, lawyer, and accountant. No pay, but excellent benefits!*

Another job description of a mom is found in Proverbs 31, which points out both character qualities and actions of the mother it portrays. It's impossible for any of us to live up to the example of this woman (or composite of women), but the chapter definitely gives us helpful principles to inspire us.

We are encouraged to be

- *Merciful to the poor.* This woman doesn't shrink from helping others.
- *Observant.* Verse 27 informs us that she watches carefully all that goes on throughout her household.
- *Trustworthy.* Her family can rely on her character and integrity.
- *Helpful.* She opens her hands to the needy.
- *Energetic.* She plants her own garden; she quilts her own bedspread.
- *Reverent toward God.* She honors, obeys, and spends time with him.
- *Wise.* She gives instructions with kindness.
- *Dignified.* She is worthy of respect because her commitment to God lies at the foundation of everything she does.

Wow! This woman is worth so much that it's hard to put a price tag on her. Don't be intimidated by this woman, moms; be inspired! With God's help, we can each be a treasure to our family.

> *God,*
> *We sometimes feel overwhelmed with all our responsibilities. We could never attempt to be an effective mom without your help. May we stay close to you, finding strength and wisdom to meet each day. Amen.*

WORK

I HAVE BROUGHT YOU GLORY ON EARTH BY COMPLETING
THE WORK YOU GAVE ME TO DO. *John 17:4, NIV*

None of us is perfect, and no mom on earth will ever do a perfect job of mothering. But when you come to the end of your mothering days, will you feel that you have completed your tasks well? When Jesus was nearing the end of his time on earth, he didn't have regrets; rather, he spoke with confidence about completing God's work. What was God's work for Jesus, and how can we be sure that *we* are completing God's work in our mothering?

Jesus gave us a lifelong pattern to follow:

1. *He pointed people to God.* John 1:18 says, "No one has ever seen God. But his only Son, who is himself God, is near to the Father's heart; he has told us about him."
2. *He modeled justice, mercy, and humility.* Micah 6:8 states, "No, O people, the Lord has already told you what is good, and this is what he requires: to do what is right, to love mercy, and to walk humbly with your God."
3. *He made disciples.* He said, "Therefore, go and make disciples of all the nations, baptizing them in the name of the Father and the Son and the Holy Spirit. Teach these new disciples to obey all the commands I have given you. And be sure of this: I am with you always, even to the end of the age" (Matthew 28:19-20).
4. *He served through sacrifice.* Philippians 2:5-8 says, "Your attitude should be the same that Christ Jesus had. Though he was God, he did not demand and cling to his rights as God. He made himself nothing; he took the humble position of a slave and appeared in human form. And in human form he obediently humbled himself even further by dying a criminal's death on a cross."

God,
Thank you that Jesus was willing to do your work so we can have a relationship with you. Please strengthen us to do the most important work of motherhood by pointing our children to you; modeling mercy, justice, and humility; discipling our kids; and serving through sacrifice. Amen.

WORK

WORK HARD AND CHEERFULLY AT WHATEVER YOU DO, AS
THOUGH YOU WERE WORKING FOR THE LORD RATHER THAN
FOR PEOPLE.   *Colossians 3:23*

Three bricklayers were hired to help build St. Paul's Cathedral in London. A curious bystander approached them and asked what they were doing. The first bricklayer responded, "I'm laying bricks—I'm making money!" The second bricklayer said, "I'm laying bricks—I'm a third-generation bricklayer. My grandpa was a bricklayer, my dad was a bricklayer, and now I'm a bricklayer too!" The third bricklayer, who had the bigger picture in mind, stepped back, looked up, and responded, "I'm assisting Sir Christopher Wren in building a great cathedral!"

Perhaps some of us can relate to those bricklayers. If a bystander came along and asked us what we were doing, we could respond, "I'm changing diapers and feeding a baby." Or, "I'm driving my kids all over town to their activities!" But a mom who has the bigger picture in mind might reply, "I'm assisting God in raising a young man or a young woman who will grow up to love and obey him."

When we complain about the drudgery of changing diapers or chauffeuring kids across town, we may have lost sight of the bigger picture. Oh, that we could step back and say, "I'm assisting God in raising my child to be a future leader!"

Father,
It's easy to lose the big picture, especially on a hectic day. Please help us to honor you as we raise our children. In the strong name of Jesus, amen.

WORK

MOSES SUMMONED BEZALEL AND OHOLIAB AND EVERY
SKILLED PERSON TO WHOM THE LORD HAD GIVEN ABILITY
AND WHO WAS WILLING TO COME AND DO THE WORK.

Exodus 36:2, NIV

When I was reading through the book of Exodus, one of the themes that jumped out at me was excellence in work. God said to Moses, "I want the people of Israel to build me a sacred residence where I can live among them. You must make this Tabernacle and its furnishings exactly according to the plans I will show you" (Exodus 25:8-9).

God trusted humans with this exacting job, for which he gave them detailed directions. Here's an example of his instructions: "Make the Tabernacle from ten sheets of fine linen. These sheets are to be decorated with blue, purple, and scarlet yarn, with figures of cherubim skillfully embroidered into them" (Exodus 26:1).

God had gifted people with skills necessary for the job, and he asked Moses to enlist their help. God was looking for two things—*skill* and *a willing heart.*

Byron Janis, one of the outstanding concert pianists of this century, said: "I believe that anyone who does something well is an artist. I don't care whether they are a shoemaker, a plumber, or a chef. Doing something exceptionally well takes talent and love of what the person does as an artist."[1]

God has given each of us varied abilities. It's up to us to discipline ourselves so that those abilities can become skills, and then to offer those skills with willing hearts. As mothers we also have the opportunity to observe our children's abilities and provide guidance and encouragement for them to develop their God-given skills.

Father,
Thank you for the gifts and abilities you have given to us. Please help us work
to develop those gifts, being good examples of stewardship to our children.
Amen.

MIND

*I*n Old Testament times God's laws were written on stones, but the stones did not provide the power to live them out. God promised blessings to those who memorized God's words and taught them to their children, and the people who chose to do so experienced the wisdom and influence that his truth provides. But having God's truth written in their minds and hearts was not something humans could experience until Jesus provided a new covenant through his death on the cross.

Christian moms have a special understanding of this principle. We realize that it is our responsibility to teach our children God's Word and to guide them with God's principles. But as they grow older and mature, we pray that they will build a personal relationship with God, through Christ, so that his Spirit will write truth in their minds and hearts. A law from the outside may guide a person, but it can never *change* him or her. For our behavior to change, God's truth must become part of our inner life, and that can happen only when God's Spirit lives inside us.

This principle about heart change is illustrated in a story about two caterpillars crawling across the grass. When a butterfly flew over them, they looked up, and one nudged the other, saying, "You couldn't get me up in one of those things for a million dollars!" It took an internal change before the caterpillars could fly, and that's necessary for us too. Changes that could never happen from the outside begin to take place when God's laws are written on our minds and hearts!

Father,
Thank you that when we enter into a relationship with you through Jesus
Christ, your laws are written on our minds and in our hearts. Please help us to
be obedient to the promptings of your truth through the help of your Spirit.
Amen.

MIND

BUT PEOPLE WHO AREN'T CHRISTIANS CAN'T UNDERSTAND THESE TRUTHS FROM GOD'S SPIRIT. IT ALL SOUNDS FOOLISH TO THEM BECAUSE ONLY THOSE WHO HAVE THE SPIRIT CAN UNDERSTAND WHAT THE SPIRIT MEANS. WE WHO HAVE THE SPIRIT UNDERSTAND THESE THINGS, BUT OTHERS CAN'T UNDERSTAND US AT ALL. HOW COULD THEY? FOR, "WHO CAN KNOW WHAT THE LORD IS THINKING? WHO CAN GIVE HIM COUNSEL?" BUT WE CAN UNDERSTAND THESE THINGS, FOR WE HAVE THE MIND OF CHRIST.

1 Corinthians 2:14-16

Just as human ears cannot hear high-frequency sounds, the person who doesn't know Christ (even though he or she may be extremely intelligent and knowledgeable by human standards) cannot understand the wisdom of God. What a huge gift to know that after we trust Christ, we receive the mind of Christ! Having the mind of Christ doesn't mean that we are perfect—our children keep us humble and honest in that regard. Rather, having the mind of Christ means that we look at life from God's perspective, keeping in mind his truth, his values, and his desires. Through the Word of God, the Holy Spirit helps us think the way Jesus thinks. A song I learned in college is one I come back to frequently:

May the mind of Christ, my Savior,
Live in me from day to day,
By His love and pow'r controlling
All I do and say.

May the word of God dwell richly
In my heart from hour to hour,
So that all may see I triumph
Only through His pow'r.

May the peace of God my Father
Rule my life in ev'rything,
That I may be calm to comfort
Sick and sorrowing.

May the love of Jesus fill me
As the waters fill the sea;
Him exalting, self abasing—
This is victory.

May I run the race before me,
Strong and brave to face the foe,
Looking only unto Jesus
As I onward go.

May His beauty rest upon me
As I seek the lost to win,
And may they forget the channel,
Seeing only Him.[2]

God,
We are so rich because of all you have done for us. Thanks for the gift of your Word, which shows us what you are like. Thanks for the gift of your Spirit, who teaches us to think like you. Amen.

MIND

DON'T COPY THE BEHAVIOR AND CUSTOMS OF THIS WORLD,
BUT LET GOD TRANSFORM YOU INTO A NEW PERSON BY
CHANGING THE WAY YOU THINK.

Romans 12:2

*M*any years ago a famous plastic surgeon, Dr. Maxwell Maltz, wrote a best-selling book, *New Faces—New Futures*. It was a collection of case histories of people for whom facial plastic surgery had opened the door to a new life. The author's theme was that amazing personality changes can take place when a person's face is changed.

As the years went by, however, Dr. Maltz began to learn something else, not from his successes but from his failures. He began to observe patient after patient whose personality, even after facial plastic surgery, did not change. People who were now beautiful kept on acting the part of the ugly duckling. They acquired new faces but went on wearing the same old personalities.

"In 1960, Dr. Maltz wrote another best-seller, *Psycho-Cybernetics*. He was still trying to change people, not by correcting jutting jawbones or smoothing out scars, but by helping them change the pictures they had of themselves."[3]

A plastic surgeon can change the nature, form, or function of our nose, ears, or jaw, but only God can transform our minds. The English word *transform* is based on the word *metamorphosis*, meaning change from within. As we spend time in God's Word, his Holy Spirit changes us from within, giving us eternal perspective and a sense of great worth, meaning, and significance. As Warren Wiersbe says, "If the world controls your thinking, you are a conformer; if God controls your thinking, you are a transformer."[4]

Father,
Thank you for your Word. May we choose to spend great amounts of time in it so that with the help of your Spirit our minds will be transformed from the inside out. Amen.

Mind

SATAN, THE GOD OF THIS EVIL WORLD, HAS BLINDED THE
MINDS OF THOSE WHO DON'T BELIEVE, SO THEY ARE UNABLE
TO SEE THE GLORIOUS LIGHT OF THE GOOD NEWS THAT IS
SHINING UPON THEM. THEY DON'T UNDERSTAND THE MESSAGE WE PREACH ABOUT
THE GLORY OF CHRIST, WHO IS THE EXACT LIKENESS OF GOD.   *2 Corinthians 4:4*

God's Spirit and God's Word can bring the knowledge of salvation to a person who is not yet a believer. Most of us are aware of grandmas and grandpas, aunts, uncles, or neighbors who haven't yet seen the light of Christ. The most powerful thing we can do as believers is spend time praying that their *minds* will be opened to God's truth.

Here are some verses that we can pray for family and friends whom God brings to our attention:

Romans 8:6: "If your sinful nature controls your mind, there is death. But if the Holy Spirit controls your mind, there is life and peace."
Prayer: Father, please bring the influence of your Spirit into _____'s mind.

Ephesians 5:8: "For though your hearts were once full of darkness, now you are full of light from the Lord, and your behavior should show it!"
Prayer: Father, in the same way that you brought me from darkness to light, please shine your light into the mind of _____.

Ephesians 4:21-22: "Since you have heard all about him and have learned the truth that is in Jesus, throw off your old evil nature and your former way of life."
Prayer: Father, thank you that I have been a recipient of your truth. I pray that you will bring the light of your truth to _____, and that your Spirit will convince him or her that your Son Jesus is the way, the truth, and the life.

Father,
Thank you that your Word is powerful. Thank you that it lends authority to our prayers and to our children's prayers. Amen.

MIND

SET YOUR MINDS ON THINGS ABOVE, NOT ON EARTHLY
THINGS.   *Colossians 3:2, NIV*

*I*n an age when women have made amazing strides in every way, depression is
still a significant problem. In fact, about 75 percent of all antidepressant medications are prescribed for women. The mom who finds herself depressed can
choose various avenues for help. Seeing a physician might be a good place to start,
since clinical depression is different from feeling discouraged. God's Word is another resource that gives direction and hope. The Bible encourages us to be completely honest with God, and it also encourages us to live up to what Christ has
already done for us. Christ has made his children rich, and yet there are things we
sometimes do to sabotage that wealth.

In Colossians 3 we discover three steps toward a healthier mind: cleansing,
filling, and healing. Verses 5 and 8 tell us to get rid of sexual immorality, impurity, lust, evil desires, greed, anger, rage, malice, slander, and filthy language.
How? We begin by exposing our hearts to God, handing over to him the things
that shouldn't be there.

Getting rid of pollutants (whenever God's Spirit points them out) is only the
beginning. The created void must be filled with Christ, and he brings compassion, kindness, humility, gentleness, patience, forgiveness, love, peace, and
thankfulness (vv. 12-15). How do we acquire these? "Let the word of Christ
dwell in you richly" (Colossians 3:16, NIV). Just as our children need food—often!—to keep them growing, our minds and hearts need Christ through time in
his Word.

Healing begins as a result of being full of Christ. His perspectives start to become our perspectives, and we begin to see life differently. Over time, we realize that there's much more to life than just our anxieties. When we're filled with
Christ, we grow to be more thankful and hopeful women.

Father,
Thank you that we can come to you with our burdens and our cares. Thanks
for the help and hope that you have given us in your Word, which makes us
rich. As we set our minds on what's important to you, please help us to view
our concerns from a heavenly perspective. Amen.

MIND

THE WEAPONS WE FIGHT WITH ARE NOT THE WEAPONS
OF THE WORLD. ON THE CONTRARY, THEY HAVE DIVINE
POWER TO DEMOLISH STRONGHOLDS. WE DEMOLISH ARGUMENTS
AND EVERY PRETENSION THAT SETS ITSELF UP AGAINST THE KNOWLEDGE OF GOD,
AND WE TAKE CAPTIVE EVERY THOUGHT TO MAKE IT OBEDIENT TO CHRIST.

2 Corinthians 10:4-5, NIV

Since September 11, 2001, our nation takes weapons seriously. If you've ever been in line behind someone who tried to get through airport security with nail clippers or a pocketknife, you've probably observed that security workers are on the lookout for weapons of all kinds.

In Paul's encouragement to believers, he reminds us that the weapons we need to confront evil strongholds in our lives are not weapons that we see and carry. Our battles are fought in the human heart, and our mind is sometimes where the battle rages the hardest. Throughout the Bible we are encouraged to guard our minds and examine our thoughts. How many times do anger, fear, pride, or anxiety challenge us each day? Sometimes these thoughts creep into our minds like guerilla warriors, silently, quietly, almost imperceptibly. But there they are, waiting for an opportune moment to battle with our better intentions and defeat us from being Christlike.

Paul recognizes the great danger in entertaining thoughts from the enemy. He teaches us that we can use supernatural weapons—prayer, God's Word, and his divine power—to "demolish" strongholds. We are not left to fight these battles in our mind with weapons that can't do the job. What a gift God's weapons are!

*Lord Jesus, commander of the Lord's army,
I submit my mind to your Word and your authority today. Please fight and
win the battle on my behalf. In Jesus' name, amen.*

MIND

FOR HE ISSUED HIS DECREE TO JACOB; HE GAVE HIS LAW
TO ISRAEL. HE COMMANDED OUR ANCESTORS TO TEACH THEM
TO THEIR CHILDREN, SO THE NEXT GENERATION MIGHT KNOW THEM—
EVEN THE CHILDREN NOT YET BORN—THAT THEY IN TURN MIGHT TEACH
THEIR CHILDREN. SO EACH GENERATION CAN SET ITS HOPE ANEW ON GOD,
REMEMBERING HIS GLORIOUS MIRACLES AND OBEYING HIS COMMANDS.

Psalm 78:5-7

When I picked up my thesaurus and flipped to the word *mind*, I was surprised to find three different noun entries. They fell into the categories of intelligence, memory, and belief. In today's devotional, I'd like to focus on the memory aspect of our minds.

When we think of remembering, we often think of looking back to a special or difficult time, to a fact retained in our mind (like 2 + 2 = 4), or to treasured memories of a special person (such as a spouse or parent who might have died). Simply put, to remember is to recall. But here in Psalm 78, the word *remember* means much more than just recalling people, events, or ideas from the past. Tyndale's *Bible Dictionary* describes it as "living in the present in the light of God's past actions." What a huge thought!

When we experience challenges and difficulties in the present, we can be strengthened to face them by seeing how God provided for people in the past. If God could make the waters of the Red Sea stand up like walls (Psalm 78:13), if he could split open rocks in the wilderness to gush with water (v. 15), and if he could rain down bread from the heavens (v. 24), then certainly he can take care of me.

These few verses remind us why we share God's Word with our children—"so each generation can set its hope anew on God, remembering his glorious miracles and obeying his commands." It's no wonder that we read Bible stories of God's power and provision to our children over and over and over again!

Father,
Thank you that memories of your power and provision to people in the past help us to set our hope in you now. Please help us to teach them to our children too. In the name of Jesus, amen.

HEART

ABOVE ALL ELSE, GUARD YOUR HEART, FOR IT IS THE
WELLSPRING OF LIFE.   *Proverbs 4:23, NIV*

*W*hat is a *wellspring*? It is the source of a stream or a spring, the point where something springs into being, or the place where things are created. What a fitting picture of our hearts, where thoughts, attitudes, and actions are initiated. The verse above begins with a weighty warning. More than anything else, we must guard our hearts. Not coddle, pamper, or indulge—but *guard*. When I guard something, I protect it, watch over it, or take necessary precautions to keep it safe.

Our hearts determine our true character. Are we pursuing purity or evil? Are we headed toward maturity or rebellion? The Bible teaches us that the most important thing we can do is to love God with our *whole hearts*—which are undivided and fixed on Jesus. Then we must guard them. Notice the common thread in these verses:

> *Be careful then, dear brothers and sisters. Make sure that your own hearts are not evil and unbelieving, turning you away from the living God. (Hebrews 3:12)*

> *Draw close to God, and God will draw close to you. Wash your hands, you sinners; purify your hearts, you hypocrites. (James 4:8)*

> *Fix your thoughts on what is true and honorable and right. Think about things that are pure and lovely and admirable. Think about things that are excellent and worthy of praise. (Philippians 4:8)*

We guard our hearts by running *to* God and running *away* from sin. Then we have a wellspring full of good things!

> Father,
> May we take the warning of your Word seriously. You are gracious to fill and cleanse our hearts when we come to you, but we must make choices to run from sin. Thank you for your Holy Spirit, who helps us. Amen.

HEART

I PRAY THAT FROM HIS GLORIOUS, UNLIMITED RESOURCES
HE WILL GIVE YOU MIGHTY INNER STRENGTH THROUGH HIS
HOLY SPIRIT. AND I PRAY THAT CHRIST WILL BE MORE AND MORE
AT HOME IN YOUR HEARTS AS YOU TRUST IN HIM. MAY YOUR ROOTS GO DOWN
DEEP INTO THE SOIL OF GOD'S MARVELOUS LOVE.

Ephesians 3:16-17

What kind of heart do we choose to have? Physically speaking, we can't choose our hearts. We live with the heart we were born with, whether it is strong, weak, defective, or in good working condition. We can choose how we care for it, however. Spiritually speaking, we are all born with sinful hearts (Romans 3:23, NIV: "For all have sinned and fall short of the glory of God"). The good news is, we now have a choice about the kind of heart we would like to have.

Left on our own, our hearts are stubborn (see Jeremiah 3:17). In fact, the Bible likens us to sheep that have gone astray, thinking they can survive without a guide. How absurd. When a sheep refuses to follow the shepherd, setting out on his own, he invites all kinds of trouble upon himself—he doesn't know where the water is, he can't get rid of parasites, and he opens himself up to destruction by his predators.

If we don't want hearts that lead us into evil thoughts, lying, sexual immorality, or theft, we must choose to ask God to cleanse our hearts and fill them with the presence of his Spirit (see Romans 5:5). This happens from start to finish by *faith*. By faith we ask God to give us a new heart, and by faith we look to him each day, exposing hearts that would easily fall into dark things if not regularly brought into the light of God's truth.

Father,
Thank you that we have a choice about the kind of heart we want to have.
Thank you that you are willing to change us as we place our faith in you.
Help us to point our children's hearts toward you. Amen.

HEART

OTHER SEEDS FELL AMONG THORNS THAT SHOT UP AND
CHOKED OUT THE TENDER BLADES. . . . THE THORNY
GROUND REPRESENTS THOSE WHO HEAR AND ACCEPT THE GOOD
NEWS, BUT ALL TOO QUICKLY THE MESSAGE IS CROWDED OUT BY THE CARES OF
THIS LIFE AND THE LURE OF WEALTH, SO NO CROP IS PRODUCED.   *Matthew 13:7, 22*

*E*ach spring, my husband and I order four or five flats of impatiens, our favorite flowering annual. We wait for a sunny Saturday in May, and then our family plants them on the north side of our home, where we enjoy them until the first freeze of November.

Looking over our impatiens early this July morning, I noticed that the plants weren't thriving. As I bent down, I saw little clover-like weeds that had been winding their way around the flowers, hindering their growth. It was time to do some serious weeding. I know that weeding is necessary, but sometimes I get so busy with other things that I forget to do it.

As I pulled weeds today, I remembered an image Jesus used while teaching his disciples. He explained that weeds and thorns in our hearts choke out good things and pose a threat to righteous, fruitful living. I thought about my own heart. When I complain, I choke out contentment. When I worry, I choke out peace. When I judge, I choke out mercy. These weeds easily wind their way around my circumstances, and when they do, they hinder my growth and my effectiveness.

I'm grateful that God uses pictures of things I recognize—like weeds—to help me understand how he wants me to cultivate my heart. I'm grateful for the power of God's Word which, when obeyed, yields a harvest of good things—not weeds.

Father,
May your Word live in our hearts. Through your power, may we triumph over things that would choke out your truth. In Jesus' name, amen.

HEART

GOD BLESSES THOSE WHOSE HEARTS ARE PURE, FOR THEY
WILL SEE GOD.   *Matthew 5:8*

*G*od didn't say, "Blessed are the pure." He said, "Blessed are the pure *in heart*."
Back in New Testament times, the Pharisees were very conscious of *ceremonial*
purity but not as concerned with purity of the heart.

The Pharisees practiced ceremonial hand washings, not for reasons of personal cleanliness, but as extra traditions that they had added to their long list of
religious rules. These washings had begun as a reminder that the people were
Jews—God's elect—and they were to keep themselves separated from sin. But
over the years they had degenerated into a ritual that made the Pharisees haughty
and arrogant. The Pharisees had become so legalistic that they were more offended when Jesus' disciples ate a meal without first washing their hands than
they were when they observed injustice or oppression.

When we consider purity, we often think first of our outward behavior. But
in the Sermon on the Mount, Jesus made it clear that holiness and purity begin on
the inside. The way to begin is by taking a look at the attitudes and affections of
our hearts, and sometimes that's not an attractive sight. We all know that it's
possible to smile on the outside when our inner attitude doesn't match. We can
fool another person, but we can't fool God.

Ceremonial purity is no substitute for spiritual purity. The washing that God
wants to see is the washing of our hearts. First John 1:9 (NIV) promises, "If we
confess our sins, he is faithful and just and will forgive our sins and *purify* us
from all unrighteousness" (emphasis added).

Father,
May we stop pretending and be honest with ourselves and with you about our
inner attitudes. We want to focus on purity in our hearts each day, because
that's when we see you. Amen.

HEART

> MY HEART IS CONFIDENT IN YOU, O GOD; NO WONDER
> I CAN SING YOUR PRAISES!
>
> *Psalm 57:7*

*G*od has given us responsibility to choose what we invite into our hearts. We can choose to focus on God and take in messages of beauty, hope, joy, and courage. Or we can choose to take in messages of pessimism and cynicism. Whichever direction we lean will determine the type of heart we grow. Only a heart that trusts in God can praise him and reflect his glory to others.

God is the author of *beauty*. We see it each day, but we don't always notice it. We see it in flowers, snow, colors, the features of our child, or music. We have little opportunities to celebrate the beauty of God's creation each day.

God is the author of *hope*. As the classic hymn reminds me, "My hope is built on nothing less than Jesus' blood and righteousness."

God is the author of *joy*. "The joy of the Lord is your strength" (Nehemiah 8:10).

God is the author of *courage*. Psalm 27:14 (NIV) teaches, "Wait for the Lord; be strong and take heart and wait for the Lord." Courage is surrounded like two bookends by waiting on the Lord.

If we want to have full hearts for our families, we will frequently run to God, who is the source of beauty, hope, joy, and courage.

Father,
Thank you that you are the author of all these qualities of the heart. May you enlarge our hearts for the roles you have given us. Amen.

HEART

NOW IS THE TIME TO GET RID OF ANGER, RAGE, MALICIOUS
BEHAVIOR, SLANDER, AND DIRTY LANGUAGE. DON'T LIE TO
EACH OTHER, FOR YOU HAVE STRIPPED OFF YOUR OLD EVIL NATURE
AND ALL ITS WICKED DEEDS. IN ITS PLACE YOU HAVE CLOTHED YOURSELVES WITH A
BRAND-NEW NATURE THAT IS CONTINUALLY BEING RENEWED AS YOU LEARN MORE
AND MORE ABOUT CHRIST, WHO CREATED THIS NEW NATURE WITHIN YOU.

Colossians 3:8-10

I'm presently waging war on clutter in my house, though I fear that it's a lifetime battle. I'm trying to get rid of as much stuff as I can by giving away, throwing away, or putting away. As I stand back and look with satisfaction on each drawer, cabinet, or closet I've tackled, I feel more energized and less weighed down.

My clutter tends to accumulate as the result of unmade decisions or unrealistic expectations. For example, I might set some papers on my dining-room table, thinking, *I'll attend to them tonight*. But five days later, the papers are still there. Or I clip a recipe out of a magazine, thinking, *I'll try it this week*. But two weeks later, the recipe is still sitting on my kitchen counter.

Over the years, I've noticed a similar pattern with clutter in my heart. If I nurse a critical thought about a friend or family member, four days later it's often worse. Or if I rehearse in my mind how someone has hurt me, not choosing to deal with it and let go, I give bitterness an opportunity to grow. God's Word reminds me that I need a throwaway pile for these things, too.

I'm learning to see clutter as an enemy. Whether it's clutter in my house or clutter in my heart, I'm beginning to ask, "How much of this stuff can I get rid of?" Just as getting rid of clutter in my home makes my house more attractive, getting rid of clutter in my heart makes my life more attractive.

Father,
Thank you for giving us new hearts. Thank you that you continually renew our hearts as we get to know you better. In Christ's name, amen.

HEART

SLAVES, OBEY YOUR EARTHLY MASTERS WITH DEEP RESPECT
AND FEAR. SERVE THEM SINCERELY AS YOU WOULD SERVE
CHRIST. WORK HARD, BUT NOT JUST TO PLEASE YOUR MASTERS
WHEN THEY ARE WATCHING. AS SLAVES OF CHRIST, DO THE WILL OF GOD WITH
ALL YOUR HEART.

Ephesians 6:5-6

"[*Doing*] the will of God with all your heart" (v. 6) was the key to a slave's ability to persevere in difficult circumstances. Slaves' service was to be motivated not by their own feeble desires to please their masters, but by what was going on *in their hearts*—their desire to do God's will.

I regret occasions when my service has been motivated by desire for approval from other people. When I approach it with that objective, my efforts are not rewarded with God's approval. When Jesus was on earth, his ministry was an expression of who he was. He knew that he was going to die for people who rejected his acts of service. He left us a great example: serve freely to please God, not to please other people. "Jesus knew that he would soon be returning to his Father. Being assured of his own destiny, he focused his attention on the disciples and showed them what it meant for him to become their servant and for them to serve one another."[5]

For our hearts to be in the right place—for our headquarters and center of operations to function for God's Kingdom—we must do what Jesus did. He focused on his *origin* and his *destiny*. When we remember daily our sin (our origin), the blood that he shed for us, and that he is coming again to take us to our real home in heaven with him (our destiny), our hearts will want to serve him regardless of outer circumstances.

Jesus,
Thank you for your purity of heart. Thank you that although God's plan for you meant death on a cross, you chose to serve your Father. Please give us your strength so that as we serve our families, we will choose to serve you from our hearts. Amen.

PRAISE

I WILL PRAISE THE LORD AT ALL TIMES. I WILL CONSTANTLY
SPEAK HIS PRAISES. *Psalm 34:1*

*I*t's important for us to teach our children that worshipping God doesn't happen only on Sundays when we're sitting or singing in church. Praising God ought to happen throughout each day. Taking a walk in the spring and admiring the daffodils is an experience that prompts our praise, whether we do it at that moment or wait until bedtime to talk to God.

My eleven-year-old and I praised God one night when we received happy news of another cousin born into the family. When we visited the new baby and parents in Des Moines, Iowa, it was a worshipful experience for me. Holding a new baby in my arms is always cause for praise that God continues the cycle of life.

Reading a book about the universe together with a child is another experience that stimulates our praise. A book I enjoyed reading with my children was *Spinning Worlds*—a child's guide to God's creation in the heavens. Does your child know that:

- God covered the earth with a substance not found anywhere else in the whole solar system (liquid water)?
- One million earths could fit inside the sun?
- God made the sun the perfect distance from the earth, so that it gives us just the right amounts of heat and light? If it were closer, we would die from heat; if it were farther away, we'd perish from the cold.

If we regularly praise God for his creation and provisions, our example may prompt our children to do the same.

> *Father,*
> *Throughout the day, as we notice something that you made or something you have done, may we remember to praise you for it. Amen.*

PRAISE

O LORD, OUR LORD, THE MAJESTY OF YOUR NAME FILLS
THE EARTH! YOUR GLORY IS HIGHER THAN THE HEAVENS.

Psalm 8:1

Imagine that you are the creator and founder of a large catering company. Not only did you form the company, but you personally crafted all the recipes being prepared and served. You selected, hired, and trained the entire staff, teaching them exactly how the food should be prepared and how the company should operate. Your company is such a success that you have been invited to prepare and serve the food at a convention.

As your staff serves the food, everyone exclaims how delicious and well-presented the meal is. In the conversation after the meal, all the ingredients are analyzed and the methods of preparation discussed, but no one ever acknowledges you as the creator, developer, and overseer of the company. You leave the event without having been recognized or affirmed by anyone—even your own staff! You would likely feel hurt or unappreciated.

I sometimes wonder if that's the way God feels when we go to the zoo and see all the animals he has created but forget to acknowledge him. I wonder how God feels when we walk outside late at night to observe the heavens, admiring the beauty of the moon and stars, but forget to praise him for designing and sustaining such beauty and glory. The next time we're admiring some of God's creation with our children, let's be sure to call attention to the Creator and give honor to him.

Father,
May we not be slow to see and praise your handiwork as we encounter it many times throughout each day. Amen.

PRAISE

PRAISE THE LORD! HOW GOOD IT IS TO SING PRAISES TO
OUR GOD! HOW DELIGHTFUL AND HOW RIGHT!   *Psalm 147:1*

I've been reading a lot about heaven recently. Consequently, I've also been reading about praise, because that's what happens continuously in heaven—now and forever. Sometimes I think of heaven as an escape from pain, disappointment, frustrating work, or stressful schedules, and I am thankful that we'll be done with all of the above when we get there. But heaven is much more than deliverance from problems—we'll be in God's presence and will enjoy and praise him forever. Forever is a very long time. I remember trying to understand the word *eternity* as a child and getting quite frustrated. Each time I thought about it, I'd think to myself, *There has to be an end!* But there isn't.

If I'm going to praise God continuously in heaven, I need more practice doing it here on earth. In my devotional time one morning, I read Psalm 150:1-6:

> *Praise the Lord! Praise God in his heavenly dwelling; praise him in his mighty heaven! Praise him for his mighty works; praise his unequaled greatness! Praise him with a blast of the trumpet; praise him with the lyre and harp! Praise him with the tambourine and dancing; praise him with stringed instruments and flutes! Praise him with a clash of cymbals; praise him with loud clanging cymbals. Let everything that lives sing praises to the Lord! Praise the Lord!*

After reading this psalm, I was prompted to do two things. The first was to read the verse about praising God with the sound of the trumpet to my eleven-year-old son, who was going to be playing his trumpet in band that day. The second was to take a walk outside after the children left for school and, while I walked, praise God. By the time I arrived back home, my heart was joyful, and I realized that praising God makes us feel full of him—as we *always* will in heaven!

> *God of forever,*
> *We have so much to praise you for. May we practice praising you regularly on earth since we will be doing it forever in heaven. Amen.*

PRAISE

PRAISE THE LORD. PRAISE THE LORD, O MY SOUL.
I WILL PRAISE THE LORD ALL MY LIFE; I WILL SING PRAISE
TO MY GOD AS LONG AS I LIVE.   *Psalm 146:1-2, NIV*

Whenever I read or recite Psalm 146, my memory wanders back to the summer of 2003. I was staying in Orlando, Florida, with my husband, Jim, where he was attending a convention. Early each morning when Jim left the hotel room for meetings, I took a long walk up and down International Boulevard.

Before walking the first morning, I read Psalm 146. The first two verses reminded me of my brother-in-law, David, who was losing his battle with cancer. Humanly speaking, David didn't seem to have much time left. As I pondered his situation, the idea of praising God as long as I live took on new meaning.

While I reflected on the psalm, an idea came to mind. Since Psalm 146 contained ten verses and I was staying in Orlando for ten days, I'd memorize one verse of the psalm each morning while I was out walking. That worked well, and in the process I discovered something new about myself: I memorize better when I'm walking than I do when I'm sitting still.

I still meditate on Psalm 146 (NIV) sometimes. And when I ponder verse 9 ("The Lord . . . sustains the fatherless and the widow") my eyes get misty. I grieve that David is no longer with us on earth, but I also praise God for the many ways he has taken care of David's wife, Joan, and her three children since David's death. "Praise the Lord, O my soul!

Father,
Thank you that we see your greatness in the way you care for us. Help us
choose to praise you every day of our lives. Amen.

PRAISE

O LORD, WHAT A VARIETY OF THINGS YOU HAVE MADE!
IN WISDOM YOU HAVE MADE THEM ALL. THE EARTH IS FULL
OF YOUR CREATURES.

Psalm 104:24

*E*arly this morning I praised God while I watched a sand crab. I had just completed an early morning walk along the oceanfront where my family is vacationing, and as I was sitting in the sand, I noticed some movement out of the corner of my eye. Looking closer, I discovered a sand crab about four or five inches in diameter with two beady eyes sticking up from the rest of its body. The crab came up out of its hole, pushed some sand out, and then sat there awhile looking at me, eventually going back underground. The routine was repeated several more times until I got up to leave.

As I watched the sand crab, I thought about how many fascinating creatures God has created. Since I am a finite creature, I can only be in one place at a time to enjoy his creation. The creatures I could see this morning included sand crabs, jellyfish, and seagulls. But God is omnipresent, able to be everywhere at once, so he can see all the creatures in the world at the same time!

When I praise God for how wonderful and big he is, my perspective changes. I'm reminded how dependent I am on him, and I'm also reminded that if he is big enough to have created and sustained the sand crab in Gulf Shores, Alabama; the giraffe in Tanzania; and the panda in China, he's big enough to take care of me.

God,
Thank you that you can be everywhere at once, watching over all your
creation, and still care about us and our families. We're encouraged to run to
you anytime, anywhere. Amen.

PRAISE

AFTER THIS I SAW A VAST CROWD, TOO GREAT TO COUNT,
FROM EVERY NATION AND TRIBE AND PEOPLE AND LANGUAGE,
STANDING IN FRONT OF THE THRONE AND BEFORE THE LAMB.
THEY WERE CLOTHED IN WHITE AND HELD PALM BRANCHES IN THEIR HANDS. AND
THEY WERE SHOUTING WITH A MIGHTY SHOUT, "SALVATION COMES FROM OUR
GOD ON THE THRONE AND FROM THE LAMB!"

Revelation 7:9-10

My husband, Jim, is grateful for the opportunity to travel to various parts of the world on business. Over the years, he has taken our sons along on some of his trips to enjoy father-son bonding times. Recently he took our youngest son, Jordan, to New York City. After completing business on Friday afternoon, they stayed over for the weekend and did some sightseeing, including visits to a NY Mets game, Wall Street, the Statue of Liberty, and more. For Sunday worship, they chose to visit the Brooklyn Tabernacle, and here's how Jim described the experience:

Thirty minutes before the service began, the Tabernacle filled with joyful people of many different nationalities—Chinese, African-Americans, Latinos, Greeks, and white Anglo Saxons, among others. Some looked wealthy, some looked impoverished, some looked healthy, and some looked disabled. They all looked like they were there to worship the Sovereign Lord.

As the worship progressed, I was struck by how this throng of people hints at what we will experience in heaven. There will be people there from every nation, but we will all be together worshipping the Lord and praising the name of Jesus Christ.

God doesn't care about our ancestry, our nationality, our health, or our wealth. He has provided redemption for all who place their faith in Christ for salvation.

Lord,
We praise you that you have given your salvation to people from every part of the world. Thank you that you didn't entrust it only to the wealthy, or the powerful, or to a certain race or nationality. Thank you that you have given it to all who place their faith in the completed work of your Son, Jesus Christ. Amen.

PRAISE

LET THE NAME OF THE LORD BE PRAISED, BOTH NOW AND
FOREVERMORE. FROM THE RISING OF THE SUN TO THE PLACE
WHERE IT SETS, THE NAME OF THE LORD IS TO BE PRAISED.

Psalm 113:2-3, NIV

I'm not real great with geography, but when I check into a hotel that has clocks on the wall showing the time in different countries of the world, I'm fascinated. I also enjoy looking at my world atlas and realizing that when it's 6 AM in Chicago, it's 7 PM in Singapore and 9 PM in Sydney, Australia.

One of the pastors in my church was extending the call to worship in a Sunday morning service recently. After he read Psalm 113:2-3, he pointed out that because the sun is always rising somewhere over the earth each hour, God is receiving praise from his people constantly! I get goose bumps just thinking about that. First someone worships God in Nairobi, then London, then Rio de Janeiro, then New York, then Chicago, and the list of cities continues, as does the praise. Of course, the angels praise God without end in heaven.

Martin Marty writes, "Christians are not the only people who can bring some justice into the world. They are not the only people who can add to the world's art or philosophy. They are not the only people who put out newsletters and go to committee meetings and play in bowling leagues. But they are the only ones who praise Jesus Christ."[6]

Praise is unique to Christians, and as long as we have breath we are privileged to be able to praise God!

Father,
I want to praise you more—both when I'm alone and when I'm with my children. Help me to see each day as a new opportunity to worship you. Amen.

INTEGRITY

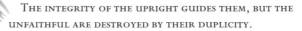

THE INTEGRITY OF THE UPRIGHT GUIDES THEM, BUT THE
UNFAITHFUL ARE DESTROYED BY THEIR DUPLICITY.

Proverbs 11:3, NIV

When I picked up this morning's newspaper, my eyes were drawn to the picture of an old schoolhouse sitting in the middle of a wide-open prairie. The article underneath the picture explained that a well-known journalist had purchased the little schoolhouse and the surrounding land for his mistress of twenty-nine years. During those twenty-nine years, he also had a wife at home on the other side of the continent. Upon becoming seriously ill, he wrote a letter to his mistress saying that if he died he wanted her to have the schoolhouse and the land. After the journalist's death, this property led to a confrontation between two women he probably hoped would never meet, and the court ended up awarding the contested land and schoolhouse to the journalist's wife.

This man left behind a reputation as a fine journalist, but double-mindedness in his private life added a bitter footnote to his character. After reading the article, I picked up my Bible and opened to the scheduled reading for the day, which included the above verse from Proverbs. Once again I was reminded that God's Word brings truth and purity to our innermost being.

As mothers, we want to be more like Christ; duplicity is not the kind of example we want for our children. Do our kids see us speaking and dealing honestly? Being loyal in our relationships? Saying what we mean and meaning what we say? When we choose integrity, we grow to be women who are whole and undivided. When we choose integrity, we choose a good path—both for ourselves and for our children.

Father,
May we be sensitive to the truth of your Word and the power of your Spirit, so
that we choose to live a life of integrity in front of you and in front of our
children. Amen.

INTEGRITY

SLAVES MUST OBEY THEIR MASTERS AND DO THEIR BEST TO
PLEASE THEM. THEY MUST NOT TALK BACK OR STEAL, BUT THEY
MUST SHOW THEMSELVES TO BE ENTIRELY TRUSTWORTHY AND GOOD.
THEN THEY WILL MAKE THE TEACHING ABOUT GOD OUR SAVIOR ATTRACTIVE
IN EVERY WAY.

Titus 2:9-10

I cannot begin to imagine the hatred, bitterness, and resentment that must have surfaced in the lives of slaves throughout history—hatred for poor treatment, bitterness over separation from family, resentment about lost rights. One of the precious few freedoms a slave possessed was the ability to choose how he or she was going to respond.

Back in the Old Testament book of 2 Kings, we read of an Israelite slave girl who lived out her integrity in a difficult and challenging situation. The girl had been taken captive—kidnapped during a raid—and now served Naaman, a commander of the army of Aram. Naaman was a very influential man, but he had leprosy. The young slave girl told Naaman's wife, "If only my master would see the prophet who is in Samaria [Elisha]! He would cure him of his leprosy" (5:3, NIV). And if you read the story, that's exactly what happened!

Warren Wiersbe describes the Jewish girl's situation: "Even though she was far from home, she did not forget her God and she was quick to witness of his great power. Had she not been a faithful worker in the house, she would not have been an effective witness, but because of her faithfulness, her witness was rewarded."[7]

Are you in the middle of a situation that prompts feelings of hatred, bitterness, or resentment because your circumstances feel unjust? Like the little slave girl, you can choose the path of integrity and beautify the truth of the Bible, even in the midst of a tough situation.

Father,
Sometimes we get stuck in angry emotions. Our hearts need the healing of your strength and grace. Please help us to make choices of integrity, beautifying your truth and expanding your kingdom of life and light to those who have not yet experienced it. Amen.

INTEGRITY

I love to walk. While I'm out walking, I often observe some interesting things. One day I came face-to-face with a fox. Since I froze, I was thankful that the fox ran off. Another day I encountered a family of ducks that included five new ducklings.

Recently I walked by a church whose parking lot signs gave conflicting messages. As I entered the driveway, a street sign read ONE WAY ONLY. But as I looked down at the pavement under my feet, I saw two distinct lanes, one with an arrow pointing toward me and one with an arrow pointing away. I tried to figure out what the signs meant, but I couldn't. I will leave that for brighter minds than mine.

I left the church wondering how many other people had been confused. I also wondered how many times my life has sent mixed messages to my children. I teach them that God wants us to show love to one another, but I criticize another person. I encourage my children to be patient with a friend, but I get impatient with my kids.

I'm grateful for God's truth, which makes the path of integrity clear. I'm also grateful for God's grace, which offers me forgiveness and redirection when I get off on the wrong path. I don't want my children to be perplexed by conflicting signs in my life. I want to walk clearly on the path of integrity.

Father,
We want to be moms of integrity. Please help us not to send mixed signals to
our children. In Jesus' name, amen.

INTEGRITY

WHY WORRY ABOUT A SPECK IN YOUR FRIEND'S EYE WHEN
YOU HAVE A LOG IN YOUR OWN? *Matthew 7:3*

Reputation is what men and women think of us; character is what God and the angels know of us.

Thomas Paine

The story is told of a prosperous young Wall Street broker who fell in love with an actress who was beautiful, talented, and dignified. He wanted to propose to her, but because he was a cautious man, he decided that before asking her to marry him he should hire a private investigator. He wanted to see if there was anything in her past or present that might threaten his fortune or harm his reputation. He made it clear to the investigator that his actress friend should not be informed about the investigation. When the report came back, it said that the actress had a fine reputation and that she chose friends of quality. The report concluded, "The only shadow is that she is often seen around town in the company of a young broker of dubious business practices and principles."

Maybe the actress should have hired the investigator! This story illustrates the importance of looking at our own hearts before we judge others. It's easy to busy ourselves with someone else's problem or flaw and ignore our own. Jesus never said there is anything wrong with careful discernment, but he said discernment must always begin with looking inside ourselves.

Father,
Forgive us for looking first to the problems in another person's life. May we look first to our own hearts with honesty and humility. Amen.

INTEGRITY

RIGHTEOUSNESS GUARDS THE MAN OF INTEGRITY, BUT
WICKEDNESS OVERTHROWS THE SINNER. *Proverbs 13:6, NIV*

*P*eople who are full of integrity are full of honesty, sincerity, and singleness of purpose. What prompts a person to have integrity, and what prohibits a person from living with integrity? Let's take a look at two of the words in the verse above: *righteousness* and *wickedness*.

Our natural bent is toward wickedness. Romans 3:10 reminds us, "As the Scriptures say, 'No one is good—not even one.'" Further down in Romans 3, we learn that the path to righteousness is not found by observing a law or moral code. Jesus had strong words for the Pharisees, people who were compulsive about following laws and codes: "You Pharisees are so careful to clean the outside of the cup and the dish, but inside you are still filthy—full of greed and wickedness" (Luke 11:39).

How do we get rid of the wickedness inside us so we can live in righteousness and integrity? The remedy is found in a relationship: "This righteousness from God comes through faith in Jesus Christ to all who believe" (Romans 3:22, NIV). The blood of Jesus poured out on the cross for us is what makes righteousness possible—we trade our unrighteousness for his righteousness. And the whole process is done by faith, from start to finish. Just as we are declared righteous when we first put our faith in Christ, we live righteously by doing the same thing. The path to integrity is found through faith in Christ.

Pray this verse for yourself and those you love:

> *"And this is my prayer: that your love may abound more and more in knowledge and depth of insight, so that you may be able to discern what is best and may be pure and blameless until the day of Christ,* filled with the fruit of righteousness that comes through Jesus Christ—*to the glory and praise of God"* (Philippians 1:9-11, NIV, emphasis added).

INTEGRITY

PEOPLE WITH INTEGRITY HAVE FIRM FOOTING, BUT THOSE
WHO FOLLOW CROOKED PATHS WILL SLIP AND FALL.

Proverbs 10:9

A person of integrity is honest, sincere, and consistent. In contrast, dishonest people take crooked paths and live in fear of being found out.

Relationships thrive on integrity. In a marriage where both husband and wife are people of integrity, there is security. Children who are blessed with parents of integrity feel secure. Security is a by-product of integrity both for ourselves and for our children.

Unfortunately, the opposite is also true. Marriages that lack integrity lack security, as is the case for children who can't trust their parents. When a person is dishonest, he or she is looking to gain an advantage by disorienting or distracting another person. Although dishonest people might think they are *gaining* something, they are actually *losing* something very valuable—trust. "It takes very little misinformation to disorient and destroy a relationship. . . . If I gave a person detailed instructions on how to go from Atlanta to New York City, and I threw in only one left turn that was a lie, they would end up in Oklahoma."⁸

Most of us have heard enough life stories to know that a lack of integrity causes untold pain in any family relationship. If our family of origin modeled integrity, we have been blessed. If not, we have the privilege of choosing a different path and modeling integrity for the next generation. Spending time in God's Word and opening our hearts to his truth will guide us in our choices to take paths that are straight, not crooked.

Father,
Please help me to be a woman who lives out your truth. I want to take straight paths. Amen.

INTEGRITY

YOU CAN BE SURE THAT NO IMMORAL, IMPURE, OR
GREEDY PERSON WILL INHERIT THE KINGDOM OF CHRIST
AND OF GOD. FOR A GREEDY PERSON IS REALLY AN IDOLATER
WHO WORSHIPS THE THINGS OF THIS WORLD. DON'T BE FOOLED BY THOSE WHO
TRY TO EXCUSE THESE SINS, FOR THE TERRIBLE ANGER OF GOD COMES UPON ALL
THOSE WHO DISOBEY HIM. DON'T PARTICIPATE IN THE THINGS THESE PEOPLE DO.
FOR THOUGH YOUR HEARTS WERE ONCE FULL OF DARKNESS, NOW YOU ARE FULL
OF LIGHT FROM THE LORD, AND YOUR BEHAVIOR SHOULD SHOW IT! FOR THIS
LIGHT WITHIN YOU PRODUCES ONLY WHAT IS GOOD AND RIGHT AND TRUE.

Ephesians 5:5-9

The only time I see lizards is when I travel. In Florida, I've seen common lizards running in and out of bushes near a swimming pool. In the Virgin Islands, I once saw an eighteen-inch iguana roaming the property where we stayed.

As a child, I was fascinated to learn about chameleons. They are a specialized group of tree-living lizards, and their eighty-five or so species reside mostly in Africa and Asia. Perhaps the most interesting thing about chameleons is their ability to change the color of their skin—usually for camouflage purposes. Camouflage makes it possible for a chameleon to stalk its prey, and it also helps it hide from its predators. Camouflage—the practice of disguising, hiding, or deceiving—is a valuable asset for the chameleon. For the Christian, though, camouflage is a problem.

Ephesians 5:6 cautions us about human chameleons who are pretending to be Christians when it warns us not to be fooled by those who try to excuse sexual immorality, impurity, or greed. The passage goes on to explain that before we know Christ, our hearts are full of darkness. But when we come to know Christ, our hearts are full of the Lord's light, and our behavior should make that clear.

Discussing the chameleon's behavior with our children provides a teachable moment. Our behavior as Christians must reflect God's gracious presence in our lives. Camouflage is not for Christians; camouflage is for chameleons.

God,
You alone have the power to bring us out of darkness and into the light.
Please help us not to be fooled into excusing dark behavior in our lives. We
need your wisdom and help. In Jesus' name, amen.

BODY

THEN HE TOOK THE CHILDREN INTO HIS ARMS AND PLACED
HIS HANDS ON THEIR HEADS AND BLESSED THEM.   *Mark 10:16*

*T*he word *hand* (or *hands*) appears about 1,800 times in our Bible and suggests images of both power and grace, blessing and curse. When Jesus lived on earth, his hands performed constant acts of love and service. With his hands he blessed children, touched and healed the eyes of a blind man, and broke loaves of bread for the hungry. Ultimately, it was into God's hands that Jesus committed his spirit as he hung on the cross, and after his resurrection he ascended to heaven, where he sits at God's right hand. Some hands mentioned in the Bible are not spoken of so kindly. Psalm 9:16 (NIV) states, "The wicked are ensnared by the work of their hands." It was by the hands of Judas that Jesus was betrayed.

A mother's hands cuddle a baby, wipe away a toddler's tear, or hold a child's Bible while reading the story of Daniel at bedtime. As the years pass, those same hands clap and cheer at ballgames or recitals, prepare pizza for a birthday party, or fold in prayer as she pours out to God her deep concerns for a child's thoughts, choices, and character.

Our hands can be instruments that help or hinder a child's life. Through our reliance on God, obedience, and good choices, our hands can bless others and contribute to the growth of God's kingdom in the lives of our families.

> *Take my hands, Lord Jesus, let them work for you;*
> *Make them strong and gentle, kind in all I do.*
> *Let me watch you, Jesus, till I'm gentle too,*
> *Till my hands are kind hands, quick to work for you.*[9] *Amen.*

BODY

> HOW BEAUTIFUL ON THE MOUNTAINS ARE THE FEET OF
> THOSE WHO BRING GOOD NEWS OF PEACE AND SALVATION,
> THE NEWS THAT THE GOD OF ISRAEL REIGNS!   *Isaiah 52:7*

This verse from Isaiah is the text for one of my favorite soprano solos from Handel's *Messiah*: "How beautiful are the feet of them that preach the gospel of peace, and bring glad tidings of good things."

This peace includes the idea of harmony between God and man, healing of the soul, and the blessings of walking with God. When a person brings peace (or *shalom*) to another, even her *feet* are beautiful! How do we keep our feet on a straight path so we can experience peace within our souls and then point our children toward healing and blessing? By following God's Word.

Psalm 119, the longest chapter in the Bible, contains 176 verses. All but five verses speak about God's Word. The message of the psalm is that if we have God's Word, we have everything we need for life and godliness. Why? Through the revelation of the New Testament we know it's because God's Word points to Christ.

Three of the chapter's verses speak of feet:

Verse 59 (NIV): "I have considered my ways and have turned my steps to your statutes."

Verse 101 (NIV): "I have kept my feet from every evil path so that I might obey your word."

Verse 105 (NIV): "Your word is a lamp to my feet and a light for my path."

If we want peace for our souls, and if we want to be the bearer of good news for our children and others around us, we must begin by spending time in God's Word.

> Father,
> Thank you for your Word that keeps our feet going in the right direction and allows us to share your good news with others. Amen.

BODY

EVIL WORDS DESTROY. GODLY SKILL REBUILDS.

Proverbs 11:9, TLB

*I*n the country church of a small village, an altar boy serving the priest at Sunday Mass accidentally dropped the cruet of wine. The village priest struck the altar boy sharply on the cheek and in a gruff voice shouted, "Leave the altar and don't come back!" The boy, Tito, became the Communist leader of Yugoslavia. In the cathedral of a large city, an altar boy serving the bishop at Sunday Mass accidentally dropped the cruet of wine. With a warm twinkle in his eyes the bishop gently whispered, "Someday you will be a priest." That boy grew up to become Archbishop Fulton Sheen. Oh, the power of words, be they written or spoken.[1]

Proverbs 11:9 points out the huge contrast between destruction and rebuilding. Our mouths can destroy, ruin, tear down, do away with—or they can rebuild, form, develop, establish, and strengthen.

When I was in junior high and high school, I studied violin with Perry Crafton, a violinist in the Chicago Symphony Orchestra. During one of my lessons, one of his fellow symphony players stopped by. Looking at me, Mr. Crafton's friend asked, "So, does she play well?" "She not only plays well, but she has an excellent sense of pitch," Perry responded. As you can imagine, I felt affirmed. Now that I'm in my fifties, I still feel encouraged by what he said.

Throughout each day we use our mouths to speak many words to our children. Are we destroying and tearing down, or building and strengthening?

Father,
Forgive me for the times when the words from my mouth have been destructive.
Please help everything I say to be affirming so that my children and others
around me will be strengthened and built up. Amen.

BODY

FOR FROM WITHIN, OUT OF A PERSON'S HEART, COME EVIL
THOUGHTS, SEXUAL IMMORALITY, THEFT, MURDER,
ADULTERY, GREED, WICKEDNESS, DECEIT, EAGERNESS FOR
LUSTFUL PLEASURE, ENVY, SLANDER, PRIDE, AND FOOLISHNESS. ALL THESE VILE
THINGS COME FROM WITHIN; THEY ARE WHAT DEFILE YOU AND MAKE YOU
UNACCEPTABLE TO GOD.

Mark 7:21-23

*D*id you know that our hearts push blood around our bodies in a complete circuit more than one thousand times every day? The heart is very complex, beating every minute of every day and night for as long as we live. This small organ, which is really a muscle, keeps our life going by pumping blood that's needed for each part of our body.

The right atrium of our heart receives *dark* blood, which is filled with waste (carbon dioxide) from other parts of our body. It is then pushed into the right ventricle, which pumps it into the lungs, where it receives fresh oxygen. The blood returns to the left atrium and flows to the left ventricle, which pumps the fresh *red* blood throughout the whole body. Then the process repeats.

Just as our physical hearts are involved in cleansing our blood from the waste and impurity of carbon dioxide, our spiritual hearts need to be cleansed from sin. God knows exactly what our hearts are like—dark without his presence and his transforming power. That's the reason Jesus came to earth—to die for our sin.

In the same way that blood moves around our physical bodies, giving oxygen to each body part and collecting impurities, so must the blood of Jesus Christ cleanse our souls, daily bringing the life of the Spirit to each part of our lives and getting rid of the impurities. We must expose our hearts to God regularly and ask him to fill them. The only thing that can cleanse our hearts from sin is the blood of Jesus.

> *What can wash away my sin?*
> *Nothing but the blood of Jesus.*
> *What can make me whole again?*
> *Nothing but the blood of Jesus.*
> *Oh! Precious is the flow*
> *That makes me white as snow;*
> *No other fount I know,*
> *Nothing but the blood of Jesus.*[2]

BODY

You made all the delicate, inner parts of my body
and knit me together in my mother's womb. Thank you
for making me so wonderfully complex! Your workman-
ship is marvelous—and how well I know it.   *Psalm 139:13-14*

*S*kateboarding down the cul-de-sac in front of our home, my ten-year-old son was enjoying a warm, sunny morning of vacation from school. When I heard one of those awful screams that a mother knows means something serious, I bolted outside and found Jordan lying in the middle of the street. He had experienced a freak fall off his skateboard, and although we didn't know it at the time, his left femur (the largest bone in the body) had horizontally snapped in two.

After a ride to the hospital in an ambulance, X-rays, and a visit by the orthopedic surgeon, Jordan had surgery to place two rods vertically through his broken femur, holding the pieces in place. Jordan's leg mended, and in the process I learned a lot about how God made the body.

After a bone breaks, an intricate process begins. "Excited repair cells invade in swarm. Within two weeks a cartilage-like sheath called callus surrounds the region and cement-laying cells enter the jellied mass. These cells are the osteoblasts, the pothole-fillers of the bone."[3] Two or three months later, a mass of new bone bulges over both sides of the broken ends of the fracture, looking like a spliced garden hose. As healing takes place, the new growth is smoothed out and the final result closely resembles the original bone.

Until that summer, I had never thought to thank God for the way he designed our bones!

> *Father,*
> *As St. Augustine said, "Men go abroad to wonder at the height of mountains, at the huge waves of the sea, at the long courses of the rivers, at the vast compass of the ocean, at the circular motion of the stars; and they pass by themselves without wondering." Thank you that we are so fearfully and wonderfully made! Amen.*

BODY

JUST AS OUR BODIES HAVE MANY PARTS AND EACH PART
HAS A SPECIAL FUNCTION, SO IT IS WITH CHRIST'S BODY. WE
ARE ALL PARTS OF HIS ONE BODY, AND EACH OF US HAS
DIFFERENT WORK TO DO. AND SINCE WE ARE ALL ONE BODY IN CHRIST, WE
BELONG TO EACH OTHER, AND EACH OF US NEEDS ALL THE OTHERS.   *Romans 12:4-5*

If you had the opportunity to read yesterday's devotional, you'll recall how much I learned about bones as a result of my son's skateboarding accident. The way God created our bodies to function is truly amazing. The way God created his church body to function is also amazing, which was another thing I learned after Jordan's accident. When my husband and I became members of College Church in Wheaton less than one week before the incident, we had no idea how much love and support our family would soon receive.

Several hours after Jordan crashed on his skateboard and was admitted to Central DuPage Hospital, our senior pastor made a visit, and for each of the next five days, various pastors from the church stopped by. Jordan received more than fifty cards, many from our church family. Interestingly enough, when he cleaned out his closet this year at the age of seventeen, he still wanted to save all those cards! Our church friends prayed, stopped by with delicious meals, and called on the phone to check up on Jordan. One family even loaned us a hospital bed for the next month while Jordan was unable to go up and down the stairs.

I'll never forget the way people in my church responded to our needs. As a result of their love, we felt a keen sense of belonging to the body of Christ. We've also discovered a sense of belonging that comes with serving others in the body of Christ. God's designs for his church are wonderful evidences of his care for us.

Father,
Thanks for times when others in your body have reached out to us. Please help us to serve you eagerly by reaching out to others. In Jesus' name, amen.

BODY

THERE IS A SPECIAL REST STILL WAITING FOR THE PEOPLE OF
GOD. FOR ALL WHO ENTER INTO GOD'S REST WILL FIND REST
FROM THEIR LABORS, JUST AS GOD RESTED AFTER CREATING THE WORLD.
LET US DO OUR BEST TO ENTER THAT PLACE OF REST. FOR ANYONE WHO DISOBEYS
GOD, AS THE PEOPLE OF ISRAEL DID, WILL FALL.

Hebrews 4:9-11

When one of our sons wrote a report about the Ten Commandments during high school, my husband noticed that something was curiously missing—the fourth commandment: "Remember the Sabbath day by keeping it holy" (Exodus 20:8, NIV). Jim and I concluded that we must not have been doing a very good job of modeling this commandment. How many times had we started the week physically weary because we hadn't relaxed on Sunday, failing to give our bodies some "Sabbath rest"?

In our goal-driven culture, the commandment to keep the Sabbath seems out of place. But before we dismiss its obligation as having passed with the coming of Christ, we might remember that we take seriously the other commandments such as those against murder, lying, and adultery. Since the Sabbath concept runs throughout the Bible from Genesis to Revelation, surely this must be important to God.

Why rest one day each week? Our bodies need a break from the day-to-day routine of work. Our souls need strength—and so we worship with other believers and spend time in fellowship. Our emotions need refreshment—so we choose to focus on different things than we do the rest of the week. Beyond this, God has commanded us to rest, and when we obey his commands, we demonstrate our willingness to submit to his authority. Resting becomes a step of faith as we trust God to help us accomplish in six days what might otherwise take seven days each week.

Keeping the Sabbath is not something we do to earn salvation. It reminds us, though, that God rested on the seventh day, and that he has prepared a "special rest" for us on that final day when he calls us to himself in heaven.

Great Creator,
Since you rested from all your work on the seventh day, help us to be faithful
and obedient in following your example. In Jesus' name, amen.

OBEDIENCE

AND HOW CAN WE BE SURE THAT WE BELONG TO HIM?
BY OBEYING HIS COMMANDMENTS. IF SOMEONE SAYS, "I
BELONG TO GOD," BUT DOESN'T OBEY GOD'S COMMANDMENTS,
THAT PERSON IS A LIAR AND DOES NOT LIVE IN THE TRUTH.   *1 John 2:3-4*

*K*nowing God involves much more than mental knowledge—it should result in obeying God.

We teach our children not to play in the street because we don't want them to be hit by a car. So we say, *many* times, "Don't play in the street" or "Look both ways twice before you cross the street." We know that our children hear us, because sometimes they even teach the same lesson to their dolls or stuffed animals. But do they really *know*? It's only when they obey us that we're sure they know.

It's that way with knowledge as a Christian. We can read the Bible, memorize the Bible, and even teach the Bible, but if we don't *do* the Bible, our knowledge is only "puff." First Corinthians 8:1 (NIV) says, "Knowledge puffs up, but love builds up." Acting in love and obedience comes as a result of knowing not just the words but the God behind the words.

A. W. Tozer writes, "The low view of God entertained almost universally among Christians is the cause of a hundred lesser evils everywhere among us. A rediscovery of the majesty of God will go a long way toward curing them."* What we believe and know about God is what determines the way we live. So if we want to live fruitful lives, we must begin by looking into the Bible to see who God is.

As we get to know and obey the God of the Bible, we will act like Jesus, who was an example of humility and self-sacrifice. Living and acting rightly—especially in front of our children—is the best evidence that we know God.

Father,
May we show evidence that we know you by the way we obey you. Amen.

OBEDIENCE

AT THIS, JOSHUA FELL WITH HIS FACE TO THE GROUND IN
REVERENCE. "I AM AT YOUR COMMAND," JOSHUA SAID. "WHAT
DO YOU WANT YOUR SERVANT TO DO?"   *Joshua 5:14*

*A*re you up against a situation in your life that feels hopeless? Are you discouraged and tempted to give up? Before Israel's conquest of the walled city of Jericho, Joshua and the Israelites must have felt the same way. But they made several good choices.

The first thing Joshua did was to humble himself before God and commit to following God's plan. Too many times when I face a problem, my first step is to draw up my own plan. This *appears* to help, but in the long run it is like putting a bandage over a wound that needs more serious attention.

Joshua took God seriously. God said that he had delivered Jericho, along with its king and fighting men, over to Joshua and the Israelites. Would I have believed that statement if I had been there? Joshua and the Israelites chose to trust God for the impossible. Although God's plan required patience, they weren't going to be delivered through sitting back and relaxing—there was some work to be done!

Their reverence for God and their faith in him prompted their ultimate obedience. They paid amazing attention to detail, including trumpets of rams' horns, marching for seven days, and circling seven times around the city on the seventh day—usually quietly, but the last time with a shout. There was no room for laziness or cynicism.

When we humble ourselves in prayer, trust God for the impossible, and obey the details, we will see God's victory over the enemy in our lives and the lives of those we love.

Father,
Thank you for the example of Joshua, who humbled himself, trusted you, and obeyed you. Please help us to do the same as we face our own challenges.
Amen.

OBEDIENCE

THE HEAVENS ARE SHOCKED AT SUCH A THING AND SHRINK
BACK IN HORROR AND DISMAY, SAYS THE LORD. FOR MY
PEOPLE HAVE DONE TWO EVIL THINGS: THEY HAVE FORSAKEN
ME—THE FOUNTAIN OF LIVING WATER. AND THEY HAVE DUG FOR THEMSELVES
CRACKED CISTERNS THAT CAN HOLD NO WATER AT ALL!

Jeremiah 2:12-13

Imagine that it's a quiet summer morning in your neighborhood. Since your children enjoy selling lemonade to friends and neighbors, you've decided to help them out. Before your kids even get out of bed, you prepare a large container of fresh lemonade—the real thing. You also bake a batch of homemade ginger cookies.

At the breakfast table, you and your children hatch a plan for selling the lemonade and cookies later in the day. Since you made the food, you suggest that they provide the signs. After lunch, you help them launch their sale outside before going back into the house to fold a load of laundry.

When you walk back outside to check on your children, you are horrified. Instead of lemonade, they're selling cups of dirty water from puddles in the front yard. And the cookies have been replaced by strange weeds that grow by the side of the road. "What are you *thinking?*" you ask.

In the Old Testament book of Jeremiah, we read that God was horrified when his people abandoned his plan for their salvation. The words Jeremiah uses are potent: God is shocked, shrinking back in horror and dismay. God's people had forsaken him, the fountain of living water. As if that wasn't bad enough, they went on to dig broken, underground water pits that couldn't even hold water. First they rejected God. Then they turned to a poor substitute. What were they *thinking?*

Children *and* adults sometimes make irrational choices, rejecting and disobeying God's plan and searching for substitutes. Only the truth and grace of God can preserve us from exchanging truth for a lie. Only the truth and grace of God can help any of us obey him.

Father,
Thank you that you are the source of life. Please help us not to go looking for
false substitutes. We don't want to exchange your truth for a lie. Amen.

OBEDIENCE

WHAT IS MORE PLEASING TO THE LORD: YOUR BURNT
OFFERINGS AND SACRIFICES OR YOUR OBEDIENCE TO HIS VOICE?
OBEDIENCE IS FAR BETTER THAN SACRIFICE. LISTENING TO HIM IS
MUCH BETTER THAN OFFERING THE FAT OF RAMS.   *1 Samuel 15:22*

*A*s our children have grown, few things have given Jim and me as much satisfaction as watching them do what we asked them to do—*especially* when we didn't have to remind them. Perhaps it was picking up their rooms, taking out the trash, or feeding the cat. What joy to "catch them" doing something right!

First Samuel 15 documents a dramatic confrontation with a man who did not do what God asked him to do. Saul, the first king of Israel, had been given instructions from God to "completely destroy" the Amalekites. While Saul started out well enough, he led the people into great sin by allowing them to keep the best of the livestock—a direct violation of God's directions.

When the prophet Samuel finally caught up with Saul, his voice dripped with sarcasm in response to Saul's claim to have carried out the command of the Lord. "Then what is all the bleating of sheep and lowing of cattle I hear?" he asked (v. 14). Even lowly animals were shouting out their accusations of Saul's disobedience! Saul claimed that his motives were good because he was going to sacrifice the livestock to the Lord. Even so, Saul's act of defiance revealed a lot about his heart. He was more concerned with himself and outward appearances than in following God obediently. Because of this, God tore the kingdom from him and gave it to a "better man" David.

If we moms experience pleasure when we watch our children obey our instructions, imagine how much joy we must bring to God when we choose to obey his Word!

> Lord,
> As we move through our day, give us the grace to follow obediently what we
> know you have called us to do. Help us to do this in big and small things.
> Amen.

OBEDIENCE

> YOU KNOW THESE THINGS—NOW DO THEM! THAT IS THE
> PATH OF BLESSING.
>
> *John 13:17*

We sometimes hear a mom say, "I feel so blessed!" What might have prompted her to feel that way? A clean bill of health from the doctor? The birth of a long-awaited child? These are wonderful blessings. But we must be careful not to limit our perception of blessings only to things we receive. In John 13 Jesus taught his disciples that obedience brings blessing. Specifically, he taught that blessing comes through humble service to others—hearing God's instructions to serve one another and putting the instructions into action.

Some years ago one of my friends died of cancer, leaving three sons who are friends of my sons. Shortly before she died, I was leaving her house and asked if there was anything more I could do. She said, "Just keep in touch with my boys." I took her request seriously, and great blessing has been mine. Whether it's been giving the boys rides, sending cards, praying for them, taking them out for donuts, giving them pizza parties for their birthdays, or giving them gifts, the joy I have received in doing those things is something I will always carry in my heart.

We are blessed (happy, joyful, fulfilled), not because of what we know, but because of what we do with what we know. We will find our greatest joy in obeying Christ by serving others.[5]

Father,
Thank you for the blessing that obedience brings to our lives. Our own souls are truly nourished. Amen.

OBEDIENCE

AS HE WAS SPEAKING, A WOMAN IN THE CROWD CALLED OUT,
"GOD BLESS YOUR MOTHER—THE WOMB FROM WHICH YOU
CAME, AND THE BREASTS THAT NURSED YOU!" HE REPLIED, "BUT EVEN
MORE BLESSED ARE ALL WHO HEAR THE WORD OF GOD AND PUT IT INTO
PRACTICE."

Luke 11:27-28

When the woman in this story pronounced a blessing on Mary, she was also complimenting Jesus. But by Jesus' response we get the impression that he desires obedience more than compliments. The woman was certainly sincere, but sincerity alone is not enough.

The order of events in this passage of Scripture is no coincidence. Notice the first words of the verse above: "As he was speaking . . ." What had he been saying? "Anyone who isn't helping me opposes me, and anyone who isn't working with me is actually working against me" (Luke 11:23). Jesus was cautioning the people against neutrality. He was teaching them that there's a spiritual war going on, and we must choose between two forces. While Jesus is building his kingdom, Satan is trying to destroy it. We must decide between the two, and if we don't make a choice, we are in essence against Christ. As Warren Wiersbe says, "We take sides with Jesus Christ when we hear his Word and obey it."

Throughout God's Word we are taught that obedience comes after hearing. God has revealed his truth to us, and he asks us to respond to it positively and actively. Isn't that exactly what we desire from our children? We want them to listen to us and obey us; the two go hand in hand. Let's not forget that Jesus used the word *blessed* in his response to the woman. That word means *happy*. When we hear God's Word and obey, that's true happiness.

Father,
May we remember that what you want most from us is our obedience. Amen.

OBEDIENCE

TO THE JEWS WHO HAD BELIEVED HIM, JESUS SAID,
"IF YOU HOLD TO MY TEACHING, YOU ARE REALLY MY
DISCIPLES. THEN YOU WILL KNOW THE TRUTH, AND THE TRUTH
WILL SET YOU FREE."

John 8:31-32, NIV

Who are Jesus' disciples? Who are people of the truth? They are the people who obey God—the people who hold to his teaching.

The Greek expression for "hold to" (*meinete en*, also translated "abide in" or "remain in") has great spiritual significance in the Gospel of John. We abide in Christ when we place ourselves in him and continue there, drawing life from his words. This produces ongoing discipleship. A true and obedient disciple will find the truth by knowing the one who is the truth, Jesus himself. This knowledge frees people from their bondage to sin.

When Jesus spoke of knowing the truth, he was speaking of knowing God's revelation to man. This revelation is embodied in Jesus himself, the Word; therefore, to know the truth is to know Jesus. The truth is not political freedom or intellectual knowledge. Knowing the truth means accepting it, obeying it, and regarding it above all earthly opinion. Doing so offers true spiritual freedom from sin and death.

Thankfully, discovering God's truth, obeying it, and honoring it are not things we are asked to do on our own. "As believers, we have the Holy Spirit living within us and guiding us on our journey through life. In fact, in John 16:13, Jesus specifically identified the Holy Spirit as 'the Spirit of truth' 'who will guide you into all truth.'"[6]

Knowing God doesn't come through intellectual activity—it comes as a result of our obedience to him.

Father,
We confess that we sometimes substitute knowing things about you for knowing you. Thanks that when we obey your Word, we really begin to know you. Please help us model obedience to you in front of our children. Amen.

FAITH 2

CONSIDER IT PURE JOY, MY BROTHERS, WHENEVER YOU
FACE TRIALS OF MANY KINDS, BECAUSE YOU KNOW THAT THE
TESTING OF YOUR FAITH DEVELOPS PERSEVERANCE. PERSEVERANCE MUST
FINISH ITS WORK SO THAT YOU MAY BE MATURE AND COMPLETE, NOT LACKING
ANYTHING.

James 1:2-4, NIV

*D*uring my college days at Moody Bible Institute, I was a resident assistant in the women's dormitory, overseeing life on the sixth floor of Houghton Hall. Returning to my room late one evening, I unlocked the door, stepped in, and was convinced that I had the wrong room. It was completely empty. After rechecking and realizing that I was in the right place, I noticed that the room wasn't *completely* empty. There was a Bible passage on the wall—James 1:2-4 (quoted above).

Well, it was pretty hard not to smile at my situation in light of the last three words of the verse. The ladies of the sixth floor had moved everything out of the room, storing half of the furniture in the shower room and the other half on the roof! (They kindly helped me move it back.) Although the incident was not a trial, it was a character building experience.

When the serious trials of life come and we choose to cry out to God for his strength and wisdom, we experience significant growth in Christian character. At a point in my life when I was going through a tough experience, a friend suggested that I begin a "faith affirmations" notebook. On days when I struggled for faith and hope, it was extremely helpful to document the many ways God had shown his love and care for me. I know difficult experiences have produced growth in character because they remind me of how much I need God and how much God cares for me.

God,
Trials are tough, and they are sometimes accompanied with gut-wrenching pain to our souls or bodies. At times when we feel like giving up, please give us faith to persevere. Amen.

FAITH 2

JESUS ALSO SAID, "HERE IS ANOTHER ILLUSTRATION OF
WHAT THE KINGDOM OF GOD IS LIKE: A FARMER PLANTED
SEEDS IN A FIELD, AND THEN HE WENT ON WITH HIS OTHER
ACTIVITIES. AS THE DAYS WENT BY, THE SEEDS SPROUTED AND GREW WITHOUT THE
FARMER'S HELP."

Mark 4:26-27

*F*or any mom who likes to garden, here's an object lesson to try with your young kids. During the fall, take your children to a gardening store and purchase tulip or daffodil bulbs. The pictures on the packages will show what colors the flowers will be.

After you plan which bulbs will go where in your yard, plant them with your children. The kids will be amazed to learn that in five or six months the bulbs will begin to shoot up from the ground, grow, and finally bloom. The activity of planting bulbs will probably raise some questions: Why do we have to wait so long for the flowers to come up? How do we know they will really be red?

The questions children have about planting bulbs are similar to some of the questions we have about our Christian faith. In both situations we learn that we need to follow the instructions and wait for God to work. When we plant bulbs, we trust the instructions on the package, wait for growth, and then enjoy the beauty. The same is true of our faith. We trust the instructions God has given us in the Bible, we choose to obey his guidelines and direction for our lives, and then we wait for the beauty! We also learn that growth doesn't happen immediately—it takes time.

God,
Thank you for your Word, which instructs us how to plant seeds of faith and godliness. Please give us patience as we trust you for growth. Amen.

Faith 2

It was by faith that Rahab the prostitute did not die
with all the others in her city who refused to obey
God. For she had given a friendly welcome to the spies.

Hebrews 11:31

*R*aising three boys who are becoming handsome young men brings with it the responsibility of building into their lives a godly desire for purity. Many years ago one of my very young sons announced that he wanted to marry me and live in our house when he grew up. Although I felt flattered, I knew that someday he would begin to notice pretty young women from other families. He has! Through the years, we've encouraged our sons to choose girls who value purity and avoid girls who behave seductively.

Why, then, do we find Rahab—a prostitute—praised in Hebrews for her faith? What is she doing on that list of heroes?

When Joshua was commanded to conquer the Promised Land (Joshua 6), the first city on the list was Jericho. It had walls at least twenty-five feet high and twenty feet wide! When Joshua sent two spies to Jericho, they found safety and lodging at Rahab's home right on the walls. Rahab was so convinced that the God of Israel was going to destroy her city that she put her hope in the spies—and their God— risking death as a traitor. Rahab's faith was significant to God because it led her to obey. "Only he who believes is obedient," wrote Dietrich Bonhoeffer, "and only he who is obedient believes."

God doesn't care what our past looks like. He can wash away our sins and give us hearts that love him fully and obediently. He is looking for faith—like Rahab's—that believes God can and will do the impossible.

Lord Jesus,
Give us the gift of daily faith. We believe that through your awesome power we can be free to live obediently in your care. Amen.

FAITH 2

JESUS SOON SAW A GREAT CROWD OF PEOPLE CLIMBING THE
HILL, LOOKING FOR HIM. TURNING TO PHILIP, HE ASKED,
"PHILIP, WHERE CAN WE BUY BREAD TO FEED ALL THESE PEOPLE?"
HE WAS TESTING PHILIP, FOR HE ALREADY KNEW WHAT HE WAS GOING TO DO.

John 6:5-6

Jesus was sitting on a hill with his disciples when he looked up and saw a large crowd coming. "Where can we buy bread for these people to eat?" he asked Philip. Jesus asked Philip this question to "test" him, because Jesus already knew there was no obvious human solution to this problem.

Philip responded with a bigger problem. He was trying to think logically, and he realized that it would take eight months' wages just to give each person one bite of food!

A note from the *Life Application Bible Commentary* reads, "As he did with Philip, Jesus sometimes tests us by putting us in difficult situations with no easy answers. At these times we feel frustrated, as Philip did. However, frustration cannot be God's intended result. The wise disciple always keeps the door open for God to work."[7]

Andrew spoke up and presented Jesus with two things—a lunch and another problem. A young boy had a lunch of five rolls and two fish; the problem was, the boy's lunch wasn't enough to feed everyone. But Jesus demonstrated that the little boy's lunch, offered in faith, was *more than enough*. Before the boy witnessed a great work of God, he had to make a sacrifice and step out in faith.

What difficult situation are you facing? Perhaps you've looked at the problem from several angles, and—humanly speaking—things look hopeless. Are you willing to set aside your limited resources and step out in faith to seek God's limitless resources?

> God of all provisions,
> Thank you that you had such patience with your disciples when they didn't
> see past human solutions, and thank you that you show the same patience to
> us. May we remember that you have limitless resources, and may we be willing
> to trust you. Amen.

FAITH 2

THEREFORE, SINCE WE ARE SURROUNDED BY SUCH A HUGE
CROWD OF WITNESSES TO THE LIFE OF FAITH, LET US STRIP OFF
EVERY WEIGHT THAT SLOWS US DOWN, ESPECIALLY THE SIN THAT SO
EASILY HINDERS OUR PROGRESS. AND LET US RUN WITH ENDURANCE THE RACE
THAT GOD HAS SET BEFORE US. WE DO THIS BY KEEPING OUR EYES ON JESUS, ON
WHOM OUR FAITH DEPENDS FROM START TO FINISH. HE WAS WILLING TO DIE A
SHAMEFUL DEATH ON THE CROSS BECAUSE OF THE JOY HE KNEW WOULD BE HIS
AFTERWARD. NOW HE IS SEATED IN THE PLACE OF HIGHEST HONOR BESIDE GOD'S
THRONE IN HEAVEN.

Hebrews 12:1-2

Born in Glasgow, Scotland, in 1867, Peter Cameron Scott grew up to establish the Africa Inland Mission, which now has more than 850 missionaries. Looking back on all the obstacles he faced, I marvel at how he kept going.

During his first trip to Africa, he came down with a severe case of malaria and had to return home. After he recuperated, he went back to Africa with his brother, John. They had been there only a short time when John was struck down with malaria and died. All alone, Peter buried his brother. Even in the pain and loneliness of those days, he recommitted himself to preaching the gospel in Africa. Sadly, his health deteriorated and he had to return to England.

Although he had pledged himself to God, he didn't know how he would ever break free from the loneliness and depression he was feeling. He wanted to go back to Africa, but he wasn't sure it would be possible.

One day he visited Scottish missionary David Livingstone's tomb in Westminster Abbey. Kneeling down in front of it, he read, "Other sheep I have which are not of this fold; them also I must bring" (John 10:16, NKJV).

This verse inspired him to rise from his knees and make plans to return to Africa. It was on this last trip that he founded the mission that is still a powerful force for the gospel in Africa today.

Are you feeling lonely or depressed? Do you feel like quitting? A mom of faith is one who focuses on God and the increase of his Kingdom amid all the hustle and bustle of each day's activities. Does that mean she never gets discouraged? No. But she prays for the perseverance she needs to keep going.

Father,
Some days we get so weary and discouraged that it's difficult to press on.
Thank you that you are always faithful. May we focus on you and run to you
for help and encouragement. Thanks that you care and listen. Amen.

FAITH 2

BE CAREFUL! WATCH OUT FOR ATTACKS FROM THE
DEVIL, YOUR GREAT ENEMY. HE PROWLS AROUND LIKE A
ROARING LION, LOOKING FOR SOME VICTIM TO DEVOUR. TAKE A
FIRM STAND AGAINST HIM, AND BE STRONG IN YOUR FAITH. REMEMBER THAT YOUR
CHRISTIAN BROTHERS AND SISTERS ALL OVER THE WORLD ARE GOING THROUGH
THE SAME KIND OF SUFFERING YOU ARE.

1 Peter 5:8-9

The Bible teaches us that Satan is our adversary—a liar and a murderer. He slanders, accuses, and deceives, and lies are his chief weapons. In order for us to recognize and counteract his deceptions, we must know and believe God's truth. We don't resist by running away from the enemy; we resist by standing up to him with the Word of God—through faith.

When Jesus was tempted by the devil (see Matthew 4), he responded to Satan's three temptations with Scripture, not with his divine power. That's encouraging to us because we too can respond with Scripture. When Satan tempted Jesus with hunger, a desire of the flesh, Jesus responded with Deuteronomy 8:3: "People need more than bread for their life; real life comes by feeding on every word of the Lord." If I cater to my physical needs and ignore God's will for me, I sin.

Satan's second temptation involved quoting Scripture out of context and daring Jesus to put himself in danger and then call to God for rescue. Jesus responded with Deuteronomy 6:16, saying it is wrong to tempt God. We should not put ourselves in circumstances where we try to force God to do something on our behalf.

The third time around, Satan offered Jesus a shortcut to power in exchange for worship, but Jesus responded with Deuteronomy 6:13, which says that whatever we worship is what we serve.

If Jesus, who is the Son of God, chose to resist the devil with faith in God and surrender to his Word, how much more do *we* need to!

Father,
When we are confronted with the devil's lies, please help us to recognize them
and counteract them with your truth. Thank you for your Word. May we hide
it in our hearts so that we will not sin. Amen.

FAITH 2

THE PEOPLE OF ISRAEL HAD WALKED THROUGH THE
MIDDLE OF THE SEA ON DRY LAND, AS THE WATER STOOD UP
LIKE A WALL ON BOTH SIDES. THIS WAS HOW THE LORD RESCUED ISRAEL
FROM THE EGYPTIANS THAT DAY. AND THE ISRAELITES COULD SEE THE BODIES OF
THE EGYPTIANS WASHED UP ON THE SHORE. WHEN THE PEOPLE OF ISRAEL SAW
THE MIGHTY POWER THAT THE LORD HAD DISPLAYED AGAINST THE EGYPTIANS,
THEY FEARED THE LORD AND PUT THEIR FAITH IN HIM AND HIS SERVANT MOSES.

Exodus 14:29-31

On a vacation to Florida, three men in my family went golfing. My husband, brother-in-law Rick, and son Nate were matched up with one other man to make a foursome. Rick was not a serious golfer, and when he approached the first tee, he was thinking, *Just let me get the ball in the air.* After he swung and heard a big ping, he felt a momentary relief. But then he watched the ball smack a nearby palm tree, fly back toward him, and land directly behind him. After a few awkward seconds of silence, the fourth man said, "I'll give you a hundred bucks if you can do that again!"

Surprising events sometimes prompt us to ask, "What are the chances of *that* happening?" We read throughout the Bible that God performed miraculous acts—supernatural occurrences packed with amazing surprises—to display his power and glory and to demonstrate that he alone is God.

Many of us and our children know the story of how God parted the Red Sea. The Israelites (God's people) were fleeing from the Egyptians (the oppressors). In an astonishing display of power, God parted the waters of the Red Sea, allowing his people to cross on dry ground. In addition, the Egyptians who were hot on their trail were drowned as the waters of the sea closed in on them.

In an astounding and wonder-working way, God demonstrated how he protects and cares for his children. He also demonstrated his wrath upon people who harden their hearts against him. God's message was not wasted on the people of Israel, and it's still a message for us today: God wants us to put our faith in him.

Powerful God,
Thank you for accounts of your might that show us who you are and prompt us to trust you. Amen.

FORGIVENESS

THEN IF MY PEOPLE WHO ARE CALLED BY MY NAME WILL
HUMBLE THEMSELVES AND PRAY AND SEEK MY FACE AND TURN
FROM THEIR WICKED WAYS, I WILL HEAR FROM HEAVEN AND
WILL FORGIVE THEIR SINS AND HEAL THEIR LAND.   *2 Chronicles 7:14*

When something isn't quite right with my child's knee, causing pain, irritation, and limited motion, I'm grateful when the doctor can take measures to help the knee function well again. It's also like that with our hearts, which are often in need of mending. God has given us steps we can take to promote healing and wholeness for the innermost parts of our souls.

The first thing God asks us to do is *humble ourselves*. When we take this posture before God, we remind ourselves that he is God and we are not. We come to him as needy human beings, admitting that we fall short of his righteous standards.

The second step we take is to *pray*. We call out to God for help that only he can give. Whether we are asking forgiveness for our own heart or asking for help in showing forgiveness to another, God's grace comes only from him—not from within ourselves.

God also asks us to *seek his face*. Seeking God is more than having a casual interest in him. It's similar to going on a hunt—pursuing something wholeheartedly. The place for us to start is God's Word, where he reveals himself to us.

Serious seeking prompts us to *turn from things that don't please God*, because his Spirit comes alongside us and shows us areas of our lives where we need to do some about-faces. As we take these steps God has given us, he is faithful to forgive us and heal us.

Father,
May we experience forgiveness and healing through humbling ourselves, praying, seeking your face, and turning from sin. Amen.

FORGIVENESS

OH, WHAT JOY FOR THOSE WHOSE REBELLION IS FORGIVEN,
WHOSE SIN IS PUT OUT OF SIGHT! YES, WHAT JOY FOR THOSE
WHOSE RECORD THE LORD HAS CLEARED OF SIN, WHOSE LIVES ARE
LIVED IN COMPLETE HONESTY!

Psalm 32:1-2

The Bible contains over one hundred direct references to forgiveness. This emphasis points out that sin needs to be removed before relationships can be restored—both our relationship with God and our relationships with others. Teaching our children about God's forgiveness is one of the most important gifts we will ever give them. Here's an overview:

1. We humans have a driving need in our hearts for forgiveness.
2. According to Psalm 32, when we are in need of forgiveness, we waste and groan, carrying around a sense of heaviness in our spirit that saps our strength.
3. God does not play games with us. Rather, when we decide to come to him for forgiveness, he decisively discards our sin, because his Son's blood has already paid our penalty on the cross.
4. Not only does God remove our sin, but he also says he removes it "as far as the east is from the west" (Psalm 103:12, NIV)—that is, immeasurably and infinitely.
5. When we quit covering up our sin, our groaning and sighing are replaced with singing. Even if there's not actual music, our hearts are glad and happiness returns.
6. God's mercy is very wide. Psalm 103:13 teaches us that God pities us the way a father pities his children.
7. Instead of fearing God and avoiding him, once we're forgiven we find him to be our hiding place. He becomes the one we run to for protection. The person who is forgiven is *blessed*!

> Father,
> *Not what these hands have done can save this guilty soul;*
> *Not what this toiling flesh has borne can make my spirit whole.*
> *Thy work alone, O Christ, can ease this weight of sin;*
> *Thy blood alone, O Lamb of God, can give me peace within.*[8]

FORGIVENESS

BUT YOU OFFER FORGIVENESS, THAT WE MIGHT LEARN
TO FEAR YOU.

Psalm 130:4

*I*f we were to research the major religions of the world, we would find that most of them teach some variation of working to obtain God's favor. But the Bible teaches that God completely forgives sins. God says that sin deserves punishment because it violates his holy character. Yet he also tells us that he is a God of grace and pardon, and that he *initiated* our forgiveness by sending Jesus to be our Savior.

God offers us forgiveness not so we will be scared of him, but so we will want to worship and honor him. He wants us to see him for who he is and respond to him with reverent and affectionate obedience.

One morning during my senior year at Moody Bible Institute, I overslept for Bible Theology class. Later that morning, I tiptoed into Dr. Luck's office with fear and trepidation. I had missed four classes that semester, and I was only supposed to have missed three. According to the student handbook, I deserved to fail the course. But Dr. Luck forgave my absence, and every time I saw him on campus after that, I felt an extreme sense of gratitude.

God's forgiveness not only prompts our gratitude but also prompts us to follow him lovingly and shrink from anything that would offend him. God does not forgive us so that we can take advantage of him and keep on sinning. In response to his forgiveness, he wants us to reverence him.

Loving Father,
Because you are so willing to forgive our sins, we want to respond with gratitude. May we not hold back from forgiving people who have wronged us. You are the one we can turn to for help in this area. In Jesus' name, amen.

FORGIVENESS

ALL OF US HAVE STRAYED AWAY LIKE SHEEP. WE HAVE LEFT
GOD'S PATHS TO FOLLOW OUR OWN. YET THE LORD LAID ON
HIM THE GUILT AND SINS OF US ALL.   *Isaiah 53:6*

How do you introduce yourself in social settings? "Hi, I'm Ellen Elwell. I'm Jordan's mom," is what I typically say if I'm attending a school event. If I'm participating in a piano teacher's convention I might say, "Hi, I'm Ellen Elwell. I teach piano in the western suburbs of Chicago."

One way I've never introduced myself is "Hi, I'm Ellen Elwell and I'm a sinful human being." Speaking those words in a social setting might feel awkward—both for me and for the listener. But the words are entirely accurate. The truth is, we're all sinners and we all need God's forgiveness. From Genesis to Revelation, we discover that the best of the patriarchs, psalmists, prophets, and disciples were sinners, just like us.

One Sunday morning, a preacher named Vance Havner spoke on the topic of sin and the depravity of man. After the service was over, one of Havner's parishioners approached him and said, "Pastor, I'm having a hard time with this idea you say the Bible teaches about the depravity of man. I just can't swallow it." The pastor smiled and replied gently, "You don't have to. It's already in you!"

It was seeing my sin that first prompted me to desire God's forgiveness. Since the day I first placed my faith in Christ, I've continued to grow in my new identity. I'm a child of God who's blessed with holiness, freedom, and wisdom—among other things—because of Christ's death on the cross. Although I'm growing and learning, I realize that I will struggle with sin until the day I die. Those struggles prompt me to depend on Christ each day because he is the only one who has power to forgive my sin and to help me live righteously. "I remember two things," said John Newton, "that I am a great sinner, and that Christ is a great Savior."

Father,
I praise you that you are a God who wants to forgive. Thank you that you
take away our guilt and replace it with joy. In the name of Jesus, amen.

FORGIVENESS

IF THEY SIN AGAINST YOU—AND WHO HAS NEVER
SINNED?—YOU MAY BECOME ANGRY WITH THEM AND LET
THEIR ENEMIES CONQUER THEM AND TAKE THEM CAPTIVE TO A
FOREIGN LAND FAR OR NEAR. BUT IN THAT LAND OF EXILE, THEY MAY TURN TO
YOU AGAIN IN REPENTANCE AND PRAY, "WE HAVE SINNED, DONE EVIL, AND ACTED
WICKEDLY." THEN IF THEY TURN TO YOU WITH THEIR WHOLE HEART AND SOUL
AND PRAY TOWARD THE LAND YOU GAVE TO THEIR ANCESTORS, TOWARD THIS CITY
YOU HAVE CHOSEN, AND TOWARD THIS TEMPLE I HAVE BUILT TO HONOR YOUR
NAME, THEN HEAR THEIR PRAYERS FROM HEAVEN WHERE YOU LIVE. UPHOLD
THEIR CAUSE AND FORGIVE YOUR PEOPLE WHO HAVE SINNED AGAINST YOU. MAKE
THEIR CAPTORS MERCIFUL TO THEM, FOR THEY ARE YOUR PEOPLE—YOUR SPECIAL
POSSESSION—WHOM YOU BROUGHT OUT OF THE IRON-SMELTING FURNACE OF
EGYPT.

1 Kings 8:46-51

Building a temple for the glory of God was a huge task for a young king. At its dedication, Solomon prayed for the people's hearts, which were more important than the new temple.

Solomon didn't say "if" in regard to sin, because he knew it was a matter of "when." His wise words gave the people—and believers today—a pattern for the cycle of sin, repentance, and forgiveness.

1. We *will* sin.
2. *When* we sin, *if* we have a change of heart and repent and plead to God, and *if* we turn back to God with all our heart and soul and pray to God, *then*:
3. God will hear our prayer, forgive the offenses we have committed against him, and show us mercy.

We must follow God's pattern for repentance and forgiveness. How gracious that God does not leave us to carry our own burden of sin—he carried it to the cross. And when we follow the pattern he gave us for repentance, we become examples of his mercy in front of our children.

Merciful God,
Thank you that we do not have to carry our sin, but that you show us mercy
when we turn to you with all our heart and soul. Amen.

Forgiveness

FORGIVE US OUR DEBTS, AS WE ALSO HAVE FORGIVEN
OUR DEBTORS.

Matthew 6:12, NIV

*O*ne day Jeanne Zechmeister, a psychologist at Loyola University, observed a woman at Mass who recited the Lord's Prayer with the rest of the congregants but very deliberately did not say the lines about forgiveness. Zechmeister was perplexed, saying, "The only thing that Jesus asks of us in the Lord's Prayer is that we forgive others; the rest of the prayer is petition. I keep wondering why the woman would not say it. I'd like to talk to her."[9]

To forgive a person is to stop blaming him or her for a wrong, to bury the hatchet, and, in releasing our desire for revenge, to be released from anger. How does this take place? For our sake and for the sake of the next generation, it's important that we know how to answer that question.

Lewis Smedes, author of *The Art of Forgiving*, has some helpful guidelines:

- Forgiving happens in stages: We rediscover the humanity of the person who wronged us, we surrender our right to get even, and we wish that person well.
- We forgive people only for what they do, never for what they are.
- We cannot forgive a wrong unless we first blame the person who wronged us.
- Forgiving is a journey; the deeper the wound, the longer the journey.
- Forgiving is not a way to avoid pain but to heal pain.
- Forgivers are not doormats. To forgive a person is not a signal that we are willing to put up with what he does.
- When we forgive, we walk in stride with the forgiving God.[10]

Forgiving is hard work, but we are probably never more like God than when we forgive.

> *Father,*
> *Learning to forgive is a challenge for all of us. Please give us your wisdom and the strength to obey your command to forgive others. Amen.*

FORGIVENESS

THAT'S WHAT MY HEAVENLY FATHER WILL DO TO YOU IF
YOU REFUSE TO FORGIVE YOUR BROTHERS AND SISTERS IN
YOUR HEART.   *Matthew 18:35*

The story in Matthew 18 offers good incentive to anyone who is struggling with forgiveness. A man had been stealing money from the king, and when the injustice was discovered, it became clear he had embezzled ten thousand talents—probably the equivalent of ten million dollars in today's terms. This was one proud man. He seemed more upset about getting caught than about having stolen. He actually thought that, given enough time, he could pay the king back. This man would have been in very deep weeds if the king hadn't been a man of compassion. He took the financial loss on himself and forgave the servant. As a result of the king's mercy, the man was not thrown into debtor's prison.

When the forgiven man left the king, he found a fellow servant who owed him a very small sum of money. Grabbing and choking the servant, he demanded payment; and when the debtor fell to his knees asking for patience, the man ordered the debtor thrown into prison until he could pay up.

When the king heard what had happened, he was furious that a man who had been forgiven so much would withhold forgiveness from another. He ordered the wicked servant thrown into jail to be tormented, and in doing so he dealt with him the way the wicked servant had dealt with his debtor.

Jesus warned us that God cannot forgive us if we do not have humble and repentant hearts. We reveal the true condition of our hearts by the way we treat others. Where there is pride and a desire for revenge, there can be no true repentance.[11]

Father,
What a graphic picture you give us in your Word of what pride does to us.
May we humble ourselves before you, so that we might find grace for ourselves
and then be willing to share it with another. Amen.

TIME

IF YOU NEED WISDOM—IF YOU WANT TO KNOW WHAT
GOD WANTS YOU TO DO—ASK HIM, AND HE WILL GLADLY TELL
YOU. HE WILL NOT RESENT YOUR ASKING.

James 1:5

I recently saw a cartoon in a women's magazine showing a little boy sitting at a kitchen table. His mother was serving him a meal, and the little boy was saying, "Mom, where did you work before you worked for Dad and me?"

I both smile and cringe at that little boy's question. I smile because, like the mom in the cartoon, I spend a lot of time serving my family, and most of the time I enjoy it. I cringe because I dislike the times when I feel like a slave to everyone else's needs and wants, having little time left over for the things I like to do. After being a mom for twenty some years, I have to admit that finding a balance is a constant challenge. I've had times when I felt overly responsible for my family and didn't take enough time to be healthy myself. At other times I was so involved in "good" things that in my busyness I neglected some of my family's needs.

For some years I have been praying daily for wisdom to know how to use my time, and it has helped immensely! I don't claim to have found the perfect balance, but when I talk to God about my schedule each morning, I'm much more conscious of making wise choices since I've already thought and prayed about it. And when things don't go well, I reevaluate and ask God for more wisdom.

Father,
Thank you that we can come to you for wisdom. Please give us help in balancing the many responsibilities of motherhood. Amen.

TIME

TEACH US TO NUMBER OUR DAYS ARIGHT, THAT WE MAY
GAIN A HEART OF WISDOM.   *Psalm 90:12, NIV*

*I*f we set out to bake cupcakes with our children, we teach them to measure correctly. Why? The way we measure affects the outcome of the cake. God's Word teaches us that the way we measure our lives affects the outcome of our hearts. In the verse above, we're taught to number our days "aright." That word is significant. We all number our days (by years), but what does it mean to do it "aright"? The preceding verses in Psalm 90 help us see the plan:

1. Realize that God lives forever. History comes and history goes, but God is eternal, and he exists far above the events on earth. No matter what generation a person lives in, he always has the opportunity to choose God as his dwelling-place, his eternal refuge.

2. Realize that our earthly lives are temporary. In verses 3-6, our lives are likened to dust, a watch in the night (about three or four hours long), and grass that springs up in the morning but withers at night.

3. Realize that our life only counts for eternity if we choose to be in proper relationship with the God of eternity. Because God made us in his image, if we choose to honor him with our lives, they can mean something and accomplish something. Our brief lives on earth can help to further his kingdom—especially through lives of the children he has given us.

Using our time correctly *now* determines the outcome of our hearts *eternally*!

Father,
Psalm 90:12 is an appropriate prayer for us each day of our earthly existence: "Teach us to number our days aright, that we may gain a heart of wisdom." Thank you that even though we are frail humans, we can choose to be connected to the eternal God through faith in Jesus Christ! Amen.

TIME

JESUS ALSO SAID, "HERE IS ANOTHER ILLUSTRATION OF WHAT THE KINGDOM OF GOD IS LIKE: A FARMER PLANTED SEEDS IN A FIELD, AND THEN HE WENT ON WITH HIS OTHER ACTIVITIES. AS THE DAYS WENT BY, THE SEEDS SPROUTED AND GREW WITHOUT THE FARMER'S HELP, BECAUSE THE EARTH PRODUCES CROPS ON ITS OWN. FIRST A LEAF BLADE PUSHES THROUGH, THEN THE HEADS OF WHEAT ARE FORMED, AND FINALLY THE GRAIN RIPENS."

Mark 4:26-28

Some years ago, we purchased two gerbils for our son Jordan, which he cared for and enjoyed for three or four years. When the second gerbil died, we promptly purchased two hamsters. Being an animal lover, my son played with the hamsters many times each day.

I was not as consumed with the little critters as he was, and when I looked at them two weeks after he brought them home, I commented that they had nearly doubled in size; their growth was amazing to me. My son hadn't noticed the growth, however, because he saw them often each day. Growth is like that; it takes time and isn't always immediately apparent.

Mark 4:26-28 gives us interesting clues about the growth process. It cannot be forced. But if the elements of God's grace, God's truth, and time are present, then God produces the growth. "If we are depressed, it does no good to be 'undepressed.' It does help, however, to cultivate the soil of our soul with the nutrients of grace, truth, and time. Only then will we gradually be transformed to greater and greater stages of joy."[12]

We cannot force growth. But when we choose to read God's Word and obey it, his Spirit teaches us his truth. And when we choose to pursue a relationship with God and his body, the church, we will experience his grace. God's grace and truth over time produce growth in the believer's life.

Father,
Thank you that as the seeds of your truth and grace are scattered in our hearts over time, we will grow! Amen.

TIME

MOSES SAID TO GOD, "SUPPOSE I GO TO THE ISRAELITES
AND SAY TO THEM, 'THE GOD OF YOUR FATHERS HAS SENT
ME TO YOU,' AND THEY ASK ME, 'WHAT IS HIS NAME?' THEN WHAT
SHALL I TELL THEM?" GOD SAID TO MOSES, "I AM WHO I AM. THIS IS WHAT YOU ARE
TO SAY TO THE ISRAELITES: 'I AM HAS SENT ME TO YOU.'" *Exodus 3:13-14, NIV*

What do the following questions have in common?

1. When is dinner?
2. How old are you?
3. Is your term paper due next week?

Time. We all measure time, and we all know that time passes, but it's impossible to say exactly what time is. One dictionary defines it as "a nonspatial continuum in which events occur in apparently irreversible succession from the past through the present to the future."

That prompted me to look up the word *continuum*: "A continuous extent, succession, or whole." It seems to me that God is the continuum—God who mentioned his full name in the Bible only once: "I am who I am."

God spoke his name to Moses when Moses was out with his sheep one day and encountered a burning bush. Moses approached because he thought it was curious that the bush was on fire but didn't burn up. Then God spoke to him from the bush, asking him to go to Pharaoh and lead the Israelites out of Egypt. Although that display of God's power took place many years ago, God hasn't changed. Hebrews 13:8 reminds us that God is the same yesterday, today, and forever.

As we face challenges in our families, it's very comforting to know that God is the I AM. What difficult situations are you facing in your piece of God's continuum? It's good to be reminded of the glory and power of the "I AM" God who is always the same, accomplishing his purposes in us as we look to him.

God,
When Moses struggled to understand how you were going to accomplish your plans through him, you came alongside him and showed him how powerful and mighty you are. We struggle with some of the same questions at times. Please encourage us with your Word and with your presence, so we will be equipped to do your Kingdom work, beginning in our home. Amen.

TIME

LORD, REMIND ME HOW BRIEF MY TIME ON EARTH WILL BE.
REMIND ME THAT MY DAYS ARE NUMBERED, AND THAT MY LIFE
IS FLEEING AWAY. MY LIFE IS NO LONGER THAN THE WIDTH OF MY HAND.
AN ENTIRE LIFETIME IS JUST A MOMENT TO YOU; HUMAN EXISTENCE IS BUT A
BREATH. WE ARE MERELY MOVING SHADOWS, AND ALL OUR BUSY RUSHING ENDS
IN NOTHING. WE HEAP UP WEALTH FOR SOMEONE ELSE TO SPEND. AND SO, LORD,
WHERE DO I PUT MY HOPE? MY ONLY HOPE IS IN YOU.   *Psalm 39:4-7*

*R*eminders of our mortality get us thinking about what's really important in life. Author Anne Lamott had a friend, Pam, who was fighting breast cancer. When Anne started complaining to Pam about the fact that she couldn't find shorts that fit, Pam gently commented, "Annie, we haven't got that kind of time."

Several years ago one of my friends had cancer. Many women I know have fought it and lived, but Marty died about a year-and-a-half after her first diagnosis. The months before and after her death were sobering and significant months of my life. Marty was the mother of three sons who are friends of my sons. I was watching a friend suffer and eventually prepare to meet her Creator and Savior.

When Marty and I visited over coffee in the early stages of her cancer, or when I sat next to her bed in the later stages, she was gracious to ask about everyday happenings in my life, but our conversations frequently turned to topics of depth and meaning. One day she said, "A lot of us went to college, married, found jobs, bought houses, had children, and have since been running our children around to all kinds of activities. These are all good things, but in the end it's our relationship with God that really matters—that's what we take with us." Marty's thoughtful words were one of the most convincing sermons I've ever heard.

God,
It's sobering for us to realize that our lives on earth are brief. Please help us to spend them wisely, remembering that our hope is in you. Amen.

TIME

> REMEMBER YOUR CREATOR IN THE DAYS OF
> YOUR YOUTH.
>
> Ecclesiastes 12:1, NIV

Jay Thomas, the college pastor at my church, recently shared an illustration he had heard from Alistair Begg. Imagine someone told you that each day he was going to place $86,400 in your bank account. Your job was to spend all of it every day, and anything you didn't spend by midnight would be lost. You'd probably spend a fair amount of time figuring out what you wanted to do with the money! Jay went on to say that even though most of us will never have $86,400 deposited in our bank accounts each day, every one of us is given 86,400 seconds of time to use each day. The question is, *How are we spending all those seconds?*

I am indebted to Sunday school teachers and youth workers who encouraged me to memorize Bible verses like the one above. I am also indebted to my parents, who built healthy opportunities, disciplines, and boundaries into my life, all of which helped me to use my time wisely. Now that I'm an adult, I'm no longer accountable to my parents for how I use my time, but I am accountable to God. And although I don't have the youth of my childhood, I don't yet have the limitations mentioned in Ecclesiastes 12:2-5 of dim eyes, trembling limbs, loss of teeth, or deafness to music. So, if God wills, I still have time to remember my Creator and honor him throughout the 86,400 seconds of each day I have left!

Little drops of water, little grains of sand,
Make the mighty ocean and the pleasant land.
So the little minutes, humble though they be,
Make the mighty ages of eternity.

Father,
Please help us to make each second of the day count for you and your Kingdom. In Jesus' name, amen.

TIME

BUT WHEN THE RIGHT TIME CAME, GOD SENT HIS SON, BORN
OF A WOMAN, SUBJECT TO THE LAW. GOD SENT HIM TO BUY
FREEDOM FOR US WHO WERE SLAVES TO THE LAW, SO THAT HE COULD
ADOPT US AS HIS VERY OWN CHILDREN. AND BECAUSE YOU GENTILES HAVE
BECOME HIS CHILDREN, GOD HAS SENT THE SPIRIT OF HIS SON INTO YOUR HEARTS,
AND NOW YOU CAN CALL GOD YOUR DEAR FATHER. NOW YOU ARE NO LONGER
A SLAVE BUT GOD'S OWN CHILD. AND SINCE YOU ARE HIS CHILD, EVERYTHING HE
HAS BELONGS TO YOU.

Galatians 4:4-7

When our oldest son, Chad, was a senior in high school, he applied to several colleges and universities. Eventually he decided to attend Grove City College in western Pennsylvania. To be admitted into their engineering school, he needed to take an entrance exam. The top three scorers would receive the equivalent of one year of college free of charge. After taking the test in March, Chad learned that he had placed fourth out of about one hundred. We were excited that he had done so well, yet sad that he had missed the scholarship by such a close margin.

At dinnertime the night before Chad's high school graduation, our telephone rang. It was the head of the engineering department from Grove City College. "One of the three finalists chose to attend another college," he said, "so Chad will now receive one of the scholarships." The timing of that "graduation gift" was incredible!

Galatians 4:4 reminds us that God sent the gift of his Son to this earth at just the right time. It was through the gift of Jesus that we became God's children, no longer obliged to live in slavery to the law. We can't yet comprehend what all that means. But we have the assurance that as God's children, our Father will not only meet our needs but will some day give to us our full spiritual inheritance, which is priceless!

Father,
Thank you that your timing is perfect, and that you have all the events of our lives under control. We're grateful for the opportunity to be your children. In the name of Jesus, amen.

ENCOURAGEMENT

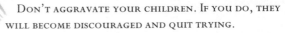

DON'T AGGRAVATE YOUR CHILDREN. IF YOU DO, THEY
WILL BECOME DISCOURAGED AND QUIT TRYING.

Colossians 3:21

*T*he story is told of a teacher who asked her students what each wanted to become when they grew up. "President." "A fireman." "A teacher." One by one they answered until it was Billy's turn. The teacher asked, "Billy, what do you want to be when you grow up?"

"Possible," Billy responded.

"Possible?" asked the teacher.

"Yes," Billy said. "My mom is always telling me I'm impossible. When I grow up I want to become *possible*."

Encouragement and discouragement are worlds apart. Encouragement brings a boost, comfort, cheer, faith, hope, optimism, support, and trust, whereas discouragement brings dejection, sadness, pessimism, and a loss of confidence.

It doesn't take me long to decide that I want to be the encouraging kind of mom, not the discouraging kind. When I'm looking for help, God's Word is a great place to start.

> *Worry weighs a person down; an encouraging word cheers a person up.*
> *(Proverbs 12:25)*

> *Gentle words bring life and health; a deceitful tongue crushes the spirit.*
> *(Proverbs 15:4)*

Every child needs to be encouraged. Every child needs to know that he has possibility. Every child needs to know that she has potential. We mothers also have potential—the potential to encourage our children. What a gift!

Father,
Please forgive us for the times we have discouraged our children. May we choose to apologize, and then look to you and your Word for the strength to be encouraging. Amen.

ENCOURAGEMENT

THEN I HEARD AGAIN WHAT SOUNDED LIKE THE SHOUT OF
A HUGE CROWD, OR THE ROAR OF MIGHTY OCEAN WAVES, OR
THE CRASH OF LOUD THUNDER: "HALLELUJAH! FOR THE LORD OUR
GOD, THE ALMIGHTY, REIGNS."

Revelation 19:6

My eleven-year-old son was seated next to me in our van when the tape we were listening to began to play the "Hallelujah Chorus" from Handel's *Messiah*. As Jordan took off his seat belt and tried to stand up, we laughed! *Everyone* knows that you stand when you hear the "Hallelujah Chorus," right? But not everyone knows of Handel's discouragement leading up to that composition.

George Frederic Handel's father was a barber who was determined that his son would become a lawyer. In spite of the fact that Handel loved music as a child, his father forbade him to take lessons. That changed when a duke who heard nine-year-old Handel play the organ strongly encouraged the father to give the boy formal music training.

Although he was enormously gifted as an organist and composer, Handel didn't have an easy existence. He fell in and out of favor with changing monarchs, dealt with unpredictable audiences, and was so deeply in debt that he thought he might end up in prison. Terribly discouraged, Handel was ready to retire from public life when he received a libretto taken entirely from the Bible. At the same time, he was given a commission from a Dublin charity to compose a work for a benefit performance.

Handel began composing, and after twenty-four days he completed 260 pages of a manuscript titled *Messiah*. One writer commented that the music and message of *Messiah* "has probably done more to convince thousands of mankind that there is a God . . . than all the theological works ever written."[2]

Just because we're discouraged doesn't mean God can't use us!

God who sees the whole picture,
It's easy for us to give up and lose heart when we're discouraged. It's easy for
our children to want to give up. Help us run to you and remember that many
people who have contributed to expanding your Kingdom were at some point
discouraged. Amen.

ENCOURAGEMENT

BUT ENCOURAGE ONE ANOTHER DAILY, AS LONG AS IT IS
CALLED TODAY, SO THAT NONE OF YOU MAY BE HARDENED
BY SIN'S DECEITFULNESS.   *Hebrews 3:13, NIV*

To understand the encouragement we are taught to give to one another, notice what the author of Hebrews wrote earlier in the chapter: "Don't harden your hearts against [God] as Israel did when they rebelled, when they tested God's patience in the wilderness" (v. 8). The children of Israel had contempt for God, and this displayed itself through negativity, grumbling, quarreling, and disobedience.

Early on, the Israelites were ready to follow God anywhere. Coming out of 430 years of slavery, they had a strong leader, and they had witnessed spectacular miracles. When things got difficult, though, they cried, "Is the Lord among us or not?" (Exodus 17:7, NIV). Grumbling, complaining, and blaming are very human reactions to difficulty, but they are not a good place for us to camp. It's healthy for us to voice our honest feelings and questions as the psalmist does (Psalm 77:7-9), but then we must move on by remembering God's mighty strength and his wonders of the past (Psalm 77:11-15).

So how do we encourage each other? To begin with, we support each other. We come alongside a fellow struggler with listening, understanding, and help. Sharing God's Word and praying are other ways to stimulate and inspire one another to have hope and courage. When my children are going through difficulties, I sometimes jot down for them specific Bible verses I am praying regarding their circumstances. This can also be helpful for husbands, for friends, and for ourselves. In our concern, we can pray that we'll have an appropriate balance of honesty and praise. How can we encourage someone today?

Father,
Thank you that you listen to our questions. Thanks for the encouragement we have received from fellow believers in times of personal discouragement. Thank you that the influence of your Word helps us with reality checks. Please help us to be an encouragement to those around us. Amen.

ENCOURAGEMENT

SO ENCOURAGE EACH OTHER AND BUILD EACH OTHER UP,
JUST AS YOU ARE ALREADY DOING.   *1 Thessalonians 5:11*

*E*ncouraging words stimulate our spirits. They give us a boost, brighten our day, and strengthen us for our tasks. Wow! All of that can be accomplished with a few encouraging words.

The other day my husband told me how much something I said had encouraged him. A few weeks ago I'd said, "I never take it for granted that we can talk about anything and everything. Our relationship feels as comfortable to me as an old pair of slippers." Apparently, those twenty-or-so words meant more to him than I had realized.

When Moses' leadership over the children of Israel was coming to a close, God asked him to encourage Joshua—God's choice for a new leader. Part of God's plan for equipping Joshua for leadership was accomplished through Moses' encouragement. That is still God's plan in our families today. What abundant opportunities we have in our homes to encourage our husbands and our children! Does your husband travel? Tuck a few cards in his suitcase—one for each day he'll be gone. And don't be fooled by age—even high school boys enjoy getting notes in their lunches! "Kind words," said Mother Teresa, "can be short and easy to speak, but their echoes are truly endless."

Father,
Thank you for people who have encouraged us. Help us to be encouraging to our families and friends. Amen.

ENCOURAGEMENT

BE MERCIFUL, O LORD, FOR I AM LOOKING UP TO
YOU IN CONSTANT HOPE. *Psalm 86:3, TLB*

When our young children are hurt, sad, lonely, or confused, they often run to us. When we moms are hurt, sad, lonely, or confused, where do *we* run?

I love the words to a song by Kurt Kaiser that I learned in college:

> *Where shall I run, Lord, when all around me, trouble and strife seem to be every-where? Haven't you said that you would protect me? Safe in your hand I will evermore be. With such protection, none can alarm me, though the storms of life almost kill. Ever to this shelter I will be fleeing. No other one can provide peace for me.[3]*

If you're feeling hurt, sad, lonely, or confused, write out the following verses on index cards and read them throughout the day to encourage your soul:

> *All those who know your mercy, Lord, will count on you for help. For you have never yet forsaken those who trust in you. (Psalm 9:10, TLB)*

> *Blessed is the Lord, for he has shown me that his never-failing love protects me like the walls of a fort! (Psalm 31:21, TLB)*

> *My protection and success come from God alone. He is my refuge, a Rock where no enemy can reach me. O my people, trust him all the time. Pour out your long-ings before him, for he can help! (Psalm 62:7-8, TLB)*

> *Lord, when doubts fill my mind, when my heart is in turmoil, quiet me and give me renewed hope and cheer. (Psalm 94:19, TLB)*

> *Father,*
> *Thank you that no matter where we are—sitting in the car, standing at the sink, lying in bed, or walking outside—we can run to you anytime we need encouragement. Thank you that you renew us with your presence and your Word. Amen.*

ENCOURAGEMENT

WHY ARE YOU DOWNCAST, O MY SOUL? WHY SO
DISTURBED WITHIN ME? PUT YOUR HOPE IN GOD, FOR I WILL
YET PRAISE HIM, MY SAVIOR AND MY GOD.

Psalm 42:11, NIV

The idea of being downcast took on new meaning to me when I learned more about sheep and their habits. A "cast" or "cast-down" sheep is one that has turned over on its back and cannot get up. It lies on its back with its feet in the air, and no matter how hard it tries to get up, it has no success. Sometimes it will bleat, but it continues to become more frightened and frustrated.

A sheep becomes downcast when it lies down and its center of gravity shifts so that its feet no longer touch the ground. At this point the sheep frequently panics, realizing that it is impossible to regain its footing on its own. In the heat of the summer, a cast-down sheep can die in a few hours. In cooler weather it might survive a few days. Shepherds are constantly on the lookout for this problem, and that is one of the reasons they count their sheep and search for any that are missing.

We too sometimes become downcast when our center of gravity shifts and we cannot get our feet back on the ground. Only our shepherd can stand us upright and get our blood circulating again. He doesn't rush toward us with a rod to beat us, but he tenderly sets us upright and longs for us to choose to follow him. What a kind shepherd we have!

Father,
Thank you that you are our Good Shepherd, who deals with us tenderly.
Thank you that you don't give up on us when we become downcast. Please
help us to follow your example and to deal tenderly with our children. Amen.

ENCOURAGEMENT

YOUR ASSISTANT, JOSHUA, SON OF NUN, WILL LEAD THE
PEOPLE INTO THE LAND. ENCOURAGE HIM AS HE PREPARES
TO ENTER IT.

Deuteronomy 1:38

Who would have thought that a red coat could have provided so much encouragement?

Back in the 1980s my sister Barbara and her husband, Jordon, went to New Delhi, India, as missionaries, and members of both of their extended families met at O'Hare International Airport to see them off. It was difficult to say good-bye; we knew we wouldn't see the young couple for at least three years.

After we all prayed together, said our tearful good-byes, and watched Barbara and Jordon board the airplane, my husband had an idea. He proposed that all of us go stand on the top level of the parking garage, which was right next to where Barbara and Jordon's airplane was parked. When we all got up there, somebody suggested that my sister Gail take off her bright red coat so we could wave it to get Barb and Jordon's attention. Guess what—it worked!

My sister Barbara remembers: "There we were, sitting on the airplane, having just said our tearful good-byes, when Jordon looked across the aisle and out the window. Something red caught his eye. He nudged me when he realized that it was both of our *families*, saying good-bye again in a dramatic way! At that point we laughed and cried all at the same time. Waving the red coat was a deliberately silly gesture, but it was an act of encouragement that still warms my heart many years later."

Who can we encourage in a creative way? Whose life can we brighten today?

Father,
Thanks for people you have sent into our lives to encourage us at times we
needed it. Please help us to be encouraging to our families and friends today.
Amen.

Prayer 2

AHAB PREPARED A FEAST. BUT ELIJAH CLIMBED TO THE TOP
OF MOUNT CARMEL AND FELL TO THE GROUND AND PRAYED.

1 Kings 18:42

There was a battle going on here, but it wasn't really between Elijah and Ahab. Ahab had declared war on God. After a three-and-a-half-year drought, God had instructed Elijah to tell Ahab that God would provide rain. When Elijah delivered the message, he challenged 450 prophets of Baal to a contest on Mount Carmel, where each side would offer a sacrifice to their God without building a fire. The true God would reveal himself by igniting the fire. All the pagan prophets' praying to Baal failed, but when Elijah prayed to the Lord (even after *water* had been poured over his offering), God sent fire from heaven to consume the sacrifice. The people of Israel praised God, and the prophets of Baal were destroyed.

But the rain still hadn't come. While Ahab went off to eat and drink, Elijah got alone to pray, bending down to the ground with his face between his knees.

Elijah knew that when God asks his people to do something, he doesn't leave them without the resources to carry out the task. We sometimes forget that prayer is our biggest and most powerful resource. Elijah's prayers were rewarded, and the rain came.

What task do you have in front of you today? Paying the bills? Dealing with a child who has a chronic problem? Whether we need wisdom with finances, insight for raising children, help in forgiving another, or strength to make obedient choices, we are wise to get on our knees and passionately ask for God's help.

God of Elijah,
Please be our helper today in the challenges set before us. May we run to you in prayer, realizing that you are our most powerful helper. Amen.

PRAYER 2

O MY PEOPLE, TRUST IN HIM AT ALL TIMES. POUR OUT
YOUR HEART TO HIM, FOR GOD IS OUR REFUGE.

Psalm 62:8

What do we do when we're up against a problem that's far bigger than anything we can handle? Some problems in life are solvable—like the time I turned on my blender when the top wasn't securely fastened. It made quite a mess in my kitchen, but in ten or fifteen minutes I had it cleaned up. Larger problems that can't be solved either quickly or easily—like giving birth to a baby who has severe medical problems—are often accompanied by overwhelming feelings.

I remember a time I encountered a life experience that I neither wanted nor understood. All I knew was that I felt a lot of pain and sadness. I decided to get alone for one day of thinking and praying. I wasn't really alone, though. I have special memories of God's presence and strength washing over me as I paced the floor with open Bible in hand, reading accounts of people in the Bible who met up with seemingly impossible circumstances. The common denominator in their prayers was that they meditated on things God had done in the past, like parting the waters of the Red Sea and protecting Daniel in the lions' den.

We too are wise to begin our prayers with reminders of things God has done in the past. That helps answer the question we all ask when we hit a snag—"Is God *really* in control?" As we remember what he has done in the past and cry out to him for help in our present situation, our hearts are stirred to trust him.

Father,
Thank you for the honesty of the psalmists and other writers in the Bible who were good examples for us of how to pray even when our hearts are heavy. May we pour out our longings to you and rehearse your faithfulness to us. Amen.

I CRY TO YOU FOR HELP, O LORD; IN THE MORNING MY
PRAYER COMES BEFORE YOU. — *Psalm 88:13, NIV*

While preparing to speak to a moms' group on the topic of spiritual nurturing, I asked my sons to help me remember some of the ways I had nurtured them during their growing-up years. One of Jordan's responses was, "Through your prayers." He explained, "I remember how nervous I was the first day of kindergarten, so I was thankful that we stood by the back door and prayed before we walked to school." I smiled, and then I asked him if he remembered what happened right after that. When he looked at me quizzically, I was thankful that he'd forgotten.

That morning Chad had started high school, Nate had started junior high, and Jordan was about to start kindergarten. I wanted to give each boy a good send-off, so before 7:00 a.m., I made breakfast for Chad, prayed with him, and drove him to school. Before 8:00 a.m., I made breakfast for Nate, prayed with him, and drove *him* to school. Thinking that I was doing a good job of sending them all off, I stood at the back door and prayed with Jordan. But as soon as I finished praying and said, "Let's walk to school!" Jordan said, "Mommy, don't I get any breakfast?"

In spite of all my preparations, I had forgotten to feed the little fella. I wanted to cry, but instead I grabbed a granola bar and a juice box on our way out the door. I think I did have a good cry when I returned home, but I laugh about the story now.

I'm thankful that Jordan remembers my prayer and not my forgetfulness. And you know what? We still pray each morning—in the car on the way to high school.

Father,
Thanks for shared moments of prayer with our kids. We all need your help throughout each day. In Jesus' name, amen.

PRAYER 2

> SO WE HAVE CONTINUED PRAYING FOR YOU EVER SINCE
> WE FIRST HEARD ABOUT YOU. WE ASK GOD TO GIVE YOU A
> COMPLETE UNDERSTANDING OF WHAT HE WANTS TO DO IN YOUR
> LIVES, AND WE ASK HIM TO MAKE YOU WISE WITH SPIRITUAL WISDOM.   *Colossians 1:9*

*M*ary, one of my friends from church, hosted a prayer time one fall for moms whose children had gone off to college. We enjoyed a wonderful time of praying together for the needs of our children. What made it particularly special was that Mary suggested we use Scripture to pray back to God some of the specific ways he wants us all to grow to be more like him.

I have found this to be helpful, not only in my prayers for my children, but also in prayers for my husband, myself, and my friends and extended family. Below I've listed several verses we can pray on behalf of our children. As you spend time in God's Word, I'm sure you will find many more prayer verses. But these are good for a start.

> *I pray that your love for each other will overflow more and more, and that you will keep on growing in your knowledge and understanding. (Philippians 1:9)*

> *And now I entrust you to God and the word of his grace—his message that is able to build you up and give you an inheritance with all those he has set apart for himself. (Acts 20:32)*

> *God of the Bible,*
> *Thank you for leaving us your Word of Truth. Thank you that your words add power to our prayer. Amen.*

Prayer 2

I WILL BE CAREFUL TO LIVE A BLAMELESS LIFE. . . . I WILL
LEAD A LIFE OF INTEGRITY IN MY OWN HOME.

Psalm 101:2

*I*n yesterday's devotional I suggested some verses from the Bible that a mom might pray back to God for her children. Today I want to focus on verses that we moms might pray for *ourselves.*

For God has not given us a spirit of fear and timidity, but of power, love, and self-discipline. (2 Timothy 1:7)

If you need wisdom—if you want to know what God wants you to do—ask him, and he will gladly tell you. He will not resent your asking. (James 1:5)

I pray that from his glorious, unlimited resources he will give you mighty inner strength through his Holy Spirit. And I pray that Christ will be more and more at home in your hearts as you trust in him. May your roots go down deep into the soil of God's marvelous love. And may you have the power to understand, as all God's people should, how wide, how long, how high, and how deep his love really is. May you experience the love of Christ, though it is so great you will never fully understand it. Then you will be filled with the fullness of life and power that comes from God. (Ephesians 3:16-19)

Your own soul is nourished when you are kind, but you destroy yourself when you are cruel. (Proverbs 11:17)

Above all else, guard your heart, for it affects everything you do. (Proverbs 4:23)

The Lord will work out his plans for my life—for your faithful love, O Lord, endures forever. Don't abandon me, for you made me. (Psalm 138:8)

Lord,
Thank you that your Word is helpful to us as moms. May we choose to walk down paths that are true and right. May we live with integrity before our children. Amen.

PRAYER 2

> AND THE HOLY SPIRIT HELPS US IN OUR DISTRESS. FOR WE
> DON'T EVEN KNOW WHAT WE SHOULD PRAY FOR, NOR HOW
> WE SHOULD PRAY. BUT THE HOLY SPIRIT PRAYS FOR US WITH
> GROANINGS THAT CANNOT BE EXPRESSED IN WORDS.
>
> Romans 8:26

Have you ever wanted to pray about a distressing or confusing matter, but you just didn't have the words? I have been so sad or perplexed at times that putting my feelings into words seemed overwhelming. At times like that, it is very comforting to realize that God knows us better than we know ourselves. Not only does God know *our* thoughts, but *he* has thoughts and intents for us that are entirely right and pure.

God is much more interested in the purity of our hearts than he is in hearing fancy prayers. When the words just won't come, groans sometimes feel more appropriate. The Bible tells us that God's Spirit groans with us, sharing the burdens of our weakness and suffering. But he doesn't stop at groaning—he also prays for us. And his prayer is that we will be led into God's will even in the middle of suffering.

It is encouraging that when I encounter situations in my life or my children's lives that I cannot analyze or pray about intelligently, groaning or pleading for God's help is a very good thing to do. How freeing it is to know that the Spirit's prayers on our behalf are *totally* in agreement with God's plans.

Father,
We thank you that when we pray, you do not evaluate our words but rather our hearts. Even when we can't find the words, your Spirit is gracious to pray for us. Thank you that you care about us very much. Amen.

PRAYER 2

[DANIEL] PRAYED THREE TIMES A DAY, JUST AS HE HAD
ALWAYS DONE, GIVING THANKS TO HIS GOD. *Daniel 6:10*

*O*ne of the joys of my life is spending time one-on-one with other women. Sometimes we walk and sometimes we sit in one another's kitchens or living rooms with a cup of coffee or a glass of water. This particular day, though, I was sitting in a restaurant having lunch with a friend.

When our meals were served, my friend and I bowed our heads while I thanked God for the food and our friendship. For the next hour or so, we enjoyed our meals and the shared conversation. While we were finishing up with a cup of coffee, a woman leaving the restaurant walked past our table, looked at me, and asked, "Are you a minister?" I smiled and said, "No, I'm not, but why do you ask?" "Well," she said, "I saw you praying before you ate, and I figured that you must be a minister!" My response to her was something like, "We were thanking God for the food and for our time together."

As the woman continued on her way, I sensed that our prayer was a positive, though surprising, phenomenon to her. Reflecting on that brief interchange, I realized that bowed heads and closed eyes are often signals to other people that we are talking to God. The challenge for all of us is to make sure that—as Daniel 6:10 expresses—the posture of our prayer reflects the gratitude to God we're experiencing on the inside.

> God,
> Thanks for people like Daniel who challenge us to pray regularly and often. We need you, and we're grateful we can talk to you. In the name of Jesus, amen.

REDEMPTION

IN HIM WE HAVE REDEMPTION THROUGH HIS BLOOD,
THE FORGIVENESS OF SINS, IN ACCORDANCE WITH THE
RICHES OF GOD'S GRACE THAT HE LAVISHED ON US WITH ALL
WISDOM AND UNDERSTANDING.

Ephesians 1:7-8, NIV

*D*uring their elementary years, my sons rode bikes to school when weather permitted. One day Nate walked home, forgetting that he'd ridden his bike. Around dinnertime he remembered, but when he went back to get the bike, it was gone. First we felt sad with him about his loss, and later we discussed the importance of locks and bike registration.

When Nate became the happy owner of a replacement bike, my husband and I made sure he used a bike lock, and we also decided to register the bike at the police station. On the Saturday my husband took Nate to register, a police auction was taking place. You can imagine their surprise when one of the items to be auctioned off was the bike that Nate had left at school! My husband spoke with the officer in charge, who said that if he could come up with some proof of ownership, Nate could have the bike back. Jim and Nate zipped home, picked up some papers, and later returned with the lost bike.

That evening at dinner we used the story of the bike to explain the meaning of redemption to our children. To redeem is to recover ownership or to rescue. When Jesus died on the cross, he provided redemption to rescue us from sin. Our family's redemption of the bike was very satisfying, but it was not costly. When Jesus redeemed us, it cost him his life's blood. That's how much he loves us!

Great Redeemer,
We are awed at how much you love us. On days when we lack hope and faith,
help us to remember your amazing gift of love. Amen.

REDEMPTION

THEREFORE, SAY TO THE ISRAELITES: "I AM THE LORD, AND
I WILL FREE YOU FROM YOUR SLAVERY IN EGYPT. I WILL
REDEEM YOU WITH MIGHTY POWER AND GREAT ACTS OF JUDGMENT."

Exodus 6:6

The Hebrew people had been slaves for four hundred years when God spoke to Moses from a burning bush, calling him to lead the Hebrews out of Egypt. Three elements of redemption, all present in the deliverance of the Israelites from Egypt, are (1) freedom from bondage, (2) the payment of a redemption price, and (3) an intermediary who secures the redemption.

In the Exodus, the children of Israel were given freedom from slavery and taskmasters. The price of redemption was the blood of a lamb sprinkled on the door frame of each home. And God was clearly the Redeemer, bringing his people out of Egypt with his outstretched arm and mighty acts of judgment.

This Old Testament story of redemption painted a picture of a much better redemption that was yet to come—redemption that would provide freedom for us and for our children.

"The lamb that was killed in every Israeli home that night was in some ways like our Savior. The lamb died for the people, and its blood saved them. That is what happened again many years later, when Christ the Savior came as the Lamb of God to die for each of us."[4]

Those of us who have Jesus' blood painted on our hearts will have nothing to fear when Jesus comes back again. In the same way that God passed over the Israelites who painted lambs' blood on their houses, he will not punish those whose hearts have been cleansed by his blood.

Father,
Thank you for the picture of lambs' blood sprinkled on door frames, which helps us explain redemption to our children. May we always remember that our freedom from sin is possible only because we trust in the blood of Jesus, our Redeemer. Amen.

REDEMPTION

ONCE WE, TOO, WERE FOOLISH AND DISOBEDIENT. WE
WERE MISLED BY OTHERS AND BECAME SLAVES TO MANY
WICKED DESIRES AND EVIL PLEASURES. OUR LIVES WERE FULL OF
EVIL AND ENVY. WE HATED OTHERS, AND THEY HATED US. BUT THEN GOD OUR
SAVIOR SHOWED US HIS KINDNESS AND LOVE. HE SAVED US, NOT BECAUSE OF THE
GOOD THINGS WE DID, BUT BECAUSE OF HIS MERCY. HE WASHED AWAY OUR SINS
AND GAVE US A NEW LIFE THROUGH THE HOLY SPIRIT. HE GENEROUSLY POURED
OUT THE SPIRIT UPON US BECAUSE OF WHAT JESUS CHRIST OUR SAVIOR DID. HE
DECLARED US NOT GUILTY BECAUSE OF HIS GREAT KINDNESS. AND NOW WE KNOW
THAT WE WILL INHERIT ETERNAL LIFE.   *Titus 3:3-7*

When I was a child, my parents collected S & H Green Stamps. The stamps were given for purchases made at various stores, and when a whole book of stamps was filled, it could be redeemed for a gift of the customer's choice. The formula for redemption was: Purchase + Stamps = Gift.

God's redemption is surprisingly different. Instead of offering our purchases to God, the things we offer are our foolishness, disobedience, deceit, enslavement, malice, envy, and hatred. Ugh! And what is God's part? What does he bring to the equation? He shows us kindness and love. Jesus Christ chose to die for us not because of anything good we had done, but because of his mercy. When we believe, he gives us the washing of rebirth and the renewal of the Holy Spirit, treats us as though we hadn't sinned, and calls us God's children.

It was this astounding realization that prompted John Newton to pen the words to the song "Amazing Grace." He was captain of his own slave ship, capturing, selling, and transporting black slaves to plantations in America and the West Indies. On one of Newton's voyages, he came across Thomas Á Kempis's book *The Imitation of Christ*, realized his debauchery, and came to Christ.

As a result he began crusading *against* slavery and became an Anglican pastor. What an amazing story we can share with our children. What an amazing change God's redemption brings to our lives!

> *Amazing grace—how sweet the sound—*
> *That saved a wretch like me!*
> *I once was lost but now am found,*
> *Was blind but now I see.*

REDEMPTION

FOR YOU KNOW THAT GOD PAID A RANSOM TO SAVE YOU
FROM THE EMPTY LIFE YOU INHERITED FROM YOUR ANCESTORS.
AND THE RANSOM HE PAID WAS NOT MERE GOLD OR SILVER. HE
PAID FOR YOU WITH THE PRECIOUS LIFEBLOOD OF CHRIST, THE SINLESS, SPOTLESS
LAMB OF GOD.

1 Peter 1:18-19

How much does redemption cost? For Loung Ung, the price for redemption was her mother's jewelry.

Loung experienced a traumatic childhood in Cambodia under the rule of the Khmer Rouge. Because her father had been a government official in a previous regime, the Khmer Rouge imprisoned him. Hoping to protect the children, Loung's mother sent them all off to different orphanages, but shortly before Vietnam invaded Cambodia in 1978, Loung's parents and some of her siblings died. Loung managed to reconnect with her brother in a refugee camp, and six months later they sold their mother's jewelry for passage to Vietnam, hiding in a boat underneath a pile of dead fish.

Loung eventually came to the United States, later graduated from college, and worked for a while with battered women. But several years ago she took a trip back to Cambodia. After sitting through a memorial service for people killed during the reign of terror, including thirty of her relatives, she decided to dedicate her life to Cambodian causes. She said, "My whole life is just about being redeemed."

Having experienced incredible trauma at the hands of a corrupt government, Loung was moved to serve because she knew what she had been redeemed from. Our redemption as believers was not paid for with jewelry—it cost Jesus his blood. When we realize what Jesus did for us and all the rottenness he has saved us from, we become motivated to serve him with grateful hearts. Like Loung, we can say, "My whole life is just about being redeemed."

Great Redeemer,
Thank you that you were willing to redeem us by paying for our sins with
your blood. May we serve you with grateful hearts. Amen.

REDEMPTION

PREACH THE WORD OF GOD. BE PERSISTENT, WHETHER
THE TIME IS FAVORABLE OR NOT. PATIENTLY CORRECT,
REBUKE, AND ENCOURAGE YOUR PEOPLE WITH GOOD
TEACHING.

2 Timothy 4:2

Are you praying for redemption in the life of one of your family members or friends? Do you know a child, a parent, a neighbor, or someone else you care about who needs Christ? When Jesus met the Samaritan woman at the well (John 4), he knew redemption was *exactly* what she needed. She was living a sinful life, having been married five times and now living with a man who wasn't her husband. It's interesting to observe how Jesus dealt with her. He knew that before she could experience saving faith, she needed to be convicted of her sin.

"The only way to prepare the soil of the heart for the seed is to plow it up with conviction. That was why Jesus told [the woman] to go get her husband: he forced her to admit her sin. There can be no conversion without conviction."[5] Saving faith takes place after a person has been convicted and has chosen to repent. Jesus convicted this woman by challenging her mind, stirring her emotions, and touching her conscience.

Since I am not God, I cannot see into other people's hearts, convict them of their sin, or change them. But there are some things I can do: I can share God's Word, and I can pray. When I do, I am joining hands with God in preparing another person's soul for the good news of God's redemption.

> *Father,*
> *I pray for _____. According to the truth of John 16:8,*
> *please convict him or her of guilt in regard to sin, righteousness, and judgment, that he or she may be drawn to you and receive your salvation. Amen.*

REDEMPTION

UNDER THE OLD SYSTEM, THE BLOOD OF GOATS AND BULLS
AND THE ASHES OF A YOUNG COW COULD CLEANSE PEOPLE'S
BODIES FROM RITUAL DEFILEMENT. JUST THINK HOW MUCH MORE THE
BLOOD OF CHRIST WILL PURIFY OUR HEARTS FROM DEEDS THAT LEAD TO DEATH SO
THAT WE CAN WORSHIP THE LIVING GOD. FOR BY THE POWER OF THE ETERNAL
SPIRIT, CHRIST OFFERED HIMSELF TO GOD AS A PERFECT SACRIFICE FOR OUR SINS.

Hebrews 9:13-14

My mom, Betty Banks, is an incredible person. For a petite woman in her seventies, she sure has a lot of pep! Some years ago, my mom and dad were having the outside of their house painted. Over the span of a week, the gentleman who painted their house saw my mom coming and going—running errands, mowing the lawn, pulling weeds, washing windows, and much more. At the end of the week, the painter said to her, "You have incredible energy! I have a favor to ask you. If I'm ever in the hospital needing a blood transfusion, may I please ask for a pint of *your* blood?"

In a blood transfusion, the donor's blood becomes a substitute for the recipient's blood. In other words, it takes the place of the original blood.

The Bible tells us that since we're all sinners, we deserve death (Romans 6:23). But in God's merciful plan, when Jesus redeemed us he became the substitute and sacrifice for our sins (1 Peter 3:18). The substitution Christ made for us isn't limited to the exchange of our sins for his righteousness. He also gave his life to purify our hearts and make it possible for us to worship God. He cleanses us from the inside out, changing our hearts and giving us new desires. The purity he brings frees us from slavery to sin, prompting us to worship and serve him. If we place our faith in Christ, his redemption brings us from death to life and replaces our stony hearts of sin with new, obedient hearts (Ezekiel 36:26).

Father,
Thank you that your redemption brings cleansing to our hearts. May we serve you joyfully because you have freed us from our sins. In Jesus' name, amen.

REDEMPTION

> BUT HE WAS WOUNDED AND CRUSHED FOR OUR SINS.
> HE WAS BEATEN THAT WE MIGHT HAVE PEACE. HE WAS
> WHIPPED, AND WE WERE HEALED!
>
> Isaiah 53:5

I wish that I owned the tattered old devotional book my parents used to read out loud when I was a child. Every now and then, they asked us children which story we'd like to hear. I chose the story about a man who lovingly took the punishment that another man deserved.

If my memory serves me correctly, the two men in the story were prisoners; the older man had been imprisoned for something he didn't do, and the younger man had committed a crime for which his prison sentence was just. The younger man was about to receive a severe beating. But just before the punishment was to be meted out, the older man stepped forward and stated that he wanted to take the beating in place of the younger man. He did, and the beating was so harsh that the older man died, sparing the younger man.

Every time I heard that story as a child, my eyes filled with tears. (They still do.) What selfless love and compassion the older man showed! That story helped me to understand Jesus' death on the cross for my sins. He died as the just for the unjust. He willingly and compassionately took the punishment of my sin upon himself so that I could be set free from the eternal consequences of sin and death. He was beaten so I could have peace. He was whipped so I could be healed. "All the kings throughout history sent their people out to die for them," said author Dave Brown. "Only one person ever died for their people willingly and lovingly." Isaiah 63:9 tells us that in his love and in his pity, Jesus redeemed us.

Father,
Thank you for the love and compassion that prompted Jesus to die in our place. We will praise you for your merciful plan forever. In Jesus' name, amen.

DISCIPLINE

DISCIPLINE YOUR CHILDREN WHILE THERE IS HOPE. IF YOU
DON'T, YOU WILL RUIN THEIR LIVES. *Proverbs 19:18*

In a scene from the classic children's book *Black Beauty* by Anna Sewell, a boy attempts to jump a pony over a gate. When the pony doesn't jump, the boy impatiently beats him with a whip. These jump attempts and subsequent whippings are repeated several times, and the boy finally hits the horse on the head. Having had quite enough, the horse puts down his head, throws up his heels, and hurls the boy into a hedge of thornbushes. A man who observes this incident reports the whole situation to the boy's parents. The mother's reaction is, "Oh, poor baby," while the father says, "This isn't the first or second time he's done that to our horse—this is a good opportunity for him to learn a lesson."

It's good for us mothers to be empathetic to the pain and feelings of our children, but when children are experiencing the natural consequences of their destructive behavior, it's not healthy to protect them from those consequences. If we do, we're basically encouraging more of the same behavior in the future.

Part of our role as mothers is to help our children see that their behavior, good or bad, has consequences. And it's much better for them to learn that in the small things now than to experience great difficulties with higher authorities down the road.

> God,
> We ask for great wisdom in teaching discipline to our children. Please help us to find a healthy balance of truth and grace as we interact with them. Amen.

Discipline

> For God has not given us a spirit of fear and
> timidity, but of power, love, and self-discipline.
>
> *2 Timothy 1:7*

When I open the newspaper each morning, I see evidence of a lack of self-discipline. I read about sex scandals in the government, bombings around the world, and fraudulent business deals in big companies. In my own community I hear about extramarital affairs, robberies, and addictive behaviors.

Discipline is defined as controlled behavior resulting from training—self-control. How we are taught—what we learned in the past and what we are presently learning—determines the way we live. And what we are presently teaching our children will influence the way they live.

Some people think, *Who needs self-discipline anyway? It's too restrictive! What I want is freedom!* If we choose to follow that path, the result isn't freedom—it's bondage. The woman I walked past at the grocery store who reeked of alcohol was not experiencing the freedom of drinking as much as she wanted; she was in bondage to her craving.

Margaret Henshaw, a distinguished American soprano and voice teacher, was once asked about the key to becoming a master performer and teacher. Her response was, "Nobody likes the word discipline; I hate it myself, but if you don't discipline yourself you're never going to accomplish anything. I think many people confuse freedom and discipline. They are not taught that *freedom is the highest form of discipline*" (emphasis added).[6]

If we wish to be free from the restraints of any kind of slavery or oppression, we must choose discipline.

Father,
The closer we walk with you, the more your Spirit helps us to want self-discipline. Please help us to grow in that quality and model it in front of our children. Amen.

DISCIPLINE

IF YOU REFUSE TO DISCIPLINE YOUR CHILDREN, IT PROVES
YOU DON'T LOVE THEM; IF YOU LOVE YOUR CHILDREN, YOU
WILL BE PROMPT TO DISCIPLINE THEM.   *Proverbs 13:24*

When my husband had a business appointment in Northern England, we took a train from London up to Carlisle. Knowing that we both had reading and paperwork to do, we chose to sit in car *F*, which was labeled the "quiet car." Ironically, several people in the quiet car were talking on cell phones or carrying on animated conversations. To add to the confusion, the conductor announced over the loudspeaker that the reservation system wasn't working properly, so there were no longer any reserved seats. He suggested that people boarding the train choose any available seat. That worked until we got to Birmingham.

At the Birmingham stop, a woman with a young child boarded, and—insisting that she was entitled to her reserved seats—made a big scene by uprooting the two people already sitting there. As if that wasn't bad enough, the woman and child made noise for the rest of the trip. By the end of the train ride, my blood pressure was up a few notches. I resented that the conductors had not exercised proper control. It didn't seem fair that people could get away with being noisy in the quiet car, or that the woman with the child could uproot two other people. The rules had not been enforced. *Where was the person in charge?* I wondered.

Thankfully, that was only a train ride. But discipline in our homes has much larger repercussions, not only for the person breaking the rules, but also for bystanders. If one child in a family is allowed to break the rules, the other children are silently (or not so silently) asking, "Who's in charge here?" Responsible parents are willing to exercise *discipline* (control, orderliness, and regulation) for the sake of *everyone* involved. As a result, everyone in the situation feels better loved and cared for.

Wise Father,
Thank you that you have left us so many sound principles of wisdom in the
Bible. Please help us to apply them. In Jesus' name, amen.

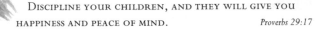

DISCIPLINE

DISCIPLINE YOUR CHILDREN, AND THEY WILL GIVE YOU HAPPINESS AND PEACE OF MIND.   *Proverbs 29:17*

The sheriff's office in a Texas city once distributed a list of rules titled "How to Raise a Juvenile Delinquent in Your Own Family":

> *Begin with infancy to give the child everything he wants. This will insure his believing that the world owes him a living. Pick up everything he leaves lying around. This will teach him that he can always throw off responsibility on others. Take his part against neighbors, teachers, and policemen. They are all prejudiced against your child. He is a "free spirit" and he's never wrong. Finally, prepare yourself for a life full of grief. You're going to have it.*[7]

Sometimes I see moms literally throw up their hands and say (in front of their child), "I don't know what to do with this child!" Every mom in the world has moments when she truly *doesn't* know what to do, but admitting it in front of the child creates more problems than it solves. For starters, the child gets the message that the mother's posture toward him is one of helplessness and disgust.

Whenever we feel overwhelmed, it's good for us to stop and ask God for his help. God promises to provide the wisdom and strength to carry out any task he gives us, if we're ready to ask for it. God's Word is another valuable resource, because it contains a huge supply of wisdom that is readily available. We also need other moms to confide in—what would we do without them? Knowing that our friends face similar challenges is immensely encouraging.

Father,
When we experience those moments of "I don't know what to do with this child," please help us remember first to run to you in our need, realizing that you will equip us with the strength and wisdom necessary to raise our children properly. Amen.

DISCIPLINE

HE WHO IGNORES DISCIPLINE DESPISES HIMSELF, BUT WHO-
EVER HEEDS CORRECTION GAINS UNDERSTANDING.

Proverbs 15:32, NIV

*I*f discipline is training that is expected to produce specific patterns of behavior in our children, we need to do a fair amount of planning, teaching, and supervising to make sure we will see the desired results.

Some of the areas I've worked on with my sons are tithing and reaching out to needy people. If we want to see growth in specific areas like these, we're wise to identify, plan, and account for each area. I read about a study at a major university that attempted to identify how people turn ideas into action. The results were enlightening:

Step	Probability of Implementation
1. Hear an idea that you like.	10 percent
2. Consciously decide to adopt the idea.	25 percent
3. Decide when you will do it.	40 percent
4. Plan how you will do it.	50 percent
5. Commit to someone else that you will do it.	65 percent
6. Have a specific future appointment with the person you committed to, at which time you will report to him whether you have done it.	95 percent [8]

The progression of these percentages is quite amazing!

Weekly planning and reviewing a young child's income helps encourage him to tithe. Encouraging a high school student to take a discouraged friend out for ice cream prompts Christian care. We all have opportunities to promote Christ-like behavior in our children.

Father,
May we promote Christian character by living it ourselves. As we see areas where our children need extra help, may we come alongside to help them plan, to encourage them, and to hold them accountable. Amen.

DISCIPLINE

PHYSICAL EXERCISE HAS SOME VALUE, BUT SPIRITUAL
EXERCISE IS MUCH MORE IMPORTANT, FOR IT PROMISES A
REWARD IN BOTH THIS LIFE AND THE NEXT.   *1 Timothy 4:8*

Where do you fall on the continuum of physical exercise? Do you relate to Robert Maynard Hutchins, who said, "Whenever I feel like exercise I lie down until the feeling passes"? Or are you training for a half-marathon? I'd like to think that I fall somewhere in the middle.

I love to walk, and I do it almost 365 days a year. It helps me to feel better, think better, and fit into my clothes better. But as beneficial as physical exercise is, the truth of the Bible has borne itself out in my experience that spiritual exercise is even better. Three disciplines have impacted my life greatly:

1. *Reading the Bible.* My testimony to its value is not original; it's from Psalm 119:92-93 (NIV): "If your law had not been my delight, I would have perished in my affliction. I will never forget your precepts, for by them you have preserved my life."
2. *Praying.* Prayer is a lifeline for me. Although I begin each day with a structured prayer time, I'm aware of God's presence all day long and enjoy talking to him about big and little things. Psalm 34:17 assures us, "The Lord hears his people when they call to him for help."
3. *Fellowshipping at church.* Whatever degree of maturity God is growing in me is due, in part, to fellowship in his body. Ephesians 4:16 reminds us, "Under his direction, the whole body is fitted together perfectly. As each part does its own special work, it helps the other parts grow, so that the whole body is healthy and growing and full of love."

God's Word reminds me that being spiritually disciplined is a win-win situation. As I invest time in spiritual disciplines, I reap rewards both now and in eternity.

Father,
Thanks for comparing physical exercise with spiritual exercise, because exercise is something we can all understand. Please help us to place a high value on spiritual fitness. Amen.

Discipline

THE WISE MAN SAVES FOR THE FUTURE, BUT THE FOOLISH
MAN SPENDS WHATEVER HE GETS. *Proverbs 21:20, TLB*

*M*anaging our money is a challenging discipline for parents and children alike. So how do we teach good principles in this area to our children? A simple method I like involves four clear glass mason jars, which are labeled *earnings*, *God*, *savings*, and *spending*. Each has a corresponding principle. When a child first earns his money or receives his allowance, he drops it in the *earnings* jar. It's good for us to remind our children that everything we have or receive comes from God in the first place.

The second principle we can teach our child is that since Old Testament times, God has asked his people to give some of their earnings back to him. A parent can help a child decide what percent of the money from the earnings jar will be given back to *God* (the second jar). The purpose of such giving is to teach us to put God first in our lives.

Saving for the future isn't advice that began with modern investment companies. God advised about *saving* (the third jar) in the verse above. When our children set aside their *spending money* (the fourth jar), we can help them avoid impulse buying by suggesting that they *think* about their purchases for a few days, a few weeks, or a few months. If they've thought ahead and priced around, they will appreciate the item or activity much more than if they acted hastily. All these principles help build a more secure child, and they also encourage self-discipline down the road.

God,
Thank you that the earth is full of your riches and your wisdom. Please give us your wisdom as we manage the money we are responsible for. Then we can pass these principles of discipline on to our children. Amen.

FOOD

"You didn't have enough faith," Jesus told them. "I assure you, even if you had faith as small as a mustard seed you could say to this mountain, 'Move from here to there,' and it would move. Nothing would be impossible."

Matthew 17:20

My family has this running joke about mustard. I like the plain variety, but everyone else in the family (my husband and three sons) likes Grey Poupon. So I shop for both kinds and try not to take it personally when they call mine the "sissy mustard."

Here's a life lesson you can teach your kids the next time they squeeze mustard on a hot dog: Even though the mustard seed is extremely small, the mustard plant can reach a height of fifteen feet. From the seeds of the mustard plant we can make a sauce (plain or spicy) to use on our favorite sandwiches.

When Jesus lived on earth, he taught his disciples spiritual truths by talking about everyday things. Mustard came up several times in his teaching. In Matthew 17 Jesus grieved over the lack of faith he saw in his disciples and told them that if they had faith as small as a mustard seed, they would do great things for God.

Great faith has very small beginnings. It begins with opening ourselves to God. When we come to him and expose our dark hearts to the light of his grace and truth, the roots of our lives are forced down into the soil of his amazing love. Then, miraculously, just as green shoots of the mustard plant come out of the ground and grow to heights of four to fifteen feet, we see shoots of faith—maybe even large ones—appearing in our lives.

Father,
Thank you for teaching us big lessons through small things. May we place our faith in you and see growth take place in our lives. Amen.

FOOD

YOU ARE THE SALT OF THE EARTH. BUT WHAT GOOD IS
SALT IF IT HAS LOST ITS FLAVOR? CAN YOU MAKE IT USEFUL
AGAIN? IT WILL BE THROWN OUT AND TRAMPLED UNDERFOOT
AS WORTHLESS.

Matthew 5:13

*H*ow do you use salt in your home? Yesterday I sprinkled it into the batter when I was baking Irish soda bread, and later in the day I used it when I prepared lasagna. In the winter my family sometimes sprinkles salt on our front step and walkway to melt the ice.

Salt was an important commodity in Old Testament times. Similar to today, it was used as a seasoning, but it was also used to preserve and purify. The expression *covenant of salt* meant the same thing as an everlasting covenant, representing faithfulness, dependability, and preservation.

When Jesus taught that his believers are the salt of the earth, he was speaking of these same properties of salt—faithfulness, dependability, and preservation. Just as salt gives flavor to our food, we Christians are God's salt in the world today. We are distinctive, and we have a unique flavor. If we lose our saltiness, we will lose effectiveness to build up God's kingdom.

Salt makes food more appetizing when it's used in appropriate measures. But if you've ever had the top of the saltshaker fly off when you were sprinkling salt on your scrambled eggs, you know that too much of a good thing can be less than appetizing. Likewise, as believers we need to realize that being overbearing in our witness is not effective. Since we are supposed to be appetizing, not offensive, we are wise to live lives that are gracious and faithful to God's truth.

God,
Thank you that you don't ask us to be salty on our own. May we walk close to you so our lives will be both tasty and tasteful. Amen.

FOOD

Do you like honey? Don't eat too much of it, or it will make you sick!

Proverbs 25:16

*M*y mom used to drizzle honey over hot biscuits she baked for us on cold winter mornings. I add honey to hot cooked carrots to sweeten the taste. (Hint: use equal parts honey and butter.) Perhaps you use it as a substitute for sugar in some of your own recipes. Simply put, honey sweetens things. But too much of it isn't a good thing. Just ask Winnie the Pooh about that! When moms across the country read Winnie the Pooh stories out loud, recounting Pooh's eating a whole pot of honey and promptly getting stuck in a doorway, even children get the idea that although honey is good, too much honey is not.

The Bible uses honey to teach us about perspective and moderation, not just in regard to food. We need healthy perspective for all of life. Proverbs 25:17 speaks to moderation in friendships: "Don't visit your neighbors too often, or you will wear out your welcome." Later in the same chapter, verse 27 warns, "Just as it is not good to eat too much honey, it is not good for people to think about all the honors they deserve." To be respected is a good thing, but to go running after recognition is not.

In Proverbs 24:13-14, a wise father encourages his son to enjoy honey, which is sweet to the taste, but even more, to enjoy wisdom, which is sweet to the soul. Honey brings instant delight, but wisdom brings lasting hope!

Father,
May we be wise and look for healthy perspective and balance in all of life.
Amen.

FOOD

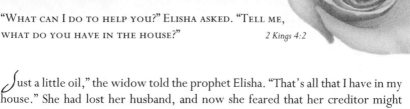

"WHAT CAN I DO TO HELP YOU?" ELISHA ASKED. "TELL ME,
WHAT DO YOU HAVE IN THE HOUSE?"
2 Kings 4:2

*J*ust a little oil," the widow told the prophet Elisha. "That's all that I have in my house." She had lost her husband, and now she feared that her creditor might come and take away her two sons as slaves. If the Israelites around this widow had been following the Levitical laws, the woman and her sons would have been provided for. Instead, sadly, their situation seemed to be headed in the wrong direction.

When the widow was feeling totally helpless, Elisha asked her two questions: "How can I help you?" and "What do you have in your house?" I appreciate the graciousness of Elisha's inquiries. He wanted to help, and he began with what she had. His questions were not patronizing or pessimistic but compassionate and hopeful.

Elisha then told her to borrow many jars from her neighbors. Next she was to pour oil into all the borrowed containers. Then the oil flowed until she and her sons filled the last jar! She sold the oil and had enough money to pay off her creditors and support her family.

Like the widow, we sometimes face situations that we think might have, could have, or should have headed in a different direction. When the painful realities of life leave us feeling needy or even hopeless, we can run to God for his gracious compassion and words of hope. He is still the God who sees and provides.

> *Father,*
> *Thank you that you saw the widow's situation and provided for her. Thank you that you see us today and that we can run to you and ask you to provide for us. Amen.*

FOOD

ALL THE WILD ANIMALS, LARGE AND SMALL, AND ALL
THE BIRDS AND FISH WILL BE AFRAID OF YOU. I HAVE
PLACED THEM IN YOUR POWER. I HAVE GIVEN THEM TO YOU FOR
FOOD, JUST AS I HAVE GIVEN YOU GRAIN AND VEGETABLES.   *Genesis 9:2-3*

Breakfast: A bowl of granola with a glass of orange juice.

Lunch: A turkey and Swiss cheese sandwich.

Dinner: Sweet-and-sour chicken, rice, green beans, and tossed salad.

Is anyone hungry? All through the Bible, we see that God uses food to provide for us, to refresh us, and to sustain us.

God provides food for us. In Genesis 1:29, God said, "Look! I have given you the seed-bearing plants throughout the earth and all the fruit trees for your food." Psalm 104:27-28 reads, "Every one of these [plants, animals, people] depends on you to give them their food as they need it. When you supply it, they gather it. You open your hand to feed them, and they are satisfied." The words *all* and *every* point out the vast extent of God's food supply throughout the world.

God refreshes us with food. The variety of foods that God has created on this earth is broad. He does more than just provide—he refreshes us with a mixture of shapes, smells, textures, colors, and flavors. Sprinkled through the Bible are foods like grapes, mandrakes, melons, figs, pomegranates, leeks, garlic, bread, quail, venison, and much more.

God sustains us with food. Perhaps the most vivid example in the Bible of food as sustenance is found in Nehemiah 9:21. Hearkening back to God's care for the children of Israel, this verse acknowledges, "For forty years you sustained them in the wilderness." God supernaturally provided manna and quail for the Israelites to eat.

It's amazing to realize that God's work of providing, refreshing, and sustaining goes back to Creation. "I realized," wrote Ingrid Trobisch, "I had never really thanked God for all the work he had done in my creation. I was overcome as I thought of how God had made plans for my life long before I was born." God is so good.

> *Gracious God who provides, refreshes, and sustains,*
> *We want our mealtime thanks to be motivated out of gratitude to you and not just habit. Thanks for the bounty you provide us. Amen.*

FOOD

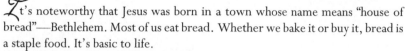

John 6:48

*I*t's noteworthy that Jesus was born in a town whose name means "house of bread"—Bethlehem. Most of us eat bread. Whether we bake it or buy it, bread is a staple food. It's basic to life.

Imagine what it would have been like to be on the hillside when Jesus blessed the five loaves of bread and two fish, multiplying them to feed thousands of hungry people. The miracle was amazing, but also amazing was the response of the crowd. After seeing Jesus provide them with food, the people wanted to make him king. Why? Not because they believed he was the Messiah, but because they thought he could provide them many material things. The people were so caught up in having their immediate physical needs met that they missed the real significance of the event—that Jesus *is* the bread of life. Jesus knew that they desired the bread more than they desired him.

May we not miss the truth that we need Jesus as our staple—that the Bread of Life who was born in the town called "house of bread" wants to be our spiritual food each day of our lives.

> *O little town of Bethlehem, how still we see thee lie!*
> *Above thy deep and dreamless sleep the silent stars go by.*
> *Yet in thy dark streets shineth the everlasting light;*
> *The hopes and fears of all the years are met in thee tonight.*[1]

Father,
Thank you that you are the bread of life and that you can meet all our hopes and fears. Amen.

FOOD

Is anyone thirsty? Come and drink—even if you have no money! Come, take your choice of wine or milk—it's all free! Why spend your money on food that does not give you strength? Why pay for food that does you no good? Listen, and I will tell you where to get food that is good for the soul!

Isaiah 55:1-2

On a bright, sunny day, our family hiked up a trail in the Colorado Rocky Mountains to Agnes Veil Falls. The falls were situated way back off the road, and it was quite a climb to get there. But the reward was worth it! With the sun high in the deep blue sky, we heard the rushing water before we saw it. Great torrents of sparkling water cascaded over the jagged rocks, coming from melting snow above our ten-thousand-foot perch.

My family loves to vacation close to water. There is something refreshing about being near it. But water is more than just good recreation; it's essential for our bodies. We may be able to live without food for some days, but not without water. That helps explain why Isaiah likened our thirst for water to our soul's thirst for God.

Sometimes we try to quench our hunger and thirst for God with other things, even good things. But Isaiah reminds us that it is only in finding the Lord that we will find satisfaction. And Jesus, in the Gospel of John, reminds us that he himself is the Living Water. God's Word and God's Son water our hearts, bringing life to us and satisfying us with God himself.

Lord,
Thank you that you have provided a way to quench the thirst in our souls.
May we daily drink in all the refreshment that it provides and be fruitful for
you. In the strong name of Jesus, amen.

WITNESS

HEAR, O ISRAEL! THE LORD IS OUR GOD, THE LORD ALONE.
AND YOU MUST LOVE THE LORD YOUR GOD WITH ALL YOUR
HEART, ALL YOUR SOUL, AND ALL YOUR STRENGTH. AND
YOU MUST COMMIT YOURSELVES WHOLEHEARTEDLY TO THESE COMMANDS I AM
GIVING YOU TODAY. REPEAT THEM AGAIN AND AGAIN TO YOUR CHILDREN. TALK
ABOUT THEM WHEN YOU ARE AT HOME AND WHEN YOU ARE AWAY ON A JOURNEY,
WHEN YOU ARE LYING DOWN AND WHEN YOU ARE GETTING UP AGAIN.

Deuteronomy 6:4-7

One of my three sons was baptized last night. As I listened to the testimonies of the seven junior and senior high school students who were baptized, I was struck by how many times they said their mothers were the ones who introduced them to Jesus. The majority of those related that it happened at bedtime, when the moms were tucking the children in for the night.

It's no surprise that our children often open up about things that are on their hearts and minds during those closing moments of the day. They don't feel the rush of getting to the next activity, and as we sit on the bed next to them, they are often interested in extending the moments of closeness.

To be effective witnesses for God in the lives of our children, we must do several things. First, we must listen to God through his Word and through prayer. Second, we must choose to love God with all our heart, soul, and strength. Third, we must open our hearts to God, exchanging our sinful ways for his righteous ways. Fourth, we must make a conscious effort to impress God's Word on our children's hearts, realizing this can happen in many different settings and postures.

As we listen to God, open our hearts to him, and share his Word with our children, we eagerly await evidences of faith and growth in their hearts.

Father,
Thank you for the great privilege of pointing and leading our children to you.
May we not cause our children to stumble by failing to walk closely with you
ourselves. Amen.

WITNESS

WE ARE CHRIST'S AMBASSADORS, AND GOD IS USING US TO
SPEAK TO YOU. WE URGE YOU, AS THOUGH CHRIST HIMSELF
WERE HERE PLEADING WITH YOU, "BE RECONCILED TO GOD!"

2 Corinthians 5:20

When I visit Washington DC, I like to drive past embassies of ambassadors from other countries. The architectural designs of the buildings reflect the countries that are represented.

Ambassadors are diplomatic officers of high rank who represent one nation in the capital of another, skillfully acting on behalf of their government. Although bound by instructions and beliefs from their homeland, ambassadors exercise considerable authority with discretion. For ambassadors to be effective, they must act acceptably in the receiving country.

When we enter into a relationship with God, we too become ambassadors with a message. As mothers, we are ambassadors first to our children, and they live in the "embassy" along with us—the embassy of our home. If God's Spirit is present in our lives, they will see whom we represent. The message we have been given is that through Christ we can have a relationship with God. When humans rebelled against God, we became his enemies, but God provided a way for us to be forgiven through Jesus' death on the cross. When we see our need for God, desire a relationship with him, and turn to Christ, he takes away our guilt and gives us his righteousness.

Our responsibility is to represent God as tactfully as we can because we are messengers of peace. Our daily briefing on God's plan for the world comes through the time we spend in his Word. We represent the King of kings, and our homes are embassies. What a privileged position we hold.

God,
Thank you that you have chosen us to represent you. May we do it with accurate information and tact that come from you. Amen.

WITNESS

INSTEAD, YOU MUST WORSHIP CHRIST AS LORD OF YOUR
LIFE. AND IF YOU ARE ASKED ABOUT YOUR CHRISTIAN HOPE,
ALWAYS BE READY TO EXPLAIN IT. *1 Peter 3:15*

While I was walking with my friend Ruthie one morning, she related something that had happened the day before. She had been to see her regular hairdresser for a trim, and the hairdresser asked, "What makes you the way you are? You live a charming life, although I know you encounter difficult things like everybody else. But you're cheerful, and you don't bad-mouth other people. So what's different about you?"

First, Ruthie laughed and jokingly suggested, "I must be blessed with lots of serotonin in my blood!" Then she offered, "My life is different because of my relationship with Jesus Christ." Her hairdresser responded that she suspected it would have something to do with religion. Ruthie later followed through on that initial question, and seeds of truth are being planted. I came away from my walk with Ruthie reminded that people notice attractive qualities in those who are part of God's Kingdom.

Each spring break my family vacations on the beach in Florida, where we spend a whole week in the sun. Upon our return to Illinois, friends often ask, "Where have you been? It must have been somewhere warm!" When we spend lots of time with God's Son, in prayer and in God's Word, people will notice that too—beginning with our families. Our lives will be different. They will see the attractive fruits of God's Spirit and find hope.

Father,
We are encouraged when people who don't know you notice there's something
different about people who do. May we walk closely to you in obedience so we
will never be a disgrace to your Kingdom. Amen.

WITNESS

I PRAY THAT YOU MAY BE ACTIVE IN SHARING YOUR
FAITH, SO THAT YOU WILL HAVE A FULL UNDERSTANDING
OF EVERY GOOD THING WE HAVE IN CHRIST. *Philemon 1:6, NIV*

If our lives are built on a vertical relationship with Christ, we will be motivated to move outward horizontally, bearing witness of that relationship to others. To be an effective communicator of our faith to those around us, we need to be aware of the good things we have in Christ.

Colossians 3:12-17 reminds us what the "wardrobe" of the Christian includes—the virtues that develop as we walk with Jesus:

1. Compassion—a tender heart
2. Kindness—thoughtfulness, understanding, and generosity
3. Humility—lack of pride and pretentiousness
4. Gentleness—a mild and pleasant nature
5. Patience—a willingness to endure
6. Forbearance—bearing with one another
7. Forgiveness—after dealing with our complaints, we stop blaming each other
8. Love—being devoted to one another, thus bringing unity and wholeness.
9. Peace—being in harmony with each other
10. Thankfulness—gratitude and appreciation
11. Love for God's Word—allowing it to dwell in our hearts, and then wanting to share it with others
12. A desire to please Jesus. Warren Wiersbe writes, "What blessings would come to our homes if each member of the family said, 'I will live each day to please Christ and make him preeminent in all things.' There would be less selfishness and more love; less impatience and more tenderness; less wasting of money on foolish things and more living for the things that matter most."[2]

These are the garments of our wardrobe that bear witness to those around us that we know Christ.

Father,
Just as we spend time taking care of our wardrobe, may we spend time with
you through your Word and prayer. We want the garments of our hearts to
point people around us to you. Amen.

WITNESS

You are the salt of the earth. But what good is salt if it has lost its flavor? Can you make it useful again? It will be thrown out and trampled underfoot as worthless. You are the light of the world—like a city on a mountain, glowing in the night for all to see. Don't hide your light under a basket! Instead, put it on a stand and let it shine for all. *Matthew 5:13-15*

While doing some last-minute shopping one week before Christmas, I stumbled on a sale at Gap. Several racks of young men's sweaters had been priced at ten dollars each—a big bargain for sweaters I knew my sons would enjoy.

After purchasing three sweaters, I left the store feeling excited about discovering such a great sale. Thinking that the news was too good to keep to myself, I mentioned it to several friends I spoke with throughout the day. If my friends still had any shopping left to do, I figured they might find something for their kids too.

Later, I got to thinking about my happy discovery and the excitement with which I shared it. Why is it, I thought, that I'll call a friend and share good news about a sale on sweaters at Gap, but sometimes I'm not as quick to share good news about gifts that Christ has given to me?

Through Christ's death and resurrection, I've received peace with God, a new identity, forgiveness of sin, the presence of God's Spirit, wisdom for the asking, and much more. I wouldn't call a friend and itemize every Christmas gift I'd bought, nor would I call a friend and describe everything Christ has done for me—the lists would be too long. But I can share *one* way that Christ is helping me today. I can witness about Christ's gifts—one person at a time.

Father,
Thank you for the privilege of representing you to others. Help us to do it with joy. Amen.

WITNESS

THE WOMAN LEFT HER WATER JAR BESIDE THE WELL AND
WENT BACK TO THE VILLAGE AND TOLD EVERYONE, "COME
AND MEET A MAN WHO TOLD ME EVERYTHING I EVER DID! CAN
THIS BE THE MESSIAH?" SO THE PEOPLE CAME STREAMING FROM THE VILLAGE
TO SEE HIM.

John 4:28-30

*H*ow ironic," we might say, "that Jesus asked the woman at the well for a drink of water!" After all, it was the *woman* who was really thirsty, right down to the bottom of her heart. She should have been asking Jesus for some of his living water—but she didn't know who he was yet.

I once asked a gentleman on a London street to take a picture of my husband and me. "Please include the red phone booth behind us in the picture," I said. "I'm very fond of them." After the man graciously took our picture, he handed me my camera, saying, "So, you like those red phone booths, do you? My great-great grandfather, Charles Gilbert Scott, was the architect who designed them!"

You can imagine how surprised and honored we felt to meet this descendant of such a famous English architect. When we returned home, I enjoyed telling the story to family and friends. My only regret was that I didn't think to ask Mr. Scott if we could take *his* picture in front of the phone booth!

As a result of that experience in London, I can better appreciate the excitement of the woman at the well when she discovered that she was talking to Christ. Here was someone she'd been waiting for her whole life. It's no wonder that she asked her friends to come and meet him too.

Father,
Please give us courage and spontaneity in sharing what you have done for us
with others who don't yet know you. In the name of Jesus, amen.

WITNESS

ONE DAY AS JESUS WAS WALKING ALONG THE SHORE BESIDE
THE SEA OF GALILEE, HE SAW TWO BROTHERS—SIMON, ALSO
CALLED PETER, AND ANDREW—FISHING WITH A NET, FOR THEY WERE
COMMERCIAL FISHERMEN. JESUS CALLED OUT TO THEM, "COME, BE MY DISCIPLES,
AND I WILL SHOW YOU HOW TO FISH FOR PEOPLE!"
Matthew 4:18-19

The phrase "fishers of men," used in many translations of this passage, was not used for the first time in the Bible. Employed for centuries by Greek and Roman philosophers, the phrase described a person seeking to "catch" others through teaching and persuasion. Since the men involved in this account in Matthew's Gospel were fishermen, it made a lot of sense for Jesus to use the analogy.

On our vacation at the ocean this past summer, one activity some of the males in the family enjoyed was fishing. Before our vacation the guys checked out a few books on fishing from the library. After glancing through one, I realized that there really *is* an art to fishing. It requires skill and knowledge, and the person who catches the most fish is probably the one who knows which fishing tackle to use, how to present the bait, where to find the fish, and how to go after them. No one ever becomes perfect at fishing—there's always something new to be learned.

People who do serious fishing are courageous and patient. Because they can't see the fish and are never exactly sure what they will encounter, they need faith to go out day after day and hope that they will catch something. Here's how Warren Wiersbe describes the fishermen who became Jesus' disciples: "They had been catching living fish and, when they caught them, the fish died. Now they would catch dead fish—sinners—and the fish would live!"[3]

If fishing for fish takes skill, patience, courage, knowledge, and faith, how much more so does fishing for people! Yet it's a responsibility and privilege God gives each of us.

God,
Thank you for pictures in your Word that point out some of our responsibilities as believers. Please help us to be concerned for the souls of people who don't know you, and may our concern begin in our families. Amen.

CHOICES

DON'T BE MISLED. REMEMBER THAT YOU CAN'T IGNORE
GOD AND GET AWAY WITH IT. YOU WILL ALWAYS REAP WHAT
YOU SOW! THOSE WHO LIVE ONLY TO SATISFY THEIR OWN
SINFUL DESIRES WILL HARVEST THE CONSEQUENCES OF DECAY AND DEATH. BUT
THOSE WHO LIVE TO PLEASE THE SPIRIT WILL HARVEST EVERLASTING LIFE FROM
THE SPIRIT. SO DON'T GET TIRED OF DOING WHAT IS GOOD. DON'T GET
DISCOURAGED AND GIVE UP, FOR WE WILL REAP A HARVEST OF BLESSING AT THE
APPROPRIATE TIME.

Galatians 6:7-9

Ben looked out the window at the garden. It looked different than it did last summer, but he wasn't sure why. He saw some large, vine-like plants spreading across the garden. They were *something* like the ones they had grown last year. But there seemed to be a difference.

"Mother," Ben asked, turning, "are those *pumpkins* growing in our garden?"

"No, Ben," she said, "they're watermelons."

"Watermelons?" Ben said in astonishment. "Where are the pumpkins?"

"We aren't having pumpkins this year."

"Why not?"

"Because we planted watermelons."

Ben looked disappointed. "But I wanted pumpkins. And now I can't ever have pumpkins." He started to cry.

Mary wiped away her small son's tears. "Yes, you can, Ben. If you like pumpkins, we'll plant them for you next year. Because each time you plant, you can grow a new harvest."⁴

Just as we reap what we sow in our gardens, we also reap what we sow in our souls. What joy to experience the harvest of a crop well-sown, but how sad to experience the loss and destruction of crops sown with bad seed.

If we're discouraged by our poor choices that have brought negative consequences, we don't need to despair. If we turn to God, repent, and with his help make choices to please him, new crops will grow, and we will experience new hope and joy.

God,
We want to honor you with good choices, not mock you with poor choices.
Please strengthen us to stand firm and sow seeds that will have eternal value.
Amen.

CHOICES

THERE IS REALLY ONLY ONE THING WORTH BEING CONCERNED
ABOUT. MARY HAS DISCOVERED IT—AND I WON'T TAKE IT AWAY
FROM HER.

Luke 10:42

Mary from Bethany is seen three times in the Gospels, and in each scene she's sitting at the feet of Jesus. On one occasion she sat and listened to his Word (Luke 10:39). On another she fell at his feet and poured out her heart to Jesus about the death of her brother, Lazarus (John 11:32). The third time she anointed Jesus' feet with expensive perfume (John 12:3).

In the first of those scenes, Jesus was visiting the home of Mary and Martha. While Martha was busy with all the meal preparations, Mary was sitting at the feet of Jesus. Martha was irritated that Mary had left her alone in the kitchen, and she wanted Jesus to order Mary to help.

As Jesus frequently did, he graciously pointed out what was most important. He didn't put down Martha's hospitality, but he certainly elevated Mary's worship. When it comes to issues of hospitality and worship, one is not "right" and the other "wrong." But we do have a choice about which is most important. Worship is the core of our Christian experience.

Before we can reflect Christ to our children, we must spend time with him and learn from him.

When we choose to spend time in personal devotion to Christ, our acts of service will follow because of the prompting of God's Spirit in our lives.

Father,
Please help us get first things first. May we worship you first, realizing that
when we are in awe of you, service will follow. Amen.

CHOICES

YOU WILL KEEP ON GUIDING ME WITH YOUR COUNSEL,
LEADING ME TO A GLORIOUS DESTINY. WHOM HAVE I IN
HEAVEN BUT YOU? I DESIRE YOU MORE THAN ANYTHING ON
EARTH. MY HEALTH MAY FAIL, AND MY SPIRIT MAY GROW WEAK, BUT GOD
REMAINS THE STRENGTH OF MY HEART; HE IS MINE FOREVER.   *Psalm 73:24-26*

When I was a student at Moody Bible Institute, I sang in the Moody Chorale. Whether we toured in England, Miami, Scotland, or Syracuse, we began each concert by singing:

> Guide me, O Thou great Jehovah,
> Pilgrim through this barren land;
> I am weak, but Thou art mighty;
> Hold me with Thy powerful hand.[5]

Weak. Perplexed. Uncertain of how to choose. Do you ever feel that way? I do. When we encounter challenging circumstances, where do we go for help with our needs and our choices?

Where we look for guidance says a lot about our character. Some people turn to the local bar or a palm reader, but a wise choice would be a pastor or a counselor—a mature person who believes in and loves God and his Word. When we have serious choices to make, we need wise counselors. One of my sons is deciding which college to attend; his guidance counselor at school is a great resource person. One of my friends is navigating through some challenges in her marriage; her marriage counselor is a huge source of help.

Human counselors are helpful, but *Jesus* is the foremost counselor in the world. He knows us, loves us, is patient with us, and encourages us. And—as any good counselor—he doesn't protect us from problems, but he equips us to face them with honesty and courage.

When you feel weak or uncertain, grab on to Jesus' hand and ask *him* to help you choose.

> *Loving Counselor,*
> *Thank you that you are the wisest counselor and guide we could ever have. In our weakness, please be our strength. Amen.*

CHOICES

LOT CHOSE THAT LAND FOR HIMSELF—THE JORDAN
VALLEY TO THE EAST OF THEM. HE WENT THERE WITH HIS
FLOCKS AND SERVANTS AND PARTED COMPANY WITH HIS UNCLE ABRAM.

Genesis 13:11

When we read the story of Abraham (here still named Abram) and Lot in Genesis 13, we are reminded that people display their true character by the choices they make. During Abraham's sojourn from Haran to Bethel, he had become very wealthy in livestock, silver, and gold. Abraham and Lot's herdsmen weren't getting along, so Abraham decided it was time to part ways. It would have been culturally appropriate for Lot, as the younger man, to show his respect to Abraham by giving him first choice of the land, but the opposite happened. Lot saw what appeared to be the most fertile land and selfishly chose it for himself, even though it included the corrupt cities of Sodom and Gomorrah. Abraham, on the other hand, allowed Lot to choose, knowing full well that from a human perspective he might receive the worse end of the bargain. He had faith that God would provide what he needed.

Through Lot's series of choices, he moved away from light and toward darkness. First he looked toward Sodom, next he pitched his tent toward Sodom, and eventually he lived in Sodom. Abraham's choices stand in great contrast to Lot's. Lot chose with his eyes and found corruption, but Abraham chose by faith and found blessing. In Lot's insecurity he chose selfishly, and his life became progressively more isolated; but Abraham's unselfishness in allowing Lot the most fertile land was rewarded with promise and abundance. After Lot made his choice, God spoke to Abraham and promised to give him all the land he could see—in *every* direction!

It is very easy and tempting to make choices based only on what we see or what is readily available. How much harder, but wiser, to seek and follow God's wisdom about a significant choice. In all our choices we need to be moving toward Christ and his light, not away from him and toward darkness. As we practice living that way, we model wise choices in front of our children.

Father,
Please help us to walk by faith and not by sight. Amen.

CHOICES

TODAY I HAVE GIVEN YOU THE CHOICE BETWEEN LIFE AND
DEATH, BETWEEN BLESSINGS AND CURSES. I CALL ON HEAVEN
AND EARTH TO WITNESS THE CHOICE YOU MAKE. OH, THAT YOU
WOULD CHOOSE LIFE, THAT YOU AND YOUR DESCENDANTS MIGHT LIVE!

Deuteronomy 30:19

To choose is to select from a number of possibilities, and we do it all day long. When my children come to the table for breakfast, will I set out cereal, or will I cook eggs? Will I walk today or not? Moving on to some bigger choices, will I send my children to private schools or public schools, or will I home school? Out of the many churches in my community, which body will I worship with?

If the breakfast issue is a "baby bear" choice, and the school and church issues are "mama bear" choices, I believe a "papa bear" choice is presented in Deuteronomy 30:19.

Moses explained to the children of Israel that they had a choice to make, and it was a choice to be made with their hearts. Moses asked the people to choose between life and death, blessings and curses. The question of the day was, "Do you choose God—yes or no?"

Paul presented that choice to his readers in Romans 10:6-10, and we have the same choice before us today. We can choose Christ and walk in his ways, or we can be drawn to other gods, bringing a curse upon ourselves. Simply stated, a choice for Christ brings life and blessing for us and for our children.

Giver of life,
Thank you that you didn't make us robots, but you created us with the ability
to choose. With the power of your Spirit, help us to make choices for you and
your Kingdom. Amen.

CHOICES

WHO ARE THOSE WHO FEAR THE LORD? HE WILL SHOW
THEM THE PATH THEY SHOULD CHOOSE.   *Psalm 25:12*

There are currently many "just say no" campaigns against drugs, premarital sex, gangs, and other issues that children face in our society. Some years ago the president of the United States and the Speaker of the House took part in a news conference that kicked off a yearlong anti-drug advertising campaign. They said the campaign would attempt to "knock America upside the head." These ads would graphically illustrate the destructiveness of drugs and point out how vulnerable children are.

I was thankful that members of our government stood against the use of drugs, but I was concerned that we might spend the $195 million pledged to the campaign on symptoms and possibly fail to deal with the root issues. I believe that teaching our children how to make healthy and God-honoring choices regarding drugs, sex, and gangs has less to do with presenting lessons about the symptoms and more to do with encouraging children to make choices from an eternal perspective.

In his book *Bold Love,* Dan Allender states, "No one will leave an addiction or compulsion unless a competing passion is offered that gives a taste of what the soul was meant to enjoy. Only heaven with the beauty of restoration is a big enough passion to draw us away from the petty distractions and cheap addictions of this sorry world."[6] Many children aren't motivated by negative consequences they doubt they'll ever experience. But they can be motivated by an understanding of the positive consequences of fellowship with God. The rewards—both now and eternally—are great.

I'm convinced that a large percentage of our focus as moms should be spent guiding our children toward God, whom we want to be the treasure of their hearts.

God,
There are many distractions and addictions that can cause our families great harm. Please help us point our children toward heaven and eternity, so that with your help they will turn from compulsions that would cause destruction. Amen.

CHOICES

I KNOW HOW TO LIVE ON ALMOST NOTHING OR WITH
EVERYTHING. I HAVE LEARNED THE SECRET OF LIVING IN
EVERY SITUATION, WHETHER IT IS WITH A FULL STOMACH OR
EMPTY, WITH PLENTY OR LITTLE. FOR I CAN DO EVERYTHING WITH THE HELP OF
CHRIST WHO GIVES ME THE STRENGTH I NEED.

Philippians 4:12-13

*God, grant me the serenity to accept the things I cannot change, courage to
change the things I can, and wisdom to know the difference.*

The mom who prays this prayer is exercising trust in God because she realizes
there are some things in life she can't change. She's not feeling trapped, though,
because she's asking for courage to make good choices about things that *can* be
changed, and she's admitting that at times it's difficult to identify which is which.

Sometimes restless discontentment can be an opportunity for change or
growth. Perhaps a mom feels she has run up against a brick wall in dealing with
her child, or she knows she's having trouble setting limits and boundaries. She
can, if necessary, make the choice to seek help from a Christian counselor or
other parenting resources. But there are some things in life we can't
change—like our families of origin, our genes, or the basic personalities of our
children or our husbands. What do we do with the situations that we'd like to
change but can't? We all encounter those. We may have no control over the situation, but we can choose the attitude of our hearts.

Our contentment will be directly proportional to our trust in God. If we have
little trust, we'll find little contentment. If we have great trust in him, we will
have great contentment, because we know he is in control. Long-term contentment in our soul is not a matter of circumstance—it is a matter of trust in God.

*Father,
May we always make the choice to trust you and be content with the circumstances of our lives that we can't change. Please give us great wisdom in all
the choices we make. Amen.*

TRUTH

JESUS TOLD HIM, "I AM THE WAY, THE TRUTH, AND THE LIFE.
NO ONE CAN COME TO THE FATHER EXCEPT THROUGH ME."

John 14:6

Imagine that you and your children are taking a hike in Colorado. You come upon a wide river, and another hiker tells you that there is only one bridge, down the river a mile or so. Will you stomp off in disgust and complain that it's unfair that there's only one bridge, or will you be grateful that there *is* a bridge, and use it to cross over?

Imagine that your child is struggling with a serious illness. You've tried every medication and treatment possible short of surgery, and now your child's doctor tells you that surgery is the only remaining option. Will you look for a surgeon who has specialized training in the area of your child's illness, or will you choose a person off the street?

The way of truth in these two situations seems obvious to us. But when it comes to matters of faith, we are not always so quick to see the truth. Many people today fight the reality of absolute truth as though it were an enemy. To be deemed "narrow-minded" is to be considered ignorant, it seems. But the reality is that truth *is* narrow. How comforting for me to know that God is truth. He's the author of truth, and the closer we get to him, the more we live truly and truly live. We trust him with our lives because he's the only one who *really* knows what life is all about.

Father,
Thank you that to know you is to know truth. Amen.

TRUTH

JESUS ANSWERED, "MY TEACHING IS NOT MY OWN. IT
COMES FROM HIM WHO SENT ME. IF ANYONE CHOOSES TO
DO GOD'S WILL, HE WILL FIND OUT WHETHER MY TEACHING
COMES FROM GOD OR WHETHER I SPEAK ON MY OWN. HE WHO SPEAKS ON HIS
OWN DOES SO TO GAIN HONOR FOR HIMSELF, BUT HE WHO WORKS FOR THE
HONOR OF THE ONE WHO SENT HIM IS A MAN OF TRUTH; THERE IS NOTHING FALSE
ABOUT HIM."

John 7:16-18, NIV

What comes to mind when you think of the word *false*? True/False sections on a test? A false alarm? Anything that is false is contrary to truth or fact. All the way through the Bible we learn that God is truth, Jesus is truth, and the Spirit is truth.

Warren Wiersbe writes, "A willingness to obey is the secret of learning God's truth." Jesus certainly exhibited that, and it is borne out in the life of the Christian as well. Too many times we do the opposite: We spend great amounts of time trying to understand and prove God's truth before we take the risk of believing and obeying. But as Jesus taught in John 11:40, "Didn't I tell you that you will see God's glory if you believe?"

Jesus wasn't asking for mindless commitment with no basis in reality, like some cults do. Rather, he was teaching that once we have seen him and have been given glimpses of his truth, we desire to respond to his will. That's the way to grow in truth.

May we strive to be women of truth who follow God's ways, not false women who are out to promote themselves or their own agenda. Each time we obey God, we grow in truth.

Father,
Please help us to respond to the truth you reveal. May we become women of
truth as a result of being women who obey. Amen.

TRUTH

MY DEAR BROTHERS AND SISTERS, HOW CAN YOU CLAIM
THAT YOU HAVE FAITH IN OUR GLORIOUS LORD JESUS CHRIST
IF YOU FAVOR SOME PEOPLE MORE THAN OTHERS? FOR INSTANCE, SUPPOSE
SOMEONE COMES INTO YOUR MEETING DRESSED IN FANCY CLOTHES AND EXPENSIVE
JEWELRY, AND ANOTHER COMES IN WHO IS POOR AND DRESSED IN SHABBY
CLOTHES. IF YOU GIVE SPECIAL ATTENTION AND A GOOD SEAT TO THE RICH
PERSON, BUT YOU SAY TO THE POOR ONE, "YOU CAN STAND OVER THERE, OR ELSE
SIT ON THE FLOOR"—WELL, DOESN'T THIS DISCRIMINATION SHOW THAT YOU ARE
GUIDED BY WRONG MOTIVES?

James 2:1-4

One of the Bible verses I pray back to God each morning comes from a little book that has only one chapter: "I could have no greater joy than to hear that my children live in the truth" (3 John 1:4). I'm grateful that my sons want to walk in God's truth, but I don't ever take that for granted. Consequently, I plan to pray 3 John 1:4 as long as I have breath.

Every now and then I get a glimpse of a choice one of my sons makes that prompts me to praise God. That's exactly what happened yesterday. One of my adult sons—who loves to golf—had been invited to play at a posh, private club. Although he'd been told that there was no cost to him, he later found out that there were strings attached. The more he thought about it, the more he felt obligated to show favoritism in a business deal. Because the whole thing left him feeling uncomfortable, he called his friend, thanked him for his offer, and declined the game. Showing favoritism might have landed Nate a prized round of golf, but he also felt that it would have compromised his values.

It's easy for us to show favoritism that's based on a desire for status, wealth, or fame. Such opportunities usually present themselves in subtle and attractive ways. But God warns us that showing favoritism and falling prey to wrong motives goes against Christ's plan for our lives. Sometimes our kids are good examples to us.

Father,
Please help us not to show favoritism but to treat each person in our lives with
fairness and truth. Amen.

TRUTH

PREACH THE WORD OF GOD. BE PERSISTENT, WHETHER
THE TIME IS FAVORABLE OR NOT. PATIENTLY CORRECT,
REBUKE, AND ENCOURAGE YOUR PEOPLE WITH GOOD TEACHING.
FOR A TIME IS COMING WHEN PEOPLE WILL NO LONGER LISTEN TO RIGHT
TEACHING. THEY WILL FOLLOW THEIR OWN DESIRES AND WILL LOOK FOR
TEACHERS WHO WILL TELL THEM WHATEVER THEY WANT TO HEAR. THEY WILL
REJECT THE TRUTH AND FOLLOW STRANGE MYTHS.   *2 Timothy 4:2-4*

"What has happened to the moms and dads who want their children to be good?
I believe they are casualties of the cultural war in our country. We live now in a
country that believes we should be nonjudgmental to the point that we won't
even fight for the souls of our own children." These words were spoken by U.S.
Senator Rick Santorum in a commencement address at Grove City College
(Pennsylvania) in 1998.

Santorum went on to say that when he was growing up in the 1950s and
1960s, parents who cared about their children's souls were called strict. Today,
those parents are called right-wing radicals. Behavior that was once seen as offensive in our culture is now openly accepted. People who question that behavior or
desire to curb it are written off as being intolerant.

Our culture is pleasure-driven. We hear people telling us to do what feels
right and to follow our desires. We have gotten away from the painful, difficult
process of discerning what is right and then acting on the truth.

So where do we go to find truth? We begin with the one who gave us truth in
the first place—God. He gave us his Word, the Bible, which he says is truth. We
are to study it and seek truth—then live it out in our families and our communities.

As we spend time with the truth-giver, we can be truth-bearers, first to our
children and then to a needy world.

Father,
May we spend time in your Word regularly, so we can be truth-bearers to a
world that needs you. Amen.

TRUTH

IF WE SAY WE HAVE NO SIN, WE ARE ONLY FOOLING OUR-
SELVES AND REFUSING TO ACCEPT THE TRUTH. BUT IF WE CONFESS
OUR SINS TO HIM, HE IS FAITHFUL AND JUST TO FORGIVE US AND TO
CLEANSE US FROM EVERY WRONG.

1 John 1:8-9

Whenever we see the word *if*, we must look closely to see what follows. In these verses, we see that if we deny that we are sinful, two things are true: (1) we are fooling ourselves; (2) we refuse to accept the truth. Simply put, if I refuse to admit my sin, I call God a liar and I lie. Before I can make any progress on a problem (whether it's anger, gossip, impatience, etc.), I must be honest with myself and with God.

God's Word teaches us that being truthful about our sin leads to hope. If instead of denying our sin we choose to confess it to God, two things happen: God forgives us and purifies us. He not only takes away the blame and grants a pardon in its place, but he also frees us and makes us clean.

The Old Testament character Jacob tricked his father and stole his brother Esau's birthright. When his blind earthly father, Isaac, asked him, "What is your name?" he lied and said that he was Esau so his father would give him an earthly blessing. Later, when Jacob was alone, afraid, and seeking God's protection, God his heavenly Father asked him, "What is your name?" This time, he responded truthfully with "Jacob," meaning *deceiver*. When he responded with the truth, God gave him a new name—Israel—and a heavenly blessing.

That gives us hope. When we respond truthfully to God, he gives us a new name—as his redeemed child—and the heavenly blessing of forgiveness as well.

> Father,
> Thank you for your patience with us. Thank you that when we are honest about our sin and confess it to you, you forgive us and cleanse us. We will offer you praise through all eternity because you paid for our sins with your blood. Amen.

TRUTH

THE PERSON WHO MADE THE IDOL NEVER STOPS TO
REFLECT, "WHY, IT'S JUST A BLOCK OF WOOD! I BURNED
HALF OF IT FOR HEAT AND USED IT TO BAKE MY BREAD AND
ROAST MY MEAT. HOW CAN THE REST OF IT BE A GOD? SHOULD I BOW DOWN TO
WORSHIP A CHUNK OF WOOD?" THE POOR, DELUDED FOOL FEEDS ON ASHES.
HE IS TRUSTING SOMETHING THAT CAN GIVE HIM NO HELP AT ALL. YET HE CANNOT
BRING HIMSELF TO ASK, "IS THIS THING, THIS IDOL THAT I'M HOLDING IN MY HAND,
A LIE?"

Isaiah 44:19-20

If we want our children to be people of truth when they're adults, we're wise to begin teaching the difference between truth and falsehood early on. The life stories we share and the way we discuss them have a profound influence on our children—probably more than we'll ever realize.

For example, without using a name, my husband and I spoke to our young children about a man we knew who lied about his expense account and lost his job. We wanted them to understand that lying is wrong and that it brings consequences. On another occasion, I had a lunchtime discussion with an older son about a false religion. I had just read an article describing a woman's excitement about the opening of a local Hindu temple. According to the article, the Hindi gods were brought in, set up on elaborate shrines, and had life breathed into them. To my surprise, my son had just been reading the above verses from Isaiah the day before, so the timing of our discussion was especially poignant.

Opportunities to differentiate between what's true and what's false are all around us. It's wise for moms to look for them and take advantage of teachable moments. "The walks and talks we have with our two-year-olds in red boots," said Edith Hunter, "have a great deal to do with the values they will cherish as adults."

Father,
Please help us to discern between truth and error. Please help us to snatch up opportunities to discuss your truth with our children. Amen.

TRUTH

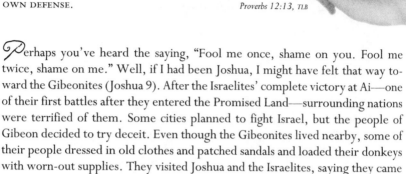

> LIES WILL GET ANY MAN INTO TROUBLE, BUT HONESTY IS ITS
> OWN DEFENSE.
> *Proverbs 12:13, TLB*

*P*erhaps you've heard the saying, "Fool me once, shame on you. Fool me twice, shame on me." Well, if I had been Joshua, I might have felt that way toward the Gibeonites (Joshua 9). After the Israelites' complete victory at Ai—one of their first battles after they entered the Promised Land—surrounding nations were terrified of them. Some cities planned to fight Israel, but the people of Gibeon decided to try deceit. Even though the Gibeonites lived nearby, some of their people dressed in old clothes and patched sandals and loaded their donkeys with worn-out supplies. They visited Joshua and the Israelites, saying they came from a distant country and asking to make a treaty with them. When the Gibeonites offered to be servants of the Israelites, the Israelites agreed to a treaty—without consulting God.

Three days later the Israelites discovered that the far-off people they had just made a treaty with were really their close neighbors! The Israelites were understandably angry about the ruse, but Joshua said the oath must stand. However, he declared that the Gibeonites would live from then on under a curse—they would be woodcutters and water carriers for the community of Israel and the house of God.

Trust in another person is only earned through consistent honesty and integrity. It's important for us to realize that deceit in our relationships with our husbands, our children, or our friends exacts a tremendous cost. Deceit erodes trust and brings a curse, but honesty, integrity, and straightforward living foster respect, trust, and thriving relationships.

Father,
We desire honesty for each member of our family. Please help us to be
straightforward and truthful in all of our relationships. Amen.

Wisdom

A WISE WOMAN BUILDS HER HOUSE; A FOOLISH WOMAN
TEARS HERS DOWN WITH HER OWN HANDS. *Proverbs 14:1*

What is a wise mom like? She has discernment for things that are true, right, and lasting.

1. Things that are *true* are consistent with fact or reality. A wise woman knows truth is found in God's Word, and she spends time there regularly. She's also willing to see things the way they really are; for example, she doesn't pretend that she or her family members are faultless.
2. Her discernment for things that are *right* helps her to practice justice with the people around her. This means she treats them fairly and with full appreciation.
3. She values things that *last*. Some things last longer than others, but two things that will endure forever are God's Word and people's souls. The wise woman values both, and the way she orders her life reflects that.

In contrast to the wise woman, a foolish woman tears down her home by

1. closing her eyes to the truth and denying the way things really are;
2. being neglectful, unfair, and unappreciative of those around her;
3. neglecting the things that last (God's Word, the souls of her family, and the souls of people around her) and spending great amounts of time on temporal things.

Taking a serious look at these two types of women is sobering and prompts us to think about how *we* want to build up our home.

Father,
Please forgive us for times when our choices do more to tear down than to build. May we be moms who, with the help of your Spirit, make choices to build wisely with truth and justice, and may we use our time, energy, and money for things that are lasting. Amen.

WISDOM

HAPPY IS THE PERSON WHO FINDS WISDOM AND GAINS
UNDERSTANDING. FOR THE PROFIT OF WISDOM IS BETTER THAN
SILVER, AND HER WAGES ARE BETTER THAN GOLD. WISDOM IS MORE
PRECIOUS THAN RUBIES; NOTHING YOU DESIRE CAN COMPARE WITH HER.

Proverbs 3:13-15

*H*ave you ever won a door prize, a drawing, or a raffle? I have, on three occasions. One time I won a small space heater. It wasn't an exciting gift, but it was functional and came in handy when our family room got a little drafty on cold winter days. Another time I won a sapphire and diamond necklace. I was at a large banquet, and when my ticket number was called and I heard a description of the necklace, I thought, *Oh, it's probably some garish piece of jewelry that I would never wear.* But to my delight it was a small, diamond-shaped pendant with one diamond surrounded by three sapphires, hanging on a beautiful gold chain. I've enjoyed wearing it for about thirty years, and I would be disappointed if I ever lost it. The third and last item I won was one ounce of gold. At the time, gold was worth about $360 an ounce, so I was rather excited!

God's Word tells me that wisdom is even more valuable than precious stones or gold; nothing can compare with it. Wisdom cannot be won at a convention or as a result of buying a raffle ticket. Proverbs 1:7 (TLB) asks, "How does a man become wise? The first step is to trust and reverence the Lord!" The next verse offers a second step in gaining wisdom: parents' teaching. "Listen, my child, to what your father teaches you. Don't neglect your mother's teaching." God's Word has given us clear steps to follow as we seek to become wise. If we *really* want wisdom and if we look for it, we will find it.

God,
Thank you that we don't have to wait to win a prize before we acquire wisdom. May we seek to trust and reverence you. As we seek you, please help us to become moms who are wise. Amen.

WISDOM

GOD SURELY KNOWS WHERE [WISDOM] CAN BE FOUND,
FOR HE LOOKS THROUGHOUT THE WHOLE EARTH, UNDER
ALL THE HEAVENS. HE MADE THE WINDS BLOW AND DETERMINED
HOW MUCH RAIN SHOULD FALL. HE MADE THE LAWS OF THE RAIN AND PREPARED
A PATH FOR THE LIGHTNING. THEN, WHEN HE HAD DONE ALL THIS, HE SAW
WISDOM AND MEASURED IT. HE ESTABLISHED IT AND EXAMINED IT THOROUGHLY.
AND THIS IS WHAT HE SAID TO ALL HUMANITY: "THE FEAR OF THE LORD IS TRUE
WISDOM; TO FORSAKE EVIL IS REAL UNDERSTANDING."

Job 28:23-28

*O*ne of my favorite books in the Bible is Job. A wealthy and upright man, Job found his integrity being tested. His sons and daughters were killed, his flocks were driven away, and he developed a terrible skin disease. Job's life had hit bottom. The rug seemed to have been pulled out from underneath him, and he had to decide how to respond.

Three of Job's friends offered their interpretations of his problems. Although it was kind of them to visit him, their idea of wisdom left something to be desired. The advice he received from Eliphaz was, in a nutshell, "I have seen firsthand how God works, and I have him figured out!" Eliphaz thought wisdom was gained by observing and experiencing life. Job's second friend, Bildad, believed wisdom was inherited from history. He reasoned, "Our forefathers figured God out, and all we have to do is use their knowledge." Zophar, the third friend, thought wisdom belonged to a select few. His attitude was, "You're lucky to have a friend who knows what God is like, because there aren't many of us around."

The comments about wisdom that ring true with me are the words spoken above by Job, the one who was tested and came away from incredibly difficult circumstances with even stronger faith. Unlike his friends, Job knew that God is the source of all wisdom and that the first step toward wisdom is to fear God. Job knew the secret: God gives wisdom to people who humbly trust him.

God of wisdom,
With the responsibility of guiding our children, we feel our need for wisdom
daily. Like Job, please help us to look up to you for wisdom and help. Because
wisdom is found in you, may we humbly trust you. Amen.

WISDOM

THE WISE ARE KNOWN FOR THEIR UNDERSTANDING, AND
INSTRUCTION IS APPRECIATED IF IT'S WELL PRESENTED.

Proverbs 16:21

*O*ne summer my husband, three young sons, and I went camping at a state park in Door County, Wisconsin. We had just spent a couple of hours setting up the camper, organizing our belongings, and building a fire for later in the evening when I heard Nate cry out in pain. While shimmying down a tree, he had snagged one of his hands on a sharp piece of bark. After looking at his nasty four-inch gash, there was not a doubt in my mind that we needed to seek medical help. We threw a clean towel over his hand, packed the family into our station wagon, and drove to the closest emergency room.

The physician on duty was kind to Nate and calmly explained what needed to happen. Before the doctor injected some necessary painkiller, he winked at my husband and me. Then he held out a large, round tray containing two needles—one mammoth and one midget. He looked at Nate and asked, "Which one would you like me to use?" You already know which one Nate chose. Jim and I were grateful that the doctor made a wise presentation in the middle of a painful situation.

By observing the emergency room doctor, I learned a helpful lesson. Hardly a day goes by in my role as a mom that I don't have to deal with some unpleasant task or situation. Spending a few moments thinking and praying about how to *present* my plans is a wise thing to do.

Father,
Please give us creative ideas about how to be wise with our children. Amen.

WISDOM

DAVID REPLIED TO ABIGAIL, "PRAISE THE LORD, THE GOD
OF ISRAEL, WHO HAS SENT YOU TO MEET ME TODAY! THANK
GOD FOR YOUR GOOD SENSE! BLESS YOU FOR KEEPING ME FROM
MURDERING THE MAN AND CARRYING OUT VENGEANCE WITH MY OWN HANDS.
FOR I SWEAR BY THE LORD, THE GOD OF ISRAEL, WHO HAS KEPT ME FROM
HURTING YOU, THAT IF YOU HAD NOT HURRIED OUT TO MEET ME, NOT ONE OF
NABAL'S MEN WOULD BE ALIVE TOMORROW MORNING." *1 Samuel 25:32-34*

Abigail, a wise woman, was married to Nabal, a perverse and immoral man.
David, God's choice to be the future king of Israel, was running from King Saul
and asked Nabal for food for himself and his men. Nabal refused rudely, and David
was very angry. David impulsively threatened to kill Nabal and take all his
possessions, but when Abigail got wind of the plan, she exercised great wisdom.
Losing no time, she bypassed her husband and took food to David. She assumed a
servant's posture before David, tactfully advising him that his plan would cost
needless bloodshed. David listened, and the outcome of the situation was amazing:
when Nabal heard what Abigail had done, he had a stroke and died, and David
asked Abigail to become his wife.

Wives and husbands whose marriages are united by the common goal and
purpose of honoring Christ are rich indeed, because both spouses are building on
the same foundation. But as with Nabal and Abigail, even if only one spouse
chooses to cooperate with God, God's grace continues to work out his good purposes
nonetheless. An uncooperative spouse is not too big a problem for God.

For any mom who is concerned about questionable patterns of behavior in her
husband or children, here are some encouraging words: "Never let the difficulties
in your home lead you to abdicate your throne. Do not step down to the level
of your circumstances, but live these to your own high calling in Jesus Christ."[1]

God,
Please give us great wisdom in dealing with family members whose lives seem
to be headed in the wrong direction. May we spend much time in prayer and
in your Word so we can live out a biblical balance of truth and grace. Amen.

WISDOM

BUT THE WISDOM THAT COMES FROM HEAVEN IS FIRST OF ALL
PURE. IT IS ALSO PEACE LOVING, GENTLE AT ALL TIMES, AND
WILLING TO YIELD TO OTHERS. IT IS FULL OF MERCY AND GOOD DEEDS.
IT SHOWS NO PARTIALITY AND IS ALWAYS SINCERE. AND THOSE WHO ARE
PEACEMAKERS WILL PLANT SEEDS OF PEACE AND REAP A HARVEST OF GOODNESS.

James 3:17-18

We identify a wise person the same way we identify a tree—by the fruit he bears. A tree is identified by the lemons, cherries, or grapefruit it bears. A wise person is identified by the following:

- *Purity*. Pure morals come from being cleansed by Christ's blood. When we receive Christ's purity, we set aside sensuality, pride, and covetousness. Purity of devotion is a result of our focus on God. We concentrate on serving and pleasing *him*.
- *Peace*. This is not a passive quality, meaning we avoid conflict and become doormats to whatever our children or husbands want. Rather, it means having a calm, tranquil spirit, which comes from a close relationship with Christ.
- *Consideration*. We treat others the way we'd like to be treated. This means that sometimes we put others' needs first.
- *Submission*. This involves a willingness to yield to another. A wise person is open to reason and doesn't always need to be right.
- *Mercy*. This is compassion that is not just thought about but is acted out toward another person at times when it would be easier to judge or condemn.
- *Impartiality*. Impartial people are unbiased and unwavering. They don't compromise the truth in a difficult situation. Wise people are steady.
- *Sincerity*. A wise mom doesn't say she believes one thing, then act out something else. Sincerity leaves no room for hypocrisy.

It would be as impossible to cultivate these qualities by ourselves as it would be to grow a garden without seeds. But when we have been cleansed by Christ's blood and we remain close to him, we—and our children—will see that these fruits grow in our lives.

> God of wisdom,
> Thank you that as we walk near you, we will grow in purity, peace, consideration, submission, mercy, impartiality, and sincerity. Amen.

WISDOM

THOSE WHO ARE WISE WILL FIND A TIME AND A WAY
TO DO WHAT IS RIGHT. YES, THERE IS A TIME AND A WAY
FOR EVERYTHING, EVEN AS PEOPLE'S TROUBLES LIE HEAVILY
UPON THEM.

Ecclesiastes 8:5-6

*H*ave you ever been so perplexed or troubled by the injustice of a situation that you

(a) had trouble eating (or ate too much)?

(b) had trouble sleeping (or slept too much)?

(c) didn't want to be around another person (or wanted to control that person's life)?

When I feel the injustice of a situation, my mind tends to work overtime. I conjure up various things I might say or do that in my opinion would "set the record straight." Sometimes I've acted on these impulses, but the problem with impulses is that they are, well, impulsive! Impulsive acts sometimes turn into careless, emotional outbursts that do more harm than good.

Have you noticed that wise people are not usually impulsive people? They've learned that we often run into trouble when we act impetuously.

The Bible is filled with examples of people who chose not to act impulsively and instead sought wisdom in the way they dealt with injustice. The Old Testament prophet Nathan is one example. God sent Nathan to confront King David with his sins of coveting, adultery, and murder after David slept with Bathsheba and then attempted to cover up his sin by having her husband killed.

Nathan wisely told David a story about a rich man who took and killed a poor man's lamb. When David heard the story, he was furious and said, "Anyone who would do a thing like that deserves to die!" "You," Nathan responded to David, "are that man!" Rather than acting impulsively, Nathan made a wise presentation—and it was highly effective.

When troubles lie heavily upon us, the wise thing to do is ask God to help us find a time and a way to do what is right. He will.

Father,
Thank you for examples of wise people in your Word. Thank you that all wisdom dwells in you. Amen.

COURAGE

"SEE," NAOMI SAID TO HER, "YOUR SISTER-IN-LAW HAS
GONE BACK TO HER PEOPLE AND TO HER GODS. YOU SHOULD
DO THE SAME." BUT RUTH REPLIED, "DON'T ASK ME TO LEAVE YOU AND
TURN BACK. I WILL GO WHEREVER YOU GO AND LIVE WHEREVER YOU LIVE. YOUR
PEOPLE WILL BE MY PEOPLE, AND YOUR GOD WILL BE MY GOD." *Ruth 1:15-16*

Woven throughout the Bible are stories of courage—stories of seemingly un-important people who accomplished great things in God's strength. God's plans and purposes are carried out from one generation to another with amazing twists, turns, and surprises, and Ruth was part of one of those plans.

A woman who had grown up in Moab, Ruth married a Jewish man, Mahlon, one of the sons of Elimelech. Elimelech, his wife, Naomi, and their two sons had left Israel to escape a famine, and while they were in Moab, both sons married Moabite women. Sadly, Elimelech and both sons died, leaving Naomi and two daughters-in-law as widows. Naomi decided to return to her hometown of Beth-lehem, assuming Ruth and Orpah would prefer to stay in Moab. But because of Ruth's love for Naomi, she insisted on going along.

An industrious woman, Ruth gleaned grain that had been dropped by harvest-ers in the field of Boaz, bringing it back to Naomi to bake bread. When Boaz found out who Ruth was, he offered her much more than the leftovers. He was kind to her because of her kindness to Naomi.

In God's plan, Ruth and Boaz ended up marrying, and a few generations later Ruth became the great-grandmother of King David. Because she had the courage to leave her homeland, accompany her mother-in-law back to Israel, and work to provide for her mother-in-law, God blessed her life. What a beautiful story of love and courage!

Father,
Thank you for the intricate way your plans unfold from one generation to another. Thank you that we can read these stories in your Word and be reminded of your great love and faithfulness. May we have faith to believe that you are weaving your purposes into our lives and courage to obey. Amen.

COURAGE

> THEN THE LORD TURNED TO HIM AND SAID, "GO WITH THE
> STRENGTH YOU HAVE AND RESCUE ISRAEL FROM THE
> MIDIANITES. I AM SENDING YOU!"
>
> *Judges 6:14*

After forty years of freedom, the children of Israel again began worshipping idols. As a result, the Midianites took over the land of Israel, treating the people poorly. When the Israelites cried out to God, he chose Gideon to help them.

One day when Gideon was threshing wheat, an angel from God visited him and stated, "The Lord is with you, mighty warrior." Gideon responded, "But sir, . . . if the Lord is with us, why has all this happened to us? Where are all his wonders that our fathers told us about when they said, 'Did not the Lord bring us up out of Egypt?' But now the Lord has abandoned us and put us into the hand of Midian" (Judges 6:12-13, NIV).

The perspective here is curious. God called Gideon a "mighty warrior," but Gideon initially saw himself as abandoned. Gideon perceived his clan to be the weakest in Manasseh, and he thought himself to be the least in his family. But God promised Gideon his presence and his strength, and he agreed to Gideon's request for a sign. After this confirmation, Gideon was willing to serve God, and God used him in incredible and powerful ways to get the Israelites back on track and defeat the Midianites.

Have you ever thought of yourself as weak or abandoned? Being human, we all experience these feelings from time to time. But when we get a glimpse of God, we realize that his presence and his strength are more than enough to accomplish what needs to be done in our part of God's bigger plan for the world.

Father,
Thanks that you were patient with Gideon's questions and that you're patient with ours too. When we feel weak or abandoned, may we gain courage by running to you, getting a glimpse of your power, and realizing your presence and strength in our lives. Amen.

COURAGE

"WE OFFER OUR OWN LIVES AS A GUARANTEE FOR YOUR SAFETY," THE MEN AGREED. "IF YOU DON'T BETRAY US, WE WILL KEEP OUR PROMISE WHEN THE LORD GIVES US THE LAND."

Joshua 2:14

I remember seeing flannel-graph pictures of Rahab when I heard the Bible story told as a young child. At the time, I didn't understand that she was a harlot, but I was fascinated by the scarlet rope hanging from her window. Joshua sent two spies to Jericho, and Rahab secretly housed them and then hid them on her roof under stalks of flax. Later Rahab lowered the two spies down the outside wall through the window of her house. She was a woman of courage, as she took great risk in hiding the spies. As a result of her help, she and her family were later spared death when the Israelites conquered Jericho.

It's interesting that Rahab, who lived in a pagan culture, called God "the Lord" in her conversation with the spies: "'I know the Lord has given you this land,' she told them. 'We are all afraid of you. Everyone is living in terror'" (Joshua 2:9).

Rahab was not saved from physical or spiritual destruction because of her character or her works. Rather, she was saved through her faith. Any woman who has had major struggles with character or behavior can find great hope and encouragement from the life of Rahab. She was a sinner who was saved through her faith, and she proved her faith by courageously risking her life to protect God's people, eventually bringing her family to belief in God. She even became part of the ancestry of Jesus (Matthew 1:5)!

Father,
To trace Rahab back in Christ's ancestry is encouraging to us, because it demonstrates that people with a sinful past can be transformed. Thank you for her example of courage, which was born through faith in you. Amen.

COURAGE

THEN THE BABY'S SISTER APPROACHED THE PRINCESS.
"SHOULD I GO AND FIND ONE OF THE HEBREW WOMEN TO
NURSE THE BABY FOR YOU?" SHE ASKED. *Exodus 2:7*

*C*ourage is found not only in older people but also in young people. Consider Miriam, the sister of Moses. Moses' mother, Jochebed, decided to do a very bold thing. In order to protect Moses from being killed by Pharaoh's soldiers, she wove some reeds into a small basket. Perhaps Miriam wondered what her mother was making—until she found out that the basket would cradle her baby brother as he floated down the river. Miriam probably watched her mother weep as she kissed her infant son and laid him in the basket, putting it into the water. I can only wonder what Miriam thought and felt as she stood on the riverbank, watching from a distance.

You know the rest of the story. Pharaoh's daughter found the baby when she went to the river to bathe, and Miriam ran to her, asking if she should find a Hebrew mother (her own!) to nurse the baby. What a brave thing for a child to do. The courage she exercised as a young girl no doubt prompted her own growth in faith. Imagine all the times that she and Jochebed must have rehearsed that story together through the years. Later in the book of Exodus we read that Miriam led the children of Israel in a song of praise after their miraculous crossing of the Red Sea.

It's often painful for mothers to sit back and watch their children struggle through difficult situations. We would much rather protect them from pain or risk. But as we see in Miriam, courage can spring from childhood difficulties, resulting in personal faith and leadership down the road.

Father,
When we know or sense that our children are struggling with some difficulty,
please give us great wisdom as moms to know how much to guide them, how
much or how little to say, and when to stand back and wait to see you work in
their hearts and lives. Amen.

COURAGE

IF I MUST DIE, I AM WILLING TO DIE. *Esther 4:16*

*E*sther was the woman of the hour. She had been chosen by the Persian king to be his new queen—but he didn't know she was Jewish. Wicked Prime Minister Haman went to the impulsive king and proposed paying the equivalent of a hundred thousand dollars into the king's treasury in exchange for the destruction of the Jews. In God's gracious providence, Esther's cousin Mordecai overheard the plot and was able to communicate it to the queen. Because Mordecai dared to act, Esther ultimately decided to go to the king on behalf of the Jews. This was a great risk because protocol dictated that anyone approaching the king without having been invited could be killed instantly, unless the king held out his golden scepter. Before going, Esther asked her people to gather together for three days of fasting. Then she said, "If I die, I die."

In the meantime, Haman had constructed a gallows on which he planned to hang Mordecai. But because of Esther's courage and trust in God's plan to save the Jews, Haman's evil was eventually exposed, and in a great reversal the king used the gallows to hang Haman.

It's important for us to see that Esther's courage was not in herself. Rather, she waited on God's providence and strength. In the same way, we don't beat Satan and his schemes with courage we muster up ourselves. We should thank God that because of Christ's victory over death and sin on the cross, the devil's schemes can be defeated in our lives.

God our preserver,
Thank you that the one who is in us is greater than the one who is in the world. Please give us your courage as we face struggles within our own families. Thanks for the victory only you can give in defeating the devil's schemes. Amen.

COURAGE

BE STRONG AND COURAGEOUS, FOR YOU WILL LEAD MY
PEOPLE TO POSSESS ALL THE LAND I SWORE TO GIVE THEIR
ANCESTORS. BE STRONG AND VERY COURAGEOUS. OBEY ALL THE
LAWS MOSES GAVE YOU. DO NOT TURN AWAY FROM THEM, AND YOU WILL BE
SUCCESSFUL IN EVERYTHING YOU DO. STUDY THIS BOOK OF THE LAW
CONTINUALLY. MEDITATE ON IT DAY AND NIGHT SO YOU MAY BE SURE TO OBEY
ALL THAT IS WRITTEN IN IT. ONLY THEN WILL YOU SUCCEED. I COMMAND
YOU—BE STRONG AND COURAGEOUS! DO NOT BE AFRAID OR DISCOURAGED. FOR
THE LORD YOUR GOD IS WITH YOU WHEREVER YOU GO.

Joshua 1: 6-9

Fear is a common human emotion. When we were children, we may have been afraid of the dark. In junior high and high school our anxieties were probably more social—we were afraid of doing anything that would cause us embarrassment. And as we mature, our fears become more sophisticated; we tend to fear things like illness, financial ruin, or abandonment.

In the verses above, Joshua is commanded three times to "be strong and courageous." Sandwiched in the middle of this command are some instructions about the Law—God's word to Israel: "Obey . . . do not turn . . . study continually . . . meditate." The passage ends with the promise of God's presence.

Joshua was facing what an earlier generation of Israel had been too frightened to confront—conquering the overwhelming might of the people in the Promised Land. The Israelites' fear led them away from God into disobedience. Because of their lack of faith, God prevented that generation from entering the land. Now, forty years later, Joshua was facing the same anxieties. God didn't minimize Joshua's fear, but he promised strength through his very presence—"For the Lord your God is with you wherever you go."

All of us face fears as we walk through life—fears that might trouble us, paralyze us, or even prompt us to disobey what we know to be right. God calls us to confront our fears, not by pretending to be brave, but rather by finding what Joshua found: God's Word to give us strength and his presence to give us peace.

> *Lord God,*
> *Thank you that I can find the courage I need to face my fears through your*
> *Word and your presence. I know that you will never leave me or forsake me. In*
> *the name of Immanuel—"God with us"—amen.*

COURAGE

BE STRONG AND COURAGEOUS! DON'T BE AFRAID OF THE
KING OF ASSYRIA OR HIS MIGHTY ARMY, FOR THERE IS A POWER
FAR GREATER ON OUR SIDE!   *2 Chronicles 32:7*

When my son Chad was about five or six, his nighttime slumber was sometimes interrupted by bad dreams. On those nights, I'd wake up to hear him crying or calling for me or my husband. I'd shuffle through the hallway to Chad's room and sit on the edge of his bed.

The first thing I did was listen to his fears, and then I told him that I had fears sometimes too. "When I'm afraid," I said, "I talk to God. God sees everything, knows everything, and can do anything. God is strong and God can help us."

After we talked for a while, I encouraged Chad to memorize the beginning of Philippians 4:6-7—"Don't worry about anything; instead, pray about everything." We also talked about Moses (crossing the Red Sea) and David (fighting Goliath); they had fears too, but God was faithful to give them help and courage.

Whenever our children have fearful experiences of any kind, it's important for them to know that we care about them, are willing to help them, and will consistently point them to God. Then they have opportunities to grow in faith and courage too.

Strong Father,
Thank you that you understand how weak we are, and that you share your
strength and courage with us. In the name of Jesus, amen.

CONTENTMENT

NOW THE SERPENT WAS THE SHREWDEST OF ALL THE
CREATURES THE LORD GOD HAD MADE. "REALLY?" HE ASKED
THE WOMAN. "DID GOD REALLY SAY YOU MUST NOT EAT ANY OF
THE FRUIT IN THE GARDEN?" "OF COURSE WE MAY EAT IT," THE WOMAN TOLD HIM.
"IT'S ONLY THE FRUIT FROM THE TREE AT THE CENTER OF THE GARDEN THAT WE
ARE NOT ALLOWED TO EAT. GOD SAYS WE MUST NOT EAT IT OR EVEN TOUCH IT, OR
WE WILL DIE."

Genesis 3:1-3

How content are we—with our children, with our abilities, with our financial situations? How do we measure contentment, anyway? Contentment is the state of being satisfied and not desiring more than we already have. Ouch! It hurts just to hear those words because I realize that discontent is something I experience too often.

In the newspaper I read about a prominent builder of upscale homes who said that one of his keys to success is always having a fabulously decorated model home to show to his customers. He said he wants them to walk away feeling terribly dissatisfied with what they already have.

Those feelings of dissatisfaction come straight from the enemy. When Satan came to Eve in the Garden of Eden, he did not remind her of all the wonderful things God had provided for her, but rather he focused on the one restriction. This is typical of Satan's behavior—he focuses on the thing we don't have instead of reminding us of all God has given us to enjoy.

God wants us to come to him with thanks for all the things that he has blessed us with. Giving heed to the "if onlys" is an awful trap, and it only causes increased dissatisfaction. When I thank God for all he has given me, I quickly gain a renewed perspective. A grateful person is usually a contented person.

God,
Please forgive us for the times we get a bad case of the "if onlys." Thank you
for your many provisions. May we remember them often. Amen.

CONTENTMENT

I AM THE GOOD SHEPHERD. THE GOOD SHEPHERD LAYS
DOWN HIS LIFE FOR THE SHEEP.   *John 10:11*

*C*ontentment should be the hallmark of the person who has put his or her affairs in the hands of God.[2] To be content, we must have an accurate picture of who God is and who we are. Looking at the relationship between a shepherd and his sheep helps us to better understand that picture.

Throughout the Bible God is described as the Good Shepherd, and people are sometimes likened to sheep. King David was a boyhood shepherd himself, and he knew that sheep are very needy. The lot in life of any one sheep depended on the shepherd who cared for it. A shepherd could be kind, thoughtful, and wise, or he could be mean, inconsiderate, and irresponsible. When we see God as our shepherd, we realize that we have the very best care available. Our shepherd is all-powerful and all-knowing. He never sleeps, and he cares about us individually because he gave us life and sustains us.

In order to be content, sheep must have freedom from fear, tension, aggravation, and hunger. It is the job of the shepherd to provide these freedoms by driving away predators, providing food and water, and keeping the sheep from other harm. God provides us with his Spirit to minister security, peace, and hope, and he gives his Word to feed us.

When we as needy people understand that we gain the very presence of God in our lives through the Holy Spirit, we realize the contentment that God intends for each one of us. He *is* the shepherd of our souls, and only he can provide true contentment.

Father,
Thank you that you describe yourself as our shepherd. We're grateful that we can find our contentment in you. Amen.

CONTENTMENT

> THEY ALL ATE AND WERE SATISFIED, AND THE DISCIPLES
> PICKED UP TWELVE BASKETFULS OF BROKEN PIECES THAT
> WERE LEFT OVER.
>
> *Luke 9:17, NIV*

I like getting up early in the morning, but I wasn't always like this. When I was in high school, I made things hard for my mom because I was stubborn about getting ready for school. Making it to my 8 AM classes in college was a huge challenge, and I'm sure I used up most of my allotted absences.

I must have begun changing my ways after becoming a mother. Getting up early has often been my only opportunity for quiet time. Quiet time for me includes reading the Bible, praying, and thinking. I don't do any of those things well when the setting is busy or noisy.

This morning I woke up at 6 AM in a hotel where my family is staying. We are on a weekend trip to take one of our sons back to college for his junior year. Since we don't have to check out of the hotel until 10 AM, it was very tempting to stay snuggled under the bedcovers. But I remembered that my attitudes and perspectives for each day are often established in the quiet of the mornings during time spent in God's Word. Once I decided to get up, my next challenge was finding a quiet spot. My family was asleep in the dark room, and the hotel lobby was too noisy. I decided to pull a comfortable chair out into the hall, and here I am with a quiet, cozy spot and a cup of coffee.

My Bible reading this morning reminded me of the power of God, the importance of my faith, and the great contentment that I experience when I am fed spiritually. In the same way that hungry people were satisfied when Jesus fed the five thousand, our souls are satisfied when we spend time with God.

God,
Thank you that when we spend time in your Word, we experience contentment. Thanks that your Word satisfies our hungry souls. Amen.

CONTENTMENT

DON'T LET ANYONE LEAD YOU ASTRAY WITH EMPTY
PHILOSOPHY AND HIGH-SOUNDING NONSENSE THAT COME FROM
HUMAN THINKING AND FROM THE EVIL POWERS OF THIS WORLD, AND
NOT FROM CHRIST. FOR IN CHRIST THE FULLNESS OF GOD LIVES IN A HUMAN
BODY, AND YOU ARE COMPLETE THROUGH YOUR UNION WITH CHRIST. HE IS THE
LORD OVER EVERY RULER AND AUTHORITY IN THE UNIVERSE. *Colossians 2:8-10*

To be discontented is to have a restless longing for better circumstances—to have a case of the "if onlys." *If only I had a better job. If only I had more money. If only I had a bigger house. If only my husband were more responsible.* The list could go on and on.

The *Chicago Tribune* recently published a weeklong series of articles examining the psychology of contentment. Some suggestions for increasing contentment were to get more rest, put on a happy face, get involved in the moment, live fully to your potential, or consider taking mood-altering medication. Whether we are reading the newspaper, going to a psychologist, or listening to a talk show host, everyone seems to have their own theory about how to find contentment and boost our personal happiness level.

So, according to God's Word, where *do* we find contentment? In a personal, growing relationship with Christ. Christ meets our needs—whether we are lonely, confused, needing forgiveness, discontented, or full of anxiety. He cares about us and wants us to come to him with our requests. Only Jesus can satisfy our longing souls.

> *Friends all around us are trying to find*
> *What the heart yearns for, by sin undermined;*
> *I have the secret, I know where 'tis found:*
> *Only in Jesus true pleasures abound.*[3]

Father,
Thank you that you are more than enough. Thank you that you have author-ity over every other power. Thanks for the contentment you bring to our souls.
Amen.

CONTENTMENT

THE LORD YOUR GOD IS WITH YOU, HE IS MIGHTY TO
SAVE. HE WILL TAKE GREAT DELIGHT IN YOU, HE WILL
QUIET YOU WITH HIS LOVE, HE WILL REJOICE OVER YOU WITH
SINGING.   *Zephaniah 3:17, NIV*

Zephaniah, an Old Testament prophet, didn't have an easy job. He needed to deliver bad news (that judgment was coming) before he could deliver good news (that salvation would follow). As you can probably guess, the verse above falls in the "good news" section of the prophet's book.

Zephaniah liked to use allusion, a literary device that makes indirect reference to another person, place, or event. This verse from his book is pregnant with allusion to a mother's love for her child and the contentment found in the mother-child relationship. Even though this short verse has only thirty-three words, it paints such a beautiful picture of our relationship with God that we're going to concentrate on it for the next three days.

The Lord your God is with you.

When I was a new mom, no one could keep me away from my baby. Even if I took a brief trip to the grocery store while my husband stayed home with our sleeping baby, I was anxious to shop quickly and get back home. If another infant in the store started crying, I was in trouble. My milk began to "let down," and I had the sudden urge to bolt home. I loved being with my baby, and sometimes it was difficult to be apart.

Isn't it curious that one of the names for Christ, first spoken by the prophet Isaiah, was Immanuel, meaning "God with us"? If I, an imperfect mom, could take so much pleasure in being with my baby, imagine how much pleasure God takes in being with me! What a comforting realization.

Father,
Thank you that you want to be with me. That thought brings me great
contentment and security. In Jesus' name, amen.

CONTENTMENT

THE LORD YOUR GOD IS WITH YOU, HE IS MIGHTY TO SAVE.
HE WILL TAKE GREAT DELIGHT IN YOU, HE WILL QUIET YOU
WITH HIS LOVE, HE WILL REJOICE OVER YOU WITH SINGING.

Zephaniah 3:17, NIV

Mighty to save.

In the language of motherhood, *mighty to save* reminds me of a nursing mom. I've heard nursing called a mother's "secret weapon." Those of you who have nursed your children understand. My baby could have been screaming at full volume, but if I picked him up and began nursing him, he stopped crying. That was immensely satisfying to me; I was saving my baby from his distress.

As wonderful as it feels for us to save our babies from hunger and tears, God sent Jesus to save us from much more than that. *Jesus* means "the Lord saves," and only he can save us from sin. Jesus did not come to help us save ourselves—he came to *be* our Savior by dying on the cross for us.

He will take great delight in you.

While my baby nursed for as long as a feeding took (and some seemed to take forever), I delighted in him. It was not unusual for me to rub my baby's head or feet during the process. I enjoyed the opportunity to study my little one's face, and I loved the eyeball-to-eyeball contact we experienced. Every now and then, my baby would stop nursing and break into a wide smile before going back to eating. What a picture of contentment!

What does it mean for God to delight in us? It means that he takes pleasure in us. He appreciates us, cherishes us, and enjoys us. Not only is that how a nursing mother feels toward her baby, but—according to this verse—it's how God feels toward us!

Father,
Thank you that you sent Jesus to save us from eternal death. Thank you that
even though you are holy and we are sinful, you actually delight in us. In the
name of Jesus, amen.

CONTENTMENT

THE LORD YOUR GOD IS WITH YOU, HE IS MIGHTY TO
SAVE. HE WILL TAKE GREAT DELIGHT IN YOU, HE WILL QUIET
YOU WITH HIS LOVE, HE WILL REJOICE OVER YOU WITH SINGING.

Zephaniah 3:17, NIV

He will quiet you with his love.

In a matter of minutes, a mother can sometimes take her baby from screaming and hungry to quiet with a full tummy. God has taken me from kicking and screaming to quiet with a content heart on many occasions as well. A verse from the Psalms that I return to again and again is, "Lord, when doubts fill my mind, when my heart is in turmoil, quiet me and give me renewed hope and cheer" (Psalm 94:19, TLB). He is the one we should run to when *our* hearts need quieting.

He will rejoice over you with singing.

I was extremely fond of singing to my children when they were little. In fact, I began singing to them when they were still in my womb. When I couldn't sleep at times during my pregnancies, I figured it was God's way of preparing me for middle-of-the-night feedings. So I put the time to good use and learned lots of Bible and nursery-rhyme songs. I sang those songs to my children for many years, and if God wills, I will enjoy singing those same songs to grandchildren someday.

I like that this verse describes God as singing over me—not with me or to me, but *over* me. It reminds me of times when my baby was tired and oh-so-fussy. I would lay him down in the crib, gently rub or pat his back or shoulder, and continue singing for as long as it took him to fall asleep. Next time you're struggling to find contentment, revisit this verse and remember that God wants to rejoice over *you* with singing!

Father,
To think that the awesome God of the universe would take time to sing over
me floods me with gratitude and contentment! Thank you that you desire a
tender relationship with each of us. In Jesus' name, amen.

THANKS

THE UNFAILING LOVE OF THE LORD NEVER ENDS! BY HIS
MERCIES WE HAVE BEEN KEPT FROM COMPLETE DESTRUCTION.
GREAT IS HIS FAITHFULNESS; HIS MERCIES BEGIN AFRESH EACH DAY.

Lamentations 3:22-23

*I*magine that I have given you a bowl full of sand and asked you to try to find the particles of iron in it. You might look for them with your eyes or run your fingers through the sand, but you wouldn't be able to detect the iron. If, however, you took a magnet and swept it through the sand, the iron particles would be irresistibly drawn to it.

An unthankful heart is like a finger trying to sift the sand for iron—it doesn't discover God's mercies. But a thankful heart, just like the magnet, sweeps through life's circumstances and finds daily blessings from God.

I do a lot of things *daily*. I walk, shower, read my Bible, feed the cat, bring in the mail, and read the newspaper. God does many things daily too, and I tried jotting some of them down one day to prompt my thankfulness. It wasn't hard. God brought the sun up this morning. He sustained the crickets that I heard chirping. He provided the pleasant breeze I enjoyed while I was out walking. He oversaw the growth of the juicy peach I had for lunch. He brought the sun down in the evening. He gave me strength to meet the needs of the day.

A thankful heart prompts a good attitude. Because God's blessings are new every morning, it's good for us to keep our thanks current for what he supplies *each day*.

God our provider,
May we choose daily to have a grateful heart because you are faithful. Amen.

THANKS

O LORD OUR GOD, SAVE US! GATHER US BACK FROM
AMONG THE NATIONS, SO WE CAN THANK YOUR HOLY NAME
AND REJOICE AND PRAISE YOU.   *Psalm 106:47*

*H*ave you ever noticed that a grateful mom is not usually a miserable mom? I'm
not suggesting that a grateful mom never gets sick, never gets angry at her kids,
or never encounters challenges in relationships. But a grateful mom has an attractive manner.

Psalm 106 encourages us to be thankful for the goodness of the Lord. It also
gives us some pictures of what life was like for the Israelites when they *weren't*
thankful. Their path toward misery included the following:

- Giving no thought to God's miracles
- Not remembering the kindness of the Lord
- Grumbling and rebelling
- Not waiting for God's counsel
- Giving in to their cravings
- Growing envious
- Worshipping false idols
- Not believing God's promises
- Provoking God by their wicked deeds
- Mingling with the pagan nations and adopting their customs
- Defiling themselves morally

In spite of the fact that the Israelites' lack of thankfulness to God led them into
all kinds of sin, when they cried to God out of their distress, he heard them and
helped them. God's patience and mercy in dealing with them was astounding.

We can learn so much from the Israelites. We easily fall into the same patterns
of grumbling, complaining, and forgetting the God who has saved and blessed us.
May we remember that God inhabits the hearts of people who thank and praise
him, but people who grumble and rebel lead miserable lives. Thankfully, the
God who showed patience and mercy to the Israelites shows patience and mercy
to us too.

Father,
We are grateful for your patience and mercy with us. May we look for things
to thank you for each day, rehearsing the blessings you have given us. Amen.

THANKS

FOR THE LORD IS GOOD. HIS UNFAILING LOVE CONTINUES
FOREVER, AND HIS FAITHFULNESS CONTINUES TO EACH
GENERATION.

Psalm 100:5

*D*o you have certain people or things in your life that remind you of how much you have to be thankful for? When I see my youngest son running around, I'm reminded how thankful I am that his left femur mended after a skateboard accident. Whenever I see or hear from our young friend Drew, I'm thankful that God healed his body after a three-year bout with leukemia.

I practiced my violin today and thanked God for providing it. About a year before I turned forty, I began praying about the possibility of purchasing a new violin, since I was still playing the same student instrument I'd had back in junior high school. I only prayed about it occasionally, probably because I didn't think of a new violin as a necessity.

Imagine my shock when my parents called me and suggested that I begin shopping around for violins because they wanted to give me one for my fortieth birthday! They had no idea I had been praying about a new instrument. I remember my knees getting all jelly-like when they told me. Not only was I grateful for the generosity of my parents, but I was amazed that God would provide a new violin in a method I wouldn't ever have imagined.

As I practice my violin this week for the prelude and offertory at church on Sunday, I offer thanks for the creative ways God answers our prayers.

God,
Thank you that you see and provide. Thanks for specific events in our lives
that strengthen our faith in you. Amen.

THANKS

IT IS GOOD TO GIVE THANKS TO THE LORD, TO SING PRAISES TO THE MOST HIGH. IT IS GOOD TO PROCLAIM YOUR UNFAILING LOVE IN THE MORNING, YOUR FAITHFULNESS IN THE EVENING.

Psalm 92:1-2

There are many ways to thank God in prayer. Here are four forms we can use and model for our children:

1. *Give thanks for provisions.* Psalm 104:13-14 says, "You send rain on the mountains from your heavenly home, and you fill the earth with the fruit of your labor. You cause grass to grow for the cattle. You cause plants to grow for people to use." We can thank God for food, breath, strength, light, encouragement, protection, and many other provisions each day.

2. *Give thanks in all situations.* First Thessalonians 5:18 urges us, "No matter what happens, always be thankful, for this is God's will for you who belong to Christ Jesus." One of my friends reminded me that the verse doesn't mean to give thanks *for* all things but *in* all things. We may not be grateful for the problem, but we thank God for what he's accomplishing in us through the problem.

3. *Give thanks for what God is doing in people's lives.* In 1 Thessalonians 1:2-3 Paul states, "We always thank God for all of you and pray for you constantly. As we talk to our God and Father about you, we think of your faithful work, your loving deeds, and your continual anticipation of the return of our Lord Jesus Christ." These are very specific areas of growth for which we can offer thanks—faithfulness, love, and hope.

4. *Give thanks in anticipation of what God will yet do.* Philippians 4:6 says, "Don't worry about anything; instead, pray about everything. Tell God what you need, and thank him for all he has done." Giving thanks to God for things yet to come indicates our trust in him.

Offer thanks for provisions, in all circumstances, for God's work in our lives, and in anticipation of what he *will* do!

Father,
Thanks for hope to keep going. Thanks that you are in control even when we feel off-balance. Thanks that you will be with us each day. Amen.

THANKS

ALL OF THESE THINGS ARE FOR YOUR BENEFIT. AND AS
GOD'S GRACE BRINGS MORE AND MORE PEOPLE TO CHRIST,
THERE WILL BE GREAT THANKSGIVING, AND GOD WILL RECEIVE MORE
AND MORE GLORY.

2 Corinthians 4:15

Have the words *thank you* ever prompted you to cry? This month I had blocked out the two weeks before a writing deadline to do nothing but write and compile. That was before my oldest son, Chad, called. He said that two of his college friends, Scott and Erin, were coming to Wheaton for a few days before Erin left on a missions trip to Africa, and would I be able to help with a little hospitality and housing? Due to putting clean sheets on beds, cleaning bathrooms, and doing some baking in preparation for my guests, I lost a little bit of work time, but the note I found on a pillow after Scott left this morning more than made up for it:

> *Mrs. Elwell, thanks so much for letting me stay here last night. It was nice having somewhere to feel welcome after our long drive yesterday. We both appreciate your hospitality, especially as Erin is a little nervous about her trip. We had a good time chatting last night. God has already blessed Erin's trip through you. Thanks again. —Scott and Erin*

That's when I cried. I realized that in God's schedule, being an encouragement to these two people was an important interlude in the middle of my work, and I was energized by the encouragement of their thanks. When we thank other people, it offers more encouragement than we will ever know.

> Father,
> Thank you for the encouragement you send us through the gratefulness of others. May we be quick to offer thanks to others and quick to offer thanks to you. Amen.

THANKS

Whenever I write, I keep a thesaurus close by. It's a treasury of words I don't like to be without. Up until today, the copy I used was a beat-up, old paperback. But now I won't need to bind that old book together with a rubber band anymore.

A few days ago I mentioned to my son Chad that I was thinking about purchasing a larger thesaurus. You can imagine my surprise, then, when I came home from walking this morning, sat down to write, and spied a new hardcover thesaurus sitting on the coffee table right in front of me. As I leafed through the pages, I felt refreshed to think that Chad would go out and purchase a new copy for me. His act of kindness put a spring in my step.

After writing a note to Chad (below), I offered thanks to God. I thanked him for blessing me with a son who's so thoughtful. I felt grateful to see the fruit of God's Spirit in Chad's life.

Dear Chad,

How do I say "Thanks" for the thesaurus? P. M. Roget suggests expressing it with acknowledgement, a benediction, a blessing, credit, grace, gramercy (that's a new word to me—it means surprise and gratitude), gratefulness, gratitude, praise, recognition, thankfulness, thanksgiving, or a thank-you note. I think I'll opt for the thank-you note.

I was surprised (would the word gramercy be appropriate here?) to discover the new hardcover thesaurus you left on the coffee table for me this morning. How thoughtful of you! I'll never forget your expression of kindness. I'm grateful to see the fruit of God's Spirit in your life.

Love,
Mom

Father,
I'm grateful for the children you've blessed me with. Thank you for the ways you bless me through their kindness. May they always walk close to you. Amen.

THANKS

PRAISE THE LORD, O MY SOUL, AND FORGET NOT ALL HIS
BENEFITS.   *Psalm 103:2, NIV*

A benefit is an advantage, an asset, or a blessing—something that makes my life better. I have numerous benefits in my life that fall into several categories.

I have benefited personally from growing up in a home where I was loved, taught the truth of Christ's gospel, and blessed through the church where my family worshipped. I also received years of violin and piano lessons, a great education from kindergarten through college, and all the benefits of growing up in an affluent country.

Another kind of benefit I realize comes as a result of my husband's job. Through Jim's company, our family is blessed with several kinds of insurance, a 401(k) plan, and a few weeks of paid vacation time each year.

The most significant and long-lasting benefits I've received are described in Psalm 103. I've done nothing to deserve them, but I've received them because of Jesus' death on the cross. Psalm 103 reminds me that God forgives, heals, ransoms me from death, surrounds me with love and tender mercies, and fills my life with good things. He is full of righteousness, justice, mercy, and compassion, and he's slow to get angry. He doesn't punish me as I deserve, and he removes my sins as far as the east is from the west. In spite of the fact that I am weak and finite, his love remains forever, and his salvation is available to my children and my children's children.

The benefits of the first two categories give me some comforts now, but the benefits I receive through Christ will never end.

Gracious Father,
Thank you that you provide us with so many blessings and benefits. May we
be quick to recognize them. Thank you most of all for sending Jesus to die on
the cross. Amen.

HEAVEN

THERE ARE MANY ROOMS IN MY FATHER'S HOME, AND
I AM GOING TO PREPARE A PLACE FOR YOU. IF THIS WERE NOT
SO, I WOULD TELL YOU PLAINLY.

John 14:2

After my grandma died, my sister and her husband had several opportunities to talk with their three-year-old son about death. They explained to Brent that Great Grandma was in heaven with God and that she was very happy there. A few days later we all went to her memorial service, which was held at a local funeral home. As we left, young Brent remarked, "I didn't think heaven would look like *that!*"

What do we expect heaven to look like? It's challenging for moms to know exactly how to respond when our children ask us about heaven because we haven't been there yet! But Scripture provides us with some facts we can share with our children:

1. Heaven is where God is (Matthew 6:9).
2. Kids love treasure chests, and heaven will be one big treasure chest. For those of us who have loved and served God with our hearts, heaven will include gift after gift after gift (Matthew 6:19-21).
3. Jesus has gone there ahead of us to make it ready and to prepare a place for us (John 14:2).
4. God is surrounded in heaven by angels who serve him. Heaven will be an experience of praising God with the angels forever (Revelation 4).
5. Heaven will feel like home to us—the place where we belong (Philippians 3:20).
6. Heaven will be a safe and happy place where there will be no end to joy. There will be no tears, no pain, no death, no weakness, and no night (Revelation 21:3-4).

God of heaven,
May we take advantage of opportunities to teach our children some of the wonderful things your Word has told us about heaven. Thank you that heaven will be a place of great joy. Amen.

HEAVEN

BUT AS FOR ME, MY CONTENTMENT IS NOT IN WEALTH BUT IN
SEEING YOU AND KNOWING ALL IS WELL BETWEEN US. AND WHEN
I AWAKE IN HEAVEN, I WILL BE FULLY SATISFIED, FOR I WILL SEE YOU
FACE TO FACE.   *Psalm 17:15, TLB*

On Valentine's Day 2003, my husband and I visited our brother-in-law, David, at Central DuPage Hospital. Just before we arrived, David's physician had broken the horrible news that he had non-smoker's lung cancer that had metastasized and permeated his brain. With David in the hospital bed, his wife, Joan, my husband, and I stood next to him, put our arms around one another, and wept for a long time. In spite of about six months of radiation, chemotherapy, and medical consultations, cancer cells eventually took over David's body.

Several weeks before David died, friends and family members offered to sit with him at the hospital when Joan or the kids couldn't be there. During one of my shifts, I asked David, "Is there anything in particular you'd like me to do while I'm here?" "Read my Bible out loud, please," was his gentle reply.

When I picked up David's well-worn *Living Bible*, it fell open to the Psalms. I noticed a verse in chapter 17 that he had underlined: "But as for me, my contentment is not in wealth but in seeing you and knowing all is well between us. And when I awake in heaven, I will be fully satisfied, for I will see you face to face."

That verse certainly characterized David's life. He had farmed in Kansas for most of his years and had seen his share of financial disappointments. But when it came to his relationship with God, David was rich. The warmth and depth of that relationship was evident to those around him. Now David experiences that relationship with Christ face-to-face. Can we, too, say that all is well between us and God?

Father,
Thank you that we will realize full satisfaction when we see you face-to-face.
Amen.

HEAVEN

FOR WE KNOW THAT ALL CREATION HAS BEEN
GROANING AS IN THE PAINS OF CHILDBIRTH RIGHT UP TO
THE PRESENT TIME. AND EVEN WE CHRISTIANS, ALTHOUGH WE
HAVE THE HOLY SPIRIT WITHIN US AS A FORETASTE OF FUTURE GLORY, ALSO
GROAN TO BE RELEASED FROM PAIN AND SUFFERING. WE, TOO, WAIT ANXIOUSLY
FOR THAT DAY WHEN GOD WILL GIVE US OUR FULL RIGHTS AS HIS CHILDREN,
INCLUDING THE NEW BODIES HE HAS PROMISED US.   Romans 8:22-23

> *There have been times when I think we do not desire heaven, but more often I find*
> *myself wondering whether in our heart of hearts, we have ever desired anything*
> *else.*   C. S. Lewis, The Problem of Pain

When we begin a relationship with God through Jesus Christ, we begin a journey to a heavenly kingdom. Seeds of God's righteousness are planted in our
souls, and we have new longings for things that are wholesome, pure, true, and
lovely. We groan to be released from the bondage this world has to sin—the
pain, decay, and death that we see as present realities.

Think of the contrasts in the following statements:

- a gorgeous summer day spent with friends at the beach, and a tornado
leaving death and destruction in its wake
- an especially tender and meaningful connection with a child, and an ugly
disagreement that leaves parent and child feeling alienated
- a hot apple pie fresh from the oven, and a container of moldy food in the
refrigerator

I like the sound of the first half of all the above, but not the second half. I like
things to be *right*! The reality of life here on earth is that although we experience
the pain of living in a fallen world, we get glimpses and tastes of heaven when we
look to God. May we be quick to see the promises of heaven in a beautiful sunset,
a treasured memory with a child, or an unexpected gift that only God could have
arranged. May we think more often about the glory that awaits us than the groaning we'll leave behind.

> *Eternal God,*
> *May the painful realities of life not lead us to bitterness or despair but rather*
> *toward hope in our eternal future with you. Thank you for moments of wonder*
> *and beauty that give us little tastes of heaven. Amen.*

HEAVEN

"LORD, REMIND ME HOW BRIEF MY TIME ON EARTH WILL
BE. REMIND ME THAT MY DAYS ARE NUMBERED, AND THAT MY
LIFE IS FLEEING AWAY. MY LIFE IS NO LONGER THAN THE WIDTH OF MY
HAND. AN ENTIRE LIFETIME IS JUST A MOMENT TO YOU; HUMAN EXISTENCE IS BUT
A BREATH." WE ARE MERELY MOVING SHADOWS, AND ALL OUR BUSY RUSHING
ENDS IN NOTHING. WE HEAP UP WEALTH FOR SOMEONE ELSE TO SPEND. AND SO,
LORD, WHERE DO I PUT MY HOPE? MY ONLY HOPE IS IN YOU.   *Psalm 39:4-7*

Alfred Nobel, a Swedish chemist, amassed his fortune by inventing dynamite
and other explosives, which he eventually sold to various governments. These
governments in turn made weapons out of the explosives. When Alfred's
brother died, one newspaper made a huge mistake and printed *Alfred's* obituary
instead of his brother's. The article described him as a man who became rich by
providing ingredients that allowed people to kill each other in huge quantities.

Alfred was sorely shaken by reading the mistaken obituary, and he determined from that point on to use his wealth to reward people for benefiting humanity. That decision led him to establish the Nobel Prize. Alfred Nobel
responded to a sobering moment by evaluating his life and resolving to move in a
different direction.

Isn't it interesting how close calls can jar us and get us thinking about what's
really important in life? Maybe a serious accident of a child reminded us that relationships are so much more important than schedules. Maybe being confronted
by a friend helped us see that our life was out of balance. Maybe reading Psalm
39:4-7 reminded us that in the end, the thing that matters most is our hope in
God—and how we've been able to influence our children to place their hope in
God.

As we assess our lives, what choices can we make today that affirm our hope in
the Lord?

God,
Today we want to pray Psalm 39:4-7 back to you. Amen.

HEAVEN

DON'T STORE UP TREASURES HERE ON EARTH, WHERE THEY
CAN BE EATEN BY MOTHS AND GET RUSTY, AND WHERE
THIEVES BREAK IN AND STEAL. STORE YOUR TREASURES IN
HEAVEN, WHERE THEY WILL NEVER BECOME MOTH-EATEN OR RUSTY AND WHERE
THEY WILL BE SAFE FROM THIEVES. WHEREVER YOUR TREASURE IS, THERE YOUR
HEART AND THOUGHTS WILL ALSO BE. *Matthew 6:19-21*

Money solved *some* of the longings of Christina Onassis. With a weekly income of about one million dollars, she was able to buy just about anything she wanted. When she was living in Europe and wanted Diet Coke, which at the time was available only in the United States, she dispatched her private jet to buy a month's supply—and it cost $30,000 per trip! She wanted twenty-four-hour companionship, so she sometimes offered friends $20,000 or $30,000 a month to stay with her. Sadly, Christina's life did not end well. She died at thirty-seven of a heart attack that was likely brought on by repeated dieting bouts and her overuse of barbiturates. All the money in the world didn't buy her happiness.

We sometimes hear people say, jokingly, "The only things certain about life are death and taxes." The only thing certain about riches is that they, like moths and rust, pass away and don't satisfy. Moths and rust are both pictures moms can identify with. We may use mothballs in some of our storage places to prevent female moths from leaving our garments full of holes. The damage these little critters cause happens slowly and quietly, like rust on our cars. Moths and rust remind us that earthly treasures don't last forever.

What are *our* treasures? What has great value to us? Is it money, clothes, our house? All the treasures in the world are not enough to satisfy our souls. Our treasures on earth can be used for eternity, however, and if we focus on God's Word and people's souls, those investments will last.

Father,
Thanks for reminders that all our earthly goods pass away. May our hearts be
focused on what's lasting and eternal. Amen.

HEAVEN

NO EYE HAS SEEN, NO EAR HAS HEARD, AND NO MIND
HAS IMAGINED WHAT GOD HAS PREPARED FOR THOSE WHO
LOVE HIM.   *1 Corinthians 2:9*

Last summer I spent a weekend visiting with my two sisters, Gail and Barbara. The three of us stayed at a hotel in Cedar Rapids, Iowa, and enjoyed a few days of walking, talking, shopping, and playing games.

The first morning we walked, we explored a neighborhood near the hotel. To our pleasant surprise, we stumbled on Noel Ridge, a sprawling park that contained acres of gorgeous flowers and groundcovers. It was a gardener's delight. The three of us walked from one tier of gardens to another, stopping to admire the beauty and variety of each section. Although I'm not the gardener that either of my sisters is, I came away with a few new planting ideas for next year: "Forever Blue" eustoma, "Lavender Lace" cuphea, and pink alteranthera. I don't know how to *pronounce* any of those names, much less grow them, but it will be fun to give them a try.

As I wandered around the colorful gardens, the words of a song came to mind:

> *Heav'n above is softer blue,*
> *Earth around is sweeter green!*
> *Something lives in ev'ry hue*
> *Christless eyes have never seen:*
> *Birds with gladder song o'erflow*
> *Flow'rs with deeper beauties shine,*
> *Since I know, as now I know,*
> *I am His and He is mine.*[1]

While living on this earth, I have opportunities to appreciate a tiny percentage of the wonders and works of our Creator. But I hope that when I get to heaven, I'll be able to admire every single flower and plant that God created. I can't imagine what it will be like to stroll through *that* garden.

> *Father in heaven,*
> *Thanks for little tastes of heaven that you give us here on earth. Amen.*

HEAVEN

NO ONE CAN LAY ANY OTHER FOUNDATION THAN THE ONE WE ALREADY HAVE—JESUS CHRIST. NOW ANYONE WHO BUILDS ON THAT FOUNDATION MAY USE GOLD, SILVER, JEWELS, WOOD, HAY, OR STRAW. BUT THERE IS GOING TO COME A TIME OF TESTING AT THE JUDGMENT DAY TO SEE WHAT KIND OF WORK EACH BUILDER HAS DONE. EVERYONE'S WORK WILL BE PUT THROUGH THE FIRE TO SEE WHETHER OR NOT IT KEEPS ITS VALUE. IF THE WORK SURVIVES THE FIRE, THAT BUILDER WILL RECEIVE A REWARD. BUT IF THE WORK IS BURNED UP, THE BUILDER WILL SUFFER GREAT LOSS. THE BUILDERS THEMSELVES WILL BE SAVED, BUT LIKE SOMEONE ESCAPING THROUGH A WALL OF FLAMES.

1 Corinthians 3:11-15

If you had unlimited resources to build your dream house, what would it look like? Would it be a small cottage by the ocean, a condominium in a high-rise close to cultural events in the city, or a brick mansion with a large, circular drive out in the country? How big would it be, what period of architecture would you choose, and what kind of building materials would you use?

Few people have the opportunity to live in their dream home. Most people are thankful for adequate shelter that houses the family. If there are extra comforts and beauties, that's great too! All of us who know Christ *will* live in a dream home someday, and spending time thinking about it now is a good thing. God's Word tells us that the way we live our lives here on earth will have an eternal effect on our dwelling in heaven.

If we want our eternal lives to be spent with Jesus, our foundation must be built on him. Having established that, our daily choices determine the kind of building materials we will use—straw, hay, wood (cheap and easy), or stone, silver, or gold (costly and valuable).

We might imagine that some of us are sending ahead sufficient materials for pup tents, some for studio apartments, some for trailer homes, some for ranch houses, and others for great mansions.[2]

What will our home in heaven be made of? We determine what it will be like by the choices we make each day.

God my foundation,
It's sobering to remember that our daily choices now will have eternal consequences. May what we think, say, and do be valuable like gold and not cheap like straw. Amen.

SERVICE

DANIEL REPLIED, "THERE ARE NO WISE MEN, ENCHANTERS,
MAGICIANS, OR FORTUNE-TELLERS WHO CAN TELL THE KING
SUCH THINGS. BUT THERE IS A GOD IN HEAVEN WHO REVEALS SECRETS,
AND HE HAS SHOWN KING NEBUCHADNEZZAR WHAT WILL HAPPEN IN THE FUTURE.
NOW I WILL TELL YOU YOUR DREAM AND THE VISIONS YOU SAW AS YOU LAY ON
YOUR BED."

Daniel 2:27-28

King Nebuchadnezzar had a dream so disturbing that he immediately called all his magicians, enchanters, sorcerers, and astrologers and demanded that they tell him its meaning. The only problem was, he also wanted them to tell him what he dreamed! When they protested that this was impossible, he gave orders that all the wise men in Babylon were to be executed.

When a guard came to kill Daniel, the Bible tells us he "handled the situation with wisdom and discretion" (vs. 14). He asked the king for extra time to interpret the dream, and God then provided the knowledge he needed.

Why might King Nebuchadnezzar have granted more time to Daniel and not to the other wise men? Perhaps it's because Daniel had the reputation of being God's servant. What was it about his life that communicated his faith?

Daniel reverenced God. The king gave Daniel extra time to interpret his dream. What did Daniel do with that time? He and his friends *prayed*.

Daniel praised God. After God gave Daniel the meaning of the king's dream, Daniel didn't rush right over to the king, and he didn't boast. Instead, he praised God for his wisdom and power.

Daniel testified about God. When the king asked for Daniel's description and interpretation of the dream, Daniel replied, "There is a God in heaven who reveals secrets" (2:28). The king was even prompted to praise God, saying to Daniel, "Truly, your God is the God of gods, the Lord over kings, a revealer of mysteries" (2:47).

As the king saw Daniel reverence God, praise God, and testify about God, he was convinced that Daniel was a servant of God. May our lives display these same qualities so that our children will learn what it means to serve God.

Father,
As we seek to be your servants, may we act in such a way that others will know
we serve you. Thank you for the example of Daniel. Amen.

SERVICE

AND SINCE I, THE LORD AND TEACHER, HAVE WASHED
YOUR FEET, YOU OUGHT TO WASH EACH OTHER'S FEET. I
HAVE GIVEN YOU AN EXAMPLE TO FOLLOW. DO AS I HAVE DONE TO
YOU. HOW TRUE IT IS THAT A SERVANT IS NOT GREATER THAN THE MASTER. NOR
ARE MESSENGERS MORE IMPORTANT THAN THE ONE WHO SENDS THEM. YOU KNOW
THESE THINGS—NOW DO THEM! THAT IS THE PATH OF BLESSING.   *John 13:14-17*

Just before Jesus performed the lowly task of washing the disciples' feet, those same disciples had been arguing about which of them was most important. How ironic that people who thought they were so important were about to behave so poorly in response to Jesus' arrest and crucifixion. This didn't take Jesus by surprise, though. He knows what we are all like deep down inside our hearts.

"Jesus knew that one of his disciples had already decided to betray him. Another would deny him by the next morning. Even this night, they would all desert him. In the next hours they would repeatedly display ignorance, laziness, and lack of trust."[3] Even though Jesus had good reasons to give up on all of them, he continued to show them his love. It was amazing, incomprehensible love because the disciples neither deserved it nor immediately appreciated it.

We are just like those disciples. We are sometimes unfaithful to Christ, and he knows the details of our experiences. But he died for us, he continues to love us, and he wants to guide us and encourage us. Do we realize how much Christ loves us? Are we willing to imitate him by serving one another in love?

Father,
Forgive us for spending too much time thinking about how important we are and not enough time serving you. Thank you for the example you left us and for the love you showed to your disciples even though they were an imperfect bunch. Amen.

SERVICE

REMAIN IN ME, AND I WILL REMAIN IN YOU. FOR A BRANCH
CANNOT PRODUCE FRUIT IF IT IS SEVERED FROM THE VINE, AND
YOU CANNOT BE FRUITFUL APART FROM ME.   *John 15:4*

As moms who walk with Christ, we realize that much of our service to people around us happens through mundane things like doing laundry, cooking, or bandaging a scraped knee. But on occasion, we also get a glimpse of something out of the ordinary God is doing that we're allowed to be a part of. That happened to me this past week.

When I sat down in the chair at the hair salon to get my hair trimmed, I sensed that the woman who was about to cut my hair had a heavy heart. "Please take off about one-half inch all over," I told her. After a few minutes of chitchat, I asked her how her week was going. She haltingly told me that a close friend of her family had committed suicide that week. *No wonder she looks so sad,* I thought.

As my hairdresser continued to talk about how she felt, she also raised some questions about God, death, and eternal life. At first, I listened and asked questions. But at an appropriate moment in the conversation, I also shared the good news about Jesus' death and resurrection. I had just read about it in Matthew two hours before my haircut.

I left the hair salon that morning with mixed feelings. I felt sad to be reminded of the awfulness of sin and death. But I also felt thankful for the opportunity to share the news that Jesus offers us forgiveness and eternal life, because we're all incredibly needy.

Later in the week, I delivered to my hairdresser a plate of homemade cookies, a card, and a copy of *Grieving a Suicide* by Albert Y. Hsu. I left the salon that day feeling grateful for the opportunity to serve Christ. I can only serve him as I remain in him.

Father,
Thanks for the joy that serving you brings. We want to stay close to you. In our Savior's name, amen.

BECAUSE OF THE SERVICE BY WHICH YOU HAVE PROVED
YOURSELVES, MEN WILL PRAISE GOD FOR THE OBEDIENCE
THAT ACCOMPANIES YOUR CONFESSION OF THE GOSPEL OF
CHRIST, AND FOR YOUR GENEROSITY IN SHARING WITH THEM AND WITH
EVERYONE ELSE.

2 Corinthians 9:13, NIV

D. Kenneth Gieser was a senior in high school. Ever since flunking fourth grade, he had struggled with his studies. He wanted very much to attend Wheaton College, but he wasn't hopeful about his prospects of being accepted. Since his father had just died, his sister went to bat for him and literally begged the college to give her brother a chance. The result? He not only graduated from Wheaton College but ended up graduating from medical school and going on to China as a missionary doctor.

To Ken's great disappointment, he became extremely ill in China and had to return home. His heart sank; he felt as though living in the United States was his "second best." But what were some of his accomplishments in this "second best" period of his life? He founded the Christian Medical/Dental Society; founded the world-renowned Wheaton Eye Clinic; helped begin the Medical Assistance Program (MAP); served on the Board of Directors of Christianity Today, the Billy Graham Evangelistic Association, TEAM Missions, and InterVarsity; and founded the Missionary Furlough Homes. He even became chairman of the Board of Trustees at Wheaton College!

The night he died, he had been visiting a Christian wilderness camp in New York. His final acts of service were humble—helping the kitchen crew wash dishes and taking out the trash. His son, Dave, reflected, "He went to sleep that night under the stars in the mountains of New York and woke up in heaven!" Ken was a servant who was ready to meet his Savior. What an inspiration for us.

Father,
Thank you for your servants who are great examples to us. Thank you that
you used a boy who once struggled in school to accomplish such wonderful
things for your kingdom. May we serve you with all of our hearts. Amen.

SERVICE

AND THEN HE TOLD THEM, "GO INTO ALL THE WORLD AND
PREACH THE GOOD NEWS TO EVERYONE, EVERYWHERE."

Mark 16:15

We can teach our children nothing more important than the gospel of Jesus
Christ, because it has eternal implications for their souls. The good news about
Jesus was prophesied in the Old Testament: Jesus was born as a man into King
David's royal family line, he lived on earth for a while, he died a terrible death on
a cross, and he was proven to be the Son of God when God raised him from the
dead through the power of the Holy Spirit. God did all this to save us from the
penalty of our sin, so that we could believe him, obey him, and bring glory to him
(Romans 1:3-5).

I'm sometimes hesitant to share God's Good News for fear that I won't deliver it perfectly or that it won't be received perfectly. But perhaps a better way
to look at it is this: If my children (or neighbors, relatives, or friends) were in a
burning building and there was plenty of time for me to warn them to get out,
would I wait until I could say, "Get out of the building and go to a safe place" with
perfect tact? Of course not! I'd deliver the message because it was urgent and because—if they acted on it—it would save their lives. So does the Good News of
Jesus Christ.

When we share the good news with our children or friends or relatives, we
tell them what Christ has done for us. As others have said, it's as though each of us
is one beggar telling another beggar where she found bread.

Father,
Thank you that the good news of Jesus gives us purpose now and hope for the
future. Please help us to serve you by spreading the good news, beginning in
our homes. Amen.

SERVICE

IT WAS REVEALED TO [THE PROPHETS] THAT THEY WERE
NOT SERVING THEMSELVES BUT YOU, WHEN THEY SPOKE OF
THE THINGS THAT HAVE NOW BEEN TOLD YOU BY THOSE WHO
HAVE PREACHED THE GOSPEL TO YOU BY THE HOLY SPIRIT SENT FROM HEAVEN.
EVEN ANGELS LONG TO LOOK INTO THESE THINGS.

1 Peter 1:12, NIV

What comes to mind when you think of the word *service*? A friend preparing a delicious meal and serving you at her dining-room table? A soldier who is contributing to the freedom of our country? A Sunday school teacher who faithfully challenges your child toward faith in God?

I offer thanks to the people around me who work and serve on my behalf. But until reading 1 Peter 1:12, I had never thought to thank God for the benefits I have received through the ancient prophets. Old Testament prophets were men of incredible service—not only to the people of their day but to us as well. They spoke of the salvation that we presently experience, and yet they never lived to see how or when it all took place. Their service must have been prompted by incredible faith.

Christians living today are privileged to have the benefit of looking back on Jesus' birth, death, and resurrection, and the entire Word of God is available to us. When we consider the faith and service of prophets of old—who had none of these benefits—we should be inspired to serve God out of gratitude and love.

Father,
Thank you for the service of the prophets and the service of people who passed on the Good News to us. May we be women who are anxious to serve you, our families, and others around us. Amen.

SERVICE

FOR EVEN I, THE SON OF MAN, CAME HERE NOT TO BE
SERVED BUT TO SERVE OTHERS. *Mark 10:45*

I presently serve as a deaconess for my church. We have fifteen women who pray, prepare the bread and juice for Communion, plan funeral luncheons, help disperse the *Care and Share* fund, write notes to encourage people in the congregation, organize baptisms, visit the shut-ins of our church, and arrange meals, rides, and child care for those who need our help. Please don't picture us as a group of old ladies with buns in our hair. We're much more spry than that. We often wear jeans, we have some good laughs, and we sip root-beer floats during committee reports.

At our meeting last night, one of our deaconesses gave us a new idea. Susan told us that she had taken her fifteen-year-old son, Andrew, along to visit an older woman in the congregation. Because I'm aware of Andrew's handsome smile and pleasant personality, I'm sure that his presence brought extra sparkle to the visit. Susan enjoyed sharing the experience with Andrew, and they were both reminded of the joy that comes from serving others. She encouraged the rest of us to consider taking our children on occasional visits too.

As we work side by side in the body of Christ, showing care and concern for others to the same degree that we would want to be cared for, we experience unity—and joy! What an enriching experience it is for me to serve alongside women who are looking not to be served, but, like Christ, to serve others.

> *Father,*
> *Thanks for the privilege of serving you. You have done so much for us through Christ, and we are grateful. Help us to look for ways to involve our children in serving you as well. In Jesus' name, amen.*

REVERENCE

THEREFORE, SINCE WE ARE RECEIVING A KINGDOM
THAT CANNOT BE SHAKEN, LET US BE THANKFUL, AND SO
WORSHIP GOD ACCEPTABLY WITH REVERENCE AND AWE, FOR OUR
"GOD IS A CONSUMING FIRE."

Hebrews 12:28-29, NIV

Reverence is a word we don't hear very often; it sounds a bit archaic to our ears. The essence of true reverence is to treasure God in our hearts and to think about him often.

When God chose Mary to be Jesus' mother, he didn't choose her for her impressive experience as a mom, because she had none. But she had great reverence toward God. When she sang about what God was doing in her life, she said, "His mercy extends to those who fear him, from generation to generation" (Luke 1:50, NIV).

When Diana, Princess of Wales, was interviewed several years before she died, her life appeared to be quite a contrast with Mary's. Diana was wealthy, and Mary was poor. Diana had a royal, fairy-tale wedding that was watched by about 750 million people around the world. Mary waited in seclusion after the angel's announcement, and her fiancé, Joseph, considered divorcing her quietly. In Diana's interview, she said she wanted to be "queen of people's hearts." Mary said she wanted to be a handmaiden of the Lord—his servant.

A *Chicago Tribune* article from August 31, 1997, stated, "The Princess of Wales was beautiful, famous and wealthy, and she won the admiration of millions, but she found simple happiness elusive." Mary led a simple life with difficult circumstances, but she had lasting joy and blessing.

What an example Mary left for us as mothers. May we always value God and be aware of his presence. Reverence is not an archaic word—it's a word for today.

God,
Thank you for Mary's example of a reverent life. Please help us treasure you in our hearts and think about you often. Amen.

REVERENCE

THOSE WHO FEAR THE LORD ARE SECURE; HE WILL BE A
PLACE OF REFUGE FOR THEIR CHILDREN.   *Proverbs 14:26*

The benefits of reverence for God don't stop with us—they are passed down to our children in some very unique ways. We're taught in this proverb that if a parent fears, or reverences, the Lord, she has a secure spiritual fortress. The refuge and protection of that fortress will be experienced by her children as well.

A fortress includes walls around a city to protect it from enemy attacks. Back in Bible times these walls were fifteen to twenty-five feet thick and twenty-five feet high. On top of these walls, towers were built at regular intervals, giving defenders a good viewpoint from which they could counter an attack. The outside walls were often protected by a moat that made direct assault almost impossible. A city inside a fortress typically had only one gate—two at the most—keeping security very tight. Since no city could last long without an adequate water supply, fortified cities were generally built near rivers or springs.

When we choose to reverence God by trusting him, spending time in his Word, and obeying what we're learning, he becomes our spiritual fortress. Our walls are built thick against temptation, we become wise about what we need to look out for, and our water supply—refreshment from God—is unending. Even if we did not experience growing up in a family fortress of faith and security, we can choose, through reverence for God, to have that security for ourselves and for our children.

Father,
Oh, how we need to be protected. Thank you that you want to be our fortress. May we choose to reverence you so we will experience security for ourselves and for our children. Amen.

REVERENCE

MAKE THIS ANNOUNCEMENT TO ISRAEL AND TO JUDAH:
LISTEN, YOU FOOLISH AND SENSELESS PEOPLE—WHO HAVE
EYES BUT DO NOT SEE, WHO HAVE EARS BUT DO NOT HEAR. DO
YOU HAVE NO RESPECT FOR ME? WHY DO YOU NOT TREMBLE IN MY PRESENCE? I,
THE LORD, AM THE ONE WHO DEFINES THE OCEAN'S SANDY SHORELINE, AN
EVERLASTING BOUNDARY THAT THE WATERS CANNOT CROSS. THE WAVES MAY TOSS
AND ROAR, BUT THEY CAN NEVER PASS THE BOUNDS I SET.   *Jeremiah 5:20-22*

*I*f you visited my friend Ruthie's home, she'd be happy to show you her sand collection. I'm not talking about samples from just two or three beaches. To date, Ruthie has 235 small glass jars of sand from places like Madras, India; Gulf Cay, Belize; Elat, Red Sea; Aran Islands, Ireland; and Mooréa, Tahiti. Because she also has pictures of the shorelines where most of her sand samples were collected, it's fun to see what some of God's beaches around the world look like.

An image of the sandy ocean shoreline was just what the Old Testament prophet Jeremiah needed to give the children of Israel a sobering wake-up call. The Israelites had a big problem: they had forgotten to show reverence and respect for their heavenly Father. All the way through the Bible, God promises blessing for those who obey and destruction for those who disobey, but the Israelites seemed to be hard of hearing.

Those of you who are mothers of teenagers might have encountered that behavior too. When we tire of saying the same things over and over, it's helpful to try a new approach. Using a word picture sometimes gets our point across, and that's exactly what Jeremiah did for the Israelites in these verses. He reminded the people that their powerful God had defined—and kept—the ocean's shorelines as an everlasting boundary between land and sea. But instead of reverencing God's awesome power, the Israelites were ignoring him.

Just like the Israelites, we sometimes ignore God and fail to treat him as he deserves. May glimpses of his wonders here on earth prompt us to show him more reverence and respect.

Father,
As our eyes and ears see and hear your wonders, may we give you the reverence
and worship you deserve. Amen.

REVERENCE

FEAR OF THE LORD IS THE BEGINNING OF KNOWLEDGE.
ONLY FOOLS DESPISE WISDOM AND DISCIPLINE.

Proverbs 1:7

*W*hile paging through the morning newspaper several Decembers ago, I stopped to read an irreverent article titled "Nativity Spoof in Need of Seasonal Forgiveness." To say that I was saddened by the article would be much too mild. Here's an excerpt:

> *"We hope God has a sense of humor," declares the program to The Madonna in Spite of Herself, Corn Production's new late-night musical Nativity spoof, "or else we're in a lot of trouble." No kidding. Given that this fringe Chicago troupe translates [the Virgin] Mary into a big-haired gum-chomping resident of Berwyn, Joseph (a.k.a. Joey) into a genial sexual predator, and the Angel Gabriel into a screaming vamp in a hot outfit, the youthful satirists at Corn Productions had better hope for some Christian forgiveness and seasonal goodwill. Otherwise, they'll have a lot more to worry about than lumps of coal in their collective stockings.[4]*

After reading the depressing article, I wondered what the people involved in the production had learned as children about the birth of Christ. Had they heard Luke 2 read at home with reverence? Had they been part of a loving body of believers where the account of Jesus' birth was portrayed respectfully? Had they ever had the chance to sense, deep in their souls, the beauty of the greatest story ever told?

What a great opportunity we moms have, while our children are living in our home, to sow seeds of respect for God and his Word.

> *Father,*
> *Sometimes we are jolted by irreverent things we see or read, and we remember that the way we think of you is not to be taken lightly. What we think about you affects the way we live. We want to show you great reverence, and by our examples and words we want to encourage our children to reverence you.*
> *Amen.*

REVERENCE

SERVE THE LORD WITH REVERENT FEAR, AND REJOICE
WITH TREMBLING.

Psalm 2:11

*R*everent fear"—now that's an interesting word combination! Let's look closely at each of the two words.

Reverence—"a feeling of profound awe and respect. Because of his majesty and holiness, God arouses a feeling of reverence in those who worship and serve him."[5]

Fear—"a feeling of reverence, awe, and respect, or an unpleasant emotion caused by a sense of danger. Fear may be directed toward God or humankind, and it may be either healthy or harmful."[6]

Reverent fear, for the Christian, is not a harmful fear that includes a sense of terror or dread. In God's Word, Christians are taught not to fear other humans, because although people may harm our bodies they cannot touch our souls. But the Bible also teaches that wicked people do fear others, acting deceitfully as they attempt to hide their sins. Unbelievers have every reason to fear God as well because they stand condemned before him. This is usually not the kind of fear that leads them to repentance. Quite the opposite; the unbeliever tries to hide from God until he or she gets a glimpse of God's love and grace.

But healthy fear includes reverence and respect. Proverbs 9:10 teaches that the "fear of the Lord is the beginning of wisdom." All of our work, all of our actions, and all of our service to God must come from a heart that has a profound sense of awe and respect for him. May our children see that in our lives so they will want to serve the Lord respectfully themselves.

Father,
May we treat you with the reverence you so deserve. When we experience your
love and grace, we want to do that. Please help us model reverence for you to
our children. Amen.

REVERENCE

IT WAS TIME FOR THE ANNUAL PASSOVER CELEBRATION, AND
JESUS WENT TO JERUSALEM. IN THE TEMPLE AREA HE SAW
MERCHANTS SELLING CATTLE, SHEEP, AND DOVES FOR SACRIFICES; AND HE
SAW MONEY CHANGERS BEHIND THEIR COUNTERS. JESUS MADE A WHIP FROM SOME
ROPES AND CHASED THEM ALL OUT OF THE TEMPLE. HE DROVE OUT THE SHEEP
AND OXEN, SCATTERED THE MONEY CHANGERS' COINS OVER THE FLOOR, AND
TURNED OVER THEIR TABLES.   *John 2:13-15*

Reverence isn't always quiet. Sometimes a display of reverence is rather surprising to those who are watching.

In Old Testament times God instructed the Israelites to bring their best animals for sacrifice. In New Testament times the Temple priests developed a market for sacrificial animals because they knew it was difficult for pilgrims to bring their own animals on the long journey to the Temple. But what began as a local farmer's market on the way to Jerusalem became a big, dishonest business that took up lots of space on the Temple grounds. With all the hustle and bustle of this dishonest and greedy trade taking place in the Temple, it was difficult to worship, which was what they were all supposed to be doing.

These greedy businessmen were making a mockery of God's house of worship, and because Jesus was zealous for the reverence of God, he displayed his reverence in a less-than-quiet manner.

He made a whip. This was a deliberate and forceful response.

He drove the money changers away. This was not loss of temper. Jesus' actions expressed anger, but he was clearly in control.

He said, "Get out of here." Jesus' reverence for God prompted him to meet mockery of God with serious consequences.

We often think of reverence as quiet, and many times it is. But there are times in our lives when our reverence for God prompts us to confront mockery of God with deliberate and carefully enforced actions.

Father,
In our parenting and in other areas of our lives, may we be zealous about not
wanting to do or give way to anything that would be mockery of you. Amen.

REVERENCE

WHEN THE PEOPLE HEARD THE THUNDER AND THE
LOUD BLAST OF THE HORN, AND WHEN THEY SAW THE
LIGHTNING AND THE SMOKE BILLOWING FROM THE MOUNTAIN,
THEY STOOD AT A DISTANCE, TREMBLING WITH FEAR. AND THEY SAID TO MOSES,
"YOU TELL US WHAT GOD SAYS, AND WE WILL LISTEN. BUT DON'T LET GOD SPEAK
DIRECTLY TO US. IF HE DOES, WE WILL DIE!" "DON'T BE AFRAID," MOSES SAID, "FOR
GOD HAS COME IN THIS WAY TO SHOW YOU HIS AWESOME POWER. FROM NOW ON,
LET YOUR FEAR OF HIM KEEP YOU FROM SINNING!"

Exodus 20:18-20

*S*ometimes we can gain our children's attention simply by raising our eyebrows
or clearing our throats. Other times, when we want to be more emphatic, we
need extra bells and whistles to do the job. Even then, what works for the oldest
child in the family might not work for the youngest, because kids' temperaments
vary.

This is true of adults as well. Some need only to see a speed limit sign to obey
it. Others try to push the limits, driving 42 miles per hour in a 30 mile-per-hour
zone, not slowing down until *after* they've seen the flashing lights of a police car
behind them. They may not have had a healthy respect for the speed limit (or the
police officer) before they received a speeding ticket, but they probably will afterward.

Throughout the events of the Bible, God chose to get people's attention in various ways. Sometimes he spoke quietly; sometimes he displayed amazing power. In
today's passage, the children of Israel witnessed God's amazing power in the thunder, the horn, the lightning, and the smoke. He had their attention! I love the
words that Moses spoke to the Israelites—once they were listening—telling them
not to be afraid, but to allow God's awesome power to produce a healthy fear and
reverence. That reverence would then foster a desire to avoid sin.

God wants the same things from us. In his good purposes, he uses various
means to get our attention, but he wants us to see him for who he is and respond
with reverent and affectionate obedience. The more time we spend in his Word,
the more we will see him as he is and want to treat him with the reverence he deserves.

Father,
Thank you for the many ways you spoke to people in history. We're grateful
for your Word, because in it we see your awesome power. May we respond to
you with reverence and obedience. In Jesus' name, amen.

CHRISTMAS

"You will become pregnant and have a son, and you are to name him Jesus. He will be very great and will be called the Son of the Most High. And the Lord God will give him the throne of his ancestor David. And he will reign over Israel forever; his Kingdom will never end!" Mary asked the angel, "But how can I have a baby? I am a virgin." The angel replied, "The Holy Spirit will come upon you, and the power of the Most High will overshadow you. So the baby born to you will be holy, and he will be called the Son of God."

Luke 1:31-35

Perhaps mothers can best understand the significance of the virgin birth of Jesus. Whether our children became part of our family through natural birth or adoption, they each had a physical father at conception. The Bible teaches us that Jesus did not. Joseph became Jesus' physical father after birth, but it was God's Spirit who miraculously provided for the Son of God to enter human existence through a virgin's womb.

When Mary was visited by an angel who explained that she was highly favored by God, she was very frightened until the angel told her not to be afraid—the Lord was with her. She was told that she would give birth to a son whom she was to name Jesus, and that he would be the Son of God. Mary's only question was, "How will this be, since I am a virgin?" She must have been a woman of great faith to ask "How?" Others might have said, "But this *can't* be!"

The angel went on to explain that the Holy Spirit would empower this divine, nonphysical act so that Jesus, a human being, could also be called the Son of God. There's huge significance for us in the angel's words to Mary. In one of the greatest miracles of all time, Jesus was born fully God and fully man—the *only* one who could later bridge the gap between God and humans!

Eternal Father,
Thank you for your magnificent plan that brought your love down to us.
Amen.

CHRISTMAS

[THE LORD] HAS RAISED UP A HORN OF SALVATION FOR US
. . . TO GIVE TO HIS PEOPLE THE KNOWLEDGE OF SALVATION
BY THE FORGIVENESS OF THEIR SINS, BECAUSE OF THE TENDER
MERCY OF OUR GOD, WITH WHICH THE SUNRISE FROM ON HIGH WILL VISIT US, TO
SHINE UPON THOSE WHO SIT IN DARKNESS AND THE SHADOW OF DEATH.

Luke 1:69, 77-79, NASB

What phrase would you use to describe the birth or adoption of your children? "The Sunrise from on high" is one of the ways Jesus' birth was depicted. Four hundred years had passed with no sign of the Savior who had been prophesied. But the dawn was about to break. Some of the characters taking part in this Sunrise to beat all sunrises were Gabriel, Zechariah and Elizabeth, Joseph and Mary, the shepherds, and Simeon. The angel Gabriel appeared to Zechariah and announced the birth of John, who would prepare the way for the Lord.

Mary was also visited by Gabriel and was told that she would give birth to God's Son. The shepherds were the first to hear the good news of Jesus' birth, seeing the light of God's glory shine on their flocks. It was no coincidence that righteous Simeon arrived at the Temple exactly when Joseph and Mary took Jesus there to present him to God, because God had promised Simeon that he would not die until he had seen Christ. In a very tender moment Simeon took the child in his arms and said that he was ready to die, now that God's promise to him had been fulfilled and he had seen Jesus, the Light.

And so dawned the Sunrise that brings light and peace to all who will accept it. Like Simeon, we must look for, have faith in, and accept Jesus, the Sunrise on high who brings spiritual birth to *our* souls.

God,
Thank you that your birth was like the dawn of sunrise, fulfilling the proph-
ecy that you came to provide forgiveness for our sins. Amen.

CHRISTMAS

AT THAT TIME THE ROMAN EMPEROR, AUGUSTUS, DECREED
THAT A CENSUS SHOULD BE TAKEN THROUGHOUT THE ROMAN
EMPIRE. (THIS WAS THE FIRST CENSUS TAKEN WHEN QUIRINIUS
WAS GOVERNOR OF SYRIA.) ALL RETURNED TO THEIR OWN TOWNS TO REGISTER
FOR THIS CENSUS. AND BECAUSE JOSEPH WAS A DESCENDANT OF KING DAVID, HE
HAD TO GO TO BETHLEHEM IN JUDEA, DAVID'S ANCIENT HOME. HE TRAVELED
THERE FROM THE VILLAGE OF NAZARETH IN GALILEE. HE TOOK WITH HIM MARY,
HIS FIANCÉE, WHO WAS OBVIOUSLY PREGNANT BY THIS TIME.   *Luke 2:1-5*

*P*alestine was under the rule of the Roman Empire, and Caesar Augustus—the
first Roman emperor—decreed that everyone must return to his ancestral home
to pay taxes. For Joseph, this meant taking an eighty-mile trip to Bethlehem.
Mary, his fiancée, who was ready to have her baby any day, went with him. Now,
I thought that pushing a shopping cart and turning over in bed were difficult at the
end of my pregnancies. I can't imagine what it would have been like to travel
eighty miles on a donkey—to pay taxes. But this inconvenient trip, as uncomfortable as it was, was yet another part of God's divine plan for the ages. You see,
back in the Old Testament, the prophet Micah had prophesied that Jesus would
come from Bethlehem, meaning "house of bread." How appropriate—that the
Bread of Life would be born in Bethlehem!

Although Joseph and Mary traveled to Bethlehem because they thought that
the Roman Empire was in control, it was really God who was in control. God always has his people in place to accomplish his purposes of bringing good news.

There's a tremendous lesson here for us about events in our lives that seem to
be huge inconveniences, or even awful tragedies. Placing our faith in God does
not mean that we try to pretend that bad things are really good. But as we grow
to trust God, we begin to see that he takes those difficult things that don't make
any sense to us and weaves them into purposes we don't yet see.

Father,
Once again we are prompted to praise you for your good plan. May we trust
your good purposes for us. Amen.

CHRISTMAS

AS HE CONSIDERED THIS, HE FELL ASLEEP, AND AN ANGEL OF THE LORD APPEARED TO HIM IN A DREAM. "JOSEPH, SON OF DAVID," THE ANGEL SAID, "DO NOT BE AFRAID TO GO AHEAD WITH YOUR MARRIAGE TO MARY. FOR THE CHILD WITHIN HER HAS BEEN CONCEIVED BY THE HOLY SPIRIT. AND SHE WILL HAVE A SON, AND YOU ARE TO NAME HIM JESUS, FOR HE WILL SAVE HIS PEOPLE FROM THEIR SINS."

Matthew 1:20-21

To think that the Creator of the universe was about to be born of a peasant virgin on cold, hard stable ground is astonishing. If I had been given the job of orchestrating Jesus' arrival on earth, I would have planned something grand. But God's designs often include humble reversals.

All the way through the Bible, we read of godly men and women whose lives were turned upside down for the sake of God's plan to deliver good news to mankind. Abraham was asked to leave his homeland, and he eventually became the father of many nations. Joseph was transplanted to Egypt, eventually rising from the pit to a high position of leadership. Moses was floated down the river in a basket to escape death by the king, and he was eventually raised by the king's daughter. Ruth's husband died, but she later remarried and became the great-grandmother of King David.

The entrance of Jesus into our human existence was one of the greatest reversals of all time. It didn't seem to make sense. Jesus—the Prince—was born into the world as a pauper. Just like all of God's truth, this example of humility gives us great encouragement. Over the course of our lives, we may experience difficult reversals. Even when they don't seem to make sense to us, we can be grateful that God sometimes uses them in our lives as part of his plan to deliver good news to mankind.

Lord Jesus,
Thank you that you didn't shun the reversal of taking on human flesh and dying for our sins. When painful reversals happen in our lives, may we run to you for help and eventually accept them as part of your good plan. Amen.

CHRISTMAS

PAY CLOSE ATTENTION TO WHAT [THE PROPHETS] WROTE,
    FOR THEIR WORDS ARE LIKE A LIGHT SHINING IN A DARK PLACE—
UNTIL THE DAY CHRIST APPEARS AND HIS BRILLIANT LIGHT SHINES IN
YOUR HEARTS.

2 Peter 1:19

When I was a child, my mom attended a women's missionary meeting at church one night each month. Little did she know that as soon as her car was out of the driveway, we kids would beg our dad to let us play hide-and-seek. This wasn't just any game of hide-and-seek. We liked to play *with all the lights in the house turned off.* We chose a night when Mom was gone because moms don't like this game. Moms are smart! They know that walking around in darkness is difficult. Being anxious both to please us and to respect my mom's wishes, my dad suggested that we leave *one* light on so we wouldn't be completely in the dark.

Perhaps that illustration helps us better understand one of the roles of the prophets in the Old Testament. Before the birth of Jesus, things had been dark for four hundred years—but not totally dark. Peter tells us that the words of the Old Testament prophets were like a light shining in a dark place. Some of the words that shone light on the nature of Christ's birth are found in Isaiah 7:14—"Look! The virgin will conceive a child! She will give birth to a son and will call him Immanuel—'God is with us.'" Other words came from Micah 5:2—"But you, O Bethlehem Ephrathah, are only a small village in Judah. Yet a ruler of Israel will come from you, one whose origins are from the distant past."

The words of those prophets have been a light to past generations, but they continue to shine for us. They remind us that God has always had people in place to accomplish his purposes of bringing others the Good News of Christ.

Father of light,
Thank you that you have never left us in the dark. Thank you for the words of
your prophets that continue to provide light for our faith. In the name of
Jesus, amen.

CHRISTMAS

NOW THERE WAS A MAN NAMED SIMEON WHO LIVED IN JERUSALEM. HE WAS A RIGHTEOUS MAN AND VERY DEVOUT. HE WAS FILLED WITH THE HOLY SPIRIT, AND HE EAGERLY EXPECTED THE MESSIAH TO COME AND RESCUE ISRAEL. THE HOLY SPIRIT HAD REVEALED TO HIM THAT HE WOULD NOT DIE UNTIL HE HAD SEEN THE LORD'S MESSIAH. THAT DAY THE SPIRIT LED HIM TO THE TEMPLE. SO WHEN MARY AND JOSEPH CAME TO PRESENT THE BABY JESUS TO THE LORD AS THE LAW REQUIRED, SIMEON WAS THERE.

Luke 2:25-28

I've always been intrigued by the Bible's accounts of lesser-known characters surrounding the birth of Christ. One of those characters was an old man named Simeon, and there's a lot of wonder packed into the ten short verses that tell his story.

Simeon was a Jew who lived in Jerusalem at the time Jesus was born. The words used to describe him—righteous and devout—are very telling. They inform us that Simeon was upright, godly, sincere, earnest, and passionate in his beliefs. The Bible goes on to tell us that God's spirit not only filled Simeon's life but had also revealed to Simeon that he would not die until he had seen the Messiah.

Eight days after Jesus was born, Mary and Joseph fulfilled the law of Moses by taking Jesus to the Temple, presenting him to the Lord. That very day, God's spirit led Simeon to the Temple, and he had a part in the ceremony! As Simeon took Jesus into his arms, he praised God, saying, "Lord, now I can die in peace! As you promised me, I have seen the Savior you have given to all people. He is a light to reveal God to the nations, and he is the glory of your people Israel!" (Luke 2:29-32).

What an example of faith Simeon is for us. He was eager for Jesus to bring light to all peoples, and as a result of his righteous and devout life he was ready to be used at just the right time for God's divine purposes. May we be every bit as eager to see the light of Jesus shine in our lives and families.

Father,
Thank you for the way you arrange for people like Simeon to be in just the right place at just the right time. We ask for your help as we cooperate with you to bring the Good News of Jesus to others. In the name of Jesus, our Savior, amen.

CHRISTMAS

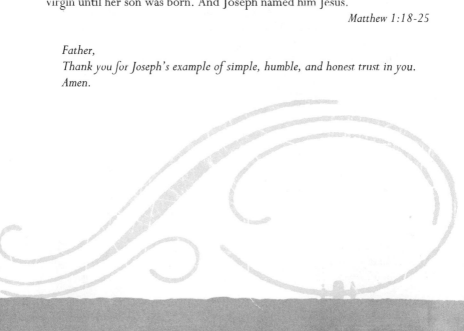

*A*s you enjoy these final days before Christmas, set aside a few minutes from your busyness and preparation to read and reflect on the familiar Christmas story.

Now this is how Jesus the Messiah was born. His mother, Mary, was engaged to be married to Joseph. But while she was still a virgin, she became pregnant by the Holy Spirit. Joseph, her fiancé, being a just man, decided to break the engagement quietly, so as not to disgrace her publicly. As he considered this, he fell asleep, and an angel of the Lord appeared to him in a dream. "Joseph, son of David," the angel said, "do not be afraid to go ahead with your marriage to Mary. For the child within her has been conceived by the Holy Spirit. And she will have a son, and you are to name him Jesus, for he will save his people from their sins." All of this happened to fulfill the Lord's message through his prophet:

"Look! The virgin will conceive a child! She will give birth to a son, and he will be called Immanuel (meaning, God is with us)."

When Joseph woke up, he did what the angel of the Lord commanded. He brought Mary home to be his wife, but she remained a virgin until her son was born. And Joseph named him Jesus.

Matthew 1:18-25

Father,
Thank you for Joseph's example of simple, humble, and honest trust in you.
Amen.

CHRISTMAS

$\mathcal{S}$ometimes when I read this passage, I try to imagine being a shepherd out there in the field. What would it have been like to see and hear armies of angels praising God for the birth of Jesus?

At that time the Roman emperor, Augustus, decreed that a census should be taken throughout the Roman Empire. (This was the first census taken when Quirinius was governor of Syria.) All returned to their own towns to register for this census. And because Joseph was a descendant of King David, he had to go to Bethlehem in Judea, David's ancient home. He traveled there from the village of Nazareth in Galilee. He took with him Mary, his fiancé, who was obviously pregnant by this time. And while they were there, the time came for her baby to be born. She gave birth to her first child, a son. She wrapped him snugly in strips of cloth and laid him in a manger, because there was no room for them in the village inn.

That night some shepherds were in the fields outside the village, guarding their flocks of sheep. Suddenly, an angel of the Lord appeared among them, and the radiance of the Lord's glory surrounded them. They were terribly frightened, but the angel reassured them. "Don't be afraid!" he said. "I bring you good news of great joy for everyone! The Savior—yes, the Messiah, the Lord—has been born tonight in Bethlehem, the city of David! And this is how you will recognize him: You will find a baby lying in a manger, wrapped snugly in strips of cloth!"

Suddenly, the angel was joined by a vast host of others—the armies of heaven—praising God: "Glory to God in the highest heaven, and peace on earth to all whom God favors." When the angels had returned to heaven, the shepherds said to each other, "Come on, let's go to Bethlehem! Let's see this wonderful thing that has happened, which the Lord has told us about." They ran to the village and found Mary and Joseph. And there was the baby, lying in the manger. Then the shepherds told everyone what had happened and what the angel had said to them about this child.

Luke 2:1-17

Father,
Thank you that your Good News is not exclusive to people with extraordinary qualifications. Thank you that your Good News is for everyone! Amen.

WORSHIP

THE SHEPHERDS WENT BACK TO THEIR FIELDS AND FLOCKS,
GLORIFYING AND PRAISING GOD FOR WHAT THE ANGELS HAD
TOLD THEM, AND BECAUSE THEY HAD SEEN THE CHILD, JUST AS THE
ANGEL HAD SAID.

Luke 2:20

*B*efore the births of my three sons, my husband and I made lists of people we wanted to call after our babies were born. The grandmas and the grandpas were at the top of the list. Next came the aunts and uncles, and then our close friends.

Who did God choose to tell first about his son's birth? Shepherds! An angel of the Lord appeared to humble shepherds who were quietly doing their jobs—tending their sheep underneath the night sky. How encouraging! God doesn't seek people with extraordinary qualifications. His good news was—and still is—for everyone. He comes to anyone with a heart humble enough to receive him.

The joyful news announced to the shepherds was that the Savior of the world had just been born in Bethlehem, and that they could find him there, lying in a manger. As soon as that announcement was made, an army of angels sang, "Glory to God in the highest"—words that have inspired more Christmas songs for the last two thousand years than we could begin to count. This was the most joyful news ever announced in history. The humble shepherds, along with the angels, were among the first to worship and praise God for sending Jesus!

The shepherds leave us a great example for our personal worship. Worship doesn't need to wait for a church service, and it doesn't need to be complicated. It is praising God for what he's done, right where we are. May we, like the shepherds, worship God with humble hearts.

> *Father,*
> *Thank you that you chose humble shepherds to praise you with the angels at Jesus' birth. We want to worship you too. In the glorious name of Jesus, amen.*

WORSHIP

AFTER THIS INTERVIEW THE WISE MEN WENT THEIR WAY.
ONCE AGAIN THE STAR APPEARED TO THEM, GUIDING THEM
TO BETHLEHEM. IT WENT AHEAD OF THEM AND STOPPED OVER
THE PLACE WHERE THE CHILD WAS. WHEN THEY SAW THE STAR, THEY WERE
FILLED WITH JOY! THEY ENTERED THE HOUSE WHERE THE CHILD AND HIS
MOTHER, MARY, WERE, AND THEY FELL DOWN BEFORE HIM AND WORSHIPED HIM.
THEN THEY OPENED THEIR TREASURE CHESTS AND GAVE HIM GIFTS OF GOLD,
FRANKINCENSE, AND MYRRH. BUT WHEN IT WAS TIME TO LEAVE, THEY WENT
HOME ANOTHER WAY, BECAUSE GOD HAD WARNED THEM IN A DREAM NOT TO
RETURN TO HEROD.
Matthew 2:9-12

The wise men were probably astrologers who, in their eagerness to observe the stars in the heavens, encountered a sign from God. In an amazing way God broke into the world of the wise men by showing them the star in the east and later redirecting their trip to thwart the murderous plans of Herod and his advisers. What was the wise men's reaction to all this? They worshipped, they opened their treasures, and they presented gifts to Jesus.

Bible scholars tell us that the gifts—gold, frankincense, and myrhh—were symbolic of who Christ is and what he would accomplish. The gold stood for royalty. Christ's royalty was much different than any royalty we observe here on earth. Isaiah 9:7 reads, "His ever expanding, peaceful government will never end. He will rule forever with fairness and justice from the throne of his ancestor David. The passionate commitment of the Lord Almighty will guarantee this!" The gift of frankincense represented deity; frankincense was used in worship at the Temple. Christ was born to be God with us. And myrrh, a spice that was used to anoint bodies for burial, signified the reason Christ came to earth—to give up his life on the cross to pay the price for our sins.

God has broken into our world and the world of our children, and he desires the same reaction from us that he did from the wise men. He wants us to see him for who he is, bow down in adoration of all he has done, open our hearts to him, and present him with our lives. How will we worship him today?

Father,
Help us worship, follow, and obey you day by day. May our example encourage others, especially our children, to worship you too. Amen.

DECEMBER 27
WORSHIP

NOW I, NEBUCHADNEZZAR, PRAISE AND GLORIFY AND
HONOR THE KING OF HEAVEN. ALL HIS ACTS ARE JUST AND TRUE,
AND HE IS ABLE TO HUMBLE THOSE WHO ARE PROUD. *Daniel 4:37*

*W*orship happens only when we're humble; true worship never happens when we're proud.

Nebuchadnezzar learned the hard way that nothing is more insane than human pride. But there is also nothing more sensible and sober than praising God. Having made an arrogant boast about all his achievements, Nebuchadnezzar was stricken down at the height of his pride by God's judgment and literally lived in insanity for a while. But when he raised his eyes to heaven and praised God, his sanity was restored. We sometimes forget one of the benefits of worship: when we lift our eyes to heaven, our perspective changes.

Nebuchadnezzar left a wonderful pattern of worship for us and for our children:

- We lift our eyes to God, taking them off our present circumstances.
- We see ourselves as nothing in comparison with him who is everything, prompting us to realize how much he loves us.
- We see that God is much bigger than we are—he is eternal.
- We thank him that his faithfulness is passed from generation to generation.
- We realize that we don't have the right to say to God, "What have you done?" because all power in heaven and earth is his.

The life of Nebuchadnezzar displays that true worship doesn't happen when we're pretending to be someone we're not, or when we feel self-righteous and deny our need for God's mercy and grace. True worship begins with humility and helps restore our perspective.

Father,
Thank you for your wonder and your splendor. Thank you that you are over everything and yet you love and care for us. May we worship you as you deserve to be worshipped. Amen.

WORSHIP

FOR THE LORD HAD MADE A COVENANT WITH THE
DESCENDANTS OF JACOB AND COMMANDED THEM: "DO NOT
WORSHIP ANY OTHER GODS OR BOW BEFORE THEM OR SERVE THEM
OR OFFER SACRIFICES TO THEM. WORSHIP ONLY THE LORD, WHO BROUGHT YOU
OUT OF EGYPT WITH SUCH MIGHTY MIRACLES AND POWER. YOU MUST WORSHIP
HIM AND BOW BEFORE HIM; OFFER SACRIFICES TO HIM ALONE." *2 Kings 17:35-36*

We see in these verses that God does not wish to share worship with anyone or anything else. After 250 years of rebellion and sin, the nation of Israel was conquered by Assyria. The Assyrians had a policy of taking the best citizens of a conquered nation to their own land and then colonizing the captive land with foreigners. This is how the Samaritan people came about—they were a mixed breed.

At first there was no universal religious faith in Samaria, so the leaders addressed the problem—but in an unusual way. They imported a Jewish priest to instruct the people about the Lord, but then they encouraged the people to worship both Jehovah and the national gods. But God didn't want mixed worship. All through the Bible he asks for undivided hearts. Many times in the Old Testament God stretched out his arm to save his people from their troubles, and yet they didn't get it. He was the only one they were supposed to worship!

"Too many people . . . attend to the outward forms of worship, lest they should lose status; but in their hearts they enthrone worldly and worthless ideals."[7]

Sometimes we think that without renouncing other gods, we can give God some sort of obligatory recognition. But—here's a lesson for us and for our children—he wants our undivided attention and praise.

Father,
Thank you for your mighty, outstretched arm that throughout the ages has reached people and saved them from distress. Forgive us for running to other things—other gods. May we serve you with undivided hearts. Amen.

WORSHIP

THEREFORE, I URGE YOU, BROTHERS, IN VIEW OF GOD'S
MERCY, TO OFFER YOUR BODIES AS LIVING SACRIFICES, HOLY
AND PLEASING TO GOD—THIS IS YOUR SPIRITUAL ACT OF WORSHIP. *Romans 12:1, NIV*

In the Old Testament, worship of God involved altars, the Tabernacle, lampstands, burnt offerings, priestly garments, priests, anointing oil, and incense. But in the New Testament, worship is characterized by joy and thanksgiving for the redemption Christ provided for us through his death on the cross. The New Testament instructs us that *where* we worship God is not so important as *how* we worship. Worship includes prayer, praise, and study of God's Word, and it must be done in spirit and in truth.

When our minds and bodies are yielded to God, every day can be a worship experience. Psalm 96:9 (TLB) says, "Worship the Lord with the beauty of holy lives." Worshipping God requires freedom from slavery or service to anything else, and if we are selfishly holding on to things in our lives that are contrary to God's instructions for us, our attempts at worship are actually mockery of God.

What prompts us to present ourselves to God? Not laws, shoulds, or ought-tos. A view of God's mercy is what motivates our true worship. It's been said that grace is getting what we don't deserve and mercy is not getting what we do deserve. As we daily thank God for his mercy to us and remember all he's done for us, we are prompted to worship him with the beauty of holy lives.

Merciful Father,
In view of all you've done for us, we pray that our lives will be characterized
by joy, thanksgiving, and worship to you. Amen.

WORSHIP

THEN HE BROUGHT ME INTO THE INNER COURTYARD OF
THE LORD'S TEMPLE. AT THE ENTRANCE, BETWEEN THE
FOYER AND THE BRONZE ALTAR, ABOUT TWENTY-FIVE MEN WERE
STANDING WITH THEIR BACKS TO THE LORD'S TEMPLE. THEY WERE FACING
EASTWARD, WORSHIPING THE SUN!

Ezekiel 8:16

*E*zekiel was a priest who, along with other citizens of Judah, lived as a captive in Babylonia. During this period of time he was a powerful messenger of God, pointing out that each person's individual response to the Lord determines his or her eternal destiny. More specifically, it's who or what we worship that determines our future.

In the verses above, Ezekiel had a vision of priests who were worshipping the sun. Admittedly, the sun is awesome. It gives us light, it rises and sets each day, it gives off heat, and it is a stable and predictable point of reference seen by human beings everywhere. But the sun is not God. Rather, the sun points *to* God.

We run into trouble when we worship the things God has made instead of worshipping him. Taking a trip to Brookfield Zoo in Chicago is a worshipful experience for me. Realizing that God imagined and created the giraffe with its long neck, the zebra with its stripes, and the polar bear who loves to play in the water helps me remember how big God is!

God deserves our worship throughout each day. Going to the grocery store with our child and acknowledging the great variety of fruits and vegetables that God created is worship. Watching a cat give birth to kittens can lead to worship. The question is, in all the exciting, awesome experiences of life, do we give credit to God, or do we consistently worship the things themselves?

Father,
Forgive us for paying more attention to things you have made than to you.
May our hearts be inspired to give you worship each day for what you have
created and provided. Amen.

WORSHIP

YOU PUT US IN CHARGE OF EVERYTHING YOU MADE,
GIVING US AUTHORITY OVER ALL THINGS—THE SHEEP AND THE
CATTLE AND ALL THE WILD ANIMALS, THE BIRDS IN THE SKY, THE
FISH IN THE SEA, AND EVERYTHING THAT SWIMS THE OCEAN CURRENTS. O LORD,
OUR LORD, THE MAJESTY OF YOUR NAME FILLS THE EARTH!   *Psalm 8:6-9*

My most vivid worship experience took place underneath the surface of the ocean.

My husband, our three sons, and I were vacationing in the Virgin Islands. Not having snorkeled before that trip, we began by kicking around in shallow waters off the coast where we were staying. We all enjoyed the experience so much that we decided to rent a boat with a captain for one day and do some serious snorkeling. When the captain first stopped the boat in what—to me—felt like the middle of the ocean, all four males in my family immediately jumped in. I, on the other hand, sat on the boat's ladder dangling my feet in the water, trying to summon enough courage to jump.

After some patient coaxing from the captain, I finally took the plunge . . . and promptly lost my fear. My only thought was *I'm in a totally different world than anything I've ever seen before*! I wanted to cry, but it wasn't because I felt sad or afraid. I felt a sense of wonder and awe at things God created that I had never seen before. As I observed the angelfish, sergeant majors, and blue tangs, the words that kept running through my mind were, "O Lord, our Lord, the majesty of your name fills the earth!"

When the five of us returned to the boat, there was one thing I was thankful that I *hadn't* seen—the three-foot barracuda that Jim and the boys described to me. It might have interrupted my worship experience.

Father,
Thank you that your majesty is evident in the fish of the sea and all the creation around us. Amen.

NOTES

January

[1] R. Kent Hughes, *1,001 Great Stories & Quotes* (Wheaton, Ill.: Tyndale House, 1998), 135.

[2] Ellen Banks Elwell, *The Christian Mom's Idea Book* (Wheaton, Ill.: Crossway Books, 1997), 202.

[3] F. B. Meyer, *F.B. Meyer Bible Commentary* (Wheaton, Ill.: Tyndale House, 1984), 587.

[4] Joanne Shetler, *And the Word Came with Power* (Portland: Multnomah, 1992), 17.

[5] Ingrid Trobisch, *The Confident Woman* (New York: HarperCollins, 1993), 63.

[6] Philip Yancey and Tim Stafford, *Unhappy Secrets of the Christian Life* (Grand Rapids, Mich./Wheaton, Ill.: Zondervan/Campus Life Books, 1979), 75.

February

[1] Gary Vanderet, *The Skill of Receiving God's Word*, quoted in Kent Hughes, *1,001 Great Stories & Quotes* (Wheaton, Ill.: Tyndale House, 1998), 256.

[2] Leland Ryken, James C. Wilhoit, and Tremper Longman III, *Dictionary of Biblical Imagery* (Downers Grove, Ill.: InterVarsity Press, 1998), 659.

[3] Bruce B. Barton, et al., *Life Application Bible Commentary, John* (Wheaton, Ill.: Tyndale House, 1993), 201.

[4] James Houston, *The Heart's Desire* (Colorado Springs: NavPress, 1996), 97.

[5] Frederick M. Lehman, "The Love of God," copyright 1917, renewed 1945 by Nazarene Publishing House. Used by permission.

[6] Kathleen Thomerson, "I Want to Walk as a Child of the Light," copyright 1966.

March

[1] R. Kent Hughes, *James* (Wheaton, Ill.: Crossway Books, 1991), 236.

[2] Ibid., 237.

[3] Helen H. Lemmel, "Turn Your Eyes Upon Jesus," copyright 1922.

[4] Warren W. Wiersbe, *The Bible Exposition Commentary, Volume 1* (Wheaton, Ill.: Victor Books, 1989), 354.

[5] Helen Russ Stough, *A Mother's Year* (Old Tappan, N.J.: Fleming H. Revell, 1905), 154.

[6] Michael Horton, *We Believe* (Nashville: Word, 1998), 101.

[7] Ibid., 131.

[8] Bruce B. Barton, et al., *Life Application Bible Commentary, John* (Wheaton, Ill.: Tyndale House, 1993), 300–301.

[9] Horton, *We Believe*, 225.

April

[1] Horatio Gates Spafford, "It Is Well with My Soul," copyright 1873.

[2] Edward H. Bickersteth, Jr., "Peace, Perfect Peace," copyright 1875.

[3] Frances Ridley Havergal, "Like a River Glorious," 1876.

[4] Gladys Hunt, *Ms. Means Myself* (Grand Rapids, Mich.: Zondervan, 1972), 21.

[5] Kay Arthur, *To Know Him by Name* (Sisters, Ore.: Multnomah, 1995), 42.

[6] Gary Smalley and John Trent, *The Blessing* (Nashville: Thomas Nelson, 1986), 81–82.

[7] *Life Application Study Bible,* NIV edition (Wheaton, Ill.: Tyndale House, 1988), 1050.

May

[1] Hughes, *James*, 193-194.

[2] James S. Hewett, *Illustrations Unlimited* (Wheaton, Ill.:Tyndale House, 1989), 380.

[3] *Life Application Bible,* NIV edition, 1933.

[4] Dr. Paul Brand and Philip Yancey, *Fearfully and Wonderfully Made* (Grand Rapids, Mich.: Zondervan, 1980), 2.

[5] Ibid., 195.

[6] Horton, *We Believe*, 26–27.

[7] Ronald F. Youngblood, ed., *Nelson's New Illustrated Bible Dictionary* (Nashville: Thomas Nelson, 1986), 503.

[8] R.V. Tasker, *The General Epistle of James* (Grand Rapids, Mich.: Eerdmans, 1983), 93.

[9] R. Kent Hughes, *Hebrews* (Wheaton, Ill.: Crossway Books, 1993), 228.

[10] Quoted in Hewett, *Illustrations Unlimited*, 256.

[11] Ronald F. Youngblood, *Nelson's New Illustrated Bible Dictionary* (Nashville: Thomas Nelson, 1995), 1126.

June

[1] Hughes, *James*, 187.

[2] Phillip W. Keller, *A Shepherd Looks at Psalm 23* (Grand Rapids, Mich.: Zondervan, 1970), 87.

[3] Connie Lauerman, "Worth a Thousand Words," *Chicago Tribune,* 8 January 1999.

[4] *Life Application Study Bible,* NIV edition (Wheaton, Ill.: Tyndale House Publishers, 1988), 1840.

[5] Joseph M. Stowell, *Perilous Pursuits* (Chicago: Moody Press, 1994), 88.

July

[1] Jeffrey Wagner, "The Indomitable Byron Janis," *Clavier*, April 1998, 9.

[2] Kate B. Wilkinson, "May the Mind of Christ, My Savior," copyright 1913.

[3] David A. Seamands, *Healing Meditations for Life* (Wheaton, Ill.: Victor Books, 1996), 29.

[4] Wiersbe, *The Bible Exposition Commentary*, Volume 1, 554.

[5] Barton, et al., *Life Application Bible Commentary, John*, 272.

[6] Martin Marty, "Elements of Worship," in *Practical Christianity* (Wheaton, Ill.: Tyndale House, 1987), 358.

[7] Warren Wiersbe, *Wiersbe's Outlines on the Old Testament* (Wheaton, Ill.: Victor Books, 1993), 331.

[8] Frank S. Pittman, *Private Lies* (New York: Norton, 1989), 59.

[9] Margaret Cropper, "Jesus' Hands Were Kind Hands," copyright 1926.

August

[1] Hewett, *Illustrations Unlimited*, 492.

[2] Robert Lowry, "Nothing but the Blood of Jesus," copyright 1876.

[3] Dr. Paul Brand and Philip Yancey, *Fearfully and Wonderfully Made* (Grand Rapids, Mich.: Zondervan, 1980), 91.

[4] A.W. Tozer, *The Knowledge of the Holy* (New York: Harper & Row, 1961), 6–7.

[5] Barton, et al., *Life Application Bible Commentary, John*, 276.

[6] Ibid., 180–181.

[7] Ibid., 123.

[8] Horatius Bonar, "Not What These Hands Have Done," 1861.

[9] *Chicago Tribune,* 31 December 1998.

[10] Lewis Smedes, *The Art of Forgiving* (New York: Ballantine, 1996), 177–178.

[11] Warren Wiersbe, *The Bible Exposition Commentary, Volume 1*, 68.

[12] Dr. Henry Cloud, *Changes That Heal* (Grand Rapids, Mich.: Zondervan, 1992), 31.

September

[1] Julia A. Fletcher, "Little Things," copyright 1845.

[2] Robert Manson Myers, *Handel's Messiah, A Touchstone of Taste* (New York: Octagon Books, 1971), 63.

[3] Kurt Kaiser, "Where Shall I Run?" Word Music, 1971.

[4] Kenneth N. Taylor, *The Book for Children* (Wheaton, Ill.: Tyndale House, 1985), 108.

[5] Wiersbe, *The Bible Exposition Commentary, Volume 1*, 300.

[6] Joan Ames, "Margaret Henshaw," *American Music Teacher*, February/March 1998, 28.

[7] Hewett, *Illustrations Unlimited*, 195.

[8] Linda & Richard Eyre, *Teaching Your Children Responsibility* (New York: Simon & Schuster, 1994), 95.

October

[1] Phillips Brooks, "O Little Town of Bethlehem," 1867.

[2] Warren W. Wiersbe, *Wiersbe's Expository Outlines on the New Testament* (Wheaton, IL: Victor Books, 1992), 583.

[3] Ibid., 158.

[4] Pat Hershey Owen, *The Genesis Principle for Parents* (Wheaton, Ill.: Tyndale House, 1985), 23.

[5] William Williams, "Guide Me, O Thou Great Jehovah," copyright 1745.

[6] Dr. Dan B. Allender and Dr. Tremper Longman III, *Bold Love* (Colorado Springs: NavPress, 1992), 175.

November

[1] Meyer, *F. B. Meyer Bible Commentary*, 129.

[2] Keller, *A Shepherd Looks at Psalm 23*, 30.

[3] Harry D. Loes, "All Things in Jesus," copyright 1916.

December

[1] George Wade Robinson, "I Am His, and He Is Mine," copyright 1876.

[2] Randy Alcorn, *Money, Possessions and Eternity* (Wheaton, Ill.: Tyndale House, 1989), 175.

[3] Barton, et al., *Life Application Bible Commentary, John*, 201.

[4] *Chicago Tribune,* December 26, 1998.

[5] Ronald F. Youngblood, ed., *Nelson's New Illustrated Bible Dictionary* (Nashville: Thomas Nelson, 1995), 1087.

[6] Ibid., 445.

[7] Meyer, *F. B. Meyer Bible Commentary*, 181.

INDEX OF TOPICS

INDEX OF
DAILY SCRIPTURE REFERENCES

Mark 7:6-7 . . . *June 3*
Mark 7:21-23 . . . *August 2*
Mark 10:16 . . . *July 30*
Mark 10:45 . . . *December 9*
Mark 15:24 . . . *March 13*
Mark 16:15 . . . *December 7*
Luke 1:31-35 . . . *December 17*
Luke 1:37 . . . *February 3*
Luke 1:39-40 . . . *January 22*
Luke 1:46-55 . . . *June 18*
Luke 1:69, 77-79 . . . *December 18*
Luke 2:1-5 . . . *December 19*
Luke 2:1-17 . . . *December 24*
Luke 2:11 . . . *May 18*
Luke 2:20 . . . *December 25*
Luke 2:25-28 . . . *December 22*
Luke 3:7-8 . . . *March 28*
Luke 4:18-19 . . . *March 31*
Luke 9:17 . . . *November 14*
Luke 10:42 . . . *October 16*
Luke 11:11-13 . . . *March 24*
Luke 11:27-28 . . . *August 11*
Luke 11:34 . . . *February 21*
Luke 12:6-7 . . . *April 18*
Luke 14:11 . . . *June 22*
Luke 18:1-5 . . . *February 26*
Luke 18:9-14 . . . *June 14*
Luke 18:14 . . . *June 20*
Luke 19:11-13 . . . *June 27*
Luke 24:50-53 . . . *March 16*
John 2:13-15 . . . *December 15*
John 4:28-30 . . . *October 13*
John 6:5-6 . . . *August 16*
John 6:48 . . . *October 6*
John 7:16-18 . . . *October 23*
John 7:37-38 . . . *May 17*
John 8:12 . . . *February 20*
John 8:31-32 . . . *August 12*
John 9:31 . . . *February 9*
John 10:11 . . . *November 13*
John 13:14-17 . . . *December 4*
John 13:17 . . . *August 10*
John 14:2 . . . *November 26*
John 14:3 . . . *February 1*
John 14:6 . . . *October 22*
John 14:26 . . . *March 21*
John 14:27 . . . *March 6, April 3*
John 15:4 . . . *December 5*
John 15:5 . . . *June 21*
John 15:12-17 . . . *February 13*

John 15:13 . . . *January 24*
John 16:33 . . . *April 6*
John 17:4 . . . *June 29*
John 19:26-27 . . . *June 5*
John 20:27 . . . *January 2*
John 21:15-17 . . . *May 26*
Romans 5:1 . . . *January 3*
Romans 5:1-2 . . . *May 19*
Romans 5:8 . . . *February 12*
Romans 5:10-11 . . . *February 15*
Romans 8:22-23 . . . *November 28*
Romans 8:26 . . . *September 15*
Romans 8:28 . . . *January 6*
Romans 12:1 . . . *December 29*
Romans 12:2 . . . *July 4*
Romans 12:4-5 . . . *August 4*
Romans 13:13-14 . . . *June 13*
Romans 15:4 . . . *January 30*
1 Corinthians 2:9 . . . *December 1*
1 Corinthians 2:14-16 . . . *July 3*
1 Corinthians 3:11-15 . . . *December 2*
1 Corinthians 10:12-13 . . . *March 4*
1 Corinthians 11:26 . . . *April 13*
1 Corinthians 15:51-52 . . . *March 22*
2 Corinthians 1:3-5 . . . *June 8*
2 Corinthians 4:4 . . . *July 5*
2 Corinthians 4:5-6 . . . *May 12*
2 Corinthians 4:7 . . . *February 24*
2 Corinthians 4:15 . . . *November 23*
2 Corinthians 5:20 . . . *October 9*
2 Corinthians 5:21 . . . *June 16*
2 Corinthians 9:13 . . . *December 6*
2 Corinthians 10:4-5 . . . *July 7*
2 Corinthians 12:9 . . . *June 23*
2 Corinthians 13:9 . . . *January 13*
Galatians 4:4-7 . . . *September 2*
Galatians 5:22-23 . . . *March 25*
Galatians 6:7-9 . . . *October 15*
Galatians 6:9 . . . *February 28*
Ephesians 1:7-8 . . . *September 17*
Ephesians 1:19-21 . . . *March 19*
Ephesians 1:22-23 . . . *March 20*
Ephesians 2:8 . . . *May 22*
Ephesians 2:10 . . . *June 25*
Ephesians 3:16-17 . . . *July 10*
Ephesians 3:17-19 . . . *February 18*
Ephesians 3:20 . . . *May 9*
Ephesians 4:23-24 . . . *April 29*
Ephesians 5:1-2 . . . *February 14*
Ephesians 5:5-9 . . . *July 29*

Keep Your
Devotional Time
fresh
with these
popular
devotionals.

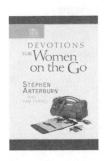
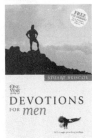
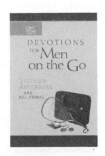

FAMILY

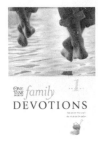

*The One Year Book of
Josh McDowell's Family
Devotions*
ISBN 0-8423-4302-4

*The One Year Book of
Family Devotions*
ISBN 0-8423-2541-7

*The One Year
Devotions for Moms*
ISBN 1-4143-0171-5

YOUTH

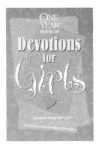

*The One Year Book of
Devotions for Kids*
ISBN 0-8423-5087-X

*The One Year Book of
Devotions for Girls*
ISBN 0-8423-3619-2

*The One Year
Devotions for Teens*
ISBN 0-8423-6202-9

*The One Year Book of
Devotions for Boys*
ISBN 0-8423-3620-6

GENERAL

COUPLES

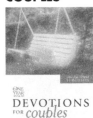

*One Year through
the Bible*
ISBN 0-8423-3553-6

*The One Year Book of
Praying through the
Bible*
ISBN 0-8423-6178-2

*The One Year Book of
Devotions for Couples*
ISBN 1-4143-0170-7